Analysing Qualitative Data *in* Psychology

SAGE was founded in 1965 by Sara Miller McCune to support the dissemination of usable knowledge by publishing innovative and high-quality research and teaching content. Today, we publish over 900 journals, including those of more than 400 learned societies, more than 800 new books per year, and a growing range of library products including archives, data, case studies, reports, and video. SAGE remains majority-owned by our founder, and after Sara's lifetime will become owned by a charitable trust that secures our continued independence.

Los Angeles | London | New Delhi | Singapore | Washington DC | Melbourne

2nd Edition

Analysing Qualitative Data *in* Psychology

Evanthia Lyons & Adrian Coyle

Los Angeles | London | New Delhi
Singapore | Washington DC | Melbourne

SAGE

Los Angeles | London | New Delhi
Singapore | Washington DC | Melbourne

SAGE Publications Ltd
1 Oliver's Yard
55 City Road
London EC1Y 1SP

SAGE Publications Inc.
2455 Teller Road
Thousand Oaks, California 91320

SAGE Publications India Pvt Ltd
B 1/I 1 Mohan Cooperative Industrial Area
Mathura Road
New Delhi 110 044

SAGE Publications Asia-Pacific Pte Ltd
3 Church Street
#10-04 Samsung Hub
Singapore 049483

Editorial arrangement © Evanthia Lyons and Adrian Coyle 2015
Chapter 1 © Evanthia Lyons 2015
Chapter 2 © Adrian Coyle 2015
Chapter 3 © Edith Steffen 2015
Preface to Section 2 © Evanthia Lyons and Adrian Coyle 2015
Chapter 4 © Jonathan A. Smith and Virginia Eatough 2015
Chapter 5 © Lesley Storey 2015
Chapter 6 © Victoria Clarke and Virginia Braun 2015
Chapter 7 © Gareth Terry 2015
Chapter 8 © Sheila Payne 2015
Chapter 9 © Sheila Hawker and Christine Kerr 2015
Chapter 10 © Adrian Coyle 2015
Chapter 11 © Chris Walton 2015
Chapter 12 © Brett Smith 2015
Chapter 13 © Nick Caddick 2015
Chapter 14 © Evanthia Lyons 2015
Appendix 1 © Arnie Reed 2015
Appendix 2 Preface © Adrian Coyle and Evanthia Lyons 2015
Appendix 2 Report 1 © Virginia Eatough and Jonathan A. Smith 2015
Appendix 2 Report 2 © Caroline Huxley, Victoria Clarke and Emma Halliwell 2015
Appendix 2 Report 3 © Magi Sque and Sheila Payne 2015
Appendix 2 Report 4 © Simon Goodman and Lottie Rowe 2015
Appendix 2 Report 5 © Nick Caddick, Brett Smith and Cassandra Phoenix 2015

First edition published 2007.
Reprinted 2007, 2012, 2014, 2015.
This second edition published 2016.

Library of Congress Control Number: 2015951598

British Library Cataloguing in Publication data

A catalogue record for this book is available from the British Library

MIX
Paper from responsible sources
FSC www.fsc.org FSC® C011748

ISBN 978-1-4462-7374-6
ISBN 978-1-4462-7375-3 (pbk)

At SAGE we take sustainability seriously. Most of our products are printed in the UK using FSC papers and boards. When we print overseas we ensure sustainable papers are used as measured by the PREPS grading system. We undertake an annual audit to monitor our sustainability.

CONTENTS

CONTENTS

CONTENTS

CONTENTS

CONTENTS

NOTES ON CONTRIBUTORS

Virginia Braun is Associate Professor in the School of Psychology at the University of Auckland (Aotearoa/New Zealand). She is a feminist and critical psychologist whose research has explored the intersecting areas of gender, bodies, sex/sexuality and health/well-being across multiple topics, and the possibilities, politics and ethics of lives lived in neoliberal times. She is currently excited to be beginning research on new food movements. She is also interested in the intersections between academia and activism. She has an ongoing interest in the doing, developing and teaching of qualitative research. With Victoria Clarke, she developed a hugely popular approach to thematic analysis (see www.psych.auckland.ac.nz/thematicanalysis), and they subsequently co-authored an award-winning textbook on qualitative research: *Successful Qualitative Research: A Practical Guide for Beginners* (SAGE, 2013). Her current book project is a book on thematic analysis for SAGE.

Nick Caddick is a Postdoctoral Research Fellow in the Veterans and Families Institute at Anglia Ruskin University in the UK. His main research interests involve exploring the impact of military life and combat trauma on veterans and their families, and understanding how various approaches to mental health and social care can promote well-being in this population. Nick utilizes narrative inquiry to understand how veterans' and families' stories shape their experiences of life post-trauma and following transition out of the armed forces. He has written and co-produced articles and book chapters on qualitative research and has taught narrative inquiry at postgraduate level and at international teaching seminars.

Victoria Clarke is Associate Professor in Sexuality Studies at the University of the West of England (UWE) in the UK. She has published three award-winning books: *Out in Psychology: Lesbian, Gay, Bisexual, Trans and Queer* [LGBTQ] *Perspectives* (Wiley, 2007); *Lesbian, Gay, Bisexual, Trans and Queer Psychology: An Introduction* (Cambridge University Press, 2010); and *Successful Qualitative Research: A Practical Guide for Beginners* (SAGE, 2013). She has published widely in the areas of LGBTQ and feminist psychology, including on lesbian and gay parenting, relationships and marriage, dress and appearance, and gender identity and education. With Virginia Braun, she developed an approach to thematic analysis that has become one of the most widely used approaches to qualitative analysis in the social and health sciences (see www.psych.auckland.ac.nz/thematicanalysis). Her current projects include research on voluntary childlessness (with Nikki Hayfield, Sonja Ellis and Gareth Terry), writing a book on thematic analysis with Virginia Braun (for SAGE) and having fun with story completion as a data generation method.

Adrian Coyle is Professor of Psychology at Kingston University, London. He is a social psychologist, and his research and publications have addressed a range of topics, principally psychological issues in identity, loss and bereavement, sexuality and religion. Much of this work has been framed in terms of social psychological approaches, theories and concepts, particularly identity process theory, discourse, and theories relevant to social inclusion and exclusion. The vast majority of his research is qualitative and has used diverse methods of data generation and data analysis. He has contributed to the promotion of qualitative research in British psychology and is a keen advocate of its value in developing insightful and useful answers to research questions. He has supervised or co-supervised the research of seven PhD graduates in social psychology and health psychology and over 80 practitioner doctorate graduates in psychotherapeutic and counselling psychology and in clinical psychology, all of whom have used qualitative methods in their work.

Virginia Eatough is Senior Lecturer in the Department of Psychological Sciences at Birkbeck, University of London where she teaches qualitative research methods, critical analysis and phenomenological philosophy. Her focus on qualitative research methods grew out of an interest in the role of subjective knowledge in understanding emotional experience. In particular, she is interested in the role of feelings in our emotional life. She is experienced in a range of phenomenological methods, especially interpretative phenomenological analysis, all of which are concerned with understanding (amongst other things) what it is like to experience something – for example, what it is like to be angry, to feel happy or to be obligated. Current projects include happiness, idiography and neurofeedback from a neuro-phenomenological perspective.

Simon Goodman is a Research Fellow at Coventry University in the UK. His research uses discursive psychology to address a number of issues, including the discursive construction of asylum seekers and refugees. His work focuses on what is and what is not considered to be racist, particularly with regard to asylum-seeking. His other interests include the British public's understanding of income inequality, and the ways in which the political far right attempts to present its policies as acceptable, non-racist, political discourse. He edits the British Psychological Society's *Qualitative Methods in Psychology Bulletin* and is the co-author of *The Language of Asylum: Refugees and Discourse* (Palgrave Macmillan, 2015).

Emma Halliwell is Senior Lecturer in the Department of Psychology at the University of the West of England (UWE) in the UK. She is a member of UWE's Centre for Appearance Research. Emma's research focuses on the impact of the mass media on body image and on the development and evaluation of interventions aimed at promoting positive body image.

Sheila Hawker received her BSc and PhD from the University of Southampton in the UK. She worked as a health services researcher on numerous projects, principally concerned with end-of-life care for older people and nurse-led chemotherapy. These included a systematic review of qualitative literature concerned with inter-professional communication when older people are discharged from hospital, a study evaluating the feasibility of a nurse-specialist-managed chemotherapy service and a multi-method examination of the provision of palliative care for older people in UK community hospitals. She was co-director of C&S Academic Services, a company offering qualitative interview and transcription services for social and health services research. Her publications include papers on 'Appraising the evidence: Reviewing disparate data systematically' (*Qualitative Health Research*, 2002) and 'End of life care in community hospitals: The perceptions of bereaved family members' (*Palliative Medicine*, 2006). She is also co-author of *Stepfamilies* (Palgrave Macmillan, 2011). She retired in 2014.

Caroline Huxley is a Senior Research Fellow at Warwick Medical School in the UK. Her current research interests lie in intersection of health sciences and psychology. She has recently worked on several funded projects that focused on the management of long-term conditions and the promotion of healthy lifestyles. Prior to this, Caroline studied for her PhD in the Centre for Appearance Research at the University of the West of England. Her research focused on lesbian and bisexual women's body image, particularly how feelings about the body were linked to health behaviours and how physical appearance was used to project sexual identity. She uses mixed methodologies for her research and has particular experience in using interviews, thematic analysis and surveys.

Christine Kerr received her BSc and PhD from the University of Southampton in the UK. She has worked on research projects focusing on health care for older people. These include a systematic review of qualitative literature concerned with inter-professional communication when older people are discharged from hospital, a multi-method examination of the provision of palliative care for older people in UK community hospitals and an evaluation of out-of-hours care in community hospitals. Her most recent, co-authored publication is 'Patient and public involvement in research and the Cancer Experiences Collaborative: Benefits and challenges' (*BMJ Supportive and Palliative Care*, 2014). She is now retired.

Evanthia Lyons is Head of the School of Psychology, Criminology and Sociology at Kingston University, London. Her research interests include identity and social representational processes in contexts of intergroup conflict and multi-cultural societies. She has used both qualitative and quantitative methods to study the development of national identities in children, the role of social memories in maintaining intergroup conflicts and the relationship between trust in political institutions and political participation amongst young people from different ethnic backgrounds in European countries. She has also used qualitative research methods to challenge existing literature on the potential impact of stigma on the self amongst members of socially devalued groups such as people with mental health problems, people with learning disabilities, older people and young mothers.

Sheila Payne is a health psychologist with a background in nursing. She is an Emeritus Professor at the International Observatory on End-of-Life Care, based in the Division of Health Research at Lancaster University in the UK. She has a long track record in palliative care research and scholarship. Her research agenda focuses on palliative and end-of-life care for older people and organizational development. She holds a number of major international grants in these areas and has supervised over 30 PhD students. She was President of the European Association for Palliative Care (2011–2015). She has published widely in academic and professional journals and has written 12 books.

Cassandra Phoenix is Reader in Critical Health Psychology at the University of Bath in the UK. Her work draws upon the sociology of ageing, the body and physical culture. The research she undertakes in this area explores the embodiment of ageing and physical activity across the life course; the impact of ageing on self, identity and well-being; disability; nature(s), exercise and the body. This work is often framed by narrative approaches, visual methods and ethnography and currently spans three complementary themes: the role of physical activity in shaping expectations and experiences of ageing; everyday experiences of chronic illness; and the use of local environments to manage and promote everyday well-being.

Arnie Reed is a chartered counselling psychologist based in Cardiff in Wales. After a full and rewarding military career, he moved into psychology, graduating from the University of Surrey in 2001 with a Practitioner Doctorate in Psychotherapeutic and Counselling Psychology. He works in a National Health Service (NHS) Trust's Community Mental Health Team and also has a private practice. He is co-director of Schema Therapy Workshops Ltd, which delivers schema therapy training and supervision to mental health practitioners in the UK and overseas. He now specializes in complex client presentations, including those clients diagnosed with borderline personality disorder (BPD) and so-called 'treatment-resistant' difficulties. He has been involved in developing a local NHS BPD service. He has also taught on various practitioner doctorate courses in clinical psychology, MSc courses in psychiatry and university trainings in cognitive behavioural therapy.

Lottie Rowe is a PhD student at Coventry University in the UK. In her research, she is discursively evaluating interactions in therapy sessions within the IAPT (Increasing Access to Psychological Therapies) programme. Her research interests include prejudice in relation to Gypsies and Travellers, therapeutic interactions, cognitive behavioural therapy, depression and discourse analysis.

Brett Smith is a Professor within the School of Sport, Exercise and Rehabilitation Sciences at the University of Birmingham in the UK. His research passion is concerned with disability, health and well-being as well as qualitative inquiry. Brett's research has been published widely in leading journals and books. In addition to over 100 publications, he has given over 150 invited talks to audiences in numerous countries around the world, including to the

Royal Society of Medicine and in the UK Houses of Parliament. Brett is editor-in-chief of the international journal *Qualitative Research in Sport, Exercise and Health.* He actively serves on nine editorial boards. He is co-author of *Qualitative Research Methods in Sport, Exercise and Health: From Process to Product* and co-editor of the forthcoming text *The Routledge International Handbook of Qualitative Methods in Sport and Exercise.* He is also passionate about teaching and has been shortlisted for and awarded various teaching honours.

Jonathan A. Smith is Professor of Psychology at Birkbeck, University of London where he leads the interpretative phenomenological analysis (IPA) research group. He has taught qualitative research methods at all levels. He has developed IPA and applied it to a range of issues primarily, but not exclusively, in health. With Paul Flowers and Michael Larkin, he has written the key text on the approach, *Interpretative Phenomenological Analysis: Theory, Method and Research* (SAGE, 2009). He has published numerous papers employing IPA and has also edited a number of books on research methods in psychology.

Magi Sque holds a joint appointment with the University of Wolverhampton in the UK and the Royal Wolverhampton National Health Service Trust as Professor of Clinical Practice and Innovation to provide research leadership for health-care practitioners in the caring sciences. She studied nursing at Guy's Hospital, London. Specializing in oncological nursing, she worked clinically in this field for 17 years at the Royal Marsden Hospitals in London and Sutton and the Princess Margaret Hospital in Toronto. Supported by a British Department of Health Nursing Research Studentship, she completed a PhD in 1996 at the University of Southampton about the organ-donation experiences of 24 bereaved family members and the attitudes, knowledge and organ-donation behaviour of almost two and a half thousand UK-registered nurses. This work was the springboard for a programme of research that gained international recognition, particularly with regard to the care of bereaved families with whom organ donation is discussed. She edited a book on the topic with Sheila Payne, entitled *Organ and Tissue Donation: An Evidence Base for Practice* (Open University Press, 2007).

Edith Steffen is Lecturer in Counselling Psychology at the University of Roehampton in the UK, having previously taught at the University of East London and the Open University. She is a chartered and Health and Care Professions Council-registered counselling psychologist and has worked in secondary and tertiary care in the National Health Service for many years. Her main research interests are in continuing bonds and meaning-making in bereavement, anomalous experience and post-traumatic growth, and practice-relevant issues concerning diversity, spirituality and religion, and social justice. She is particularly interested in qualitative research. Her doctoral research at the University of Surrey, from which she graduated in 2011, focused on the experience of sensing the presence of the deceased in bereavement and incorporated a pluralistic approach as part of its methodological stance. As Associate Editor of the journal *Counselling Psychology Review,* she has been responsible for co-ordinating peer reviews and has taken editorial leadership on special issues on 'Power and equality' (2013), 'Existential approaches' (2014) and 'Positive psychology' (2015).

Lesley Storey is Lecturer in Political and Social Psychology at Queen's University Belfast in Northern Ireland. Her research has focused on identity, intergroup relations and the importance of social factors in a wide range of behaviours and states, including illness and well-being, particularly cancer. She has a special interest in qualitative research methods.

Gareth Terry is a Senior Research Officer in the Centre for Person Centred Research at AUT University (the Auckland University of Technology) in New Zealand. His work fits broadly within the areas of critical health and critical social psychologies. He has particular research interests in people living with chronic health conditions, men's health, body image, reproductive decision making (particularly the decision not to have children) and masculine identities. He has methodological interests in thematic analysis, critical discursive psychology and qualitative survey development, and has contributed to edited volumes in these areas.

Chris Walton is Lecturer in Social Psychology at Lancaster University in the UK. His research and publications have addressed a variety of topics, from masculinity and emotion to new genetic technologies to interactions involving people with intellectual disabilities. A commitment to the development of qualitative research methods has been a consistent feature across his research interests and publications, particularly the incorporation of non-verbal behaviour into conversation analysis.

SECTION I

Qualitative Research
in Psychology:
Setting the Scene

1

DOING QUALITATIVE RESEARCH: INITIAL QUESTIONS

Evanthia Lyons

This chapter outlines the aims of this book and provides an overview of the contents. It describes the main decisions and uncertainties that researchers face when conducting qualitative research at the different stages of the research process. It raises some of the questions that you, as a reader, should bear in mind when you attend to each chapter to help you make the most effective use of the book.

Background to the book

As a teacher and a researcher, I have often been faced with excited and anxious students and colleagues who were either about to embark on qualitative research or were in the midst of conducting qualitative research. In talking about their anxieties and excitement, they often commented on the uncertainties associated with making the decisions involved in the research process. Qualitative researchers soon realize that there are no universally-agreed right answers to questions such as the style of interviewing they should use to collect their data or which approach to data analysis they should adopt or how they can identify a theme in their analysis or the exact criteria they should use to evaluate their research.

This book aims to provide researchers who are new (or relatively new) to qualitative research with the methodological tools and conceptual maps they need to navigate their way through the process of qualitative research. It describes the uncertainties surrounding qualitative research and the many dilemmas faced by researchers. It illustrates these by drawing on the experiences of researchers with varying degrees of expertise in qualitative research. It also provides readers with the necessary background knowledge and raises their awareness of the questions they will need to address to help them make informed decisions about how to deal with these uncertainties and dilemmas.

Conducting qualitative research: quandaries and uncertainties

Qualitative research methods do not easily provide firm and incontestable answers to questions about the research process and data interpretation. This in part results from their underlying philosophical assumptions concerning how we should produce psychological knowledge. Although 'qualitative research' is a term that covers a number of different methods, as a bare minimum most of these methods share the assumption that there is no 'objective' reality or universal truths. Rather they are underpinned by the belief that knowledge and the processes that lead to its production are context specific. Furthermore there is the assumption that researchers and participants – together with other related individuals and groups of individuals, ideologies and social structures – are integral and dynamic parts of the context of the phenomenon under investigation (Dallos and Draper, 2010; Harré and Secord, 1972). Therefore there is no formulaic way, no blueprint, of how qualitative research ought to be conceptualized and conducted as the choices and decisions made throughout the research process are likely to define and influence what is researched, the data that are collected, how data are made sense of and the conclusions that are drawn.

However, it is important to emphasize that qualitative research is not a homogeneous domain. It is a domain that includes different research approaches and methods that are based on different philosophical assumptions concerning how we should produce psychological knowledge and what *can* be known, and have different scientific goals and guidelines for good practice (Denzin and Lincoln, 2011a; Henwood and Pidgeon, 1994; Willig, 2013). Furthermore, they are based on differing conceptualizations of the relationship between language, cognitions and reality. These sets of assumptions are the focus of a domain of the philosophy of science that is referred to as **epistemology** (Benton and Craib, 2001). Chapter 2 provides a fuller discussion of what epistemology is and the various epistemological stances underlying the different research methods.

The assumption that the production of knowledge and how we make sense of and talk about our social world is context specific, together with the wide range of methods available to those who want to conduct qualitative research, give rise to a number of questions at each stage of the research journey. For example, at an early stage, you have to decide whether you should use a qualitative methodological approach or a quantitative approach or a combination of these – which is called **mixed methods research** – to investigate a topic. If you decide to conduct qualitative research, then you are faced with a decision about which particular method(s) you should use.

At the stage of designing your research, you have to make decisions about how to use existing theory and knowledge gained from others' research findings. Do we take this knowledge into account when we, for example, formulate our research questions and/or design our interview schedule or choose which texts will form the data we plan to analyse (if we decide to analyse pre-existing data)? Do we engage with existing knowledge before, during or after the stage of interpreting our data and how do we ensure that pre-existing ideas do not overly influence how we make sense of what participants tell us – or should we? Should we give existing theory the same status that we give to what participants tell us (or, if we are not conducting interviews for data, what other sources of qualitative data tell us)? Furthermore, we need to reflect on how we conceptualize our role as a researcher. Do we see the researcher as a mere perceiver of the participants' meaning-making endeavours? Do we see the researcher as a perceiver *and* interpreter of what participants express? Do we see the researcher's role as one of taking apart accounts of a phenomenon provided by participants or other sources, identifying the assumptions that those accounts are based on, offering a social critique of the status quo and identifying alternative ways of conceptualizing our social world?

Both relatively novice and more experienced researchers feel a sense of excitement, perhaps bewilderment, and quite often anxiety when they face the task of analysing pages and pages of qualitative data. They may of course have a textbook that outlines a step-by-step guide and techniques for how to analyse qualitative data using their chosen analytic approach. But how do you apply these to your own data? Qualitative researchers quickly come to realize that this is not a straightforward process. No matter which approach to qualitative research you use, identifying a '**theme**' or a '**category**' or a '**discourse**' or a '**narrative**' from the data is not easy. However clearly the analytical steps are described in a textbook, applying them to a data set is not a mechanical process. It is a **meaning-making** process. It requires the researcher to immerse themselves in the data, make sense of the data and identify the 'themes', 'categories', 'discourses' or 'narratives' that would provide a recognizable and useful account of the data. However, what is recognizable and what is useful are to a great extent subjective judgements. In this sense, no single interpretation is the 'correct' or 'true' one.

This does not mean *any* interpretation is a good interpretation. We could argue that a piece of qualitative research should be evaluated along two main dimensions: firstly, its **rigour** and quality and, secondly, its usefulness (see Chapters 2 and 14 for more on this). So how does a researcher know which themes, categories, discourses or narratives are relevant and/or useful? Should their relevance and usefulness be determined by how good they are at providing a **descriptive** or an **explanatory account** of the data? Or should their relevance and usefulness be judged on how they engage with existing theoretical and empirical knowledge or their applicability to real-life situations? In any case, should they be relevant and useful to those who participated in the research or to those who funded it or to other potential users of the research findings?

Furthermore, qualitative researchers also face the task of disseminating their findings in a way that it is recognized by the participants, colleagues and other interested audiences as making a useful contribution. Given the diversity of the potential audience, how we present our findings orally or in a written form again raises a lot of questions. For instance, how can we show the rigour and quality of our research so that our academic peers accept the credibility and usefulness of our findings? How do we make our findings accessible to the groups of people who participated in the research? How do we persuade policy-makers to take notice of the findings of a research study that is based on perhaps just a few individuals, as often qualitative research involves small size samples? How can we ensure that our research has the desired political and social implications and avoid others exploiting the research for purposes we do not agree with?

These are just a few of the issues that qualitative researchers face and we as a research community do not have precise and universally-agreed answers. These issues are often resolved on the basis of the questions researchers seek to address and their exact assumptions about what can be known, what are valid ways of producing knowledge and the relationship between language, cognition and 'reality'.

The structure of the book

The contents of the book are organized in a way that reflects the three main objectives that Adrian Coyle and I had when we initially conceptualized this book. Our first objective was to provide readers with the necessary background knowledge and an awareness of the questions they will need to address in order to make informed decisions about whether to conduct qualitative rather than quantitative research and, if they decide to follow a qualitative path, which particular qualitative approach(es) would best suit their research goals. Our second objective was to equip readers with the basic tools to carry out their analysis by providing detailed, contextualized coverage of the practicalities of each of five qualitative methods/approaches: interpretative phenomenological analysis (IPA) (Smith, 1996, 2004), thematic analysis (Braun and Clarke, 2006, 2013), grounded theory (Charmaz, 2014; Corbin and Strauss, 2015; Glaser and Strauss, 1967), discourse analysis (Parker, 1992; Potter and Wetherell, 1987) and narrative analysis (Crossley, 2000; Frank, 2012; McAdams, 2013). In addition, the book includes accounts of an actual analysis of a specific data set in a step-by-step manner using the five approaches.[1] Our third objective was to provide the reader with

---

[1]The first edition of this book was a product of a workshop funded by the Economic and Social Research Council's 'Advanced Training in Social Psychological Research Methods' and organized by the editors in 2002. At that workshop, the data set presented in Appendix 1 was analysed by four groups of postgraduate students using interpretative phenomenological analysis, grounded theory, discourse analysis and narrative analysis under the guidance of expert facilitators. Since then both this work and the life circumstances of the original workshop facilitators have changed. This led to the inclusion of chapters on an additional analytic method, thematic analysis, and the involvement of new 'expert' and 'novice' authors. In this edition of the book, the authors of the 'theoretical' chapters on the methods (Chapters 4, 6, 8, 10 and 12) have supervised the analysis of the data set using the method in which they are experts and which is reported in Chapters 5, 7, 9, 11 and 13.

guidance as to how to write up qualitative research in general and how to report studies employing each of the five approaches in particular.

Thus, in addition to this chapter, Section I includes a chapter by Adrian Coyle that gives an account of the historical development of qualitative research methods in Britain and discusses in some detail some of the central issues underlying qualitative research. It also includes a chapter by Edith Steffen on ethical considerations in qualitative research. The chapter by Coyle aims to sensitize the reader to issues such as the value of qualitative research in psychology, the relationship between epistemology and method, and how qualitative research might be evaluated. The chapter provides a general background to qualitative research and raises questions that the reader may want to bear in mind when reading the theoretical and analytic chapters included in Section II in order to note how each of the five approaches deals with them. In Chapter 3, Steffen discusses some of the ethical issues that often arise in qualitative research as well as reminding us that ethical considerations should be at the centre of our thinking at all stages of research and not only at the time when we apply to an ethics committee for ethical review of our proposed research.

Section II includes five chapters (Chapters 4, 6, 8, 10 and 12) outlining the theoretical underpinnings and methodological issues involved in employing each of the five approaches to qualitative research that are focused on in this volume. These chapters contextualize the discussion of these issues by giving ample examples of the main questions and challenges faced by researchers who employ each of the analytical approaches and examples of how these were dealt with in particular projects.

Each theoretical chapter is followed by a chapter presenting the reflections of a member of a group or a relatively junior researcher (at the time) who analysed a specific data set using the approach described in the theoretical chapter. The main aims of these chapters are twofold. Firstly they reflect on the experiences of relatively novice researchers who used each method and secondly they provide a comparative context within which the reader can explore the similarities and differences amongst the five approaches. The data set used in this exercise can be found in Appendix 1. There the researcher who originally generated the data, Arnie Reed, provides a preface that places the data set in context.

The final chapter in Section II (Chapter 14) offers some reflections on the similarities and differences between the five focal analytic approaches. It extends the discussion on some of the issues raised in the introductory chapters as well as the subsequent theoretical and analytic chapters. In Chapter 14, I summarize and compare the position that each approach takes on these issues. Also, I consider the political implications of the choices we make in the research process, especially in relation to how we conceptualize the relationship between ourselves, as researchers, and the participants.

Finally, Appendix 2 includes examples of published work by researchers who used each of the research methods, with reflective commentaries on aspects of the writing-up process. These reports provide the reader with useful examples of and tips on how to write up qualitative research, thus completing the research process.

Doing qualitative research is certainly an exciting and challenging process. Its appeal is partly due to the rich data it produces and the opportunities it opens up for exploring the complex, ambivalent and often contradictory ways in which we make sense of and construct our social worlds. Reading this volume will, we hope, make it easier to explore issues that are important not only in a social and political sense but to you personally. However, it does not promise to answer all your questions as there are many that still remain unanswered by the research communities and there are others that are specific to particular research methods and that could not be covered in the space available in this book. Also, some questions can really only be answered through your own experience of qualitative research and your reflections on your experiences. We hope that the book inspires and equips you to roll up your sleeves and get your hands metaphorically dirty as you gather and analyse your own qualitative data to answer your own research questions. Through that process, what we give you here will be developed, refined and maybe even challenged.

CHAPTER SUMMARY

This chapter has emphasized the diversity of the research methods covered under the umbrella of qualitative research and has described some of the key assumptions these methods share. It argued that the assumptions that qualitative research approaches make about how we produce knowledge and its context specificity can leave researchers feeling uncertain about how to conduct research and to engage with qualitative data. The chapter has raised some of the questions that qualitative researchers often grapple with and has outlined the structure of the book.

Further reading

A volume that covers many approaches to qualitative research and deals with debates and tensions within the qualitative research paradigm is Denzin and Lincoln's (2011b), *The SAGE Handbook of Qualitative Research*. Willig's (2013) *Introducing Qualitative Research in Psychology* and Smith's (2015), *Qualitative Psychology: A Practical Guide to Research Methods* provide very clear and rigorous accounts of some widely used qualitative research methods and methodological debates within the field of qualitative research.

2

INTRODUCTION TO QUALITATIVE PSYCHOLOGICAL RESEARCH

Adrian Coyle

This chapter introduces the reader to some key issues in qualitative psychological research. It begins by reviewing the assumptions made by the standard 'scientific method' within psychology concerning *how* we can know and *what* we can know. These are contrasted with the assumptions that underpin different qualitative approaches. This discussion includes an historical account of the development and use of qualitative research in psychology. Attention then turns to some key issues in qualitative psychological research, including reflexivity, appropriate criteria for the evaluation of qualitative research and combining methods.

Introduction

The methodological repertoire of psychological research has undergone a remarkable change over the last few decades. I recall that when I was an undergraduate student in the mid-1980s, we received a very clear message from our lecturers that acceptable psychological research involved, among other things, the careful measurement of variables, the control of other variables and the appropriate statistical analysis of quantitative data. The possibility of conducting psychological research using qualitative methods was never entertained. Indeed, I remember thinking that qualitative work was something done by some of my unfortunate peers in sociology, who, I thought, did not seem to realize that their research could never be properly 'scientific'. How times have changed!

Beginning in a concerted way in the 1990s, British psychology developed an openness to qualitative work and a growing recognition of the contribution that qualitative research makes to a rich and broad disciplinary research profile. This can be seen, for example, in the frequency with which psychology conference papers and symposia feature qualitative work without methodology being a focal issue, the increasing number of qualitative articles in many peer-reviewed psychology journals, the plethora of books on the use of qualitative methods in psychology and the establishment of modules within psychology degree programmes and entire courses devoted to qualitative methods. In 2005 a Qualitative Methods in Psychology Section was established within the British Psychological Society which remains among the Society's largest sections. (The American Psychological Association now has a Society for Qualitative Inquiry in Psychology within its Division 5: Quantitative and Qualitative Methods.) Qualitative work has become a standard feature of many branches of psychology, especially in social psychology, health psychology, feminist psychology, psychotherapeutic and counselling psychology, clinical psychology and educational psychology. As a result, it is fair to say that psychology students in British universities today have a different methodological socialization compared to the one I experienced as an undergraduate, although coverage of qualitative methods can be tokenistic and there are some outposts where qualitative approaches are still resisted.

This chapter examines the development of psychological interest in qualitative methods in historical context and point to the benefits that psychology gains from qualitative research. It also looks at some important issues and developments in qualitative psychology. First, though, we will consider a vitally important matter that cannot be overlooked in any consideration of qualitative research – epistemology. This takes us into philosophical territory that might be a bit off-putting but I will try to make it as painless as possible. Try to stick with me because, if you can understand some basic points about epistemology, this will give you a framework for understanding important differences between approaches to research and for applying different approaches in a coherent way. Also, the term will reappear across the chapters in this book, which is why it is important from the outset to grasp what it means and its implications.

Epistemology and the 'scientific method'

At its most basic, qualitative psychological research may be regarded as involving the collection and analysis of non-numerical data through a psychological lens (however we define that) in order to provide rich descriptions and possibly explanations of people's meaning-making – how they make sense of the world and how they experience particular events. As Willig (2013: 8) notes, qualitative researchers 'aim to understand "what it is like" to experience particular conditions (e.g. what it means and how it feels to live with chronic illness or to be unemployed) and how people manage certain conditions (e.g. how people negotiate family life or relations with work colleagues)' – although this does not capture all qualitative research in psychology, as we shall see. The chapters outlining the principles and practicalities of the five focal methods in this volume specify the kinds of research questions that each method most readily addresses. However, qualitative psychological research involves more than this.

Qualitative research is bound up with particular sets of assumptions about the bases or possibilities for knowledge, in other words **epistemology**. The term 'epistemology' refers to a branch of philosophy that is concerned with the theory of knowledge and that tries to answer questions about *how* we can know and *what* we can know. All research approaches and methods are based on a set of epistemological assumptions that specify what kinds of things can be discovered by research which uses those approaches and methods. Epistemology is often discussed alongside **ontology**, which refers to the assumptions we make about the nature of being, existence or reality (and discussions often slip between the two).

I want to repeat a key point here: different research approaches and methods are associated with different epistemologies. It is important to bear this in mind because otherwise it is easy to assume that we are talking about a homogeneous domain when we refer to 'qualitative research'. Instead, the term 'qualitative research' covers a variety of methods with a range of epistemologies, resulting in a domain that is characterized by (potentially creative) difference and tension. In this section and the next, we shall examine the main epistemologies associated with both quantitative and qualitative research.

The epistemology adopted by a particular study can be determined by a number of factors. A researcher may have a favoured epistemological outlook or position and may locate their research within this, choosing methods that accord with that position (or that can be made to accord with it). Alternatively, the researcher may be keen to use a particular qualitative method in their research and so they frame their study according to the epistemology that is usually associated with that method (although note that many qualitative methods have some degree of epistemological flexibility, most notably thematic analysis – see Chapter 6 in this volume). Whatever epistemological position is adopted in a study, it is usually desirable to ensure that you maintain this position (with its assumptions about the sort of knowledge that the research is producing) consistently throughout the write-up to help produce a coherent research report. Sometimes a more flexible position on this is needed – for example, when using methods with different epistemologies within the same study. We shall return to this later.

If you are still reading and have not given up in despair at all this philosophical talk, you might be thinking that this concern with epistemology needlessly complicates qualitative research. If you have been using experimental approaches or other research designs in which you have been gathering and analysing quantitative data, you may not have encountered any major discussions about epistemology. This does not mean that those types of research have no epistemological position. It just means that those research approaches adopt an epistemology that is often taken for granted both in research and in life more generally. That epistemology can be referred to as positivist-empiricist and hypothetico-deductive, although, strictly speaking, positivism and empiricism are slightly different.

Positivism holds that the relationship between the world (that is events, objects and other phenomena) and our sense perception of the world is straightforward: there is a direct correspondence between things in the world and our perception of them, provided that our perception is not skewed by factors that might damage that correspondence, such as our vested interests in the things we are perceiving. Thus, it is thought possible to obtain accurate knowledge of things in the world, provided we can adopt an impartial, unbiased, objective viewpoint. The related domain of **empiricism** holds that our knowledge of the world must arise from the collection and categorization of our sense perceptions/observations of the world. This categorization allows us to develop more complex knowledge of the world and to develop theories to explain the world. Few scientists today adopt an unqualified positivist or empiricist outlook because it is generally recognized that our observations and perceptions do not provide pure and direct 'facts' about the world. Yet one fundamental claim from empiricism remains central in research, namely the idea that the development of knowledge requires the collection and analysis of data. This is something shared by qualitative researchers, although, compared with empiricists, we have very different ideas about what constitutes appropriate data and about how those data should be generated and analysed.

Researchers and students who have been exposed to a traditional methodological socialization within psychology (especially experimental psychology) will be very familiar with the theory of knowledge that developed in response to the shortcomings of positivism and empiricism – **hypothetico-deductivism**. The figure most closely associated with the development of hypothetico-deductivism, Karl Popper (1969), believed that no scientific theory could be definitively verified. Hence, the aim is not to obtain evidence that supports a theory but rather to identify theoretical claims (hypotheses) that are false and ultimately theories that are false. Research that adopts a hypothetico-deductive stance therefore operates by developing hypotheses from theories and testing these hypotheses. The assumption is that by identifying false claims, we can develop a clearer sense of the truth.

This approach involves **deductive** reasoning. In research, this means reasoning which begins with theories, which are refined into hypotheses, which are tested through observations of some sort, which leads to a confirmation or rejection of the hypotheses. This is sometimes referred to as a 'top-down' approach because it involves starting at a general theoretical level and taking claims from that level through more specific levels of reasoning – going down from general to specific.

As psychology developed as a discipline, it became identified with the assumptions of positivism, empiricism and hypothetico-deductivism – in short, the '**scientific method**'. This assumed that a reality exists independent of the observer (the ontological assumption of **realism**) and that we can access this reality through research. The research approach that would access reality accurately was held to be one that was characterized by objectivity and neutrality and precise measurement in hypothesis-testing. It was assumed that this would enable the researcher to obtain accurate, unclouded information about the psychological and social worlds. It was believed that objectivity and neutrality could be achieved by having researchers remain detached from their research so that they would not contaminate the research process with whatever personal investments they may have had in the research topic. So, for example, contact between researchers and participants was either minimized or standardized, so that each participant received the same instructions. In writing up research reports, the researcher was usually erased from the research process by the use of the passive voice rather than personal pronouns. Hence, rather than saying 'I developed a questionnaire', researchers would write 'A questionnaire was developed', erasing the agent in the process and creating the impression that the work was 'untainted' by human involvement on the researcher's side. Precision in measurement was assumed to be possible for any psychological dimension that existed. It was assumed that, through the development of progressively refined tests and measures, any psychological dimension that actually existed could be measured with precision.

Where qualitative work was undertaken within the 'scientific method', this was very much as a preliminary step before the 'real' research. For example, when researching an area that had not been researched before or that had been minimally researched, qualitative work might be conducted to identify the key elements in that area which could then form the basis of measurement instruments such as questionnaires. However, a few qualitative research methods embraced the 'scientific method' and all its apparatus. One example is Krippendorf's (2013) structured form of content analysis, which categorizes and quantifies qualitative data very systematically and is concerned with reliability in a way that is not shared by many other qualitative methods. This is an example of what has been called **'small q' qualitative research** (Kidder and Fine, 1987). This is research that uses qualitative tools and techniques but within a hypothetico-deductive framework. In contrast, **'Big Q' qualitative research** refers to the use of qualitative techniques within a qualitative paradigm which rejects notions of objective reality or universal truth and emphasizes contextualized understandings. All five research approaches that are examined in this book are examples of 'Big Q' qualitative research. We will now consider the historical development of that type of qualitative work.

We have started our consideration of qualitative research in psychology by noting how important it is to understand the assumptions that different research approaches and methods make about knowledge – what it is based upon and how it can be achieved. We looked at the assumptions that underpin the research designs that have long dominated psychology, such as experimental approaches and survey work. These have been referred to as the 'scientific method'. We noted that some types of qualitative research share these assumptions. In this book, though, we are concerned with approaches to qualitative research that are based on quite different assumptions and are *distinctively* qualitative – what has been called 'Big Q' qualitative research.

BITE-SIZED SUMMARY

··················

1

Resistance to the 'scientific method': alternative epistemologies and research foci

The 'scientific method' approach to psychological research has been resisted in some branches of the discipline. For example, in versions of psychotherapeutic psychology, from its early days emphasis was placed on qualitative case studies as a route to knowledge development. Freud (1909/1955) used that approach as a way of testing his theories. However, the truly 'scientific' status of this work was seen as dubious by the arbiters of scientific practice and it remained the methodological exception rather than the rule. Beginning in the 1960s and 1970s but becoming more evident in the latter part of the 1980s and the 1990s, there was a slow, incremental shift in British psychology as the discipline moved towards acceptance of at least some versions of qualitative research. This was the culmination of a long history of debate about what sort of knowledge psychologists can and should aim for in research (in other words, epistemological debate), even if this debate did not occur in the foreground of mainstream psychology.

Understanding individuals in context on their terms

In their concise historical account of the development of qualitative psychology, Henwood and Pidgeon (1994) trace this debate back to the work of Wilhelm Dilthey in 1894 who argued that the human sciences should aim to establish understanding rather than causal explanation (see also Denzin and Lincoln's, 2011a, review of the history of qualitative research across disciplines). This challenge proved persistent and it can be heard echoed in the nomothetic-idiographic debate of the 1950s and 1960s. This debate concerned the relative merits of **nomothetic research** approaches which seek generalizable findings that uncover laws to explain objective phenomena and **idiographic research** approaches which seek to examine individual cases in detail to understand an outcome. Researchers such as Allport (1962) argued that we cannot capture the uniqueness of an individual's personality simply by abstracting dimensions from aggregate statistical scores.

These themes can also be discerned within some influential early texts that advocated a shift towards qualitative methods within psychology. For example, in their 1972 book *The Explanation of Social Behaviour*, Harré and Secord expressed concern about the focus on the manipulation of variables and the dominance of quantification in psychological research. They saw this as reflecting a limited, mechanistic understanding of human beings whose complex humanity could never be captured by such an approach to research. In their classic 1981 text *Human Inquiry*, Reason and Rowan drew upon these and other ideas to advocate what they called a 'new paradigm' for psychology. Similarly, in their 1985 book, Lincoln and Guba called for a 'naturalistic' paradigm based upon the search for detailed description, which aimed to represent reality through the eyes of research participants and attend to the complexities of behaviour and meaning in **context**.

These concerns were also characteristic of psychological research informed by second-wave feminism in the 1960s and 1970s. One of the chief aims of feminist psychology is to reveal and challenge the ways in which male power has operated and continues to operate within psychology and the ways in which it has overlooked or misrepresented women's experiences. For example, psychology has long evaluated women's experiences in terms of male norms and, unsurprisingly, has found that women 'fall short'. It has looked for 'sex differences' in various domains and has turned up differences that represent women as inferior to men – except when those differences are in domains that allow women to excel in their 'natural' roles as wives and mothers (Wilkinson, 1996).

In a desire to explore women's experiences on their own terms and to allow women's voices to be presented without imposing pre-existent, ill-fitting frameworks of meaning, many feminist psychologists turned to qualitative methods that had a **phenomenological** emphasis. Such methods focus on obtaining detailed descriptions of experience as understood by those who *have* that experience in order to discern its essence. These methods are not concerned with producing an objective statement of an experience but rather with obtaining an individual's personal perception or account of the experience on their own terms. For example, one explicitly feminist qualitative method that was developed was the voice relational method, which has as one of its aims the hearing of voices that have often been suppressed and silenced such as those of adolescent girls (McLean Taylor et al., 1996). It does this through a careful, guided 'listening' to transcripts of interviews with those whose voices are not usually listened to and hence who have played no meaningful role within public debate. Some of the research methods covered in the present volume can be seen as practical responses to the concerns raised by these critics of the use of the 'scientific method' within psychology. For example, interpretative phenomenological analysis (IPA) has an explicitly phenomenological and idiographic commitment to discerning individual meaning-making within qualitative data (see Chapter 4).

These approaches involve **inductive** reasoning. In research, this means reasoning that begins with data, which are examined in light of a study's research questions. Patterns in the data are discerned and labelled. Some approaches link these patterns to existing theory or use them to create new theory. Inductive research is sometimes referred to as a 'bottom up' approach because it involves starting with the specific (that is, the data) and moving up from this level towards conceptual and theoretical levels.

Any type of qualitative research that seeks to uncover people's meanings and experiences in an inductive way has been described as embodying an 'experiential' approach (Braun and Clarke, 2013). Most of these forms of qualitative research have retained the realist commitment of the scientific method to some degree. They assume that a reality exists independent of the observer which can be accessed in some way through research and that participants' language provides us with a 'window' to that reality. This is not a straightforward, unqualified realism: many of these methods have adopted a **critical realist** outlook which assumes that, while a reality exists independent of the observer, we cannot know that reality with certainty. These are ontological and epistemological assumptions about reality and how we can know reality. However, feminist and other psychological researchers sought approaches that were critical in a different way and that allowed not just a phenomenological understanding of experience but also a critical understanding of the social and economic factors that determined experience. Both the voice-relational method and IPA permit this but the major focus for those who wanted to undertake thoroughly critical work was research methods that had a radically different epistemology – **social constructionism**.

Critical stance on the construction of reality

The milestone in the popularization of a social constructionist approach to psychological research was the publication of Potter and Wetherell's book *Discourse and Social Psychology: Beyond Attitudes and Behaviour* in 1987. This was to have a profound and unsettling influence on social psychology and sparked much debate and controversy within this and other branches of the discipline as it challenged the very foundations of what was regarded as legitimate psychological research. In broad terms, the social constructionist perspective adopts a critical stance towards the taken-for-granted ways in which we understand the world and ourselves, such as the assumption that the categories we use to interpret the world correspond to 'real', 'objective' entities (Burr, 2015). From a social constructionist perspective, the ways in which we understand the world and ourselves are built up through social processes, especially through linguistic interactions, and so there is nothing fixed or necessary about them: they are the products of particular cultural and historical contexts.

This is a **relativist** stance in which 'reality' is seen as dependent on the ways we come to know it. Research conducted within a social constructionist framework focuses on examining the ways of constructing social reality that are available within a particular cultural and historical context, the conditions within which these ways of constructing are used and the implications they hold for human experience and social practice (Willig, 2013). In contrast with an 'experiential' approach, relativist, social constructionist research has been described as embodying a 'critical' or 'discursive' approach to qualitative research (Braun and Clarke, 2013; Reicher, 2000).

Relativism and social constructionism contrast with the ontology and epistemology of other approaches to qualitative research which tend to assume that there is some relationship between the outcome of the analysis of research data and the *actualities* of which the analysis speaks. So, for example, if I were to analyse qualitative data from men on their experiences of expressing emotion, many analytic approaches would assume that the analysis reflects some sort of underlying truth or reality about these experiences. Many approaches may see the correspondence between the analysis and those experiences as not being an exact one because the men may have forgotten some of the details of what they described or because they engaged in particular self-presentations or because the analysis represents an interaction between the data and the **interpretative framework** (that is my professional and personal investments in the research) that I brought to bear on the data. Nevertheless, some relationship is usually assumed between the analysis and truth or reality from these realist and critical realist perspectives.

Social constructionism views things rather differently. Some qualitative methods that adopt a social constructionist epistemology hold on to the idea of data representing things that have an existence outside the data. Others are largely disinterested in whether there is a reality existing 'out there' to which qualitative data correspond and instead locate their focus of interest elsewhere. So, to return to our example, from a social constructionist perspective, data on emotions are not seen as reflecting some reality about emotions. Instead they are seen as accounts that construct emotions in particular ways and that use 'emotion talk' to perform particular social functions. Social constructionism can be quite difficult to grasp as its understandings run counter to so much that we take for granted in our world and in much psychological research. To find out more about it, turn to Chapters 10 and 11 in this volume which examine the main social constructionist research approach – discourse analysis.

You have now moved right across a spectrum of ontology and epistemology, starting with the realism of the scientific method, through critical realism and finally the relativism of social constructionism. You have also encountered other ways of categorizing types of research (deductive and inductive) and qualitative research (experiential and critical). All these terms might be a little confusing because they overlap in what they refer to. However, if you continue reading about qualitative research, you will encounter them again and again so it is useful to have them defined and related together in one place. The core commitments of each ontological position are summarized in Figure 2.1. I have not mapped the five qualitative approaches that are covered in this book onto this figure, partly because some approaches can be located in more than one position and partly because Evanthia Lyons

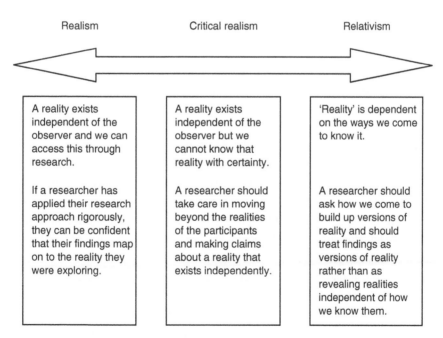

Figure 2.1   An ontological and epistemological continuum (based on material from Braun and Clarke, 2013)

examines this in Chapter 14. Also, the authors of the chapters that present the principles of each approach (Chapters 4, 6, 8, 10 and 12) discuss the ontology and epistemology of their approach in specific terms.

BOX 2.1 **Mapping ontology and epistemology onto actual research**

Below you will find modified versions of abstracts from three published qualitative studies. Information about the specific approach to analysis that was adopted in each study has been removed.

Consider each abstract and try to map the study onto the ontological and epistemological positions presented in Figure 2.1. Think about how the authors write about their findings and the relationship they assume between their findings and a definitive 'reality'.

You may find this tricky, partly because you only have a short summary of key points from each study and also because, as Evanthia Lyons observes in Chapter 14, researchers do not always adopt ontological and epistemological positions consistently in their research. If you need more information on the studies and how the researchers wrote about their findings, look up the whole articles and read them.

Consider the other ways in which we have categorized (qualitative) research – as deductive or inductive, as experiential or critical – and try to map the abstracts onto those categories too.

- This study explored what it is actually like to be depressed, that is, to capture the content and complexity of this experience from the view point of the sufferer. We present a case study of one man diagnosed with reactive depression. A semi-structured interview explored the experience of depression. The interview was transcribed and qualitatively analysed. We describe how his depression occurred in the context of work and financial difficulties and note how a sense of vulnerability emerged and contrast this with his reported experience of conventional masculinity. The process of becoming depressed involved the eruption of old negative memories and a catastrophic view of the present and future involving failure and death. We present a detailed analysis of two metaphorical constructions of depression. The features of depression form an interconnected whole. The experience of depression is so extreme that it is reported as if the person or self is dying. Onset appears to involve the destruction of highly valued life projects of the person. For some individuals, metaphors and images may be an actual part of the experience itself and contribute to it. (From Rhodes and Smith, 2010)

- Weight management services in the UK's National Health Service (NHS) are on the increase, partly due to rising rates of patients classified as obese. Those attending such services are held accountable, on some level, for their weight, although this issue is rarely addressed in clinical research in this area. By contrast, critical social research on obesity considers blame a prominent issue, though it has yet to examine this in interactions between patients and health professionals. This paper examines how blame is managed in the turn-by-turn interaction in group meetings within NHS weight management treatment. The data corpus consists of digital audio recordings of 27 discussion-based group meetings between patients and practitioners in a specialist weight-management service in central Scotland. The analysis focuses on those moments in which patients appear to resist the notion that they are responsible for their weight gain. Such moments are typically managed by patients in one of two ways: by denying having performed the blameworthy activity, or locating the blame as outside of individual control. Both strategies, however, rely on an individualistic concept of weight that reifies the medical model, while at the same time, troubling that model and its efficacy. The paper concludes with a consideration of the implications of these discursive practices and their relevance within the field. (From Wiggins, 2009)

- Two young adults' experiences of deliberate personal change in the realms of study habits and social interaction were examined using a qualitative, interview-based case study approach. Both talked about an aspect of their behaviour that they had changed and one that they would like to change. Qualitative analysis was used to interpret their stories and reach an integrative and contextualized understanding of their individual developmental trajectories. Our analysis explored the use of motivated reasoning to avoid or reinforce change, and the role of emotion in decision-making under uncertainty. These two themes are integrated in our discussion of the role of self-regulation in deliberate change, which sheds light on the experience of ambivalence about change and on the unpredictability of individual development trajectories. Building on theory and research on affective forecasting biases, we propose that a failure of 'experiential emotional anticipation' can explain ambivalence about personal change and why people sometimes do not act upon their rational beliefs. (From Lopes et al., 2014)

BITE-SIZED SUMMARY 2	We have traced the history of qualitative approaches to research in psychology. As the scientific method was found to be too limited in the insights that it could provide into human life, calls were made for approaches to research that would allow us to understand people in context, on their own terms and in all their human complexity. Such approaches were developed and some contemporary qualitative approaches to psychological research embody the same commitments. The psychology that arose from second-wave feminism sought research approaches that offered critical understandings of the social and economic factors that determine experience. Social constructionist approaches helped to answer that need. This historical account takes us from realist approaches to critical realist approaches to relativist, social constructionist approaches – right the way across the ontological and epistemological spectrum.

Reflexivity in qualitative research

If you have made it this far and are still reading, you deserve to be congratulated on your persistence and determination. We have covered some demanding philosophical ground and, if you have understood it, this will equip you to engage with qualitative approaches to psychological research in an informed way. You can relax now because we move onto less demanding terrain as we attend to a key feature of qualitative research: **reflexivity**.

Reflexivity refers to the acknowledgement by the researcher of the role played by their interpretative framework or **speaking position** (including theoretical commitments, personal understandings and personal experiences) in creating their analytic account. The role of the researcher's interpretative framework in generating data and producing the analysis is often regarded as a contaminating factor in most quantitative research – particularly the personal aspects of that framework. In contrast, many qualitative methods are characterized by an expectation that the researcher will make explicit their speaking position. In some research, there is a tokenistic engagement with this, where researchers present a mini-biography and fail to identify which aspects of their speaking position were salient in their research and in what ways these commitments influenced the research process and the research outcome (to the extent that this is available to the researcher's conscious awareness). However, properly done, this can acknowledge the role of the researcher and it can increase the **transparency** of the research process and so help readers to understand and evaluate the work. For an example of a researcher reflecting on their speaking position, see Box 2.2.

Reflections such as these can be readily incorporated within qualitative studies undertaken by undergraduate and postgraduate students, especially in disciplines such as

---

BOX 2.2

A researcher reflects on her speaking position

In her doctoral study of Pentecostal Christians' representations of and responses to people with mental health conditions, Victoria Uwannah (2015) offered some reflections on how her positions as a researcher and a Pentecostal Christian played out in her research. For example, she reflected on what she noticed about how she positioned herself during focus group interviews and the dilemma that this presented:

> During the interviews I noticed that I sometimes slipped into addressing the groups as 'we' in reference to Pentecostal Christians and later, as I listened to the recordings, I wondered why I did this and what effect it had on the interview process. I think at times I may have felt like I wanted the participants to know that I was on their side, that I shared an identity and commitment with them, that I wasn't there to 'catch them out'. This may have positively affected how at ease the participants felt but it also could have prevented certain material from coming up if there was an assumption that I would know all about Pentecostalism and wouldn't have to have Pentecostal beliefs, views and behaviours explained to me.

> I became particularly aware of my position and investment when interviewing people from my own church. At times when the group used words or expressed views that I knew would be classed as stigmatizing or negative, I inwardly cringed, thinking how best I could interpret or gloss over parts of the data that made it sound like 'we' were ignorant or insensitive to matters of difference. This feeling was present to some extent in all the focus group work. I felt I would be pulled in two directions when it came to the analysis – whether to be a researcher of integrity whose interpretations were determined by the data in productive interaction with my subjectivity or whether to defend 'my people'. As someone who was engaged in doctoral research and who is committed to psychological practice being based on good research evidence, I felt there shouldn't have been any question about priorities in my mind – but it *did* feel very much an 'either/or' situation at that point.

> A shift came when I began to read more deeply about how our realities are shaped or constituted by our interactions with others and with dominant

(Continued)

discourses. To put it simply, I realised that we are what we know. If we don't know possible alternative ways of seeing, feeling and acting, how can change occur? Instead of viewing my research as a potential exposé of Pentecostal Christians, I started to see it as a potentially positive situation in that, if I fed my research findings back to Pentecostal communities, this could create an impetus for forging new realities around how those communities understand and respond to mental health issues and to people with mental health histories in Pentecostal congregations. That realization enabled me to engage with the data in an open way and with a sense of integrity and 'mission' as a researcher *and* as a Pentecostal Christian.

counselling psychology and clinical psychology where personal reflectiveness is usually expected. Students can work these reflections into their research narrative at appropriate points. For example, the reflections in Box 2.2 could be located within an account of the analytic procedure and process. The only difficulty with this is that, if the rest of the account is written in a more detached style, the use of 'I' in the personal reflections can be rather jarring. In this case, it is necessary to think carefully about how best to achieve a consistent tone throughout the research report – for example, by writing in a more personal way throughout. Alternatively, personal reflections can be kept separate from the main body of the text. This, however, runs the risk of suggesting that the personal dimension is not really very important or that it somehow contaminates the qualitative research process and so has to be kept separate from the 'real' business of the research (that is the analyses). Instead, the personal dimension is an integral aspect of many qualitative methods.

While personal reflections can and should be included in student research reports, it is usually a different matter when writing for publication. Relatively few academic journals carry articles that feature analyses that include consistent personal reflections. This may be because tight word limits for articles mean that researchers prefer to focus on presenting findings. It does mean, though, that those findings lack an important contextual aspect and readers may be deprived of something that would help them to understand and evaluate the research. For more on reflexivity, see Finlay and Gough (2003).

Evaluative criteria for qualitative research

Having noted that a researcher's acknowledgement of their speaking position within a study can help the reader to evaluate the research, we now examine that issue further and consider how consumers of qualitative research (whether they be students, academics or service providers) can evaluate the worth of a qualitative study. Positivist-empiricist, hypothetico-deductive, quantitative psychological research tends to be assessed in terms of criteria such as reliability and internal and external validity. These rely on an assumption of objectivity – that the researcher and the research topic can be independent of each other. Hence the aim in this research paradigm is to limit researcher 'bias', with 'bias' being defined in terms of deviation from some definitive truth or fact. Given the contention in most qualitative research that the researcher is inevitably present in their research, any evaluative criteria that relate to strategies for eliminating 'bias' are inappropriate.

Using inappropriate traditional criteria to evaluate qualitative research means that inevitably the research will be found wanting. It is as if a music critic who is a specialist in heavy metal evaluates an opera in terms of its pounding, driving rhythm and loud elemental physical sound, expecting fast and furious screaming guitar lines. Inevitably an opera will fail to meet these criteria – but that means that the wrong criteria have been applied, not that the opera was of poor musical quality. For this reason, in their research reports qualitative researchers may wish to specify alternative criteria by which they wish their research to be evaluated. There is now a variety of such criteria available but I still find myself drawn back to criteria developed at the turn of the millennium by Elliott et al. (1999) and Yardley (2000). Together these sets of criteria have a scope and usefulness that have not been bettered.

Through a thorough process of consultation, Elliott et al. (1999) developed seven evaluative criteria that are considered common to qualitative and quantitative methods and seven criteria that are particularly pertinent to qualitative research. Some qualitative researchers have expressed reservations about these criteria (Reicher, 2000) and have favoured looser evaluative schemes such as that of Yardley (2000) whose criteria overlap with those of Elliott et al. (1999) in some respects. See Table 2.1 for both sets of criteria.

Yardley held that good qualitative research should embody elements of 'sensitivity to context', 'commitment and rigour', 'transparency and coherence' and 'impact and importance'. By **'sensitivity to context'**, she means that, among other matters, the research should make clear the context of theory and the understandings created by previous researchers using similar methods and/or analysing similar topics; the socio-cultural setting of the study (for example, the ideological, historical and socio-economic influences on the beliefs, expectations and talk of all participants, including the researchers); and the social context of the relationship between the researchers and the participants (see Box 2.3). **'Commitment'** is said to involve demonstrating prolonged engagement with the research topic and **'rigour'** relates to the completeness of the data collection and analysis. 'Transparency' entails detailing every aspect of the processes of data collection and analysis and disclosing/discussing all aspects of the research process; **'coherence'** refers to the quality of the research narrative, the 'fit' between the research question and the philosophical perspective adopted, and the method of investigation and analysis undertaken. **'Impact and importance'** relate to the theoretical, practical and socio-cultural impact of the study.

ADRIAN COYLE

Table 2.1 Evaluative criteria for qualitative research presented by Elliott et al. (1999) and Yardley (2000)

Elliott et al.'s criteria	Yardley's criteria
Criteria applicable to qualitative and quantitative research:	• Sensitivity to context
	• Commitment and rigour
• Explicit scientific context and purpose	• Transparency and coherence
• Appropriate methods	• Impact and importance
• Respect for participants	
• Specification of methods	
• Appropriate discussion	
• Clarity of presentation	
• Contribution to knowledge	
Criteria especially pertinent to qualitative research:	
• Owning one's perspective	
• Situating the sample	
• Grounding in examples	
• Providing credibility checks	
• Coherence	
• Accomplishing general versus specific research tasks	
• Resonating with readers	

BOX 2.3

'Sensitivity to context' in a study of perceptions of bystanders held by people who experienced workplace bullying

To take an example of what one of Yardley's (2000) evaluative criteria might refer to in practice, let us consider a qualitative study that sought to develop an understanding of how people who had been bullied in the workplace perceived the role played by bystanders to this experience – that is, workmates who witnessed the bullying or were aware of it but did not intervene to prevent it. Let us say that the researcher obtained their data by conducting individual interviews with people who reported that they had been subjected to workplace bullying.

In order for this study to demonstrate 'sensitivity to context', the researcher would need to relate the study to other relevant research and theory on bullying in general, workplace bullying in particular and the bystander phenomenon. We would expect the

24

researcher to note not only where the findings echo this previous work but also where they differ from it and to suggest new ways of conceptualizing the bystander effect in workplace bullying.

We would also expect that the participants and the researcher would be placed in context. This would involve describing the participants' demographic and other relevant 'background' details (such as sex, age, ethnicity, educational attainment and occupational history) and, in presenting the findings, orienting to how these factors may have shaped the reports that participants provided. So, for example, a female employee may not have expected male bystanders to intervene when she was subjected to bullying by a male supervisor for 'not being competitive enough' because she may have perceived the bully and the bystanders to share the same ideas about the necessity of a competitive ethic in the workplace and about women not being ideally suited to this. We would also expect the researcher to disclose whether they had experienced bullying in the workplace or in other settings and, if so, to suggest how these experiences might have shaped their expectations of the study and influenced the analysis.

We may also wish to see the researcher reflect upon the social context of their relationship with the participants, especially in terms of any power differentials. Although research participants have power during interviews as they possess something that the researcher wants, the researcher is usually on familiar terrain in the interview context and may use this familiarity to exert control. In this particular study, we would expect the researcher to be carefully attuned to issues of power because, if the researcher were overly controlling, the participant may experience this as replicating the bullying that they are talking about. Hence, we would hope to see the researcher discuss how issues of power were managed during the interviews and afterwards (for example, they may have sent draft analyses to participants to allow them to play an active role in interpreting the data).

As yet, there is no consensus about the best criteria for evaluating qualitative research, although there are recurrent themes among the criteria that have been developed relating to the provision of contextualized accounts of the participants, detailed accounts of the analytic process, an account of the researcher's speaking position and how this influenced the analysis and the consistent grounding of interpretations in research data. Indeed, it has been claimed that reaching consensus is impossible because of the heterogeneity of qualitative methods in psychology (Madill and Gough, 2008, have identified 32 methods of analysing qualitative data). Moreover, it has been contended that any attempt to specify generic evaluative criteria risks having qualitative studies evaluated by criteria that do not suit the particular form of qualitative research they have employed (Madill and Gough, 2008). This assumes, however, that the researcher exerts no control over the criteria that are applied to their work. The evaluative schemes that have been suggested should be seen as giving the researcher a range of credible criteria that have been tested through usage. The researcher can select those criteria that are most appropriate to their study, justify their choice of criteria and allow readers to assess that rationale and, if they agree, evaluate the study using those criteria.

Another criterion that appears in the schemes of Elliott et al. (1999) and Yardley (2000) relates to the practical utility of qualitative research. This is an important consideration that overlaps with Elliott et al.'s criterion about resonating with readers and is part of Yardley's 'impact and importance' criterion. This is sometimes referred to as the 'So what?' question, which arises from the view that good psychological research should inform professional practice, the delivery of public services or social policy or make some other sort of demonstrable or potential positive difference. For example, a clinical psychologist specializing in working with people with chronic conditions may enjoy reading a detailed qualitative analysis of an account offered by one person of their experience of living with Parkinson's disease (see Bramley and Eatough, 2005). However, they may then wonder, 'So what? What does this tell me about the experiences of the many people with Parkinson's disease whom I encounter in my work? How can my practice be improved by this study?' Given that relatively few qualitative studies

---

BOX 2.4	Applying Yardley's (2000) evaluative criteria

Choose one of the three studies presented in Box 2.1 and download the full article. (At the time of writing, two of three articles can be found through a Google Scholar search if your library does not have access to the relevant journals.) Read the article carefully and evaluate it using Yardley's (2000) four criteria.

- How did the article fare when evaluated using these criteria? What can you now conclude about the quality of the research presented in the article?

- Based on your initial reading of the article, do you think the assessment produced by these criteria is justified?

- Did any of the criteria seem more appropriate to the article than others?

can confidently claim to have charted the full diversity of their research topic, these 'So what?' questions can be frequently encountered. Various responses are possible. The researcher could explain that a more general picture of a research topic is progressively built up through a series of complementary qualitative studies, with each adding something new to that developing picture. Hence, an individual study represents a step in the process of building up a more general picture that could be used to inform therapeutic intervention. In addition, there is always the possibility of glimpsing something of the universal through the particular.

'Methodolatry' and flexibility in qualitative research

In her reflections upon her evolving understanding of the research process, Willig (2013: 4) talked about how, as an undergraduate, she thought of research methods as 'recipes'. These recipes specified the right ingredients (for example, a representative sample, a suitable measurement instrument and a relevant statistical test) and the order in which they had to be used to produce the right outcome. However, over the years, through her experience of research, she has come to view the research process as a much more creative enterprise centred not on the correct application of techniques but on the best ways of answering research questions. For her, the focus has shifted from the method to the questions that the research seeks to answer. Those of us who find methodology fascinating can sometimes lose sight of what is ultimately important in research and can become more concerned with using as pure a version of our favoured methods as possible. We can become guilty of methodolatry – a slavish attachment and devotion to method (Chamberlain, 2000).

This, of course, raises a question about the value of this book. With its focus on presenting the principles and practicalities of five popular qualitative research approaches and methods in psychology, does this book run the risk of promoting qualitative methodolatry within psychology? The answer to that depends partly on the way in which the material in this book is used.

For students and researchers who are using a particular qualitative method for the first time, it can be useful to have a set of steps that can be followed. Otherwise, lacking a clear sense of where to begin and how to move an analysis forward, students or researchers may experience anxiety about whether what they are doing qualifies as a legitimate version of whatever approach or method they are using. This can lead to the researcher becoming analytically immobilized. Hence, each of the five chapters that present the focal methods in this book (Chapters 4, 6, 8, 10 and 12) outlines steps or strategies that can be useful 'road maps' to guide the student or researcher who is new to these methods. However, continuing the analogy, it is important to remember that each of these maps represents only one route to an analysis. If the researcher becomes fixated on that route and regards it as the only possible way to achieve a legitimate analysis using that particular method, they are in danger of slipping into a methodolatrous stance. They are also in danger of producing a limited analysis, which could have been improved if they had explored different analytic routes that might have taken them along more creative and unexpected paths. It is worth noting that there is a theme of flexibility running across the five chapters that present the focal methods. Each of the writers on these methods acknowledges that there is more than one acceptable way to conduct an analysis using their approach.

So, it is fair to say that this book does not necessarily contribute to methodolatry, provided its chapters are not regarded as presenting the sole and definitive ways of applying the focal methods. Instead, the chapters should be seen as providing useful initial routes through the methods for novice researchers. With time and experience, these researchers should devise their own 'takes' on these methods and might even creatively develop the methods for future researchers.

BITE-SIZED SUMMARY 3

We have noted the importance accorded to reflexivity in qualitative research. The researcher's reflections on how their speaking position shaped the research process and outcome are not seen as indicating 'bias' in qualitative research but as acknowledging a necessary and important dimension of the research process and enhancing the transparency of the research. We have considered criteria by which qualitative research might be appropriately evaluated. Evaluative schemes for qualitative research centre on the contextualization of participants, the provision of detailed accounts of the analytic process, the consistent grounding of interpretations in research data, and reflexivity. Finally we noted the risks of lapsing into methodolatry – a slavish attachment and devotion to method – and recommended that researchers should ultimately aim to apply qualitative methods with flexibility and with a consistent focus on the research question.

Combining research methods and approaches

In recent years, it has become increasingly common to see both qualitative and quantitative methods being used in the same research project. Such a **mixed-methods** approach is a welcome development because it guards against methodolatry and can enrich research outcomes. Quantitative research and qualitative research perform different functions and so a project that incorporates both can benefit from what each offers, most obviously breadth and depth.

What can be challenging, though, is to integrate qualitative and quantitative findings that may have been generated by approaches and methods based on quite different epistemological assumptions. If we see integration as requiring all the findings from a research project to be united within one framework, that will be difficult to achieve. However, if we are more modest about what integration involves, possibilities open up. For example, Moran-Ellis et al. (2006) suggested that integration requires that different methods, which are oriented to the same research goal or question, are given equal weight within a project. Using this definition, a project could consist of relatively discrete qualitative and quantitative elements, with each equally contributing something different to the task of answering the research question(s).

I know from experience that this can work effectively: I was part of a team that examined public attitudes to new genetic technologies through a quantitative national survey, a quantitative study involving vignettes and qualitative studies using data from focus group interviews and the media. The data were analysed using statistical approaches, content analysis and discourse analysis but in ways that enabled the findings to 'speak' to each other (for example, see Shepherd et al., 2007). For more on the place of qualitative methods in mixed methods research, see Frost and Shaw (2014).

It should not be assumed that a combination of qualitative and quantitative methods is inherently superior to research that adopts a single approach. The sorts of research questions that are presented in the chapters on the focal methods (and in the empirical reports in Appendix 2) in this volume could not have been addressed using quantitative methods without losing richness and detail. The decision to use a combination of qualitative and quantitative methods should be determined by how best to answer particular research question(s).

In recent years, work has been conducted in psychology on a purely qualitative mixed methods approach. This has been undertaken by Frost and colleagues (Frost, 2011; Frost and Nolas, 2011; Frost et al., 2010) who have explored the value of applying different qualitative methods with different ontologies and epistemologies to a single data set. This has been termed a **pluralistic analysis**. Its aim is to produce rich, multi-layered, multi-perspective readings of any qualitative data set through the application of diverse 'ways of seeing'. Differences between the methods are not ignored: instead the task is to find ways of working creatively with differences to advance the research aims. Although we never intended it, the present volume can be seen as embodying a pluralistic approach. In Chapters 5, 7, 9, 11 and 13, researchers report on the process and outcome of applying each of the five qualitative methods addressed by this book to a common data set of two interview transcripts (which can be found in Appendix 1).

These developments in combining research approaches and methods may point to a new phase in the story of qualitative psychology. It may be the case that I belong to a generation of psychologists who have had to adopt a purist approach to qualitative research as part of a process of advocacy in order to shift the methodological terrain in British psychology. That process has come a long way and we should never assume that the advances that have been made are secure, especially given how enamoured the discipline has become with cognitive neuroscience perspectives. Nonetheless, it may be the case that new generations of researchers will be able to adopt a routine, pragmatic stance towards the selection of research methods, whether qualitative approaches (singly or in combination), quantitative approaches or a mixture of qualitative and quantitative, while remaining attentive to epistemological considerations, to produce comprehensive, creative and useful answers to psychological research questions.

If you are of that generation, I wish you well as you carry forward the work that my generation has undertaken in qualitative psychology and I hope that this book will help equip you for the journey.

CHAPTER SUMMARY

This chapter has presented some core issues that are relevant to and will help to contextualize the five qualitative research methods that are addressed in this volume. Readers who attend carefully to the material presented and who consult other important work that is cited here will find themselves equipped to undertake good qualitative research. However, the key factors in determining the ultimate quality of their research will be the skill and creativity with which they apply the principles of the various methods.

Further reading

Those who are coming to qualitative research for the first time are in a fortunate position because there are now many good-quality books available that, like the present volume, provide a background to the emergence of qualitative research in psychology and details of specific approaches and methods. The *magnum opus* of qualitative research across disciplines is Denzin and Lincoln's (2011b) edited volume, *The SAGE Handbook of Qualitative Research*. In the UK, noteworthy examples include Willig's (2013) *Introducing Qualitative Research in Psychology* and the edited volumes by Willig and Stainton-Rogers (2008), entitled *The SAGE Handbook of Qualitative Research in Psychology*, and by Smith (2015), entitled *Qualitative Psychology: A Practical Guide to Research Methods*. Further reflections on assessing the quality of qualitative research can be found in an article by Meyrick (2006). To help guard against becoming fixated on method, it is worth reading Chamberlain's (2000) article about the dangers of methodolatry.

3

ETHICAL CONSIDERATIONS IN QUALITATIVE RESEARCH

Edith Steffen

Ethical questions arise at every stage of the research process from initial design, through fieldwork and analysis to the dissemination of research findings. This chapter considers principles and levels of research ethics and how these apply in qualitative research contexts, focusing on the fieldwork and data analysis stages. The analysis stage tends to be relatively overlooked in writing on qualitative research ethics but it requires a high level of reflexivity and ethical responsibility as researchers are in a powerful position when interpreting participants' words.

Introduction

'Ethics' literally translates as 'the study of morals' and is a term that is used synonymously with moral philosophy – a branch of philosophy that is concerned with the theory of morals and how we ought to live our lives. Deciding how to behave from a moral or ethical perspective in a given situation is not a simple matter. Morals and values can clash and compete with one another, in which case we are faced with a moral dilemma. If you take a moment to think about your own life, you may be able to think of a number of moral dilemmas that you have faced or could face. For example, you might be committed to attending a very special family event but find that your best friend is heart-broken and needs your comfort. What would be the most ethical thing to do? While ethics cannot make that decision for you, it could help you raise your awareness of what exactly the dilemma is about and how the decision could be approached, so you become clearer about what may be the most important course of action in a given situation.

How can ethics achieve this? It depends on the branch of ethics. There are at least five different positions within the field of ethics (Hammersley and Traianou, 2012; Wiles, 2013):

1. the study of duty ('deontology'), which focuses on the action or behaviour itself;

2. the study of the outcome of action ('**consequentialism**'), which focuses on which action would get the best result;

3. studying each case separately ('**situationism**');

4. the study of the actor ('**virtue ethics**'), which seeks to develop moral judgement and virtue in the person;

5. the ethics of care ('**relational ethics**'), which focuses on relationships, interdependence and process.

Research ethics

Although making ethics-related decisions as a researcher is different from making decisions about moral priorities in our personal lives, one of the important commonalities is that, as researchers, we may sometimes not be aware that what we are faced with is a moral or ethical dilemma. In the pursuit of knowledge, researchers can lose sight of the values and commitments that are at stake or the moral and ethical boundaries that might inadvertently or, indeed, intentionally be broken. There are many examples in the history of research in which the relentless pursuit of data and discoveries was accompanied by ethical blunders. For example, the development of the 'HeLa cell line' from a cancer cell taken from a patient called Henrietta Lacks led to major medical discoveries such as the polio vaccine and advances in the treatment of cancer and AIDS. However, neither Henrietta Lacks nor her family gave consent to having her tissue appropriated in this way, nor did she or her family agree for her name to be made public, nor was any compensation made (see Skloot, 2010).

Apart from accidental and intentional ethical omissions, the darker side of the history of science includes many examples of harmful research. The 'experiments' carried out by Nazi doctors on their victims are among the most harrowing examples of such practices. As a result of the public outcry at the harm done in the name of science, the second half of the twentieth century saw the development of research ethics codes and legislation to regulate research conduct and protect participants against abuse and exploitation. Before that, it had been up to the researcher to show the required responsibility, in line with a virtue ethics position. The emergence of ethics codes brought about a shift towards duty ethics or deontology. While the new ethical systems initially regulated medical research only, social research soon adopted similar frameworks.

In psychology, we have some famous examples of psychological research that caused harm or could have caused harm to participants such as Milgram's (1963) study of obedience to authority and the Stanford Prison Experiment (Zimbardo, 1973). These are often cited as lending support to the need for ethical frameworks and regulations in psychology. It may be reassuring that such research designs would not pass ethical review now in their original form.

The most prominent ethics codes that are relevant to psychology in the UK today are the British Psychological Society's (BPS) (2009) *Code of Ethics and Conduct*, the BPS (2010) *Code of Human Research Ethics* and the Economic and Social Research Council's (2015) *Framework for Research Ethics*. While these ethical frameworks cannot prescribe what counts as ethical or unethical behaviour in every instance and at every stage of different research processes, they lay down particular principles of conduct – that is fundamental assumptions that those researchers to whom the code applies are required to adopt. They are therefore essential reading for anyone wanting to conduct psychological research in the UK.

Some have criticized the increasingly regulatory climate in which research with human participants now takes place, taking issue with what has been termed an 'accountability regime' (Hammersley and Traianou, 2012: 7) which could lead to 'dull conformity', 'an end to serious creative thinking, an end to ethics' (Parker, 2005: 18). It could perhaps be maintained that there may sometimes be a conflict between the arguably 'defensive practice' of ethics committees which evaluate the ethical implications of proposed research and the spirit in which the general ethics codes have been written. For example, the BPS (2010) *Code of Human Research Ethics* lists just four basic principles:

- respect for the autonomy and dignity of persons;
- scientific value;
- social responsibility;
- maximizing benefit (**beneficence**) and minimizing harm (**non-maleficence**).

The code provides some explanation of these principles but it is left to the individual researcher to take responsibility for their application and to use ethical reasoning to think through dilemmas that may arise during the research. In fact, it defines ethical research conduct as 'in essence, the application of informed moral reasoning, founded on a set of moral principles' (BPS, 2010: 7). This is important, as ethics is not just a stage in the research that can be resolved once and for all by satisfying the relevant ethics committee. It is essential for researchers to continue to reflect on the ethical dimensions of their research at all stages and on multiple levels. Ethical frameworks may be used to regulate and constrain research but they can also be seen as aids to ethical thinking (Wiles, 2013), especially when faced with the unexpected, as is often the case in qualitative research.

BITE-SIZED SUMMARY

1

There are different branches of ethics that focus on different aspects of an action or situation: deontology or duty ethics, consequentialism or outcome ethics, virtue ethics, situationism and relational ethics. Ethics codes tend to be deontological, that is concerned with regulating the way research is carried out. They provide ethical principles that need to underpin the entire research process. Psychological researchers in the UK need to abide by the BPS *Code of Ethics and Conduct* and the BPS *Code of Human Research Ethics*. Ethical principles underpinning psychological research include respect, scientific value, social responsibility, beneficence and non-maleficence.

Ethics and research design

The design stage of research often causes novice researchers the greatest worry. There is a great deal to think about and to take into consideration. As stated above, the science aspect and the ethics aspect of research go hand in hand, and the proposed design of the study needs to be suitable to answer the questions that are being asked. Otherwise the study would be a waste of everyone's time and involvement. We therefore owe it to those who support our research – whether funders, supervisors or participants as well as to ourselves and the relevant knowledge communities and wider society – to ensure that our study makes sense and is workable.

The different ethical questions that need to be addressed at the design stage are sometimes thought of in terms of micro and macro ethics (Brinkmann and Kvale, 2008). The level of **micro ethics** is about our relationships with participants, particularly at the fieldwork stage. This includes details around sampling and access to participants, **informed consent**, **confidentiality** and anonymity, potential risks and safety measures. Micro ethical matters are unlikely to get overlooked because they are institutionalized in the ethics review process that almost all research involving human participants now needs to undergo. The level of **macro ethics** addresses our relationships with the wider world. Here it can be asked: 'How can the findings be applied?'; 'Who is likely to benefit from the research?'; 'What potential harm may the dissemination of the findings cause?' The macro level is not always given the attention it deserves. Novice researchers in particular sometimes suffer from a lack of researcher self-esteem and so are reluctant to believe their research could make a difference. However, by not acknowledging the potential impact of our research, we may not only deny its potential for benefit but also its potential for harm.

In between micro and macro ethics, the level of **meso ethics** could be added, as addressing our relationships with knowledge communities. Questions to ask here include: 'Have I searched the literature enough to know that my research can really add something to existing knowledge?'; 'Is my research question likely to produce the knowledge that I am looking for?'; 'Is there a match between my research question, the methods I want to use and my epistemological position?'; 'Do I have the skills to carry out the proposed research and, if not, do I know how to acquire them?' While these questions tend to be viewed as related to science rather than ethics, it is suggested here that these also need to be seen as part of the researcher's ethical accountability, relating directly to the ethical principle of 'scientific value'.

Research ethics in qualitative research

The general principles laid out in the ethics codes mentioned above apply to all research, whether quantitative or qualitative. However, there are also specific ethical issues that apply only or particularly to qualitative research. Before looking at these in more detail, let us consider the ethics of qualitative research at a general level. One view that could be taken is to see qualitative research as intrinsically ethical. Extreme as it may seem, such a perspective may have some foundations. For example, researchers who conduct 'Big Q' qualitative research (Kidder and Fine, 1987) – that is, those who do not simply import qualitative data into a positivist framework but who embrace a qualitative orientation to the research process as a whole and cultivate 'a qualitative sensibility' (Braun and Clarke, 2013: 9) – may be likely to apply critical reflection to the research process and to value the subjectivity of their participants and the context-dependent nature of the data. This could be seen, by its very nature, to embody an ethical stance of respect for the dignity of persons within a relational focus. However, there are some problems with such a view, which has been labelled 'qualitative ethicism' (Hammersley, 1999). Brinkmann and Kvale (2008: 8) have argued, for example, that qualitative research is in fact 'saturated with ethical issues' and that researchers need to be even more attentive to ethics here due to concealed forms of power exertion that may operate. We shall return to this point. Table 3.1 lists some of the aspects of qualitative research that lead to specific ethical considerations.

Ethical considerations for fieldwork in qualitative research

The following issues should be considered *prior to* starting the research. In fact, these issues should be thought about at the proposal-writing stage but often this is not dealt with until the stage of applying for ethical review. University ethics committees are particularly concerned with the safety of participants but also the safety of researchers. There are some general considerations that apply across different designs but it is just as, if not more, important to consider the ethical issues that are specific to the proposed individual research project.

Table 3.1 Specifics of qualitative research and associated ethical issues

Issue	What this means	What risks are implied	How to address this
Uncertainty of outcome	We cannot predict what exactly will happen, whether during fieldwork or during the analysis.	There are limits to how informed 'informed consent' can be.	Being transparent. Procedures can be detailed but not the final outcome.
Interest in personal detail and in the actual words that people use	Private information will be made public.	There may be a risk to confidentiality.	Protecting participants' identity though anonymization.
Interest in 'real' people within the contexts of their actual lives	We may ask questions about participants' circumstances and wider contexts.	Risk of higher disclosure than intended and unexpected impact of research on context.	Informed consent as an ongoing process.
Importance of the researcher–participant relationship	Participants need to be able to trust researchers to treat them with respect.	Risk of abuse of power.	Need to adhere to principles of honesty and respect.
Possibility of 'dual relationships'	The researcher may know the participant in another capacity outside the research context.	Conflict of interest could be damaging to both the research and the other relationship.	To avoid if possible. If unavoidable, agree with the participant how to handle any conflict.
Researchers make decisions about how to analyse the participants' words	Researchers decide what aspects of the data to focus on, how to read and make sense of the data.	Data analysis is often invisible, giving researchers much power, with the potential to abuse it.	Informing participants about the general approach to data analysis prior to fieldwork.
Researchers may be personally highly involved in their research	'Insider' research: researchers may feel personally affected by the issues and participants' disclosures.	There is a risk of researchers pursuing a 'personal agenda' and/or experiencing emotional distress.	Reflexivity: keeping a research journal; discussing issues with a research supervisor; seeking help with own emotions if needed.
Researching 'the other'	The opposite to insider research: researching a member of a group one does not belong to.	When 'studying down' (participants with lesser power), there is a risk of misrepresentation, paternalism and abuse.	Involving participants in research as researcher-participants who share decision-making.

Sampling and access to participants

Researchers need to consider who their participants will be and how they will access them, which is tied to the research aims and questions. Thus, if my research wishes to explore how pregnant commuters experience travelling to work on overcrowded trains, the broad category of 'pregnant commuter who uses trains' can be further broken down in terms of stage of pregnancy, years of commuting prior to pregnancy or type of train travelled on, whether I am interested in those covering a longer or a shorter distance to work, and other potentially relevant considerations, thus defining clear inclusion and exclusion criteria. Amongst these should be criteria directly concerned with participants' well-being. For example, the researcher may decide to interview only women who are experiencing 'uncomplicated' pregnancies.

Accessing participants can be fraught with ethical issues, especially when it involves making contact with and gaining approval from so-called 'gatekeepers' (that is, people who can open up (or close off) access to your sample population) before participants can be contacted. Possible power relationships between gatekeepers and participants need to be taken into consideration to ensure the research is not 'tacitly "coercive"' (Miller and Bell, 2012: 64). It may be helpful to ask how participants would be able to resist participation, especially if they are vulnerable. In the example of pregnant commuters, advertising the research in GP surgeries would enable participants to 'self-select' freely. However, if access is gained via their midwife, they may find it harder to resist complying because they may fear that this would adversely affect their relationship with their midwife and thus their treatment.

Informed consent

Respect for the autonomy of participants demands that sufficient information is provided so they can make an informed decision about whether or not to participate in the research. Note, however, that this is not a one-off decision. Not only do participants have the 'right to withdraw' at any time, as in all research with human participants, but, due to the open-ended nature of qualitative research, there is also a need for ongoing or 'process consent' (Wiles, 2013: 28). The principle of informed consent requires researchers to explain clearly:

- what the research is about;
- what is involved;
- what the potential advantages and disadvantages are;
- whether there are any risks and how they will be addressed;
- who participants can contact for further information or to make complaints about how they have been treated;
- how confidential their participation is;
- how personal information is anonymized;

- how the data are used;
- how the data are stored;
- whether and how the research will be disseminated;
- what potential impact the findings may have.

Potential participants need to be given sufficient time to read, consider and possibly discuss with others the implications of taking part in the research and to ask for further explanations and information. Thus, letting participants have the necessary information at least one week in advance of any interviews is considered good practice.

Although the points above may seem like a comprehensive list, there are many unknowns at the outset, meaning that 'fully' informed consent is unrealistic. For example, government-funded research now tends to require digital data sharing, which implies that participants would also need to consent to their data being stored for as yet unknown future uses, presenting a host of additional ethical issues (see Mauthner, 2012). Another issue that has been debated in the qualitative research literature is whether or not to disclose how the data will be analysed, as this has implications for how participants are 'represented' in the eventual findings (Doucet and Mauthner, 2012). A desire for transparency and openness would call for disclosure. Yet there is a limit to what can be disclosed prior to the fieldwork, as most analytic decisions cannot be made until the actual data are available. Thus, participants may only be able to consent to researchers' broad interests and approach, not to the final form and content of the analysis.

Confidentiality and anonymity

The issue of confidentiality is closely tied up with informed consent. Participants need to know whether their material will be kept confidential. In qualitative research, there is an increased risk of identification due to the reporting of the actual words of real-life individuals in most research outputs. While **anonymization** strategies can be employed to reduce the risk of identification (see Howitt, 2013, for a helpful list), there are exceptions where confidentiality may need to be broken (for example, the disclosure of risk to life). There are other threats to confidentiality. For example, Saunders et al. (2015: 1) have pointed out that it is becoming increasingly possible to 'cross-link' online information on individuals which can lead to 'jigsaw identification' (the identification of someone by assembling different information from different sources). Ethical dilemmas about identification can also be presented by the opposite case, namely when participants actually *want* to be identifiable. Qualitative research has often been used to 'give voice' to participants from marginalized groups whose voices are seldom heard or attended to in the public square. Insisting on anonymity could be seen as denying participants their voice or attributing fragility to them on the basis of their group membership, whereas a 'positive ethics' view (Nolas, 2011: 139) could entail treating participants as 'moral agents' who can make their own choices.

Interviewing and debriefing

Fieldwork ethics in qualitative research has its most poignant application in the face-to-face meeting between researcher and participant which tends to revolve around the research interview in most cases. Different ethical questions arise for one-to-one interviews and for focus group interviews. However, some common ethical recommendations apply. These include treating participants with respect throughout, giving them space to ask questions, allowing time to settle in as well as for **debriefing** at the end, asking open and clear questions and ensuring participants' well-being at all times. If participants become distressed during the interview when addressing personally sensitive issues, it is of utmost importance to respond empathically and sensitively, to ask if they would like to stop and take a break, skip to another question, postpone the interview to another time or withdraw altogether.

In a focus group interview, additional ethical challenges may include managing hostility or discord between participants or, more likely, managing the extremes of very quiet and very outspoken participants. Talking about sensitive issues in a group setting can be more difficult. Participants may be left feeling exposed if they disclose more than they meant to or they may find their distress about difficult experiences echoed and amplified by hearing other participants reflect on similar experiences. Specific guidance on facilitating focus groups and managing group dynamics should be consulted when planning focus group research (for example, Stewart and Shamdasani, 2014).

As regards the researcher–participant relationship, an interesting point has been put forward by Duncombe and Jessop (2002). They have observed a tendency for 'faking friendships' (p. 109) in qualitative fieldwork through the deliberate use of certain interpersonal skills for building rapport. Similarly, Brinkmann and Kvale (2008: 267) discuss the seductiveness of 'semi-therapeutic relationships'. The concern expressed by these authors is that there may be a danger of creating an atmosphere of intimacy in order to 'draw' intimate disclosures from participants when in fact such relationships cannot be maintained post-interview. However, there is a difference between 'faking friendship' and using therapeutic or counselling skills such as empathic reflection. The use of counselling skills in qualitative interviews can have significant benefits, especially when researching sensitive issues, as this could increase the sense of safety for participants – although care needs to be taken not to mislead participants that explicitly therapeutic input is on offer (Coyle and Wright, 1996).

Online research

Online qualitative research is a growing area that is accompanied by specific ethical issues. King (2010) has identified four areas of particular concern: the establishment of participant identity, the effects of visual anonymity, maintaining confidentiality online and managing online relationships. Different strategies can be used to manage these newer ethical issues. It is recommended that researchers follow the *Ethics Guidelines for Internet-Mediated Research* (BPS, 2013).

BITE-SIZED
SUMMARY
....
2

At the stage of designing and planning a research project, ethical questions arise at different levels that need to be considered, ranging from local fieldwork questions to questions about the broader impact of the research. In relation to qualitative fieldwork, researchers need to consider the ethical aspects of inclusion and exclusion criteria for sampling and any ethical issues in gaining access to participants. Participants need to be equipped to provide informed consent to take part in a research project, having considered what is involved and its implications as fully as possible. Researchers have a duty to keep confidential any information that could identify participants to anyone outside the project (with some exceptions). Interviewing requires the use of interpersonal skills including empathy and sensitive responsiveness to the interviewees' needs. Researchers conducting focus group interviews or online qualitative research need to consult ethical guidance specific to the demands of those contexts.

Ethical issues in qualitative data analysis

Much of the attention of ethics codes and ethics committees is concerned with the safety of research participants during fieldwork. In the research ethics literature, there is a general neglect of issues that arise during the data analysis process, with some notable exceptions. For example, Willig (2012: 45) has pointed out that qualitative data analysis always involves interpretation, whichever analytic stance is taken, and this necessarily includes some appropriation and misrepresentation, including the risk of 'interpretative violence' (see also Chapter 14 in this volume). Doucet and Mauthner (2012: 127) similarly state that it is during the analysis that 'the power and privilege of the researcher are particularly pronounced [ ] because of the largely invisible nature of the interpretive process'. Taking a feminist relational stance to research, they view this issue as part of the accountability that researchers hold in terms of their relationships with participants and wider research communities.

One frequently raised question concerns the extent to which researchers' interpretations *represent* their participants. Analysis has been described as 'an act of betrayal, no matter how well intentioned or integrated the researcher' (Miles and Huberman, 1994: 265). Partly this could be due to a mismatch between the participants' expectations and the kinds of findings the analysis is likely to produce, leading one researcher to express fear about possibly encountering 'a participant's anger or pain in hearing my interpretation of their experience' (Price, 1996: 209). For example, imagine you have interviewed participants about their experience of calling in sick at work and your interpretations discuss the 'different types of excuses people come up with when they pretend to be ill'. This kind of interpretation is unlikely to represent the participants' own understandings and could lead to anger and distress if they read the research report. Participants' expectations of what they thought they were contributing to may be violated here, depending on what they were told at the outset about the nature of the research question and potential analytic foci.

Some analytic stances may be more prone than others to lead to a conflict of perspectives between researchers and participants. Hammersley (2014) has used the example of interviewing for discourse analysis as a potential case in point. He draws attention to the possibility that participants might not give consent if they realized that the accounts they provided would not be used to gather information about a phenomenon but 'to obtain a sample of the discursive practices they employ' (p. 532). However, he argues, gaining **informed consent** for discursive interpretation would not be very practicable, as participants would become self-conscious, thus undermining the aim of the research.

An important distinction to draw here is between an empathic and a suspicious hermeneutic or interpretative stance. Willig (2012) has used this distinction to point out the different interpretative attitudes underlying different analytic approaches, which could be seen as located on a continuum (see Figure 3.1). For example, a phenomenological approach would be located at the empathic end of the continuum as it seeks to understand people's own meaning-making as closely as possible, whereas a discursive or psycho-social perspective would be located at the more 'suspicious' end of the continuum as these approaches tend to interpret data in the light of theoretical frameworks that seek to explain participants' experiences and language behaviour rather than understand them from participants' own viewpoint.

Different strategies for managing the ethical dilemmas that may arise for researchers in the analytic process have been put forward. Doucet and Mauthner (2012) advocate a

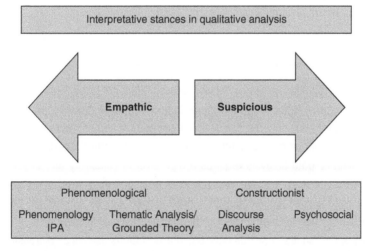

Figure 3.1 A continuum of empathic-suspicious interpretative stances (based on Willig's, 2012, continuum of interpretative styles)

particularly thoroughgoing level of **reflexivity**, the maintenance of relationships throughout the research process and the need to attend particularly to the justification of knowledge claims. Willig (2012: 56) has suggested three strategies:

> (1) keeping the research question in mind and being modest about what the research can reveal, (2) ensuring that the participant's voice is not lost, and (3) remaining open to alternative interpretations.

Willig (2012) also refers to pluralistic research as a potential way forward – that is, research involving the application of different qualitative methods to a single data set with the aim of producing rich, multi-layered, multi-perspective analyses (Frost, 2011; Frost and Nolas, 2011). Rather than assuming 'one truth' or attempting to merge different epistemological stances into one, pluralism can move between different levels of interpretation, holding in mind that 'qualitative research is about attempting to discover new aspects of a totality that can never be accessed directly or captured in its entirety' (Willig, 2012: 162). To illustrate, when studying the experiences of bereaved people who had sensed the presence of a deceased loved one, Adrian Coyle and I applied both a phenomenological and a discursive analytic lens to the same data set (Steffen and Coyle, 2011, in press). While the phenomenological perspective captured how participants described the lived experience of the phenomenon and what the experiences meant to them, the discursive perspective revealed that participants worked to justify the veridicality of their experiences and to ward off alternative explanations. This could be seen in the context of dominant conceptualizations of such phenomena, which tend to pathologize these experiences as intrapsychic phenomena, dismissing perceivers' own understandings. Taking one stance alone when researching sensitive or controversial experiences can prove reductionist, while a pluralistic approach can offer a more holistic understanding.

BITE-SIZED SUMMARY

3

The analytic process in qualitative research tends not to be routinely thought of as an enterprise that poses ethical challenges. Data analysis involves interpretation. This implies not only the risk of misinterpretation and misrepresentation but also the potential to do harm through what can be termed interpretative violence. Qualitative data analysis requires a high level of reflexivity and ethical responsibility, as researchers are in a powerful position when interpreting participants' words. Different analytic stances adopted by researchers can be seen as lying on a continuum between a hermeneutic of empathy and a hermeneutic of suspicion.

Modesty and openness towards different interpretations as well as pluralistic research approaches may offer a way forward.

> ### BOX 3.1 | Applying the principles of ethical research
>
> Consider the following scenario:
>
> You are seeking to study how immigrant families talk about and construct the experience of being ostracized. A father of an immigrant family has told you that he and his family would like to take part. When you arrive for the interview, the teenage children seem reluctant to participate. Furthermore, the father tells you his reason for volunteering is 'to let the world know'.
>
> - What ethical dilemmas may arise here?
> - Which dilemmas may arise at which stage of the research process?
> - How could you address them?
>
> Draw on the five different approaches to ethics set out at the start of the chapter as well as the fundamental research ethics principles listed in the BPS (2010) *Code of Human Research Ethics*.

CHAPTER SUMMARY

- Ethical research conduct is the application of informed moral reasoning based on moral principles.

- Learning from the history of unethical research on human participants, research ethics codes have been developed which researchers need to abide by.

- Qualitative research generates particular ethical issues, for example around confidentiality and informed consent, safety of participants and the researcher–participant relationship.

- Researchers need to give thought to general ethical issues as well as to the different dilemmas that may arise within the context of their specific research project.

- While researchers tend to focus more on ethics when seeking ethical review, ethical thinking needs to permeate the entire research process from the design stage to fieldwork to analysis and dissemination.

Further reading

Oliver's (2010) introductory text *The Student's Guide to Research Ethics* is comprehensive and reader-friendly. Wiles's (2013) book *What Are Qualitative Research Ethics?* is very informative on broader as well as more specific ethical issues. King's (2010) book chapter provides a basic introduction to research ethics, gives specific advice on completing forms for ethical review and includes a section on internet/online research. Willig's (2012) *Qualitative Interpretation and Analysis in Psychology* is unusual in its serious consideration of the ethics of data analysis and interpretation. Miller et al.'s (2012) thought-provoking edited volume *Ethics in Qualitative Research* considers research ethics from a feminist perspective.

Turning to articles on specific ethical issues, Nind et al. (2013) report on an interview study on cases of methodological innovation and highlight the need for reflexivity to manage risks. Drawing on an 'ethics of care', Holland et al. (2014) navigate ethically sensitive moments when researching substance misuse with parents and their children.

SECTION II

Approaches to Data Analysis

PREFACE TO SECTION II

Evanthia Lyons and Adrian Coyle

There is a large number of research methods that fall under the umbrella of qualitative research and that have been employed within psychological studies. These include content analysis (Krippendorf, 2013), the data-display approach (Miles et al., 2014), protocol analysis (Gilhooly and Green, 1996; Green and Gilhooly, 1996), grounded theory (Glaser and Strauss, 1967), interpretative phenomenological analysis (Smith, 1996, 2004), thematic analysis (Braun and Clarke, 2006, 2013), the voice relational method (McLean Taylor et al., 1996), discourse analysis (Parker, 1992; Potter and Wetherell, 1987), narrative analysis (Crossley, 2000; McAdams, 2013) and conversation analysis (Hutchby and Wooffitt, 2008; Sidnell and Stivers, 2013). Indeed, Madill and Gough (2008) have identified 32 methods of analysing qualitative data. Furthermore, some of these are not unitary methods/approaches but exist in several different forms. No single book could hope to cover in depth all the qualitative methods that have been used or could be used in psychological research.

In this volume, we have chosen to focus on five methods/approaches: interpretative phenomenological analysis, thematic analysis, grounded theory, discourse analysis and narrative analysis. The reasons for this were twofold. Firstly, each of these methods is widely used by researchers in many sub-disciplines within psychology. Secondly, these methods vary in terms of their underlying epistemological assumptions. We expect the comparison of these methods to facilitate an understanding of the relationship between epistemology and method and, in turn, its impact on different aspects of the research process.

The principles and practicalities of each approach are discussed first by researchers with considerable experience of using them in their own work. Interpretative phenomenological analysis (IPA) is presented by Jonathan A. Smith and Virginia Eatough, thematic analysis by Victoria Clarke and Virginia Braun, grounded theory by Sheila Payne, discourse analysis by Adrian Coyle and narrative analysis by Brett Smith.

These chapters present a detailed discussion of the epistemological and methodological issues pertaining to each method. They introduce the theoretical and philosophical backgrounds to the method and, where there are different versions of the method, the authors discuss these in relation to their favoured version (if they have one). For example, in Chapter 6, Victoria Clarke and Virginia Braun discuss how thematic analysis has developed since the early 1990s, highlighting two broad approaches that they term the 'small q' and 'Big Q' versions. They then focus their discussion on the 'Big Q' approach stressing the flexibility of this method of analysis which can be used from different epistemological standpoints. In Chapter 8, Sheila Payne talks about the historical development of grounded theory and distinguishes between the approach first put forward by Glaser and Strauss in 1967 and subsequent versions that were developed independently by Glaser and by Strauss, as well as more recent developments such as Rennie's (2000) methodical hermeneutics, Clarke's (2003) postmodern version and Charmaz's (2014) social constructivist version. In Chapter 10 on discourse analysis, Adrian Coyle distinguishes between the two major variants in the UK – discursive psychology (Edwards and Potter, 1992) and Foucauldian discourse analysis (Parker, 1992) – while attending also to a synthesis of the two. In Chapter 12, Brett Smith focuses on dialogical narrative analysis, although he acknowledges the different theoretical positions taken and types of analysis conducted by narrative researchers as well as the wide range of definitions of narratives that can be found in the literature.

Each of the chapters that present the methods includes a discussion of the type of research questions that their focal method is best suited to addressing and gives examples of research questions that have been explored using that method. They also consider the type of data that are most amenable to analysis using the particular method. For example, in Chapter 4, Jonathan A. Smith and Virginia Eatough discuss in some detail different types of interviewing and argue that semi-structured interviewing is the most appropriate method of data collection for IPA. Hence, readers should consult that chapter for some useful material on qualitative interviewing, although the basic principles outlined there may need to be altered in light of the demands of other methods. In Chapters 6, 8, 10 and 12, the authors discuss the optimal ways of collecting data for the analytic approach they discuss. Each of these chapters also gives an invaluable guide to the analytic process and illustrates different analytic principles and strategies by giving examples from past research projects.

Each of the methods presented in this book has been applied to a common data set by researchers who have experience in using the particular method, working under the guidance of a more experienced expert in the method. The aim of this was to allow a clear comparison between the methods in terms of how the analytic focus was framed, what the analytic task involved and what was produced at the end of the process. The interview transcripts used for this exercise are presented in Appendix 1, together with an introduction to the data set by Arnie Reed, who collected the data for research that he conducted as part of his doctoral training in counselling psychology at the University of Surrey. The research project was a qualitative study of ex-soldiers' accounts of renegotiating their identities after leaving the army. Prior to this exercise, most of the researchers who analysed the data had relatively little experience of using the method that they applied to the data set.

In each of the 'Doing …' chapters, the authors wrote up the findings of their analysis and reflected on their experiences of the analytic process. All of these authors recognize that, inevitably, their account is their personal interpretation of that process, and highlight some of the dilemmas they faced during the analytic process.

These writers have not been hesitant in pointing to the difficulties they encountered and the ways in which they tried to overcome these difficulties. It is almost as if the initial chapters on each method present the 'theory' of what it is like to analyse data using these approaches whereas the 'Doing …' chapters suggest, through the practical experience of novice researchers, what it is *really* like to grapple with these methods! We recommend that readers study both chapters on each approach together so that they can get a more complete picture and understanding of the method. In order to follow the 'Doing ...' chapters fully, though, it is important that readers familiarize themselves with the data set in Appendix 1 first.

Finally in this section, in Chapter 14 Evanthia Lyons discusses the major similarities and differences between the five approaches. She pays particular attention to how each of the five approaches conceptualizes and deals with the way researchers should use existing psychological knowledge and their personal experiences and speaking positions in the process of conducting qualitative research. She also discusses the goals of psychological inquiry and the question of what are the most appropriate criteria for evaluating research conducted within each approach.

Across the chapters in this section, the reader will find detailed discussion of the theoretical and philosophical underpinnings of the five research approaches as well as rich and detailed technical information on how to apply these in research projects. We invite the reader to pay equal attention to each of these aspects and, perhaps most importantly, to reflect on the relationship between them.

4

INTERPRETATIVE
PHENOMENOLOGICAL ANALYSIS

Jonathan A. Smith and Virginia Eatough

In this chapter, we outline the theoretical underpinnings of interpretative phenomenological analysis (IPA). We discuss the type of research questions for which IPA
is suitable and consider sampling and data collection methods. We offer some
guidelines for conducting an IPA study, focusing on interviewing and analysis. The
chapter concludes with a consideration of those features which make for a high
quality IPA study.

Introduction: theoretical underpinnings

Interpretative phenomenological analysis (IPA) has theoretical origins in **phenomenology** (Moran, 2000), **hermeneutics** (Palmer, 1969) and **idiography** (Smith et al., 1995). Over the last 20 years, IPA has produced a distinctive approach to psychological research, supported by a growing corpus of psychological studies (Smith, 2011a). IPA is now also being used in many disciplines beyond psychology.

The aim of IPA is to explore in detail individual personal and lived experience and to examine how participants are making sense of their personal and social world. The main currency for an IPA study is the meanings that particular experiences, events and states hold for participants. For example, IPA is particularly well suited to exploring topics within health, social and clinical psychology where there is a need to understand how people perceive and understand significant events in their lives. This reflects its phenomenological lens – a concern with an individual's personal perception or account of an object or event as opposed to an attempt to produce an objective statement of the object or event itself.

At the same time, IPA also emphasizes that research is a dynamic process with an active role for the researcher in that process. Access to the participant's experience depends on and is complicated by the researcher's own conceptions. Indeed these are *required* in order to make sense of that other personal world through a process of interpretative activity. Thus a two-stage interpretation process, or a **double hermeneutic**, is involved. 'The participants are trying to make sense of their world; the researcher is trying to make sense of the participants trying to make sense of their world' (Smith and Osborn, 2015: 53). This double hermeneutic neatly illustrates the dual role of the researcher. In one sense the researcher is like the participant, drawing on mental faculties they share. At the same time, the researcher is different to the participant, always engaging in second-order sense-making of someone else's experience. See Palmer (1969) for a history of hermeneutics.

One can also look at this double hermeneutic another way as IPA combines an empathic hermeneutics with something of a critical hermeneutics (Ricoeur, 1970). Thus, consistent with its phenomenological origins, IPA is concerned with trying to understand what it is like from the point of view of the person, to take their side, to stand as far as is possible (which is never completely possible) in the shoes of the participant. At the same time, a detailed IPA analysis can also involve standing a little back from the participant and asking curious and critical questions of their accounts – for example, 'What is the person trying to achieve here?', 'Is something leaking out here that wasn't intended?', 'Do I have a sense of something going on here that maybe the person themselves is less aware of?' Both styles of interpretation can be part of sustained qualitative inquiry and IPA studies will often contain elements of each. Allowing for both aspects in the inquiry is likely to lead to a richer analysis and to do greater justice to the totality of the person, 'warts and all'. However it is necessary for an IPA analysis to begin with an empathic stance before adding a critical layer during later stages of analysis.

IPA has a theoretical commitment to the person as a cognitive, linguistic, affective and physical being and assumes a chain of connection between people's talk and their thinking and emotional state (Smith, 1996). At the same time, IPA researchers realize this chain of connection is not at all straightforward. People struggle to express what they are thinking and feeling; there may be reasons why they do not wish to self-disclose. The researcher has to interpret the person's mental and emotional state from what they say. In practice, this involves the researcher adopting different ways of thinking interpretatively about the data – for example, moving between building up rich experiential descriptions heavily grounded in the participant's own words and developing a more interrogative alternative account. In other words, it involves not uncritically accepting at face value what has been said.

The holism inherent in this portrait of the person also connects IPA with humanistic psychology (Graham, 1986) which developed in the 1960s and 1970s as a reaction against the conceptualization of the person within the experimental and laboratory paradigm. Humanistic psychology also had a political commitment to personal and social activity outside the academic world, promoting, for example, self-actualization, group therapy and connections with Eastern philosophy. IPA has a humanistically-informed holistic model of the person but is still oriented to research within academia and within psychology as a discipline. Thus IPA is trying to help broaden psychology's conceptualization both of what the person is and of how research on this person is to be conducted.

IPA's emphasis on sense-making by both participant and researcher means that it can be described as having cognition as a central analytic concern. This suggests an interesting theoretical alliance with the dominant cognitive paradigm in contemporary psychology (Smith, 1996). However while IPA does share with cognitive psychology and social cognition (Fiske and Taylor, 1991) a concern with mental processes, IPA strongly diverges from mainstream psychology when it comes to deciding the appropriate methodology for examining such phenomena. While mainstream psychology is still strongly committed to quantitative and experimental methodology, IPA employs in-depth qualitative analysis. In this context, it is interesting to see an alignment with Bruner (1990), who was one of the founders of the cognitive approach and who regrets how it swiftly moved from a central concern with meaning and meaning-making into the science of information processing.

IPA is an idiographic mode of inquiry as opposed to the nomothetic approach that dominates in psychology (Smith et al., 1995). In a nomothetic study, analysis is at the level of groups and populations and one can only make probabilistic claims about individuals: for example, that there is a 70 per cent chance that person X will respond in this way. In an idiographic study, because it has been derived from the examination of individual case studies, it is also possible to make specific statements about those individuals. Thus, for IPA, the analysis always begins with the detailed reading of the single case. You can then write that case up as a case study or you can move to an equally attentive analysis of the second case and so on. Assuming your analysis is of a group of individuals, a good IPA study will always allow itself to be parsed in two different ways. The reader should be able to learn something about both the important generic themes in the analysis but also still about the narrative life world of the particular participants who have told their stories. For more on the theoretical foundations of IPA, see Smith (1996) and Smith et al. (2009).

BITE-SIZED SUMMARY

1

It is important to understand the basic commitments that characterize a research approach in order to use that approach in an informed and appropriate way. We have noted IPA's theoretical commitments in phenomenology, hermeneutics and idiography and have described how these operate in IPA research to provide deep insights into how participants are making sense of their personal and social world. The researcher is actively involved in generating these insights as s/he makes sense of the participant's sense-making. The idiographic commitment means that, in a good IPA study, it is possible to learn about both convergences and divergences, that is about both commonalities of experience across participants and also about the life world of individual participants.

Research questions

As has been stated above, IPA is concerned with the in-depth exploration of the personal and lived experience of the individual and with how participants are making sense of that lived experience. This helps define the type of research question that is suitable for an IPA study. Box 4.1 illustrates some specific research questions that guided IPA projects and that have resulted in subsequent publication.

BOX 4.1 **Examples of psychological research questions addressed in IPA studies**

- How does a woman's sense of identity change during the transition to motherhood? (Smith, 1999)

- What sense do people who have had a heart attack make of what has happened? (French et al., 2005)

- What is it like to experience addiction to alcohol and how does this affect self and identity? (Shinebourne and Smith, 2009)

- How do young people with psychosis experience and interpret personal romantic relationships? (Redmond et al., 2010)

- What is the experience of deciding whether to take a genetic test or not like? (Smith et al., 2013)

As can be seen, IPA studies are usually concerned with big questions, questions of considerable importance to the participant either on an ongoing basis or at this critical juncture. Often these issues are transformative and often they are about identity because careful, in-depth, holistic analyses of individual accounts of significant experiences or events almost always impact on personal and social identity. IPA studies can be concerned with questions that are apparently quite particular or well defined (for example, 'How does someone who is at risk decide whether to take a genetic test or not?') or much broader (for example, 'How will changing career affect this person's life more generally?'). Good IPA studies tend to tap into **'hot cognition'**, engaging with issues that are current, emotive and sometimes dilemmatic. Studies can be single snapshots or can follow participants longitudinally. What all of these studies and all of these research questions would have in common is a concern with the detailed exploration of the personal and social experience of the participant in the study.

Sampling and sample size

IPA studies are conducted on relatively small sample sizes. The priority is to do justice to each case and the detailed case-by-case analysis of individual transcripts or accounts takes a long time. Sometimes students try to 'play safe' by having a large sample size, hoping they will thereby overcome the anxieties of examiners who may be more comfortable with quantitative research. In our experience, this almost always misfires: you can end up in the trap of being swamped with data and only producing a superficial qualitative analysis but still not having an adequate sample to satisfy quantitative criteria.

Before continuing on the question of sample size, we should say that we have also argued for the value of a sample of one (Smith, 2004). Consequently, there is a growing number of published single-person case studies examining, for example, the experience of living with Parkinson's disease (Bramley and Eatough, 2005), health behaviours and masculine identity (de Visser and Smith, 2006), and addiction (Shinebourne and Smith, 2009). This is indeed a logical step if the idiographic commitment is taken seriously. The single case study has been sorely neglected in psychology (Radley and Chamberlain, 2001; Smith, 1993; Yin, 1989) and we would argue that it has an important intellectual role to play in its own right. Of course, if you are submitting work for a degree, conducting a single case study is a high-risk strategy and should not be undertaken lightly. Pragmatically, it makes sense to be careful in the selection of the case that is put under such intense scrutiny. However, increasingly students are finding that there is value in sticking with a fascinating, troubling, complex case and attempting to do justice to it in its own right before moving on to another.

The value of a detailed case study like this is two-fold. Obviously the reader of the research report learns a great deal about that particular person and their response to this specific situation. There is also space to see connections between different aspects of the participant's account. However, we are also thereby better positioned to think about how we and other people might deal with the particular situation being explored, how at the deepest level we share some things with a person whose personal circumstances may at face value seem entirely separate and different from our own. Thus the detail of the individual can also bring us closer to significant aspects of the general; connecting with their individual unique life also connects with a shared humanity.

However assuming that a researcher resists the temptation of sticking with a single case study, how many participants should be included in an IPA study? There is no *right* answer to this question. It partly depends on the degree of commitment to the case-study level of analysis and reporting, the richness of the individual cases and the constraints under which you are operating. There seems to have been some consensus that between six and eight participants is an appropriate number for an IPA study as part of a professional doctorate (Thompson et al., 2011; Turpin et al., 1997). For the present, we think this is acceptable. It provides enough cases to examine similarities and differences between participants but not so many that the researcher is in danger of being overwhelmed by the amount of data generated. It is important, though, that a certain figure or band does not become a fixed expectation. As we have said above, in certain cases, an 'n of 1' can be argued for; in other cases, a detailed examination of convergences and divergences within a set of three cases would be the best way to proceed. Indeed, our experience tells us that three cases work very well for undergraduate projects, encouraging students to do justice to the data whilst giving them a sense of how patterns can be discerned across the material. It is more difficult to give an indicative number for PhDs because there is so much variation in their research questions, design and scope.

IPA researchers usually try and find a fairly **homogeneous sample**. The basic logic is that if one is interviewing, for example, six participants, it is not very helpful to think in terms of random or representative sampling. IPA therefore goes in the opposite direction and, through purposive sampling, finds a more closely defined group for whom the research question will be significant. How the specificity of a sample is defined will depend on the study. In some cases, the topic under investigation may itself be rare and/or under-researched (for example, the experience of living with a rare genetic disorder) and will thus define the boundaries of the relevant sample. In other cases where a less specific issue is under investigation, the sample may be drawn from a population with similar demographic/socio-economic status profiles – for example, if you are interested in how people respond to government advice on healthy eating. It is also possible to think in terms of theoretical rather than empirical generalizability. In this case, the reader makes links between the findings of an IPA study, their own personal and professional experience, and the claims in the extant literature. The power of the IPA study is judged by the light it sheds within this broader context.

As ever, these issues must be tempered with a strong dose of pragmatism. Your research sample selects itself in the sense that potential participants are, or should be, free agents who choose to participate or not. So you may have to adapt or redraw the criteria for inclusion if it transpires that you are unable to get enough members of the originally defined group to agree to take part in your study.

Data collection: semi-structured interviews

What about the method of data collection? The vast majority of IPA studies have been conducted on data obtained from **semi-structured interviews**, and this form of data collection might be considered the exemplary one for this type of research. The advantage of semi-structured interviewing for IPA is that the researcher is, in real time, in a position to follow up interesting and important issues that come up during the interview. However, it is important not to be doctrinaire about this. It is possible to collect rich verbal accounts by other means. For example, participants can be asked to write autobiographical or other personal accounts or to keep diaries for a period of time. The first author used all these forms of data collection during a study of the transition to motherhood and the diaries in particular were an important source for the analysis (Smith, 1999).

Given that most IPA studies at present use semi-structured interviewing, we will con-centrate on the practicalities of this form of data collection here. While it is probably obvious that semi-structured interviewing lies on a continuum from unstructured to structured, just what people mean by these terms can vary considerably. Therefore to assist in understand-ing the particular features of what IPA means by 'semi-structured', we will contrast it with structured interviewing.

The structured interview shares much of the logic of the experiment in psychology. The researcher usually decides in advance exactly what form the data will take. Sometimes the investigator will provide the respondent with a set of possible answers to choose from and the questions are constructed in such a way as to elicit answers corresponding to, and easily contained within, predetermined categories that can then be numerically analysed. In other cases the respondent is allowed a free response that can be categorized subsequently. In order to enhance reliability, the interviewer is supposed to stick closely to the interview sched-ule and behave with as little variation as possible between interviews. While the structured interview offers maximal control to the investigator, the format clearly puts considerable constraints on the encounter between the researcher and participant.

With semi-structured interviews, the investigator works from a pre-constructed sched-ule but the interview will be *guided* by the schedule rather than dictated by it. Hence the ordering of questions is less important. The interviewer is freer to probe interesting areas that arise and can follow the participant's interests or concerns. These differences follow from what IPA is trying to do. The researcher wants to find out about something but the process of finding out depends on establishing an empathic relationship with the participant and facilitating their giving their account of the topic of interest in their own words and in their own way. Therefore the participant is an active agent in shaping how the interview goes. The participant can be seen as the experiential expert and should therefore be allowed maximum opportunity to tell his/her own story. Of course, this form of interviewing reduces the control the investigator has over the situation.

Why is a schedule produced before interviewing? Working on a schedule enables you to be explicit about what might be covered in the interview. It also helps you to think about problems that might arise, for example, around addressing sensitive issues and how those issues could be addressed. Having thought in advance about the different ways the interview may proceed means that when it comes to the interview itself, you can focus more thoroughly and more confidently on what the participant is actually saying. As an example, Box 4.2 presents the first half of a schedule from a project by the authors on women's experience of anger and aggression.

Good interview technique often involves a gentle nudge from the interviewer rather than being very explicit. While constructing your schedule, you may realize that your first draft questions are too explicit (for example, 'What happened when you were made redun-dant?'). Redrafting enables you to make them gentler and less direct (for example, 'Can you describe the day you were made redundant, starting with when you first became aware it

> ## BOX 4.2 — Interview schedule (abridged)
>
> 1. Can you tell me about what your life was like as a child and when you were growing up?
>
>   Prompt: might want focus on particular age points – child/teenager/young adult family/school/college/work/relationships
>
>   What about more recently?
>
> 2. Can you tell me about times when you have been involved in a conflictual situation when you were growing up?
>
>   Prompt: maybe focus on particular age points/contexts – family/school, etc. description/cause/protagonist/actions/affect/cognitive response then
>
>   What about more recently?
>
> 3. Can you tell me what the word 'anger' means to you?
>
> 4. Can you tell me about times when you've been angry when you were growing up?
>
>   Prompt: maybe focus on particular age points/contexts – family/school, etc. description/cause/protagonist/actions/affect/cognitive response then
>
>   What about more recently?
>
> 5. Can you tell me how you have acted on that anger?
>
>   Prompt: age points/contexts

might happen?'). The intention is to assure the participant of the value of what they have to say about the topic in the context of their lives in order to facilitate the giving of rich experiential accounts.

Sometimes participants may have difficulties in understanding or responding to questions. For example, for some, a particular question may be too open. In order to be ready for this, you can write more explicit or specific prompts. So, for example, in Box 4.2, question 1 has prompts relating to areas the participant may wish to consider. Questions 2 and 4 have a set of reminders to the interviewer of domains that it may be useful to ask the participant about.

Once you have completed your schedule, you should learn it by heart like a play script before beginning to interview so, when it comes to the interview, the schedule acts as a mental prompt, if needed, and not something to which you are constantly referring.

Semi-structured interviews of this type usually last for an hour or more and are usually better done in a quiet place without other people being present. Of course there will be exceptions to this – for example, it may not be advisable or possible with young children. Where the interview takes place can also affect the ambience. Participants are usually most at ease somewhere familiar but again sometimes this may not be the case or may not be possible. The early part of the interview is taken up with making the participant comfortable. If you are expecting participants to talk in detail about an important experience, then they will need to be relaxed.

Interviews are flexible and dynamic. The aim is not to follow the schedule robotically. Rather you adapt the schedule according to what is happening. Thus you may well change the sequence of questioning because it works better on this particular occasion. Questions will be rephrased to follow the flow of the conversation. Much of the interview is taken up with probing the participant on issues which arise and this means it is normal to move away from the schedule. In practice the interview is usually a type of dance, moving seamlessly between questions predicted and prepared in advance and unanticipated avenues which come up spontaneously. At the same time, the researcher needs to monitor how things are going to make sure the conversation does not stray too far from the agreed topic.

It is important to try and establish a slow and comfortable pace to the interview. Try not to talk too quickly; let the participant take their time in answering a question before you move on to the next one. Finally, you need to check that the participant is comfortable as the interview proceeds. If there is an indication of some discomfort, expressed either non-verbally or in how the participant replies, you need to deal with this. Usually it is a matter of backing off, pausing and asking in a more gentle way or moving to a different topic area. However if the participant becomes quite distressed then you would need to discuss this explicitly with them and contemplate stopping the interview. In our experience this is a very rare occurrence. These considerations are about respecting the participant and reducing the risk of the interview experience being harmful to him/her. This is part of ethical research practice. For more on this, see Chapter 3 in this volume where Edith Steffen examines ethical considerations in qualitative research.

For IPA, it is necessary to audio-record and transcribe the whole interview. Transcription is a time-consuming business: you can expect an hour of interviewing to take seven hours or more to transcribe. Of course this depends on how good your typing skills are. When preparing to print the transcript, make sure you leave a wide enough margin on both sides of the transcript to make your analytic comments.

IPA research usually addresses questions that are or have been important in participants' lives. These may be either relatively broad or particular. IPA studies have relatively small samples in order to do justice to the meaning-making of each participant. These samples are homogeneous to allow a specific type of experience to be examined in depth. Case studies, focusing on one participant's meaning-making, are also suited to IPA work. Data for IPA research are usually generated through semi-structured interviews, with the interview schedule used in a flexible way to allow interesting and/or unexpected issues to be followed up. Good interviewing technique involves gently encouraging and helping the participant to talk about their experiences, with a slow and comfortable pace being maintained throughout the interview. Interviews should be audio-recorded and then transcribed in preparation for analysis.

BITE-SIZED SUMMARY

2

Analysis

IPA is not a prescriptive approach; rather, it provides a set of flexible guidelines which can be adapted by individual researchers in light of their research aims. This is particularly true when it comes to analysis. This section describes the analytic steps we went through in the anger and aggression study in order to help the reader see how the analysis unfolds but this should not be treated as the 'correct recipe' for doing IPA. Instead it should be seen as an illustration of *one* way of doing it.

This project was a detailed, idiographic examination of participants' experience of anger and aggression, its interpersonal context and models of etiology. In brief, the analytic stages involved (a) several close and detailed readings of the data to obtain a holistic perspective so that future interpretations stayed grounded within the participants' accounts; (b) identifying initial themes, organizing these into clusters and checking them against the data; (c) refining and condensing themes and examining them to discern connections between them; (d) the production of a narrative account of the interplay between the interpretative activity of the researcher and the participants' account of their experiences in their own words (Smith and Osborn, 2015). The detailed outcome of the analysis can be found in Eatough et al. (2008). A case study from the project is presented in Appendix 2 (Report 1) in this volume.

The stages used throughout the analysis were as follows and were applied to the transcript of each participant. First, during transcription, the interviewer kept a record of initial thoughts, comments and points of potential significance. It was felt they might be useful to return to and check against later interpretations during analysis. Second, each transcript was read several times and the right-hand margin was used to make notes on anything that appeared significant and of interest. With each reading, the researcher should expect to feel more immersed in the data, becoming more responsive to what is being said.

Box 4.3 demonstrates this stage of analysis for a small section of the interview with Debbie (a participant whose name has been changed here) who was the first woman who was interviewed. The interviewer is responding to a topic introduced by the participant.

BOX 4.3 ▷ **Annotating the transcript with initial notes**

Int.:	Can you tell me about an argument with your sister?
Debbie:	I've got a system, I mean I do it now, I always wash glasses first and my sister just came along with cups full of tea and coffee and poured them straight into the sink and I just lost my temper. I just remember I was so angry with her I wasn't going to let her push me around any more that I just did a role reversal with her. And I just sort of pinned her against the wall and started slamming her head against the wall to see how she felt like, to see what it felt like to her.
Int.:	What happened next?
Debbie:	I don't know whether it was because I'd done it to my sister but I just broke up into tears and I just had to <u>get out</u>. I mean, I've never had a fight with my sister like that since. We have like verbal fights but I just felt like, I had a lot of mixed emotions after I'd done that. I felt happy that I'd stuck up to myself with her but I also felt annoyed with myself because I'd hurt her and then I felt happy again because she'd got a taste of her own medicine and knew how I felt. It's dead weird. I'd so many emotions in one go that I'd never felt so many at the same time before. It was a really strange feeling. But I broke down into tears and I knew then I had to get out. And I just went for a walk.

Right-hand margin notes:

Lost my temper – instant
Anger

Switched roles D is aggressor
Physical aggression

Wants her sister to feel the same

Broke into tears/
Desire to escape

Verbal aggression
Felt happy

Felt annoyed
Felt happy again
Wants sister to feel like her
Multiple emotions

Strange, unusual experience/
Tears
Left the situation

The next stage involved returning to the transcript and using the left-hand margin to transform initial notes and ideas into more specific themes or phrases (see Box 4.4). This stage calls upon psychological concepts and abstractions. Caution is essential at this point so that the connection between the participant's own words and the researcher's interpretations is not lost. These early stages of analysis require the researcher to be thorough and painstaking.

BOX 4.4

Documenting themes

	Int.:	Can you tell me about an argument with your sister?
	Debbie:	I've got a system, I mean I do it now, I always wash glasses first and my sister just came along with cups full of tea and coffee and poured them straight into the sink and I just lost my temper. I just remember I was so angry with her I wasn't going to let her push me around any more that I just did a role reversal with her. And I just sort of pinned her against the wall and started slamming her head against the wall to see how she felt like, to see what it felt like to her.
Rapid emotional shift into anger		
Power dynamics		
Physical aggression		
	Int.:	What happened next?
	Debbie:	I don't know whether it was because I'd done it to my sister but I just broke up into tears and I just had to <u>get out</u>. I mean, I've never had a fight with my sister like that since. We have like verbal fights but I just felt like, I had a lot of mixed emotions after I'd done that. I felt happy that I'd stuck up to myself with her but I also felt annoyed with myself because I'd hurt her and then I felt happy again because she'd got a taste of her own medicine and knew how I felt. It's dead weird. I'd so many emotions in one go that I'd never felt so many at the same time before. It was a really strange feeling. But I broke down into tears and I knew then I had to get out. And I just went for a walk.
Crying/Desire for escape		
Verbal aggression		
Conflicting emotions		
Projecting self-feelings		
Multiple emotions		
Crying		
Avoidance		

The next stage consists of establishing connections between the preliminary themes and clustering them appropriately (see Box 4.5). As part of this process, it may be useful to 'imagine a magnet with some of the themes pulling others in and helping to make sense of them' (Smith, 2004: 71). This process is inevitably selective so that some of the themes may be dropped either because they do not fit well with the emerging structure or because, within the emerging analysis, they do not have a strong enough evidence base.

BOX 4.5 ▸ **Clustering of themes**

Physical aggression

Verbal aggression

Rapid emotional shift into anger

Crying

Conflicting/multiple emotions

Desire for escape

Power dynamics

Projection of self-feelings

Finally, a table is produced that shows each **superordinate theme** and the themes that comprise it (see Box 4.6). These clusters are given a label (a superordinate theme title) that conveys the conceptual nature of the themes therein. Key words from the participant are used to remind the researcher what prompted the themes.

For the researcher, this table is the outcome of an iterative process in which she/he has moved back and forth between the various analytic stages ensuring that the integrity of what the participant said has been preserved as far as possible. If the researcher has been success-ful, it should be possible for someone else to track the analytic journey from the raw data through to the end table. This is referred to as an independent audit. Only after we felt some measure of 'gestalt' (Smith, 2004) had been reached for each participant was a cross-case analysis carried out and a final table of superordinate themes put together that represented the whole data set.

Analysis continues into the formal process of writing up a narrative report of the inter-play between the interpretative activity of the researcher and the participant's account of her experience in her own words. Writing and re-writing tends to take the analysis deeper as the researcher is focusing closely on making explicit their interpretative commentary on key things the participants are saying. The aim is to provide a close textual reading of the participant's account, moving between description and different levels of interpretation, at all times clearly differentiating between account and interpretation. Enough data should be presented for the reader to assess the usefulness of the interpretations. Box 4.7 shows a very short piece from the final write-up. The excerpt begins with the consideration of a different participant – Angela.

BOX 4.6 **Final table of themes**

Forms of aggression

Physical aggression: *I just sort of pinned her against the wall*

Verbal aggression: *We have like verbal fights*

The anger experience

Rapid emotional shift into anger: *I just lost my temper*

Crying: *I just broke up into tears*

Conflicting/multiple emotions: *I'd so many emotions in one go*

Relationship between self and other

Power dynamics: *I just did a role reversal with her*

Projection of self-feelings: *She'd got a taste of her own medicine*

BOX 4.7 **Short excerpt from the final write-up**

When emotions are felt intensely such as extreme anger and grief, they can feel unbearable:

> I was thinking I want to get rid of this anger and I think what do I do so I just lay in the bed and I could feel it building up and my heart was killing me.

Angela's anger combined with her grief at the loss of her child is deeply felt. The experience is centred in her heart and she indicates that the experience is one of actual

---

(Continued)

physical pain. Feeling several emotions at a single time is a tumultuous experience in itself. The effect is one of confusion, which is enhanced when the emotions are antagonistic:

> I had a lot of mixed emotions after I'd done that. I felt happy that I'd stuck up to myself with her [sic] but I also felt annoyed with myself because I'd hurt her I and then I felt happy again because she got a taste of her own medicine and knew how I felt. It's dead weird. I'd so many emotions in one go that I'd never felt so many at the same time before. It was a really strange feeling.

In this extract, Debbie is describing how she felt after a fight with her sister. As with the previous episode, happiness accompanied anger but there is a lot more going on besides. Debbie has conflicting feelings, which shift from annoyance to satisfaction, and it appears that some form of internal dissonance ('weird' and 'strange') further complicates the emotional confusion.

BITE-SIZED SUMMARY 3

IPA offers a set of flexible guidelines for data analysis rather than a rigid set of analytic procedures. We have described the steps that we followed in analysing data from the study of anger and aggression that we have been using as an example of IPA work in this chapter. We first selected one transcript, read it closely several times and, in one margin, made notes on anything that seemed of interest. Next we condensed the notes into themes or phrases in the other margin while ensuring they reflected the participant's words. We clustered these preliminary themes on the basis of connections between them. We gave each cluster a superordinate theme title and created a table of superordinate themes and the themes that constituted them. We repeated the process with other transcripts and drew up a final table of superordinate themes that reflected the whole data set. Finally, we wrote these up.

Doing high quality IPA

There is now a considerable corpus of research using IPA. Jonathan Smith (2011a, 2011b) has published an overview of some of that literature, together with guidelines for evaluating IPA studies. Emerging from this is an account of the qualities required to do high quality IPA (briefly summarized in Box 4.8) together with, in the 2011a paper, illustrated summaries of good IPA papers. In another paper (Smith, 2011c), Jonathan points to the important role of the **gem**, a small but powerful extract from a participant that captures key qualities of the phenomenon under investigation and shines light on the broader corpus of data collected. He points to different types of gem and connects these to hermeneutic theory. It is hoped that these papers will help students and researchers in their endeavours to produce high quality IPA.

BOX 4.8 — **What makes a good IPA paper?**

- The paper focuses in detail on a particular topic.

- The researcher has obtained and presents high quality data.

- Sufficient extracts from participants are presented to make a plausible case.

- The analysis must be interpretative, not just descriptive.

- The paper is engaging and well written.

BOX 4.9 — **An exercise in constructing interview questions**

If you are a student who is studying IPA in a class, work in a small group of three or four students. Imagine you have designed an IPA study where you will talk to new undergraduates about their experience of the first term or semester at university. Construct the first three questions of an interview schedule. To do this, first draft some questions, then discuss them among yourselves and revise them until you think they are fit for purpose. Construct prompts for each question; these will be used if a particular participant has difficulties with one of the main questions.

(Continued)

- How easy or difficult did you find it to construct the questions for the interview schedule?

- Before you actually start interviewing participants, how might you find out whether your questions work?

If you found it difficult to construct good interview questions, do not be discouraged. Creating good interview questions is a real skill that takes time and experience to develop. Even the most experienced researchers sometimes find that questions they have carefully created do not work well in practice and need to be revised!

CHAPTER SUMMARY

This chapter has:

- presented the theoretical foundations for IPA – phenomenology, hermeneutics and idiography

- considered how to design an IPA study – appropriate research questions, sampling and data collection

- illustrated how to conduct an IPA interview and analysis

- given pointers to producing and evaluating high quality IPA.

We hope that readers now feel they have a good sense of the particular qualities of IPA – something that will be refined and developed by drawing comparisons between IPA and the other approaches in this book. Hopefully, too, after reading this chapter, Lesley Storey's reflections on doing IPA in Chapter 5 and the IPA study in Appendix 2 (Report 1), some readers will feel inspired to have a go at conducting an IPA project themselves.

Further reading

For a comprehensive guide to IPA, see Smith, Flowers and Larkin's (2009) book *Interpretative Phenomenological Analysis: Theory, Method and Research*. This book provides extensive coverage of the theoretical underpinnings of IPA, step-by-step guidance to carrying out an IPA study and detailed illustrations of completed studies. Other useful guides to the theoretical aspects of IPA are offered by Smith (1996) and Eatough and Smith (2008). For more on the practicalities of doing IPA, see Smith and Osborn (2015). Two examples of good IPA studies are de Visser and Smith's (2006) detailed case study of a young man's ambivalent attitudes towards alcohol, and Turner et al.'s (2002) paper exploring the experience of ex-professional footballers who have subsequently suffered osteoarthritis. For other examples of IPA studies, see the studies cited in Box 4.1 in this chapter.

5

DOING INTERPRETATIVE PHENOMENOLOGICAL ANALYSIS

Lesley Storey

This chapter presents an account of one researcher's experience of working in an analytic group that applied the principles of interpretative phenomenological analysis (IPA) to one interview transcript. This interview had been conducted with an ex-solider and examined his experiences of being in and leaving the army and his post-army life. The chapter describes the application of the different steps in IPA, illustrating these with reference to the data, and offers some reflections upon the analytic process. It also considers some broader issues raised by IPA, such as the role of theory in the analysis.

Introduction

Qualitative methods have a number of advantages over quantitative methods in some areas of research. They are concerned with meaning, sense-making and subjective experience rather than imposing preconceived variables. Qualitative methods involving interaction between researchers and participants (usually face-to-face interaction in individual or group interview contexts) avoid the need to specify the meaning of core research concerns in advance. Instead, participants can determine (and revise) these meanings themselves during data collection and, in that process, potentially contest the researcher's interpretations of these core concerns. This openness and dialogue (which is not intrinsic to qualitative methods but depends upon the researcher's skills) also mean that the researcher is less likely to misinterpret participants' responses.

In this chapter, I discuss aspects of these advantages in relation to interpretative phenomenological analysis (IPA). I then focus on the practicalities of applying IPA to interview data from an ex-soldier which examined his experiences of being in and leaving the army and his post-army life (see Appendix 1 in this volume). Thus the chapter considers what it was like to apply the principles outlined by Jonathan A. Smith and Virginia Eatough in Chapter 4 and offers some 'hands-on' observations from the research 'coalface'. For this analysis, I worked as part of a group of six female researchers of different ages from different educational establishments who had not met prior to working on the data over the course of two days. We had different levels of experience with qualitative research in general and with IPA specifically. Throughout this chapter, although I talk about the work of our group, these are my personal interpretations of the group process and other group members may have perceived the group's interactions in a different but equally valid way.

It is worth noting that, early in the analytic task, the group decided to focus attention on *one* interview transcript (the interview with David), even though transcripts from interviews with two ex-soldiers were available to us. We felt that, within the limited analytic time available to us, we would have difficulty in completing a meaningful analysis of more than one transcript. The adoption of a case study approach fits with the idiographic commitment of IPA, which, when aiming for a group-level analysis, begins with the analysis of an individual case and moves from there to the analysis of further cases. Therefore we felt that this chapter would provide readers who have not used IPA before (and who are considering applying it to more than one transcript in a non-case-study analysis) with a good sense of what it may be like to conduct the important first analysis in the IPA process. Also, as Smith and Eatough noted in Chapter 4, IPA has increasingly been applied to single cases and has generated detailed, rich insights through such a focus.

Stage 1: initial readings of the transcript

One of the most challenging aspects of dealing with qualitative data can be knowing how and where to start. Often the researcher is presented with a mass of text that can feel overwhelming and it can seem an impossible task to find any coherent meaning in the transcript (which may sometimes be due to the nature of the data: see Box 5.1). The identification of central concerns within the data is a principal aim of many versions of qualitative analysis (for example, in the form of **superordinate themes** in IPA and core categories in grounded theory). IPA offers a series of steps – not in a prescriptive way – that are designed to allow the analyst to identify central concerns within the data. Therefore, even if the data set appears overwhelming and even if at first you doubt whether you will ever be able to discern coherent meaning in it and present this as superordinate themes, it is important to trust the analytic process and trust that eventually meaning will be created from the data. Otherwise you may never dare to begin the analysis!

BOX 5.1	Dealing with fragmented interview data

Some interview transcripts can be quite fragmented, with the participant covering many seemingly unrelated issues, darting from issue to issue and apparently contradicting themselves. This can result from a poorly focused interview schedule, in which case the schedule can be revised before the next interview if the project is still in progress. However, it may also happen with a well-organized interview schedule, despite the interviewer having done their best to keep the participant focused on the research topic. Most qualitative researchers will attempt to do this with a relative lightness of touch, trying to strike a balance between ensuring that the issues specified on the interview schedule are covered and allowing the participant to identify and pursue issues relevant to the research topic that were not considered when the schedule was compiled. Still, some research participants may use the interview setting as a chance to rehearse other issues that are either unrelated or only minimally related to the research topic. This may happen if a participant is suffering from a physiological, neurological or psychological disorder that has detrimentally affected their processing and attentional capacities. Yet it may also occur if the research is dealing with a particular aspect of a topic that might be considered sensitive and if the participant has never or seldom had the opportunity to discuss the general topic with an attentive listener before. In this case, the participant may wish to talk about *all* of their experience and may have difficulty in organizing such substantial information. As well as following standard ethical procedures during the interview (see Chapter 3 in this volume) and revisiting recruitment criteria for future interviews, the researcher may subsequently have to apply the analytic procedures to the transcript to whatever extent is possible or, in a worst-case scenario, disregard highly fragmented interview data. The interview transcript analysed in this chapter posed no such problems.

IPA starts with an iterative process of reading and re-reading a transcript with a view to getting an overall 'feel' for the interview. With the transcript of the interview with David, despite the fact that we were analysing data that we had not collected, we experienced emotional reactions to him of different strengths and valences as a result of the account that he provided in the interview. It is possible that these reactions were a result of varying degrees of identification with David and his circumstances. Identification can potentially cause problems in analysis: an over-identification with an interviewee on the basis of shared or similar experiences may lead the analyst to force the data to conform to *their* experiences. Equally, a negative dis-identification with the interviewee can make it difficult to empathize (or at least sympathize) with the interviewee and thus attain the sort of 'insider' perspective on the research topic to which IPA aspires in its phenomenological commitment.

Our predominant reaction to the transcript was one of sadness for David who seemed to have been abandoned by the army which had been his home for many years. However, our sadness was counterbalanced by frustration, as David seemed to feel that all his problems would be solved if only he were able to return to army life. We discussed the fact that these reactions were very much *our* reactions to the data, whereas we had initially hoped to identify a 'feel' for the transcript from *David's* perspective. Nevertheless, we felt that it was useful to have identified these responses and to have considered their origins because this alerted us to aspects of the **interpretative frameworks** that we would bring to bear upon the data – the personal 'lenses' through which we might view the data, including our understandings, emotions and experiences. We were able to consider how some aspects might prove useful in the analytic process in terms of furthering our understanding of David's experiences and how others might prove problematic and would have to be closely monitored (for example, in causing us to dismiss some of David's reactions to the situations he described).

This process of reflecting upon and acknowledging the interpretative framework that the analyst applies to the data is called **reflexivity**. It is important because it helps to increase the **transparency** of the analysis, although some aspects of an analyst's framework may be unconscious and so may not be readily identifiable by them. We were fortunate to have had a group context in which to consider these issues and question each other closely and we wondered about the extent to which we could have done this if we had been working alone as individual analysts.

Following the initial reading, we continued by re-reading the transcript to produce wide-ranging notes on anything that appeared significant and of interest; we carried out this task as a group. These notes/questions were recorded on the right-hand margin of the transcript. For example, the powerful passage in which David referred metaphorically to seeing ghosts (lines 105–107) elicited the words 'death' and 'bereavement', although we were not clear at this stage who we felt had died or had been bereaved.

In Box 5.1, it was noted that data can sometimes be fragmented and contradictory. However, contradictions can be discerned in many interviews without this being associated with problematic fragmentation. One observation that the group made following the initial reading related to the contradictions that analysts had observed within David's account. There were occasions when David identified a quality or a skill that had been useful in the army and which he had grown to value over the years. Sometimes consciously and in other places perhaps less consciously, the same quality or skill was represented as a handicap in the new, post-army phase of his life. There was a tragi-comic self-realization some way into the interview when David was talking about how having been in the army gave him a sense of self-confidence when it came to job interviews but he recognized some of the downsides:

Where it hinders me is the fact that I like things in lines. I like things in neat packages and so when I go – like when I was driving the truck, when I used to come back at night, I used to park all the wagons up so all the bumpers were level. (Lines 238–241)

This attention to detail had undoubtedly been important in the regimented world of the army but it may have appeared unusual and may even have been negatively evaluated in a civilian context. At this stage, we simply noted this observation and set it aside as a possibly fruitful line of inquiry that might be followed later.

BITE-SIZED SUMMARY

1

In this chapter, I draw upon my experience of working as part of a group of researchers who applied IPA to the transcript of an interview with an ex-soldier called David. The account of our experience that I offer will help you to develop a sense of what it is like to conduct IPA 'for real'. We began by reading the transcript, trying to develop a 'feel' for the data. We realized that our responses to the transcript said more about us and our emotional responses to the data than about David's sense-making. I have noted the importance of acknowledging these responses to enhance the transparency of the analysis. We then re-read the transcript and, in the right-hand margin, we made notes about anything that appeared significant and of interest. We also noted variability and contradiction in the account that David gave.

Stage 2: identifying and labelling themes

The next stage of analysis involved returning to the transcript and using the notes that had previously been made in the right-hand margin to produce **themes** in the left-hand margin. In this process, we spent some time discussing the advantages and disadvantages of using concepts from psychological theory in producing themes which reflected David's meaning-making. We struggled with what we saw as a need to move beyond producing descriptive themes and to come up with themes that were 'properly psychological', at least in some cases. In our discussion, this was balanced against a concern about moving too far away from the data and possibly violating IPA's phenomenological commitment if we were to over-write David's subjectivity with our favourite theories. Other researchers who have used psychological theory in IPA have faced the same dilemma concerning how best to avoid having it over-write participants' phenomenologies in the analysis (see Box 5.2).

Ultimately we decided that, as we were conducting psychological research for a psychological audience, it was necessary to use concepts derived from psychological theory where appropriate to produce an analysis that would be credible and possibly useful to our audience. We adopted two strategies to reduce the risk of violating David's subjectivity. The first was to use theoretical constructs in an eclectic way in our interpretations rather than restrict ourselves to one particular theory because we felt that an over-investment in any single theory would make us more liable to squeeze David's data into that theory – as well as needlessly limiting our interpretative power. 'Locus of control', 'possible selves', 'self-efficacy' and psycho-dynamic approaches were all suggested as possible theoretical concepts

BOX 5.2 ▸ **The use of psychological theory in IPA research**

Researchers who have used IPA to analyse qualitative data and who wished to make explicit use of psychological theory in their analysis but also to avoid violating participants' sense-making have responded to this dilemma in various ways. The standard response has been to invoke theory when discussing the findings arising from an analysis of participants' sense-making undertaken, as far as possible, on their own terms (for example, Flowers et al., 1997; Senior et al., 2002). Hence, theory does not *drive* the analysis but is invoked as an explanatory resource after participants' subjectivities and meaning-making have been engaged with. As IPA has refined its commitments over the years, this has become the usual and acceptable approach to incorporating theoretical insights into IPA research. It should be noted, though, that it is acceptable to present relevant theories and theoretical concepts in the introduction to an IPA report to contextualize the study (see Box R1.1 in Report 1, Appendix 2 in this volume).

Earlier examples of IPA research saw researchers identifying a range of potential theoretical perspectives from which the data could be interpreted before the analysis began but refusing to privilege any single perspective in advance of engaging with the data (for example, Vignoles et al., 2004). This may be acceptable depending on how it is implemented. A more a priori theoretically-committed approach involved choosing a single theory in advance and using it to inform the analysis but without trying to *test* the theory through the data (for example, Turner and Coyle, 2000). Today that approach is unlikely to be seen as sufficiently aligned with IPA's phenomenological commitments and would probably be considered a type of thematic analysis rather than IPA.

and approaches for making psychological sense of the data. Secondly, we resolved to ensure that any theoretical interpretation arose clearly from the data. As a result, during the analysis, I remember the questions 'But is it in the data?' and 'Where does it say that in the transcript?' being voiced again and again in relation to possible theoretical interpretations.

In the case of David's interview, there was one particular section of text that was interpreted from different theoretical perspectives. One of the issues that came up in discussion of the data was the way in which joining a total institution like the army at a relatively young age can create problems for soldiers when it comes to dealing with the complexities of adult life on discharge. Group members coming from different theoretical perspectives interpreted this situation in terms of 'the army as mother', 'external locus of control', 'army as disempowering and emasculating', 'lack of self-efficacy' and 'external attribution of power'. It was exciting to pursue these interpretations and to see how far the data would allow us legitimately to 'stretch' them because we felt that here we were moving beyond a literal interpretation of the data into a more psychological interpretation. Nowhere in the transcript did David say that he saw the army as a substitute mother but he did ascribe to the army various nurturing qualities that are often associated with parenting, such as authority and the provision of protection, material shelter and comforts. It might be considered surprising that the group specified 'the army as mother' rather than 'the army as parent', especially as the stereotype of father as disciplinarian might seem closer to the army's image. However, David particularly commented on the deficits left by his mother's early death and the practical skills that he said he had acquired in the army (such as cooking and cleaning) seemed to us to be more associated with a traditional maternal role. This allowed us to explore the idea that leaving the army was experienced by David as a form of extreme separation anxiety or even bereavement.

Following agreement on how to use theoretical constructs, we identified, as individuals, what we felt to be the most important themes in the transcript and then discussed them as a group. We all used different ways of describing themes and one of the major differences was in the level of analysis represented by our suggested theme titles. Some group members suggested very general themes such as 'loss', while others identified much more detailed themes around the specifics of the army's exit programme. Following discussion, we agreed on five initial themes, which were:

- what the army gave David;
- what the army took away from David;
- the differences between army and civilian life;
- the similarities between army and civilian life;
- identity transition as a work in progress/absence of closure.

We were aware that the aim of the interview had been to look at identity issues and we were concerned that only one of our themes at this stage seemed directly to concern identity. However, recognizing that an interview characterized by openness on the part of the interviewer may well elicit material that was not originally considered to be relevant to the research topic or research question(s), we decided to set this concern aside and concentrate on (our readings of) David's sense-making in the transcript.

Stage 3: linking themes and identifying thematic clusters

During this stage, connections were identified between the preliminary themes. This enabled us to amalgamate some themes and, where appropriate, to incorporate into other themes material from those themes that had been jettisoned. For example, we decided that the two themes concerning differences and similarities between army and civilian life fitted within the two themes concerning gains and losses associated with (leaving) army life. This was because the elements that we drew upon to provide examples of differences and similarities were actually illustrating the way in which David identified what he had gained and lost through (leaving) army life. For example, his sense that he had lost a sense of team membership when he left the army was exemplified by his identification of differences between the collective sense of 'team' in the army ('I was a member of a team and I was an important member of a team' – lines 17–18) and the more narrowly-defined sense of 'team' in his civilian job ('You're not a team member within the school because you're not a teacher' – lines 48–49). We also felt that the provisional superordinate theme relating to 'Identity transition as a work in progress/absence of closure' was better dealt with as themes within a broader superordinate theme entitled 'The end of a relationship'. We felt that this broad theme also allowed us to explore some of the emotional issues that had been raised and identified during the initial read-through of the transcript. So, our three final superordinate themes were:

- what the army gave David;
- what the army took away from David;
- the end of a relationship.

We had some concerns that the first two might simply be different sides of the same coin and so one might turn out to be redundant or the themes might need to be combined. However, when we identified each superordinate theme's constituent themes during the analysis, we found them to be sufficiently distinctive, with each relating to different aspects of the interview and, therefore, worthy of separate inclusion. This is a vital point because it showed us as a group how important it was to 'try out' an analysis to see whether or not it worked. If we could not identify data from the transcript to support a potential superordinate theme (or theme), we dropped it.

We found the experiential aspect of the analytic exercise to be fundamental. We learned as much from actually doing the analysis and resolving analytic problems and dilemmas *in vivo* as we did from discussing it as a group. For example, we had initially identified 'absence of closure' as a superordinate theme but we were only able to find one data extract which referred to this. We felt that this was a significant issue but would work better as a theme.

Stage 4: producing a summary table of superordinate themes

At the end of our analysis, we organized our superordinate themes into a table, together with their constituent themes and illustrative quotations (see Table 5.1).

Table 5.1 Superordinate themes and constituent themes

Superordinate theme	Themes	Example of illustrative quotation
Theme 1: What the army gave David	A sense of being someone special	
	A structure to his life which allowed him to plan	
	Confidence and pride	'It gave me more confidence. As a nipper when I first joined the army, I wasn't confident at all.' (Lines 4–5)
	Sense of belonging and being part of a team	
	Parenting	
Theme 2: What the army took away from David	Health	
	Ability to relate to civilians	
	Practical skills	
	A future/sense of purpose	'sometimes I don't feel as though there's a purpose to it … thinking "What the hell am I doing here? Bugger this" … But I've got to do this yet again, today and tomorrow. And you think to yourself, "This is me for the rest of my life".' (Lines 218–223)
	(Almost) his marriage	
Theme 3: The end of a relationship	Abandonment and betrayal	'Once you're out that gate, that's it. I know I can't even get back into the camp where, not ten minutes ago, I was a serving sergeant. I can't get back in. You know, you … it's like they're throwing you outside and locked the gate, you know, and that's it – you're on your own. That was painful.' (Lines 95–99)
	Bereavement/death	
	No closure	

The analytic process continued as we drew together initial notes and created provisional themes. We debated whether and how we could use concepts derived from psychological theory in creating themes. We decided to make use of theoretical concepts provided they readily fitted the data and had interpretative value. We identified five initial themes that were consolidated into three superordinate themes after we had taken account of connections between them. In all of this, our learning about IPA came as much from actually doing the analysis as from the discussions that we had about the analysis. The three superordinate themes were then presented in a table.

Presentation of the analysis in narrative form

A summary of the group's IPA analysis of the transcript is provided below. Given the time constraints under which we worked, this is not in any way intended to be read as a complete in-depth IPA analysis (for a more extended example of such an analysis, see Report 1 in Appendix 2 in this volume). Rather, it is designed to convey the essence of our analysis of David's transcript and is presented in a simplified form. Each section starts with a superordinate theme, followed by its constituent themes and then a brief discussion (see Box 5.3).

BOX 5.3 ▶ **The structure of the analytic narrative**

The superordinate themes, themes and associated quotations in our analytic narrative do not follow the chronology of the interview. Data from different parts of the transcript are used to exemplify any individual theme. There is a sense in which the interview is reconstructed to form a coherent analytic narrative, which is perfectly acceptable provided the meaning of data excerpts is not misrepresented or distorted. Great care needs to be taken with this because there can be a temptation to extort maximum evidence in support of a central or favoured theme by citing data out of context. As we reflected upon this in our analytic group, we realized that, if assessors of qualitative interview-based analyses have the study's interview transcripts available to them, they would do well to check at least some of the quotations that have been used to illustrate themes to ensure that they have been used appropriately and have not been taken out of context.

Superordinate theme 1: what the army gave David

We know that David felt that the army gave him a lot and it was easy to identify these elements because they were clear and unambiguously stated. It gave him:

- Theme: a sense of being someone special

  'I was an important member of a team and I was recognized as doing something for my country.' (Lines 17–18)

- Theme: a structure to his life which allowed him to plan

  'Like, we've got days when we're on exercise for a few weeks. Get there and you could plan your life. You knew you were going on exercise and you thought, um, you knew that 18 weekends out of the 52 … you knew you were going to kill a few beers and you knew you were going to have a good time.' (Lines 313–317)

- Theme: confidence and pride

  'It gave me more confidence. As a nipper when I first joined the army, I wasn't confident at all.' (Lines 4–5)

  'so we were important and I was proud of that.' (Lines 29–30)

The reference to having lacked confidence before joining the army would seem to be particularly relevant as it indicates that David does not have a positively-evaluated prior possible self to draw on from his life before joining the army when it came to constructing a new identity in civilian life.

- Theme: sense of belonging and being part of a team

  'It's like, as I say, I had an identity and I belonged to somewhere.' (Lines 22–23)

  'I was a member of a team and I was an important member of a team.' (Lines 17–18)

David compares his high status within his collective army team membership with his current position as a school caretaker. Having been a sergeant in the army and a member of the driving corps, he is now what he considers to be a lowly member of the school staff:

  'You're not a team member within the school because you're not a teacher.' (Lines 48–49)

  'as if to say, "Ah, it's only the caretaker and his staff – they'll do it." It annoys me because being part of a team as we should be, as we were in the army, you know, we would have all helped right from the top all the way down.' (Lines 54–57)

However, there is a suspicion that his memories of team spirit in the army are somewhat rose-tinted and later he does make a distinction between the way the officers and ordinary soldiers are treated at the end of the careers:

  'You know, I think some of the officers at the top don't realize just how hard it is for someone to get out because I know when they finish, they don't really finish.' (Lines 188–190)

Here we have an indication that it is not merely team membership that is important to him. It also matters which team he is a member of and what position he holds within any team hierarchy.

- Theme: parenting

'Yeah, I think I learned a great majority of them [values] being in the army. Ah, I wouldn't say I could have learned them at home because my mother died when I was young, when I was little, you know, um, so being brought up by my grandmother, right, I don't think she had a great deal of time so, so yeah, I think I got a lot of them being in the army.' (Lines 69–74)

This nurturing also included training in practical skills which again he might otherwise have expected to have learned from his mother. There is something almost childlike in his listing of his practical skills, which is emphasized by his repeated use of the words 'I can':

'I can make my breakfast, I can make my dinner, I can sew, I can iron, I can wash.' (Lines 208–209)

Superordinate theme 2: what the army took away from David

While we had a very strong sense that the army took away as much as it had given David, these losses were less explicitly stated and needed to be teased out from the data.

- Theme: health

'I got damaged knees and other things and I'm knackered.' (Lines 122–123)

- Theme: ability to relate to civilians

'Well one of the reasons why I think I was moonlighting was to get to know my civilian counterparts and try and get into how they thought and how they worked and how they operated.' (Lines 368–370)

David presents this as though he were an anthropologist exploring an alien civilization. He puts this in stronger terms a few lines later and emphasizes his sense of being excluded by his use of a simile in which he likens his attempts to join a civilian organization (in this case as a lorry driver) to those of a Black person trying to join a racist organization:

'it's how can I put it, a bit like a Black trying to join the Klu Klux Klan [sic], you know.' (Lines 375–376)

- Theme: practical skills

While we see above that the army provided him with the skills needed by a young person which he might not otherwise have learned, having lost his mother at an early age, later on it became clear that the army did not give him the practical skills to enable him to take on a more adult role outside the army. He discovered this in dramatic terms when buying a house:

'You just had to go out and try and find your own feet and make lots of mistakes – expensive ones at that.' (Lines 261–263)

'what you see on paper and what happens on the ground are two different things. Um, we bought a house and it collapsed and we lost everything.' (Lines 271–273)

- Theme: a future/sense of purpose

'sometimes I don't feel as though there's a purpose to it … thinking "What the hell am I doing here? Bugger this" … But I've got to do this yet again, today and tomorrow. And you think to yourself, "This is me for the rest of my life."' (Lines 218–223)

Earlier in the interview, David had described how he had known exactly what lay ahead when he was in the army, which had enabled him to plan and had been evaluated in positive terms. However, knowing what the future holds for him in his present job is seen negatively. This suggests that it is not simply the ability to plan which is important to him: the content of the plan is equally significant.

- Theme: (almost) his marriage

'I tended to be a little wild for about a couple of months after I got out, which one does. Uh, it nearly broke the marriage up at one stage.' (Lines 135–137)

Our research group was entirely female and we were all struck by the paucity of references by David to his wife and children: they are practically invisible in the transcript. The fact that the difficulties he experienced after leaving the army jeopardized his marriage was dealt with in only one sentence – something that did not endear him to us. I do not know whether it was solely gender that prompted this reaction, despite comments such as 'typical man' from group members, but we did have to work to find strong grounds for empathizing with David after this. Once again, this offers an example of how the reactions that data elicit in an analyst need to be monitored and worked with if it is felt that they could adversely affect the analysis. Here, our reaction served to alert us to the near absence of references to David's wife and children in the data.

Superordinate theme 3: the end of a relationship

Having discussed earlier the contention that the army gave him a sense of being parented which had been missing following the premature death of his mother, there is also a sense that, for David, leaving the army had much more emotional significance than might be associated with the end of a career. The themes, which are discussed here, all relate to emotions commonly felt at the end of a deeply important personal relationship. Having theorized that the army fulfilled a motherly role for him, it seems therefore that having to leave the army against his will (we infer because of restructuring) has resulted in a sense of a second bereavement with which he has not yet come to terms.

- Theme: abandonment and betrayal

  'Once you're out that gate, that's it. I know I can't even get back into the camp where, not ten minutes ago, I was a serving sergeant. I can't get back in. You know, you…it's like they're throwing you outside and locked the gate, you know, and that's it – you're on your own. That was painful.' (Lines 95–99)

  'And you know they don't realize that you've given the best time of your life to them and you give, which I did, I gave 150 per cent.' (Lines 120–122)

There is no sense in the interview that David left the army of his own volition. He specifies that his demobbing was under 'Options for change' but there is a very strong flavour of having been abandoned and indeed betrayed by the army. There is a very strong visual image generated by being locked out and physically excluded from the army premises showing how, despite attempts at negotiating a transition from army to civilian life, there comes a point at which the separation is crystallized and becomes final.

- Theme: bereavement/death

  'like we were saying, you walk round and you walk down the street and you see ghosts. You know, you walk down the streets where you walked down as a serving soldier and you can see all these ghosts.' (Lines 105–107)

David does not use the words 'death' or 'bereavement' to describe his feelings but he does refer twice to seeing ghosts. We interpreted this as the ghost of his former life but it also sets up a metaphorical separation between the world of the dead and the world of the living and we believed that David felt himself to be more dead than alive.

- Theme: no closure

  'I think we're still in the army.' (Line 461)

This statement comes very near the end of the interview and seems to indicate clearly that, despite his articulate way of describing his situation, it is a situation which has not yet been resolved, emphasized by his use of the present tense. In Chapter 4 in this volume, Jonathan A. Smith and Virginia Eatough state that 'a detailed IPA analysis can also involve standing a little back from the participant and asking curious and critical questions of their accounts – for example, "What is the person trying to achieve here?", "Is something leaking out here that wasn't intended?", "Do I have a sense of something going on here that maybe the person themselves is less aware of?"' On the whole we were cautious about reading too much into the words of the interviewee but in this case we felt that David's statement about still being in the army possibly indicated a need for psychological closure. We felt it was possible that, because in the interview he focuses on the practical problems of leaving the army, he has not yet had an opportunity or the support he needs to address the emotional legacy of leaving the army.

The quotations that have been presented to illustrate the themes of 'Abandonment and betrayal' and 'No closure' could be regarded as examples of what Smith (2011c) calls a **gem**. By this he means a small but powerful data extract that captures key qualities of the phenomenon under investigation.

Our outline of our analysis ends here. Usually in IPA work, having analysed the first transcript, the researcher would proceed to analyse transcripts from other interviewees, conduct cross-case comparisons and produce a final group-level table of superordinate themes. However, here we opted to focus on one case only and, in doing so, developed a real familiarity and engagement with his story, even within the relatively short time for which we worked on the data. I hope that my reflections on our analysis will provide guidance and reassurance to those who are considering using IPA in their own research in the future.

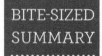

BITE-SIZED SUMMARY

3

The superordinate themes that we generated through our analysis have been presented in narrative form, together with the themes that constituted them and illustrative quotations. We have identified two instances of data 'gems' which seemed to capture core features of David's experience of leaving the army and post-army life. The write-up of our analysis has only been presented in skeletal form but it should provide an indication of the basic structure of an IPA write-up.

BOX 5.4

Explaining the value of an IPA approach

Imagine that you are a researcher who has applied for funding for an IPA study of people's understandings and experiences of a particular health-related condition or phenomenon. (For the purposes of this exercise, select a particular health condition or phenomenon that your proposed research will focus on.) Your application has received some fairly positive reviews but you have been asked to provide a specific justification for choosing an IPA approach for the proposed project.

How would you justify the use of IPA to a funding body where the reviewers might not be familiar with the approach or indeed with qualitative research? Emphasize the fit between your proposed research focus and IPA and explain what would be gained by using IPA here rather than another qualitative approach.

CHAPTER SUMMARY

This chapter has provided some reflections on the process of applying the principles of IPA to one interview transcript within a group context and within a limited time frame. Readers have been taken through the analytic stages so that they can understand how the final superordinate themes, which reflect the core concerns of the interview (and the analysts' interpretative frameworks), were identified. Some general issues raised by the analytic process (the problem of fragmented data, the use of theory and the structure of the analytic narrative) have also been explored. These have relevance beyond an IPA context and it is hoped that researchers using other qualitative methods may find these useful.

Further reading

Smith, Flowers and Larkin's (2009) book, *Interpretative Phenomenological Analysis: Theory, Method and Research*, is written by the originator of the approach and by two researchers who have been using it from its earliest days. It remains the obvious resource for anyone wishing to explore IPA in depth. Two examples of good IPA studies are Hadfield et al.'s (2009) research exploring how doctors working in accident and emergency departments respond to treating people who self-harm, and Fox et al.'s (2011) research on the personal meanings ascribed to eating-disorder symptoms by a group of women with various eating issues.

6

THEMATIC ANALYSIS

Victoria Clarke and Virginia Braun

This chapter provides an introduction to thematic analysis as a method for identifying and interpreting patterns in qualitative data. We distinguish between two main 'schools' of thematic analysis: (1) approaches with a foothold in quantitative research which are concerned with the 'reliability' of coding and theme development and (2) our thoroughly qualitative approach which views coding and theme development as organic and fluid and as ultimately and inescapably subjective. In this chapter we focus on the latter. Another hallmark of our approach to thematic analysis is that it offers a theoretically flexible method with wide-ranging applications rather than a theoretically-informed methodology that necessarily sets limits on application. We describe different ways of implementing thematic analysis and then outline a six phase process for conducting a thematic analysis involving: (1) data familiarization; (2) coding; (3) searching for themes; (4) reviewing themes; (5) defining and naming themes; and (6) writing up.

Introduction

Thematic analysis is a technique or method for identifying and interpreting patterns of meaning (or 'themes') in qualitative data. We outline our approach to thematic analysis, highlighting particular aspects of the process with examples from our study of gay men's clothing and appearance practices (Clarke and Smith, 2015). This study used qualitative surveys (see Braun and Clarke, 2013) to collect data from a convenience sample of 20 British men who were mostly young (aged 25 or under), white and middle class, and self-identified as gay (n = 18) or bisexual (n = 2). The initial research question was 'How do gay men make sense of their clothing and appearance practices?' but, after coding and initial theme development, this was refined to 'What concerns and appearance pressures do gay men attend to in making sense of their clothing and appearance practices?' The reflective report in Appendix 2 (Report 2) by Caroline Huxley and colleagues provides another example of an appearance-focused thematic analysis study. Before outlining the six phases of our approach to thematic analysis, we first discuss how thematic analysis developed as a qualitative analytic method and its 'unique selling point' compared to other qualitative analytic approaches, that is, its flexibility and potentially wide-ranging application.

The history and development of thematic analysis

Unlike with other qualitative approaches – such as interpretative phenomenological analysis (IPA) (see Chapter 4) or grounded theory (see Chapter 8) – no one person or group of people can claim to have developed or 'invented' thematic analysis. Systematic procedures for analysing qualitative data began to be developed in the 1960s and 1970s and around that time lots of different versions of thematic analysis were in use. Furthermore, thematic analysis was not only used as a term to describe an analytic technique centred on generating themes from qualitative data (for early examples of this type of thematic analysis, see Benner, 1985, and Dapkus, 1985). It was also used inter-changeably with the term 'content analysis' to describe a method for quantifying the content of qualitative data (Christ, 1970), as well as being used to describe particular forms of content analysis, including interpretative (or qualitative) content analysis (Baxter, 1991; Woodrum, 1984). Furthermore, the term 'thematic analysis' has had many other uses in a wide variety of disciplines from the philosophy of science (Holton, 1973) to education studies (Winter and McClelland, 1978).

Another confusion in the history of thematic analysis is that qualitative researchers have often simply referred to themes 'emerging' from data, typically with no discussion of the analytic procedures they followed. The notion that themes just emerge from data like bubbles rising to the surface of a pot of boiling water is too good to be true. If only it were possible to collect our data then leave it somewhere to self-analyse! Analysis requires the active and systematic engagement of the researcher with the data and this is where analytic procedures come in. Systematic procedures for coding and theme development in thematic analysis began to be outlined in the 1990s (see Aronson, 1994, for an early example), and there are now a number of different sets of procedures for and approaches to thematic analysis (see, for example, Boyatzis, 1998; Guest et al., 2012; Joffé, 2011), including our own (Braun and Clarke, 2006, 2012, 2013). The students we teach often tell us that one thing that makes qualitative approaches confusing, complex and anxiety-provoking is the seemingly endless range of possibilities for analysing data and the lack of a clear, accessible and definitive set of guidelines. Here we provide some clear guidelines for thematic analysis and, in Chapter 7, Gareth Terry offers some reflections on the experience of applying thematic analysis to the data set in Appendix 1.

Looking across the different approaches to thematic analysis, it is possible to identify two broad 'schools': what we call 'small q' and 'Big Q' thematic analysis. Most contemporary approaches to thematic analysis fall under the small q umbrella. 'Small q' refers to the use of qualitative techniques within a broadly quantitative framework or paradigm (for further discussion of the distinction between small q and Big Q qualitative research, see Kidder and Fine, 1987). This means that researchers doing small q thematic analysis try to ensure the 'reliability' of their analyses in ways that would make sense to a quantitative researcher. For example, when coding their data, they use a 'codebook' or 'coding frame'. After an initial process of **data familiarization** (reading and making notes on the data), they develop all the codes they will use to analyse their data, writing clear and concrete definitions for each code. This coding frame is then applied to the entire data set by two or more researchers working independently. 'Inter-rater reliability' scores are calculated using Cohen's Kappa to determine the level of agreement between the independent coders. A Kappa greater than .80 indicates a very good level of agreement and supposedly 'reliable' coding. This 'triangulation' of coding is thought to be a hallmark of quality. This approach to coding probably sounds rather appealing as it removes subjectivity from data analysis – and psychology students are often told that subjectivity has no place in research. However, as qualitative researchers, we think researcher subjectivity should be embraced rather than eliminated. We shall explain why in relation to our approach to thematic analysis.

The other 'school' of thematic analysis, 'Big Q thematic analysis' – which our approach exemplifies – is one that acknowledges and indeed welcomes researcher subjectivity. It is 'Big Q' because it is a qualitative technique used within a qualitative paradigm that emphasizes contextualized understandings and rejects notions of objective reality or universal truth (for more on this, see Chapter 2). The difference between the two approaches is evident in how coding is approached (we introduce our approach here but discuss it further below). Rather than developing a (rigid and inflexible) coding frame that is then applied to the whole data set, coding in Big Q thematic analysis is a fluid, flexible and organic process that evolves as the analysis progresses. Although it can be useful to code data with another researcher (to discuss and compare analytic observations), it is normal and acceptable for one researcher to code the data set. This is what Victoria did in the gay men and appearance study, even though it was a collaborative project. The aim of coding here is not to code 'accurately' (whatever that might mean here) with the intention of unearthing *the* codes buried within the data. Instead the aim is to use the researcher's skills and standpoint to produce a plausible and coherent coding of the data from which a number of different analyses could be developed.

This is an important point to grasp. Within a qualitative paradigm, there is no single definitive analysis that the intrepid researcher discovers in the data: the researcher is not seen as working as a metaphorical archaeologist. Rather the researcher uses their skills, combined with the content of the data, to create their analysis. Here the researcher is seen as a metaphorical sculptor. This means that various different analyses are possible (Braun and Clarke, 2013). However, this does not mean that an analysis is just 'made up' or that 'anything goes' with Big Q thematic analysis. Rather, it recognizes that the analysis is the result of a researcher with a particular set of skills, training, disciplinary knowledge, biography and socio-demographic positioning actively engaging with their data. If an analysis is plausible and coherent, it is because of the researcher's unique standpoint, not in spite of it. 'Reliability' or trustworthiness in Big Q thematic analysis stems from a systematic and scholarly approach to analysis (see below), not from checking the 'accuracy' of coding using statistics (Braun and Clarke, 2013). At best, a 'very good' inter-rater reliability score simply shows that researchers have been trained to code in the same way, not that the analysis is 'reliable' (Yardley, 2008).

> We have outlined two broad 'schools' of thematic analysis: (1) a 'small q' approach with a basis in quantitative research that seeks to produce qualitative analyses that are 'reliable' in ways that make sense to quantitative researchers and (2) a 'Big Q' approach – the focus of the remainder of this chapter – that embraces and is enhanced by the subjectivity of the researcher.

BITE-SIZED SUMMARY
....
1

The flexibility of thematic analysis

We will now describe the distinctive features of our approach to thematic analysis in more detail. Thematic analysis is unique among qualitative analytic approaches because it is a method whereas most other approaches are best described as methodologies. The terms 'method' and 'methodology' are often used interchangeably but they mean something rather different. A method is a technique – a set of procedures for collecting data (such as interviewing) or for analysing data. A methodology is a theoretically-informed framework for conducting research. A methodology tells you what your guiding theoretical assumptions are, what kinds of questions you can ask, how you should construct your sample, how (ideally) you should collect data from this sample, as well as specifying a range of procedures for (appropriately) analysing data (Braun and Clarke, 2013).

Some 'methods' of qualitative data analysis (such as IPA, narrative analysis and discourse analysis) are better conceptualized as methodologies: they come 'ready-packaged' with a set of theories, appropriate questions and ideal methods for data collection (see Chapters 4, 10 and 12 on IPA, discourse analysis and narrative analysis respectively). Thematic analysis, in contrast, can be flexibly applied within any of the major ontological, epistemological and theoretical frameworks underpinning qualitative research (see Chapter 2), from realism and essentialism to relativism and social constructionism. For example, Huxley et al.'s (2014) thematic analysis of the appearance pressures faced by lesbian and bisexual women is underpinned by a critical realist framework (see Report 2 in Appendix 2), as is Gareth Terry's worked thematic analysis of the data set for this book (see Chapter 7). Our thematic analysis on the appearance concerns of gay men is by contrast informed by a social constructionist position.

Thematic analysis can be used to answer most types of research question that are of interest to qualitative researchers: see Table 6.1 for a **typology** of qualitative research questions and examples of studies that have used thematic analysis to address these types of questions. There is no ideal type of data for a thematic analysis study: the method can be and has been used to analyse everything from interviews (for example, Huxley et al., 2014) to secondary sources (for example, Farvid and Braun, 2006). There are no particular sampling requirements for thematic analysis, although some degree of homogeneity in sampling is useful for identifying patterned meaning in smaller samples, and the method can be used to analyse both smaller and larger data sets. However, if using interviews, we generally recommend a sample of at least six because of the emphasis on patterned meaning across cases rather than idiographic meaning (see Braun and Clarke, 2013, for a more detailed discussion of sample size). This is one respect in which thematic analysis differs from IPA where the emphasis is on the analysis of data from small samples, including samples of one (see Chapter 4).

When it comes to analysis, thematic analysis can be used to capture the surface (semantic) meanings in data, to stay close to participants' perspectives (see Report 2 in

Table 6.1 A typology of research questions suitable for studies using thematic analysis

Type of research question	Example of a thematic analysis study
Experiences: research questions focused on individual lived experiences	How do people experience online gaming? (Hussain and Griffiths, 2009)
Understandings and perceptions: research questions focused on individual views on and conceptualizations of particular phenomena	Do lesbian and bisexual women think they are protected from socio-cultural pressures to be thin? (Huxley et al., 2014)
Influencing factors: research questions that explore the individual and social factors that underpin particular phenomena	Why do people participate in longitudinal qualitative (health) research? (Peel et al., 2006)
Practices/accounts of practices: research questions that explore the things people do in the world and/or how people make sense of the things they do in the world	What concerns and pressures do gay men attend to in making sense of their clothing and appearance practices? (Clarke and Smith, 2015)
Representation: research questions that explore the ideas that surround particular phenomena in particular media	How is climate change represented in British broadsheet newspapers? (Jaspal and Nerlich, 2014)
Construction: research questions focused on the role of language (or 'discourse') in constituting particular versions of 'reality'	How do New Zealand men construct their masculine identities in relation to the choice to have a vasectomy? (Terry and Braun, 2011)

Appendix 2). It can also be used to examine the assumptions and logic frameworks (latent meanings) underpinning the surface meanings: this was the focus of our analysis of gay men and appearance. This means that thematic analysis can be used both to describe and summarize data and to interpret and interrogate data.

Finally, thematic analysis can be used both **inductively** and **deductively**. Although pure induction is not possible because qualitative analysis is always guided by broad onto-logical and epistemological frameworks and the researcher's standpoints, analysis can be primarily anchored in the data (see Report 2 in Appendix 2). Alternatively, analysis can be deductive in the sense that existing theories and concepts provide a lens through which to read and interpret the data. For example, we used concepts like 'compulsory heterosexuality' (Rich, 1980) to help us make sense of the ways in which the participants in our study were reluctant to appear 'too gay'.

Because there are many different ways of using thematic analysis, before commencing analysis you need to decide

- what ontological, epistemological and theoretical frameworks will inform your use of thematic analysis;
- whether you will code the data for and describe **semantic** meaning or whether you will code for and interrogate **latent** meaning;
- whether your analysis will be grounded in the data or whether it will be guided by exist-ing theory.

Answering these questions can be challenging and frustrating if you are new to qualitative research but making these elements explicit gives you an extra insight into the 'inner work-ings' of qualitative analysis and how theoretical assumptions inform analytic observations. Although this might seem to give an inordinate range of variations of thematic analysis, in practice relativist, constructionist, latent and 'deductive' approaches to thematic analysis tend to cluster together, and realist, essentialist, semantic and 'inductive' approaches cluster together. However, most analyses contain elements of both semantic and latent coding.

We outlined thematic analysis as a flexible technique for qualitative analysis with a wide range of applications. Because thematic analysis is not a theoretically informed methodology, the researcher should decide how they will use thematic analysis before commencing data analysis. The decisions here will include answer-ing questions about guiding theoretical assumptions, coding semantic or latent meaning and analysing data inductively or deductively.

BITE-SIZED
SUMMARY
. . . .
2

Doing thematic analysis

Our approach to thematic analysis offers a six-phase process that systematically builds from data familiarization through to coding and theme development. Although we outline distinctive phases, the process can be more recursive than linear: sometimes you might go back and forth between phases rather than strictly progressing from one to the next. It is very useful to follow these phases closely when learning but, with more analytic experience, some phases may blur into each other.

Data familiarization

Data familiarization is like jumping into the deep end of a swimming pool: it is about immersion – and it can feel similarly anxiety-provoking if you have not done it before! It involves reading and re-reading your data to develop a deep and familiar sense of the semantic, obvious meanings of the data. This is fairly easy to achieve but familiarization also asks you to go a step further and to start engaging analytically with the data. This can be trickier as you have to move from a mode of simple consumption of the data to a more questioning mode. It is about treating your data as data, where you take a position of distance from the explicit meanings and begin to think about the broader assumptions and ideas and what these might mean – all in relation to your research question. Try not to worry if you feel you cannot get enough distance at this stage to see beyond the obvious content of the data. The next coding phase will facilitate that.

In practical terms, as you read your data, you make notes when something of interest occurs to you. That might sound fairly unstructured – and it is. The notes you make are casual observations about the data; they are like personal memos that you use to remind yourself of potential analytic insights or things you might want to explore during coding and theme development. For example, reading the gay men and appearance data, Victoria immediately noted an emphasis on the importance of authentic individuality, something she had previously written about in relation to lesbian women and appearance (Clarke and Spence, 2013).

Data coding

Coding switches your mode of engagement with the data from casual to systematic and involves working through the data set, developing codes for segments of data. A **code** is a succinct label (a word or a short phrase) that captures a key analytic idea in the data that is of potential interest to the research question. Coding is a short-hand but it is not just about data reduction in the sense of summarizing the (surface) meanings in the data. Codes also capture your interpretations of the data. Furthermore, a good code will pass the 'remove the data' coding test (Clarke and Braun, 2013). Imagine we come along and take away your data (as we often do to our students!). Would your codes evoke the meanings they are designed to capture? Using the gay men and appearance study as an example, a code like 'more positive' could be fairly meaningless without the data to explain it. However, the code 'more positive about appearance post-coming out' clearly evokes the data, identifying both the issue (appearance after 'coming out' as gay) and what the participant's experience is (he has become more confident in his appearance) (see Table 6.2).

Table 6.2 An excerpt of coded data from the gay men and appearance study

Extract	Codes
Question: Have you made any changes in your appearance after coming out as a gay man? Please explain.	
Response: Well in a way I have. I have become a lot more confident about my appearance. I have changed my hairstyle, my sense of self and fashion wise as well. I do admit I have taken things from different subcultures. I like to make it seem as if I were following the latest trends but at the end of the day I have changed cos I have really like what I have seen.	Changes made to appearance post-coming out More positive about appearance post-coming out Subcultural influences on appearance (Not) a dedicated follower of fashion Conformity = loss of individuality Importance of appearance reflecting the real me
But on a different level I have also joined a gym and gone on diets to make myself thinner as in this modern day world no one really gives you a second look unless you are the size of a cotton bud. This has also made me a lot more happy in myself as well.	Appearance pressures in the gay community Changes made to appearance post-coming out Gay body ideals – thin Securing the right kind of gaze The comfort of (body) conformity More positive about appearance post-coming out

As we noted above, codes vary in what they capture. Some simply identify and summarize the obvious things that the participant says, as is the case with the code 'more positive about appearance post-coming out'. These codes can be termed semantic or descriptive. Other codes are more latent or interpretative: they capture the researcher's interpretation of the assumptions and logic frameworks that underpin the semantic content. The code 'the comfort of (body) conformity' in Table 6.2 is an example of this kind of code. It not only identifies the broad issue the participant is talking about (that is, changing his body to fit gay subcultural appearance norms) and his feelings about it (positive). It also signals an analytic view by the researcher, that conformity with body norms is at least part of the explanation for why this is experienced positively. Ultimately you want your codes to capture both the diversity of perspectives evident in the data set and the patterning of meaning (Braun and Clarke, 2012), and some will be more descriptive, others more interpretative.

In practical terms, the process of coding requires you to 'tag' segments of data with a code as you sequentially work through the data set. Every time you identify something of interest in the data, you should decide whether you can use an existing code or need to create a new one (in Table 6.2 some of the codes are used more than once). We suggest writing on hard copy data items or typing into an electronic document (like in Table 6.2).

Increasingly, though, we get asked about doing coding electronically and about the role of computer assisted qualitative data analysis software (CAQDAS) designed to facilitate qualitative analysis (see Silver and Fielding, 2008), and whether thematic analysis is amenable to CAQDAS use. Although we will continue to describe the process of analysis as if you were coding the data manually, using CAQDAS is indeed possible. If using CAQDAS, as with the other qualitative approaches presented in this book, the essential process remains the same but the mechanics change. However, note that CAQDAS will be most useful in the coding and theme identification phases but is less relevant in the later phases of thematic analysis.

You need to code systematically, working through each data item, until the whole data set has been coded. You do not need to code every single bit of the data, just the segments that are potentially relevant to answering your research question. However, research questions can evolve alongside coding and theme development in thematic analysis so it is important to interpret your research question very broadly and code inclusively. The basic advice here is that if there is something even potentially relevant to your research question in the data, you should code it. For instance, in our example, if a participant talked about their musical tastes, you probably would not code it but if they talked about their musical tastes in a way that related to their own appearance, it might be relevant and so you would code it.

There is one other issue to be aware of with coding, which we might term 'coding drift'. Coding deepens our analytic engagement with the data and, as coding develops, we often start to have new analytic insights that are produced as a result of coding. For example, during the coding of the data on gay men and appearance, Victoria noticed that the participants often made implicit and explicit comparisons to and distanced themselves from other (straight and gay) men. What this means is that we start to code data in new and different ways because we see additional analytic possibilities in the data. Yet, because this usually happens some way through the coding phase, relevant data in data items that we coded earlier may have been missed. For this reason, it is important not just to go through the data once when coding it. We recommend a double round of coding so that coding drift can be counterbalanced and you can be confident that the data are coded comprehensively and consistently. Once you are satisfied that the coding is thorough and consistent, you need to prepare for theme identification and development. This involves compiling all the codes from your coding phase into a long list of codes and compiling data associated with each code.

BITE-SIZED SUMMARY

3

We described the dual process of immersion and distance that characterizes the familiarization phase of thematic analysis where you start to read your data as data. The coding phase moves to a more systematic way of working with the data where you identify key aspects of the data – both obvious, semantic ones and less obvious, latent ones – that are relevant to answering your research question.

Searching for themes

Codes can be understood as the building blocks of your themes. While a code relates typically to a very specific aspect of the data, a theme identifies a general patterning of meaning. So this phase requires you to step back from the minutiae of the data and think about the broader patterns that you can identify in the data. Any 'themes' that you start to identify are very provisional so think about them as candidate themes. They often evolve and may even be rejected as the analysis progresses so it pays not to get too attached to them at this early stage.

Practically, the first step of identifying potential themes is usually to cluster together codes that relate to a particular issue (although sometimes if a code is rich or complex enough, it might get 'promoted' to become a theme: see Charmaz, 2014). The initial way to do this is to see whether you can identify certain repeated ideas, concepts or meanings in the list of codes that you compiled at the end of the last phase. For example, Victoria initially clustered together lots of codes relating to appearance norms on the 'gay scene'. In identifying candidate themes, there are three useful guiding questions to consider (Braun et al., 2014):

- Is this candidate theme centrally relevant to answering my research question? With many potential themes in data, the ones you identify should individually but also collectively offer the fullest account of the data to answer your question.

- Is this candidate theme evident across more than one or two data items? As thematic analysis is concerned with patterned meaning, it is important that themes are evident across multiple data items. That said, frequency is not the sole criterion for determining themes. Themes may sometimes be important to your research question even if they are only evident across a few data items (Braun and Clarke, 2006; Buetow, 2010).

- Can I easily identify a **central organizing concept** for this candidate theme? A central organizing concept is a key analytic tool in thematic analysis. It refers to a clear core idea or concept that underpins a theme – the essence of what the theme is all about (Braun and Clarke, 2013). Identifying a central organizing concept for each theme ensures that each theme is internally coherent and distinctive.

A good theme will identify an area of the data and tell you something about it. Furthermore, a good theme is distinctive but relates to the other themes: together the themes provide a clear image of your data set and your interpretation of it. You can think of each theme as a piece in a jigsaw puzzle, with the whole analysis as a completed jigsaw (Braun and Clarke, 2012).

Up to this point, your theme development has relied on your in-depth knowledge of the data – developed through familiarization and coding – and the data codes themselves. This means you are at least one degree removed from the data and it is really important to go back to the data to explore the fit between what you have provisionally identified and the meanings expressed within the data. This is the main focus of the review phase and, in preparation for the first part of the review, you need to compile all the data extracts associated with all codes relevant to the developing analysis.

Reviewing themes

The review phase develops your thematic analysis in relation to the data set as a whole as well as the coded data. It offers a double layer of quality control to ensure your candidate themes closely represent the content of the data set and that these themes tell the fullest story about the data in relation to your research question. The first aspect of the review process is to check the candidate themes against all coded data relevant to each theme to ensure a good fit between your candidate themes and coded data. The second aspect of the review is to check your candidate themes against the entire data set to ensure a good fit between this and your final themes. This is not a quick process but it is crucial to ensure that (a) your coding has not missed some particular aspect of the data; (b) in the analytic process, you have not 'drifted' away from the data set and inadvertently presented an analysis that does not represent the data; and (c) the analysis provides as thorough, meaningful and nuanced an account of the data set as possible.

Through the review process, the 'shape' of your analysis is likely to change: remember we advised not to get too attached to your candidate themes! In going back to the data, you might discard a theme, combine two (or more) themes, split a theme into two themes, retain but refine a theme, or some combination of these. For example, when reviewing 'the gay "look"' candidate theme, Victoria noticed two distinct elements: discussion of various stereotyped 'gay' appearances on which the men expressed different opinions and an acknowledgement that the gay scene emphasizes the importance of 'looking good'. Given these quite different elements, she decided to split this theme into two subthemes.

To reiterate, you need to be open to changing your candidate themes on the basis of their fit with the data and how well they answer your research question. It is crucial to keep this latter point in mind. Thematic analysis is a method for reporting patterns in data but it is not just about reporting any or all patterns. Instead, you should identify patterns (themes) that meaningfully answer your research question and that provide the richest account of the data in doing so. This means that in developing but especially in **reviewing themes**, you need to keep your research question at the forefront of your mind. This can help you determine whether or not some feature or pattern in the data is worth developing in the analysis. If it does not address the research question and add something to the overall analysis, it probably should be discarded at this stage. There is always far more that can be said about data than any one analysis can capture.

Other questions that may help you when revising and developing your themes include:

- Is this a theme? What you are dealing with could just be a code. If it is a theme, it may be helpful to ask the questions below.

- What is the nature of this theme? Does it tell me something useful about the data set and about my research question?

- What are the boundaries of this theme? What does it include and what does it exclude?

- Are there enough (meaningful) data to support this theme? In other words, is the theme 'thick' or 'thin'?

- Are the data too diverse and wide-ranging? Does the theme lack coherence? (Braun and Clarke, 2012: 65)

Another useful tool for developing the analysis is the central organizing concept, which we previously described. If you can identify the central organizing concept for each theme, it is relatively easy to determine whether or not some aspect of the data is part of a theme. In our data, the central organizing concept for the theme 'the gay "look"' is captured in the theme title, namely the notion that there is a distinct visual identity associated with gay men.

At this point in the analysis, you also want to think about the structure of the over-all analysis and thus the relationships between themes. A **thematic map** (see Figure 6.1) provides a useful tool for mapping out candidate themes and the relationships between them – both 'horizontal' and 'vertical' relationships. You could also do this with a table if you are less visually oriented but we find visual mapping really useful. The concept of horizontal relationships relates to how the themes in your analysis fit together. The concept of vertical relationships captures the relationships between themes and the subthemes that sometimes sit 'within' themes. A **subtheme** shares a central organizing concept with a theme but highlights one particular aspect of it (Braun and Clarke, 2013), such as 'the pleasure of being myself' in Figure 6.1. If you have an element of a theme that is particularly salient and offers information you want to emphasize in answering your research question, identifying it as a subtheme can be useful. Our general advice is to use subthemes judiciously because lots of subthemes risk creating an analysis that lacks coherence and analytic depth. However, this is a guide not a rule and becoming good at thematic analysis involves learning when a 'rule' should be broken. For example, the outcome of our revision of the gay men and appearance analysis resulted in the thematic map in Figure 6.1. This is about as complex as a thematic analysis should be. It demonstrates an analysis with two main themes – 'the gay "look"' and 'the pleasures and dangers of looking gay' (which together are captured in the overarching theme of 'not hiding, not shouting, just me'), with one or two levels of subthemes within each. This analytic 'shape' resulted from a theme review process where we realized that many of the candidate themes shared a broader, central organizing concept. Hence it made sense to cluster them under two themes but they also contained particular aspects relevant to the analysis that we wished to emphasize; for this reason, we had multiple subthemes.

In general, in response to the frequently asked question of 'How many themes should I have?', we advise reporting no more than between two and six themes in an analysis (Braun and Clarke, 2013). Also, keep in mind the practical constraints of word limits when writing for student course work and for publication: the more themes you have, the less detailed your analysis will be and the less space there will be for developing subthemes. Ultimately, the number of themes also needs to be determined by how best you can answer your research question within the constraints of the context for which you are writing. Not all elements need to be reported in detail. In report-ing the gay men and appearance analysis, the main themes only structure the analysis and it is the

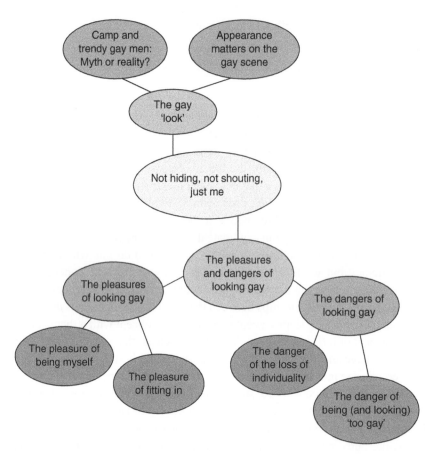

Figure 6.1 A thematic map from the gay men and appearance study

subthemes that are discussed in depth. However, and somewhat creatively, the overarching theme is discussed at the end of the analysis, where it is revealed as an analytic conclusion reached by making sense of the patterning of the subthemes (see Clarke and Smith, 2015).

BITE-SIZED SUMMARY
·················
4

Developing and reviewing themes is a flexible and recursive process of mapping and revising patterned meaning, first across the codes, then across the coded data and ultimately in relation to the whole data set. As the analysis evolves through this process, it is important not to get too attached to early ideas about themes and subthemes. Thematic maps and central organizing concepts are useful tools for refining the shape of your thematic analysis.

Defining and naming themes

Once you have decided on the overall structure for your analysis, you move on to the phase of developing a detailed analysis of the data in each theme. Our students often comment that this is where the real analytic work begins. Here you refine the focus and scope of your analysis and determine the exact '**story**' you will tell for each theme and overall. Your 'story' is the analytic narrative that you build around your data excerpts to tell the reader what you think is going on in the data, why this is important for your research question and why the reader should care about it. As part of this, you select the data extracts that you will present in the write-up of the report: good extracts are those that provide clear, compelling and vivid illustrations of the issue or point you are demonstrating in your analysis. For example, in Table 6.2, the participant's comment about the importance of being 'the size of a cotton bud' on the gay scene is beautifully evocative of the extremity of gay appearance norms. With a participant as articulate and expressive as this, it would be tempting to quote him over and over again. But in selecting excerpts, you should also try to draw widely from across your data set because you want to demonstrate the patterned nature of the themes you report. Only quoting one or two data items would undermine that. Remember also that data are just data until you tell the reader why they are important and relevant. An absolutely crucial maxim in developing and refining the analysis is that 'data do not speak for themselves'. Doing analysis means you need to provide an interpretation of the data.

A useful exercise in this phase can be writing a definition for each theme as it tests your analytic clarity and quickly identifies if the boundaries and scope of a theme are not clear. A **theme definition** is like an extended central organizing concept – extended because it highlights the analytic interpretation of the data as well as describing the key concept encapsulated in the theme. The material in Box 6.1 provides an example from our gay men and appearance study.

The other useful thing to finalize at this point is the name you will give to each theme (and subtheme). A good name signals the focus of the theme and the analytic scope or content of it. Through this, it is informative to a reader before they read the whole analysis. In the gay men and appearance study, the theme name 'the gay "look"' orients the reader to a focus on appearance stereotypes and practices within the gay subculture that the men are part of. The name 'the pleasures and dangers of looking gay' signals a more psychological orientation and a focus on the experiences and meanings of the participants themselves.

Writing up thematic analysis

This is the final phase. You are almost there: you just have to produce the final report (for example, a dissertation or a journal article). In quantitative research, this phase would be a

> ## BOX 6.1 | Definition of the core theme of 'Not hiding, not shouting, just me'
>
> The overarching or core theme in the analysis of the data on gay men and appearance is 'Not hiding, not shouting, just me'. This theme captures the way most of the participants made sense of their visual identities as neither closeted (hiding) nor 'too gay' (shouting); they were just ordinary men who happened to be gay. In making sense of their clothing and appearance practices in this way, the men oriented both to the importance of being an authentic individual (which is threatened by conformity to gay appearance mandates) and the 'coming out imperative' (Rasmussen, 2004) in the gay community (where a fully developed sexual identity and comfort with sexual identity are equated with and communicated by openness about sexuality and are threatened by an over-emphasis on individuality). This meant that, for example, men who did not conform to gay appearance mandates (for example, men who identified as 'straight-acting') ironically made sense of their appearance as an authentic expression of their inner selves, often asserted pride in their sexuality and contrasted their appearance with that of gay men who were 'too gay' in appearance (and thus not authentically individual).

big one but because qualitative research requires you to write as you develop your analysis, this phase is more about producing a polished analysis and a polished report.

In qualitative research, the traditional 'results' and 'discussion' sections are typically (but not always) combined into one (see Report 2 by Huxley et al. in Appendix 2). As discussed above, the analytic section presents your reading of the data and tells the reader why that is interesting and important. It effectively presents the evidence base from your data and an analytic narrative that 'answers' your research question. In thematic analysis, there are two different ways of treating your data extracts (Braun and Clarke, 2013). One is an illustrative approach where data extracts are used to illustrate the claims that you make but you do not actually say anything in your analytic narrative about the specifics of each extract (this is the approach taken in the reflective report by Huxley et al.). What this means in practice is that you could remove your data extracts or replace them with similar others and your analytic narrative would still be coherent. The other way of treating your data extracts is an analytic approach where your analytic comments relate to the specifics of the actual data excerpts. What this means is that if you replaced your data extracts with others or removed them, your analysis would not make sense: your data extracts and analytic narrative are enmeshed (for an example of this, see Eatough and Smith's reflective report on an IPA study in Appendix 2). Although thematic analysis often uses data extracts in one of these ways, both approaches can be combined. For example, the report of the gay men and appearance study combines both illustrative and analytic approaches (see Clarke and Smith, 2015).

Another aspect of writing up relates to the way your overall research report needs to explain, locate and contextualize your analysis in relation to existing theory and research. Not only do you need to provide a literature 'review' (see Braun and Clarke, 2013) but in the analysis section (or in the discussion if this is separate from the presentation of the analysis), you need to re-engage with relevant literature, highlighting continuities and discontinuities, using existing literature to extend the insights gained from the data and, if relevant, providing reinterpretations of earlier research on the basis of your analysis. If you do not do this, your analysis will be limited in terms of analytic insight, contribution to scholarship and scholarly quality.

Quality control in thematic analysis

One of the common criticisms levelled at qualitative research, typically by those unfamiliar with Big Q approaches, is that 'anything goes' and analyses can be effectively 'made up'. In thematic analysis and other qualitative approaches, demonstrating a systematic and thorough analytic process goes a long way in protecting your analysis against this type of critique. However, there are many ways in which thematic analysis can still be done poorly. Using our 15-point checklist of criteria for 'good' thematic analysis (see Table 6.3) will orient you to some of the potential pitfalls you need to avoid to ensure that the outcome of your analytic efforts represents a good thematic analysis. Despite providing this clear checklist, over the years we have encountered innumerable examples where researchers have claimed to be doing thematic analysis according to our approach, yet have published work that falls short in important ways.

Looking across the common problems we have encountered, we emphasize the following as particularly important quality control issues and explain why this is the case:

- As we have highlighted, thematic analysis is an active process. This means that you need to make decisions about what form of thematic analysis you use and to be explicit about your role in shaping the analysis into its exact form. What this means in 'quality control' terms is not claiming that 'themes emerge' (point 15 in Table 6.3) but being explicit about your process of theme identification and development. It also means being explicit about the version of thematic analysis you are using (point 12)

Table 6.3 Fifteen-point checklist for a good thematic analysis (Braun and Clarke, 2006: 96)

Process	No.	Criterion
Transcription	1	The data have been transcribed to an appropriate level of detail and the transcripts have been checked against the recordings for 'accuracy'.
Coding	2	Each data item has been given equal attention in the coding process.
	3	Themes have not been generated from a few vivid examples (an anecdotal approach) but instead the coding process has been thorough, inclusive and comprehensive.
	4	All relevant extracts for each theme have been collated.
	5	Themes have been checked against each other and back to the original data set.
	6	Themes are internally coherent, consistent and distinctive.
Analysis	7	Data have been analysed (interpreted, made sense of) rather than just paraphrased or re-described.
	8	Analysis and data match each other: the data extracts illustrate the analytic claims.
	9	The analysis tells a convincing and well-organized story about the data and topic.
	10	A good balance between analytic narrative and illustrative extracts is provided.
Overall	11	Enough time has been allocated to complete all phases of the analysis adequately without rushing a phase or giving it a light 'once-over'.
Written report	12	The assumptions about and specific approach to thematic analysis are clearly explicated.
	13	There is a good fit between what you claim you do and what you show you have done, that is, the described method and reported analysis are consistent.
	14	The language and concepts used in the report are consistent with the epistemological position of the analysis.
	15	The researcher is positioned as active in the research process; themes are not just said to have 'emerged'.

and making sure that the overall analysis is theoretically coherent (for example, you should not use constructionist language if you are doing a more realist/essentialist thematic analysis, or vice versa) (points 13 and 14).

- Presenting a thematic analysis is about telling your story about the data, not about presenting data that 'speak for themselves'. So it is really important that you provide enough narrative around your data extracts to tell the reader what your analytic story is. Aim for an equal balance of data extracts and analytic narrative or perhaps even

BOX
6.2

Coding practice

The data extracts below were generated by the gay men and appearance study in response to the question, 'Is it important to you to be recognizable or visible as a gay man in terms of your appearance? Please explain.' Have a go at coding these extracts, keeping in mind our research question: 'What concerns and pressures do gay men attend to in making sense of their visual identities?' Try to generate a mixture of semantic and latent codes. If you are reading this chapter as part of a course in qualitative research, invite a classmate to code the data as well and compare your two sets of codes. What are the differences and similarities between your sets of codes? Think about why this might be, then work together to develop an overall interpretation of the data extracts that focuses on what they tell us about the ways in which gay men make sense of their appearance and clothing practices. Note that the data were generated in response to a survey question and so we have not altered the participants' original spelling and punctuation.

'Not really. There are times when I do wish it to be more obvious, simply because I like people to know without me having to tell them. Additionally, if I'm in a situation where I'm making a political statement, and may wish to be more obvious about it, but I don't need to wave the flag to be gay. Besides, one of the things people don't like about some elements of the gay community is the way some of us throw our sexuality around and make bold statements about it. I'm not the kind of person to go round wearing a T-shirt that says "I'm not gay, but my boyfriend is." I prefer more subtle ways of letting people know if I'm ever in a situation where I feel I want people to know. Most of the time it's none of their business anyway.' (Participant 5)

'No because I don't want to be seen as different. Again I don't like labels and straight people do not have "straight" written on their forehead, in the same way I don't want to paint myself as "gay" even though I'm not ashamed of it. It doesn't need to be advertised. I am very open with my sexuality, now, but there are many other aspects to me that are important. Being gay isn't the only one.' (Participant 8)

'Not really, it's easier than having to tell people you're gay all the time if they can already tell, but at the same time you don't want being gay to be your entire identity, sometimes you want to blend in with the crowd. So sometimes being overtly gay is easier than not being, but other times it's better to just be recognised as another person, not for people's first impression of you to be "Oh he's obviously gay".' (Participant 9) a greater proportion of narrative if you are doing a more constructionist version of thematic analysis.

- Following on from this, your story is not just a summary of the content of the data extracts: it needs to tell the reader why and how the data answer your research question. Even if you take a more descriptive and semantic approach to thematic analysis, you still need to interpret the data for the reader. This means you need to make sure you tell the reader what is interesting about the data and how the data answer your research question; you need to go beyond paraphrasing the content of the data (points 7 and 9).

CHAPTER SUMMARY

This chapter has distinguished between different approaches to thematic analysis and foregrounded Braun and Clarke's (2006) theoretically flexible approach. The status of thematic analysis as a theoretically flexible method rather than a theoretically informed methodology has been identified as its key distinctive quality. The chapter has outlined the questions that the researcher must answer before beginning thematic analysis. Moving into practicalities, it has described and demonstrated six phases of thematic analysis, from data familiarization to writing up, using examples from a study of gay men and appearance. Finally, the chapter has discussed issues of quality control in thematic analysis and has considered what makes a good thematic analysis.

Further reading

The original article in which we outlined our approach to thematic analysis remains the obvious starting point for anyone wishing to become familiar with the method (Braun and Clarke, 2006). For a more extensive discussion and demonstration of thematic analysis (and other aspects of qualitative research), see our 2013 book *Successful Qualitative Research: A Practical Guide for Beginners*. The companion website for this book includes data sets for practising thematic analysis: www.sagepub.co.uk/braunandclarke. Our thematic analysis website may also be useful as it includes frequently-asked questions about the method: www.psych.auckland.ac.nz/thematicanalysis. Two articles that offer good examples of different forms of thematic analysis on the topic of appearance are those of Harcourt and Frith (2008) and Carey et al. (2010). The former presents an essentialist, descriptive thematic analysis of women's experiences of changes in appearance during chemotherapy. The latter offers a more critical, theoretically-driven thematic analysis of girls' reflections about the appearance culture within an all-girls' school.

7

DOING THEMATIC ANALYSIS

Gareth Terry

This chapter uses the approach to thematic analysis described by Victoria Clarke and Virginia Braun in Chapter 6 to analyse the interview accounts of two men who had transitioned from the army to civilian life. Using the six phases of thematic analysis to structure the chapter, I demonstrate how I generated three themes from the data: (1) the superiority of army skills and values; (2) 'translation' as essential to success; and (3) neither soldier nor civilian. This example demonstrates the flexibility of thematic analysis as a method, its relative ease of use and the rich, textured descriptions of a data set that can be produced through thematic analysis.

Introduction

As an early-career researcher who has used and continues to use qualitative methods, I have found thematic analysis to be an essential tool for analysing qualitative data. Thematic analysis has been the core of all the qualitative analyses I have undertaken, sometimes used as a stand-alone method (Terry and Braun, 2009, 2011, 2012a) and at other times in conjunction with other analytic techniques such as critical discursive psychology (see Wetherell and Edley, 2009, and Chapter 10 in this volume). The theoretical flexibility of thematic analysis makes it ideally suited to such a pluralistic analytic approach (see Chapter 14 for more on pluralism). Even when my primary analytic focus has been a discursive analysis of a short segment of interaction (for example, Terry and Braun, 2013), I have found a preliminary thematic analysis of the data useful for identifying an analytic focus and selecting a data corpus. In short, I am now a committed fan of thematic analysis!

Thematic analysis has no inbuilt restrictions with regard to the size of data set it can handle. Some researchers have used thematic analysis to analyse large data sets, such as those generated by qualitative surveys (see Braun and Clarke, 2013, for a discussion of the qualitative survey method). For example, Toerien and Wilkinson (2004) used thematic analysis to analyse survey responses from 678 women. However, Braun and Clarke (2013) generally recommend a minimum sample of six for an interview study because thematic analysis emphasizes patterned meaning across data items. Although thematic analysis provided a useful tool for analysing the interview transcripts from David and Brian in Appendix 1 and allowed the identification of patterns, a larger data set would ideally be needed to draw more substantive conclusions.

This chapter demonstrates the approach to thematic analysis that Victoria Clarke and Virginia Braun describe in Chapter 6, using the interview transcripts from David and Brian. Clarke and Braun argue that there are a number of questions that analysts need to answer before beginning a thematic analysis – questions that orient the analysis and the analyst to a particular theoretical framework. My responses to these questions are as follows:

- What is my theoretical framework? I performed this thematic analysis from a critical realist perspective which recognizes the socially constructed nature of our understandings of reality and theorizes language as shaping the meaning of social and interpersonal worlds and as having material limits and implications (Burr, 2015; Parker, 2002). Critical realism sits between what Clarke and Braun (see Chapter 6) describe as a constructionist position and an essentialist position (see also Chapter 2, this volume). It is a framework I have used before and one I often choose as I find it useful to ground the analysis in the experiences that the two men describe while still allowing for a critical, contextualized analysis.

- Am I analysing the data inductively or deductively? I took an inductive approach to the data, which means that codes and themes were derived from the data, focusing on the experiences of the participants, rather than having me come to the data with a pre-defined set of concepts and assumptions.

- Am I coding semantic or latent meaning or both? At this point in the process I will generally code at both levels and establish at a later point which direction I will ultimately take.

- What is my research question? At the earliest phases of analysis, my research question was simple and broad: 'What were the men's experiences of transitioning from the army to civilian life?' To some degree, this broadness was a result of my positioning in relation to the data. I was not involved in the collection of the data nor in the generation of the original research question, which would have been informed by a comprehensive engagement with the literature surrounding the topic. As such, I needed breadth in my 'naive' research question to facilitate the first phase of thematic analysis: data familiarization.

- What are my assumptions about the topic? Having never been in the armed forces, I came to these data as a naïve outsider in regard to the specific experiences of the men in respect to this context. However, I have lived in two cultural contexts other than my own (New Zealand), one vastly different (Taiwan) and one relatively similar (United Kingdom). My experience of these sorts of transitions is likely to have been brought to my analysis of the data.

Phase 1: familiarizing yourself with the data

In reading text of any kind, we most often treat it as a source of information or a relatively transparent medium of communication between the author and the reader. We may agree or disagree with what has been written or even the way it has been written but writing and reading serve primarily as a means of transmitting ideas. In thematic analysis, familiarizing yourself with the data involves treating text in another way – as a subject of critical analysis. Making the mental shift from one form of reading to another can be harder than it might seem in the abstract, and the process of familiarization has been integral to my own experiences of doing a thematic analysis well.

When I do a thematic analysis, my first reading of a data set is generally not particularly concerned with a systematic analysis of the data. Instead my aim is to immerse myself in the data set. At this point, I have my broad research question in mind and I may have some very rough ideas about what the data might contain. If I collected or transcribed the data myself, I may even have some expectations about codes that I might develop. However, looking for codes without being familiar with the data tends to lead to making analytic leaps prematurely, without the benefit of evidence to back them up or missing the less obvious meanings in the data that become apparent through repeated engagement with the data. Familiarization helps me to engage with the data as data, without the need to begin coding or worrying about the shape of potential themes.

In my first reading of the two interview transcripts in Appendix 1, a number of ideas began to form about the overall shape of the data and I noted these in the margins of hard copies of the transcripts (examples included 'sense of belonging to something is lost', 'army life as over-arching identity?', 'struggling without support structures'). At this stage, I did not want to overdo the note taking (and risk 'unfamiliarized' coding) and I found the physical limitations of the margin helpful in this regard. One of the features of the data that was initially apparent was the repeated reference to difference in cultures (armed forces versus 'civvies'). This is likely to have been an artefact of the interview schedule in that the interviewer's questions explicitly framed the discussion this way. Both David and Brian, in various ways, seemed to be describing a form of 'culture shock' from which it took them some time to recover. In re-entering the culture they grew up in, they now found themselves bewildered and frustrated, and the culture of the armed forces was their reference point. Like many who immigrate or travel into another cultural context, they would often maintain the superiority of their 'home' values over those of the 'new' context in which they found themselves (for example, see Sam and Berry, 2010).

For instance, Brian talked about the difficulties in finding work to 'fit' his skills and experience, despite the re-entry training the army gave him. Both men argued that these difficulties were such that much more comprehensive retraining was necessary but that they had been left to do this process themselves:

> Brian: And the problem is everything you do in the forces, all the experience you gain, it doesn't transfer very well to civilian life so you need to sort of adapt all your skills and qualifications into such a way as civilian employers can actually pick up on it and understand. And that's what I didn't have time to do, you just don't have time to do it in the year. (Lines 161–165)

Here Brian argues that there needs to be a process of 'translation' between army and civilian life and values. That he had not gained all the necessary knowledge to make that translation effectively was causing him problems. The notion of two cultures with different languages is aptly demonstrated by Brian referring to having to work hard to enable civilian employers to 'pick up on' and 'understand' his skills.

During the process of familiarization, ideas in the data that reinforced this notion of culture shock occurred time and again. However, as I am quite aware, this may simply have been a reflection of my unconscious search for patterns as a way of making sense of an unfamiliar data set. In the same way that we 'notice' a type of car that we have newly bought and then begin to see it 'everywhere' (sometimes called the 'frequency illusion': Denison, 2008), it can be easy to see what seems to be a theme occurring when in fact it is only an interesting or vivid feature of the data. Whether the idea of cultural difference would persist throughout the next phases of the analytic process was yet to be determined. It can be tempting, when seeing these sorts of patterns, to develop them into proto-themes. This needs to be vigorously avoided because, more often than not, it will undermine the potential for a good thematic analysis.

Another feature of the data that stood out during the familiarization process was the way in which the men 'did' masculine identity. Performance of gender is often something that can be identified in talk and men will often 'make sense' of their masculine identities in patterned, recognizable ways (Wetherell and Edley, 2009). Noticing this feature of the data was likely to have been a consequence of my experience of working within the field of masculinities research (see Terry and Braun, 2009, 2011, 2012b, 2013). This sort of 'noticing' is a typical event in thematic analysis as your disciplinary knowledge and research interests can shape what you see in the data. This is why familiarization is such an important phase: you have the time to allow this type of noticing to occur without the need to rush into coding or theme development too early. What I was identifying in the extracts was their potential candidacy for forms of discourse analysis that identify gendered patterns of communication and/or the shared cultural resources men use to make sense of their masculine identities (see, for instance, Mankayi, 2008; for more on discourse analysis, see Chapter 10 in this volume). Although this was an interesting feature of the data, it was not an indication of a coherent theme that might be generated.

BITE-SIZED SUMMARY
1

I have outlined my experience of the process of familiarizing myself with the data set as the first phase in thematic analysis. This involves learning to read the data as data. It is also important to keep your research question in mind when reading the data. My key initial observation gained through this process concerned a notion of cultural difference and 'culture shock' for the men.

Phase 2: generating initial codes

Someone new to thematic analysis may fall into the trap of not engaging properly with the earlier, crucial phases of the analytic process. This is most likely to occur through the researcher trying to define themes too early and providing examples that are **anecdotal** rather than the product of a systematic and comprehensive thematic analysis of the data. Braun and Clarke (2012) argue that codes are the building blocks of analysis; without them, your analysis has shaky foundations. Although 'cultural difference/culture shock' and 'masculine sense-making' were defining features of the familiarization phase, they may not recur consistently enough throughout the whole data set to constitute themes. Coding is essential to avoiding the pitfall of being drawn into anecdotalism or creating 'pseudo-themes' out of interesting features of the data.

It is always important to remember one core understanding shared by most forms of qualitative research: coding is not about finding meaning hidden within the text. Instead it is concerned with creating meaning at the intersection between the data set and the interpretative resources that you bring to the data set. For this reason, coding needs to be systematic; code names or 'labels' need to be well constructed because the meanings that codes evoke may not be obvious to you (and certainly not to any co-researchers) in the later stages of analysis when you work much more with the codes than with the data. Codes are attached to extracts that may become exemplars of a theme further down the analytic track but for now provide evidence for the code. Table 7.1 gives an example of what coding looks like using an extract from one of the interview transcripts.

As noted above, I approached the men's interviews by simultaneously examining both the semantic and latent levels of meaning. At the **semantic** level, I coded what the men were saying, describing the explicit responses to the interviewer's questions. For example, David argued that being in the army gave him a sense of confidence in himself and his abilities that enabled him to find work easily. At the **latent** level, I was looking for implicit ideas, interpreting the men's sense-making and their underlying frameworks of logic. Here, an example might be 'resisting work culture of civilian colleagues'. This can be seen in the ways that David struggled against the work culture of the other drivers and set out to improve it, even though it became clear that doing so was a 'hindrance' for him in some unspoken way. For me, these two levels of coding are not done sequentially but simultaneously. This

Table 7.1 An example of coded data from David's interview

Data	Codes
Arnie: Can you say something about how, if at all, being an ex-soldier helped you or caused problems for you, or if you feel it made no difference?	Interviewer gives opportunity to talk about similarities, differences, possibility of ambivalence
David: In civvy street, being an ex-soldier gives you the confidence. Um, I went for an interview for a job. As I said, I've never been out of work. I've had more jobs than I thought I ever would and I think that the simple fact is that when I go on the interviews, I say, 'Right, this is me. This is what you're getting. Take me and I'll be a great team player', and I tell them that. Where it hinders me is the fact that I like things in lines. I like things in neat packages and so when I go – like when I was driving the truck, when I used to come back at night, I used to park all the wagons up so all the bumpers were level. Funny as it may seem, they had them parked all over the car park. It made it harder to get out. They couldn't see the fact that by lining them all up it was easy to get them out. Um, it was other little things like your paperwork. Keep your paperwork in order – it makes it easy. I think that side of life used to hinder me because all I would do was spend an extra ten minutes. All they wanted to do was in, out and go. Um, so yeah, there is a hindrance somewhere way along the line, in some aspects. I think in most aspects it certainly stood me in good stead.	Sense of confidence in self and abilities Having a large number of jobs (or job interviews) Getting jobs is easier than keeping them Structure is important Civvy colleagues are disorganized/inefficient 'Fixing' the work of civvy colleagues Superiority of army approach Army approach to work more efficient Army values can hinder in new life Alienating civvy colleagues Collective values of army remain essential to identity Resisting work culture of civilian colleagues

tendency may reflect my own experience with thematic analysis and so others may find it simpler to code these levels separately.

At this point in the analysis, the initially very broad research question was becoming more refined through the coding process. Now the question was: 'How do the men portray the transition between the armed forces and civilian life?' This change in the research question meant I began to identify elements in the data that were not obvious in my earlier familiarization readings. As a result, I began another coding round with this new research question in mind, as Braun and Clarke (2006) suggest.

Coding should not only identify similarity across data items but also difference. Within this data, the key similarities between the men's accounts (the superiority of army values, finding it difficult to transition between 'cultures') were often not as stark as the differences. Although both interviews are dealing with the difficulty of transition, David's account is very much defined by struggle and a lack of success in his integration into civilian life, whereas Brian's account is much more positive. Coding these differences between the two accounts and the various ways the two men made sense of their experience is just as likely to translate into themes as the more obvious similarities between them.

BITE-SIZED SUMMARY

2

Codes are the foundations upon which themes are built. Coding should be guided by your research question but it can also serve to refine that question. Coding is not about identifying pre-existing meaning in the data; instead it is about the researcher generating meaning as they engage with the data. Codes can focus on semantic meaning, latent meaning or both.

Phase 3: searching for themes

Quite simply, 'searching for themes' involves identifying patterns that allow you to make sense of the codes that have been generated. Although the phase is described as a 'search' this is not a passive experience and can therefore require more work than the coding process that precedes it. 'Searching' is an active, constructive phase, shaping the codes into a coherent story that makes sense of the data (Braun and Clarke, 2012). As the generation of themes begins, the quality of codes can make a great difference. If coding has been haphazard, the process of sculpting a theme can be much slower and more laborious and may require several more rounds of coding. Even with high quality coding, it can take time to develop a **central organizing concept** (that is, a core idea or concept that underpins a theme) for a group of codes that brings them together into a theme. There will be attempts and failures, new attempts and returns to older attempts to determine whether there is something 'recoverable' and useful in them.

As a consequence, the emphasis in this phase should be on developing 'candidate' themes. These are often tentative and temporary. There may be some degree of overlap between the themes and the themes may not capture all or most of the coded data. During this period, you need to keep referring back to the research question to clarify the direction of the theme development process and to establish whether the themes being generated are relevant and useful interpretations of the data. In Table 7.2, I show the three candidate themes that I generated initially and (some of) the codes that I clustered within them. At this stage, I was quite unsure about themes 2 ('Strategies to transition successfully') and 3 ('Obstacles to successful transition') and so they offer a good illustration of themes being 'tried out'.

The codes seemed to fit well within three candidate themes and together the three themes seemed to capture most of the coded data. Theme 1 ('Army values constructed as superior to civilian ones') is a good example of a theme that captures the coding of latent ideas across the data set. While not always explicitly articulated, the theme of superiority

Table 7.2 Initial candidate themes

Candidate theme	Army values constructed as superior to civilian ones	Strategies to transition successfully	Obstacles to successful transition
Associated codes	Ex-servicemen work harder 'You can tell the difference just by looking' Need to translate army skills and values to civvy world Civilians unable to do basic life tasks Pre-army life/values unhelpful (for David) – all worthwhile value from army	Adapted personal style to fit civilian expectations Found support that helped Found similarities between army world and civvy world Is treated as of more value in current role than in army role Finding a 'middle ground' where he can be both army and civilian (at the mess)	'Prejudice' against ex-service people Transition portrayed as poorly managed by others Taking an adversarial approach to teachers and officers Treated as lower status than when in army Getting jobs is easier than keeping them

was nonetheless a powerful feature of the data. At no point in either transcript was there a sense that civilian life was better than military life: it could be successfully transitioned into but it was almost inherently an inferior way of life according to both men. Furthermore both men seemed to resent leaving the army. This was apparent in Brian's explicit comments about making the best of a bad situation. David, on the other hand, demonstrated his resentment through references to the poor transition, blaming first the army's exiting procedures and then the attitudes of those in 'civvy' life with whom and around whom he worked.

Although I was happy with theme 1, there were aspects of themes 2 and 3 that I was less sure about. While they helped 'explain' the data in many ways, they lacked some of the features of good themes that were suggested in Chapter 6, such as the patterning of meaning across the data set. Weakness with themes can become evident in any number of ways. Developing a thematic map (see Figure 7.1) is one option as it visually represents the location and boundaries of candidate themes in relation to one another and the codes attached to these. In this exercise, mapping out the themes enabled me to see that each of the two 'problem' themes contained many codes and data extracts from just one interview. It was highly problematic that they did not capture data from across both interviews, as I will discuss in the next section.

Generating themes is an active process. As with coding, theme development should be informed by the research question. You need to develop candidate themes: do not become too attached to emerging themes at this stage because you may need to amend or abandon them. Finish the process of theme development by identifying which aspects of your analysis you feel more confident about and which aspects need to be reconsidered in the next 'review' phase.

BITE-SIZED
SUMMARY
....
3

Phase 4: reviewing potential themes

This phase involves reviewing your candidate themes in relation to your codes and the data extracts associated with them and exploring whether the themes 'work' in relation to the entire data set. Here the boundaries between phases 3 and 4 blurred quite a lot which has been a relatively common feature of my experience of doing thematic analysis. As noted above, I had some concerns about two of the candidate themes identified in my 'searching' phase. Even without this sort of 'obvious' issue to address, the reviewing phase is still essential to a good thematic analysis, especially for those new to the method. Thematic analysis is hardly ever a linear process and returning to the research question and the data extracts in a recursive fashion ensures a degree of quality control. In my case, the review did not mean totally throwing out the existing themes and starting from scratch (as sometimes may be required) because the ideas they captured had some explanatory power in relation to the data set and could be reworked.

Although the second and third themes were distinctive, what they crystallized were the differences between David's and Brian's descriptions of the relative 'successes' of their transitions (in other words, a 'Brian' theme and a 'David' theme). Braun and Clarke (2006) argue that themes need to reflect patterns across the data set rather than simply within a data item and this is where themes 2 and 3 seemed to fail as themes. As a consequence, I collapsed themes 2 and 3 together, cutting and pasting the codes and data extracts allocated to them into one document. I then placed theme 1 and the collapsed 'theme' (2 + 3) side by side and assessed them in light of the research question's focus on cultural difference. My core question to myself at this point was: 'Is there a story I can tell about the data that makes sense of these themes?'

As you can see, there is some risk attached to the review phase: strong themes that you like may not 'work' and, as one or two themes shift, another may not have the strength it seemed to have before the reviewing process. This may leave you feeling that the analysis is unravelling, which can be disconcerting. However, as long as the earlier phases of a thematic analysis are of good quality (for example, the codes are clearly labelled and thoughtful, data extracts have been collated and the research question is well defined), it is unlikely that your analysis will completely unravel.

In fact, in this particular analysis, the review process reinforced the strength of the theme of 'superiority of army life over civilian life' but the collapse of the boundaries between themes 2 and 3 also highlighted two new candidate themes. The first suggested that transitioning between the army and civilian worlds involved a translation process and that success or failure was dependent on the ability to translate between 'languages'. For instance, Brian summed up his 'successful' transition as follows:

> Brian: I've mellowed to such an extent and I suppose you have to … in such a way to ... you have to sort of change your style. A lot of my work, I train people up ... my work is training and I've had to adapt my training style to be more civilian friendly

than in the military because it was ... people used to say, 'Well, we come to you and you don't teach us – you shout at us', which was – all I was doing was projecting my voice so that people would hear me at the back but I've had to adapt it in such a way that people are more happy with it and it's slightly less structured than what it was when I was in the forces – a bit more casual.

This was more than simple adaptation. In Brian's interview, he referred to a number of 'translation points' that could have led to success or failure in which the ability to reflect on his army experience and to understand clearly the context he was in were each essential. Even elements such as the lack of identifiable 'uniform' among senior management needed to be negotiated and understood in the new context. This theme also helped explain some of David's problems and sense of isolation but more importantly it helped explain his response to them. In many ways he seemed to be resisting the need for translation, insisting instead on the superiority of the values and skills he had gained in the army. This difference between the two men may have been a consequence of the length of time they had been outside the army, although this is unclear from the data or the introduction to the transcripts.

The original theme of superiority and the new theme of translation accounted for much of the data. However, there were still a number of 'miscellaneous' codes and, in particular, codes that seemed to relate explicitly to the concept of identity. There were also a number of data extracts that had multiple codes attached to them and, when pooled together, I could identify enough data to sustain a new theme that explicitly captured the notion of having a liminal or 'in-between' identity: both of the men, in various ways, spoke of being neither in the army nor a civilian.

As the two new themes still had candidate status, I went through the revision phase one more time, checking their boundaries, determining whether there were enough meaningful data to support them, identifying how they related to one another and, most importantly, what they said about the research question. Using thematic maps helped with this process of determining themes and capturing the overall 'shape' of the analysis. Figure 7.1 shows my final map with the three final themes identified (note there were no subthemes in my analysis; otherwise they would also be indicated).

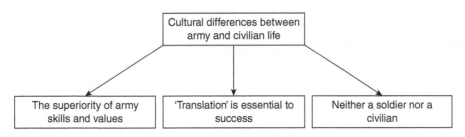

Figure 7.1   Example of a thematic map: final three themes following review phase

After this second revision phase, I was confident that the themes I had developed told the type of story I thought was appropriate to the data, the research question and the critical realist orientation of my analysis. It captured the experiences of the men without losing the sense that these accounts were constructed from existing, readily available ideas about their social worlds, such as the notion of 'civvy street' and ideas of social class that David in particular drew upon to explain his situation. With the review process complete, I felt ready to move on to the next phase of analysis.

BITE-SIZED SUMMARY

4

Themes need to be coherent and capture meaning across the data set. The research question can help identify weaknesses in your themes by determining the boundaries of your research focus. Return to the data extracts to determine the 'fit' of the themes and the quality of the story that they tell. Following a review, two new themes were developed that fulfilled the criteria for good themes in thematic analysis: '"translation" is essential to success' and 'neither a soldier nor a civilian'.

Phase 5: defining and naming themes

This is perhaps my favourite part of thematic analysis. A lot of the hard work has been done, providing a solid foundation for creativity. It is the start of the formal writing process and all my notes and thoughts about the data (including about the earlier candidate themes) are pulled together to make something meaningful. It is time to select the data extracts that best demonstrate the key aspects of each theme. This phase provides an opportunity to interpret the data extracts for your imagined reader. Most importantly, it is also where the final story of your analysis is pulled together, making sure that it works on paper as well as it does in your head! The naming and defining task essentially provides the scaffolding on which the next phase rests.

Due to the work I had put into developing and reviewing the themes, naming the themes was a fairly straightforward process. In order to establish how the new versions of theme 2 and 3 differed from the earlier versions, I had already thought quite carefully about the central organizing concept of the themes. This is really what the task of defining and naming is about – articulating what is distinct about the themes and how they relate to one another. Braun and Clarke (2012) argue that theme names need to be concise, informative and catchy. They suggest that using data quotations can provide a great way to make the meaning of the themes clear. Box 7.1 shows how I named and defined the final themes.

These theme names and definitions give clear direction for the writing process. In much the same way as the research question guided the analysis until this point, the themes provide a framework for the final selection of data extracts to be included in the report and for the direction the analysis needs to move in to shape the analytic conclusions.

> ## BOX 7.1 Developing definitions and names for the final three themes
>
> *Theme 1: 'We seem to be much more flexible, much more adaptable to situations' – the superiority of army skills and values.* This theme captured some of the explicit references by the two men to the value of their army training and the character qualities they had developed in the army and had retained from their army experience. It also maps some of the latent features of the data where the men assumed their army values were superior to those of civilian contexts. This was particularly the case for David who found it difficult to understand why his co-workers did not follow similar patterns and protocols to him, especially when he demonstrated the obvious 'superiority' of these.
>
> *Theme 2: 'You need to … adapt all your skills and qualifications' – 'translation' as essential to success.* This theme captured what united Brian's and David's differing experiences of 'success' in adapting to the civilian context. In it, there was an underlying premise that the army and civilian contexts were as distinct as two different 'ethnic' cultures. Learning to understand what was valued in the civilian context and translating the skills and values they had gained in the army to meet these expectations was essential to success for the two men. Brian's account was marked by struggling with this but ultimately succeeding; David's was more immersed in the ongoing nature of the struggle (not helped by some rather difficult life experiences). This may reflect the lengths of time they had been outside the army or other differences between the two men.
>
> *Theme 3: 'Once you're out that gate, that's it' – neither a soldier nor a civilian.* Both men spoke of being caught between the two worlds of soldier and civilian and of their identities as being in a somewhat liminal state as a consequence. Although they more closely identified with the values of the army and the skills they had learned there, they had both left that world and, in David's case, had been rejected by it.

Phase 6: writing the report

Writing happens through the analytic process: the final stage involves weaving together all your analytic notes and the extracts you have selected to illustrate the themes into an argument that answers the research question (Braun and Clarke, 2012). The final research report is the evidence of all your earlier work and will be where your analysis stands or falls. In light of this, it is usually a good idea to go through a number of drafts to get to the finished product (for a discussion of the importance of editing, see Braun and Clarke, 2013).

> **BOX 7.2**
>
> ## Excerpt of write-up of theme 2: 'You need to ... adapt all your skills and qualifications' – 'translation' as essential to success

The second theme generated from the data was built around the motif of 'translation'. Both men described experiencing something akin to culture shock when they moved from the army world to the civilian one, where the rules they had come to rely on to make sense of their worlds seemed no longer to apply or at least were interpreted differently. Often they framed this in terms akin to learning a new language, that a person needed to understand the new context well enough to be able to translate their 'native tongue' for the benefit of those around them:

> And the problem is everything you do in the forces, all the experience you gain, it doesn't transfer very well to civilian life so you need to sort of adapt all your skills and qualifications into such a way as civilian employers can actually pick up on it and understand. (Brian)

The disjuncture between 'everything you do in the forces' and approaches used in the civilian world were identified as the biggest obstacles in Brian's experience of transitioning out of the army (see also Verey and Smith, 2012). However, what was evident across the interview was his ability to reflect on this issue and make the changes to his 'style', translating his army-honed skills into ones that fitted 'civilian' life. For instance, he commented:

> I've mellowed to such an extent and I suppose you have to ... in such a way to ... you have to sort of change your style. A lot of my work, I train people up ... my work is training and I've had to adapt my training style to be more civilian friendly than in the military. (Brian)

The relationship between this theme and the previous one is particularly strong in this extract. Here the adaptation in styles is orientated towards the civilian style and away from the army style. There was a sense that Brian's army-learned training style was inherently superior and simply needed adaptation to be more palatable to his civilian audience (see also Woodward and Jenkings, 2011). Following this logic, the need to translate is essential to his success, as taking on board the skills and values of the civilian context was rendered unthinkable.

There is not enough space within the scope of this chapter to provide a full report of a theme, so Box 7.2 provides an extract from the write-up of the translation theme. As you can see, I wove literature into the analysis to support my points, which is important for locating new research in relation to existing work. Following Braun and Clarke's (2006, 2012, Chapter 6) guidelines, I tried to maintain roughly a 50:50 ratio between data extracts and analysis, making sure to interpret the data rather than simply paraphrasing it and to demonstrate the relationship between the three themes and their relationship to the research question. An example of a more fully worked up version of a thematic analysis report can be found in Appendix 2, Report 2.

BOX 7.3 ▶ (More) coding practice

Choose an online version of a national newspaper or use an online database such as LexisNexis to collate a data set of between five and ten articles on a topic of your choice. For example, use the search terms 'ex-soldier' or 'former military personnel' to focus on the coverage of issues faced by former members of the armed services. Practise coding these using the research question, 'How do the media represent the issues facing ex-service personnel?' Applying the principles outlined in this chapter and in Chapter 6, thoroughly code your data set.

CHAPTER SUMMARY

In this chapter, I used Braun and Clarke's (2006, 2012, Chapter 6) approach to thematic analysis to analyse the accounts of two men who had left the army and acculturated into civilian life. Following coding, theme development and review, three themes were generated that told a meaningful and coherent story about the data that emphasized: (1) the superiority of army values and skills; (2) the need to learn the 'language' of the civilian world and 'translate' their army skills and values into the new culture; and (3) an in-between identity of being neither a soldier nor a civilian. These themes told a story of cultural difference (identified during the familiarization phase of analysis) between civilian and army worlds – but one that could be transitioned through successfully if the men were able to reflect upon and adapt to their new situation.

Further reading

A detailed worked example of a thematic analysis of interview data is provided by Braun and Clarke (2012). An example of a 'straightforward' thematic analysis that I conducted can be found in Terry and Braun (2011). For a more complex example of the possibilities offered by thematic analysis, see Terry and Braun's (2012b) work which starts with thematic analysis but moves on to poststructuralist discourse analysis. Readers who are interested in contexts of transition in military life will find an excellent thematic analysis of data on one particular context in Verey and Smith's (2012) research on 'post-combat adjustment'.

8

GROUNDED THEORY

Sheila Payne

This chapter introduces the philosophical background and historical development of grounded theory. It highlights the different versions of the method originally produced by Glaser and Strauss (1967) and the tensions between them. The majority of the chapter discusses the principles and practice of grounded theory analysis, including the sorts of research questions best suited to this approach, the types of data and sampling approach to use, the timing of data collection and the distinctive analytic procedures. The chapter ends by considering the development and testing of new theory, the assessment of quality and how to present a grounded theory study. Throughout the chapter, examples are drawn from a specific research project in order to illustrate analytic decisions.

Introduction

Grounded theory developed out of a programme of research concerned with exploring the experience of dying patients in American hospitals during the 1950s and 1960s (Glaser and Strauss, 1965). At this time, medical practice was predominantly paternalistic and information about the diagnosis and the dying prognosis was not routinely shared with patients. The research team therefore had the difficult dilemma of how to investigate a phenomenon that was not openly acknowledged, although it was physically present in the dying trajectories of patients. The lack of 'grand' theories and the inappropriateness of survey methods (which were popular at the time in sociology) provided the impetus for the development of new ways of doing qualitative research.

Glaser and Strauss's (1967) book *The Discovery of Grounded Theory* offered a critique of a number of features of research practice at the time, including the hypothetico-deductive method in which research was designed to test existing theory. Instead they proposed a method of developing or 'discovering' theory **inductively** from close examination of data. They were also critical of the way qualitative research was regarded as merely descriptive and sought to demonstrate the analytical and explanatory power of qualitative analysis.

It is widely believed that grounded theory has derived its philosophical roots from **symbolic interactionism** and pragmatism (Bartlett and Payne, 1997). The ideas of scholars such as Dewey, Cooley, James and Mead provide the foundation, in particular the notions explicated by Mead (1934) that individuals are self-aware and that intersubjectivity (the psychological relation between people) influences behaviours. Symbolic interactionism takes the position that people act towards things based on the meanings those things have for them, that these meanings are derived from social interaction and that these shared meanings are influential in society. According to Rennie (2000: 492), 'pragmatism holds that knowledge production is a matter of perspective and that warrants to truth are a matter of consensus among the members of the community of inquirers'. Strauss's background was in the 'Chicago school' of sociology. This perspective saw human behaviour as determined by social structures and physical environmental factors rather than by genetic and personal characteristics. Its research combined theory and ethnographic methods which involve the researcher using systematic observation to study people and cultures, trying as much as possible to observe things from the point of view of the subjects of the study. This background influenced Strauss in his use of in-depth case studies and ethnographic methods.

Early formulations of grounded theory have been regarded as based on the **epistemological** position of **positivism**, in which it is assumed that there is a straightforward relationship between objects in the world and our perception of them (see Chapter 2 in this volume). From this position, it is regarded as possible to describe what is 'out there' and that there is an ultimate 'truth'. In their original exposition of grounded theory, Glaser and Strauss (1967) suggested that hypotheses derived from a grounded theory may be empirically tested and that methods of verification should rely on external objective procedures. However, later formulations have emphasized a more interpretative stance (Corbin and Strauss, 2015; Strauss and Corbin, 1990). Henwood and Pigeon (1994) have highlighted the tension that can be seen between the epistemological positions of 'realism' and 'constructivism' in literature on grounded theory. Realism can be seen in contentions that grounded theory inductively reflects participants' accounts. Constructivism can be seen in the recognition that it is the researcher who creates and interprets the data to develop new theory.

Different versions of grounded theory: variations on a theme

It was some time before grounded theory methodology was widely taken up but in the last 20–25 years it has become one of the most popular methods of qualitative research. It has now spread across a number of disciplines (for example, psychology, education, social work and nursing) and has been developed in a number of ways. This section will briefly summarize the diversity of grounded theory methods.

> **BOX 8.1**
>
> **Key differences between main approaches in the conceptualization and conduct of grounded theory analysis**
>
> Version advocated by Glaser and followers:
>
> - great value placed on simple systematic procedures to allow emergence of theory;
>
> - argues that theory generation arises directly and rigorously out of the data (Glaser is critical of Strauss for 'forcing' coding by having preconceived ideas; Glaser describes this as full conceptual description of data rather than an emergent theory);
>
> - argues for verification of theory by returning to the data;
>
> - rejects interpretivism (the contention that there are multiple realities of phenomena, that these can differ across time and place and that the meaning of action can be understood from actors' perspectives);
>
> - great emphasis placed on the final stage of theoretical coding;
>
> - great importance attached to memo writing;
>
> - advocates a simple version of theoretical sampling.
>
> Version advocated by Strauss and followers:
>
> - offers fairly complex analytic procedures;
>
> - advocates direct questioning during development of theory;
>
> - articulates an array of techniques to facilitate constant comparison;
>
> - proposes complex tools for theoretical comparison;
>
> - less emphasis placed on final stage of selective coding;
>
> - suggests a number of types of memos including code notes, theoretical notes and logical notes;
>
> - offers more complex types of theoretical sampling.

Glaser and Strauss's (1967) book is regarded as offering the original version and, by some, the 'classic' account of the method. However, the methodological procedures are poorly articulated and there are ambiguities in how researchers should conduct analyses.

Following the success of that book, Glaser and Strauss developed divergent views on what constitutes 'correct' approaches to analysis. A more explicit version of the analytic procedures was published by Strauss and Corbin (1990) that departed in some ways from the original version. (For the latest edition, see Corbin and Strauss, 2015: from here on, I will mostly refer to the earlier edition because it was the first detailed exposition of Strauss's distinctive perspective on grounded theory and the fundamentals remain the same.) This was greeted by an angry reaction from Glaser who considered their approach to be too prescriptive. It is not my intention to offer a full account of the history of this conflict as others have summarized the key issues (for example, Bryant and Charmaz, 2007; Charmaz, 2014). The main differences in opinion have been around the role of induction, the degree to which theory 'emerges' or is 'forced' from the data, and procedural variations (see Box 8.1: the meaning of some terms used there will become clear later in the chapter). Where they influence analytic processes, I have highlighted them in this chapter. There have been numerous others who have contributed to the development of the grounded theory method, resulting, for example, in Charmaz's (1990, 2014) social constructivist version, Rennie's (2000) methodical hermeneutics version and Clarke's (2003) postmodern version.

BITE-SIZED SUMMARY 1

Grounded theory was developed in the 1960s in response to perceived problems with existing research approaches. Its fundamental concern was to develop theory on a given topic inductively, working up from a close examination of qualitative data. Theory produced in this way would be *grounded* in the data and would explain the phenomenon expressed in the data. As a research approach, grounded theory grew from the philosophical traditions of symbolic interactionism and pragmatism. Different versions of grounded theory analysis have developed over time, with the originators of the approach and others producing versions based on different assumptions about research and with different emphases.

Method and methodological issues

Having considered the philosophical basis for grounded theory and reviewed some of the debates on how grounded theory has developed since its inception, the remainder of the chapter offers practical suggestions about how to 'do' grounded theory analysis. In common with some writers on other qualitative methods, in my view it is not helpful to present grounded theory as a fixed method in which there is only one 'right' way to conduct an analysis. Instead, I offer suggestions as to how researchers might proceed if they wish to label their method as 'grounded theory'. At the outset, it is important to recognize that, in this chapter, I will be describing the procedures that characterize research which aims to develop new theory – in other words, the 'full version' of grounded theory – and not the modified version in which initial open coding is used only. The latter is often described as a grounded theory approach to analysis too (see Foster et al., 2004, for a good example). 'Full' grounded theory has the development of new theory as its aim rather than just using grounded theory's procedures for the coding and organization of data. It is, however, possible to use grounded theory approaches to generate new theory but not to do this exhaustively. This abbreviated approach can be seen as producing something that is an important step *towards* a grounded theory. For example, Karlsen et al. (2014) describe the outcome of their research on the role played by trusted adults in the spiritual lives of children as a *contribution* towards a grounded theory on the topic because of the study's limited sample (see Box 8.4 later in the chapter).

The following section is presented in linear order. There are early decisions and steps that need to be conducted in sequence but one of the unique features of grounded theory analysis is the dynamic interplay of data collection and analysis. To illustrate some of these issues, I will draw on data from a study exploring the understandings of cancer and end-of-life care of older Chinese people resident in the United Kingdom (Payne et al., 2004). The research design is described in Box 8.2.

BOX 8.2	Exploring and understanding the views of older Chinese people about cancer and end-of-life care (Payne et al., 2004)

Rationale for study

Minority ethnic groups make up about 6 per cent of the population of Britain, with Chinese people constituting about 5 per cent of all minority ethnic people living in the UK. There are concerns about equity of access to cancer and palliative care services for Black and minority ethnic groups. Issues of English language competence, socio-economic deprivation, institutional ageism and cultural insensitivity may mean that older Chinese people are multiply disadvantaged in accessing acceptable cancer and end-of-life care services. Little is known about their understanding of cancer and end-of-life care.

(Continued)

Research question

What are older Chinese people's beliefs and perceptions regarding cancer and its treatment, and their preferences (if any) about end-of-life care?

Research design

Qualitative study using grounded theory analysis.

Phase 1

Focus group interviews with members of existing community groups to elicit understandings of cancer and develop culturally appropriate vignettes.

Phase 2

Individual interviews using vignettes (that is, fictional or real-life 'cases' or scenarios relevant to the research topic/question to which interviewees are invited to respond) as prompts to explore understandings and preferences. Both focus group interviews and individual interviews were conducted in participants' preferred dialect (Cantonese, Hakka or Mandarin).

Research design

Types of research questions

All research should seek to address one or more specific research questions. For pragmatic reasons, by focusing on specific objectives, the research is more likely to be achievable within the constraints of finite resources such as time, money and energy. Students and new researchers may find this one of the most demanding aspects of designing their research but it is essential that a clear focus on a topic area is defined before embarking upon data collection. Because grounded theory is suitable for exploratory research, the research question may become more refined and specific during the course of data collection and analysis as the researcher gains a greater awareness of the key issues. The wording of the research question and research objectives should make it clear 'what, who, when and how' will be researched. Typically, research questions that seek to explore processes and/or meanings lend themselves to grounded theory analysis (see Box 8.3). If the research questions are predominantly concerned with 'how many' or 'how often', these may be better answered using quantitative methods of inquiry.

BOX 8.3 — **Examples of research questions addressed in grounded theory studies**

- How does chronic illness impact on perceptions of the self? (Charmaz, 1990)

- How do women with advanced breast or ovarian cancer cope with palliative chemotherapy? (Payne, 1992)

- How do families of deceased people decide whether to donate their loved one's organs for transplantation? (Sque and Payne, 1996: see Appendix 2 (Report 3) in this volume for more details)

- How do college students who are living away from the family home cope when a family member is diagnosed with or treated for cancer? (Basinger et al., 2015)

- How do health-care professionals who work with children and adolescents with chronic fatigue syndrome/myalgic encephalomyelitis understand the condition? (Marks et al., 2015)

When to use grounded theory

Researchers may consider using grounded theory when:

- relatively little is known about the topic area;

- there are no 'grand' theories to explain adequately the specific psychological constructs or behaviours under investigation;

- researchers wish to challenge existing theories;

- researchers are interested in eliciting participants' understandings, perceptions and experiences of the world;

- the research aims to develop new theories.

The aims of grounded theory analysis are to develop inductive theory which is closely derived from the data rather than deductive theory which is supported by hypothesis testing.

Therefore grounded theory is a suitable method for exploratory research and explanatory research but it should be more than descriptive. If the intention of your research is merely to describe a set of behaviours, perceptions or experiences, then thematic analysis (see Chapter 6 in this volume) is likely to be a better option – although thematic analysis can produce explanatory as well as descriptive research. With reference to the study described in Box 8.2, we selected grounded theory analysis because not only were we interested in describing older Chinese people's views but we wished to develop theoretical explanations about why they held these views and how they influenced behaviours such as seeking screening and treatment for cancer. For example, we wished to account for preferences about the role played by Western medicine and Chinese traditional medicine in cancer.

When to review the literature

In many paradigms, it is usual to conduct a literature review and plan all stages of the research before gathering data but in grounded theory there is debate about the extent and nature of literature reviewing that is desirable and appropriate before embarking upon data collection. It has been argued that the researcher should commence data collection early and delay the literature review to enhance their naivety and their sensitivity to the issues emerging from the data. An alternative view is that some awareness of the existing literature and relevant theories is required if only to confirm that the topic is not already theoretically well developed and understood. Researchers should be sufficiently aware of the literature to enable them to be sure that their research will contribute new knowledge. Awareness of the empirical and theoretical literature is essential during the latter stages of the analysis to ensure that new theoretical constructs are linked to existing work. In my view, novice researchers need to spend some time doing a preliminary search of the literature and they also need to be aware of the preconceptions and assumptions that they bring to their data collection and analysis based upon their disciplinary background (see more about this and reflexivity later). Another pragmatic reason to undertake some reviewing of the literature is that this is often a requirement for students in presenting research proposals and for all researchers in obtaining ethical approval for their study. If external funding is being sought for the project, a literature review will also be an essential requirement.

With regard to the study with older Chinese people, we undertook a preliminary literature review during the process of developing the application for funding and as part of the procedures required to obtain ethical approval. However, we delayed the writing of a full literature review so that it ran concurrently with data collection during the initial focus group interviews in Phase 1. We considered that this strategy allowed us to comply with external constraints (for example, funding bodies and ethics committees) while retaining some openness to new ideas and concepts during initial data collection and analysis. By undertaking the literature review concurrently with data collection in Phase 1, we were able to use both emerging analytic insights and existing theoretical and empirical information to shape the Phase 2 interviews.

> Grounded theory analysis is directed towards developing new theory that is derived from and grounded in research data. This is an inductive process, working from data and moving progressively up to theory. The grounded theory approach is suitable for exploratory and explanatory research, undertaken in areas where there are no suitable theories available to explain the phenomena of interest. It is best suited to research questions that seek to explore processes and/or meanings. There are various views on when a literature review should be conducted in grounded theory research: at least a preliminary search of the literature is recommended before starting data collection. These points have been illustrated with reference to a grounded theory study that explored understandings of cancer and end-of-life care among older Chinese people resident in the United Kingdom.
>
> **BITE-SIZED SUMMARY**
> ....
> **2**

Data collection

Types of data

There are four common types of qualitative data:

- Language in the form of written text or spoken words

- Observations of behaviours (involving talk and non-verbal interactions)

- Images which may be dynamic events (captured digitally, on videos or films, photographs, drawings or paintings)

- Artefacts such as sculptures or objects.

Grounded theory requires data that are or can be transformed into text. Therefore the first two types of data are most commonly used. It is important to recognize the difference between *elicited* data, which are specifically requested and collected by researchers for the purpose of answering the research question, and *naturally-occurring* data. Most data used for grounded theory analysis are elicited for the purpose of the project by talking to people during individual or focus group interviews. However, it is also possible to conduct a grounded theory analysis based on recorded conversations, counselling sessions or other naturally-occurring data. A grounded theory analysis of printed materials such as government policy documents, diaries or inspection reports may also yield useful insights.

How to collect suitable data

Interviews

Interviews are a suitable method of collecting elicited data for grounded theory analysis for a number of reasons. Firstly, they build upon everyday experience of conversations and generally people are pleased to have the opportunity to talk with an attentive person in a face-to-face situation. Participating in interviews requires the ability to talk and understand the questions. Language and comprehension difficulties may exclude people who have learning difficulties/disabilities (Finlay and Lyons, 2001, 2002) or low educational attainment and people who do not understand the language or accent of the interviewer. Typically, face-to-face interviews are popular with researchers because they tend to generate a higher response rate than other methods and there is likely to be less missing data than in questionnaires but they can be expensive and time consuming to conduct. The principles of semi-structured interviews described by Jonathan A. Smith and Virginia Eatough (see Chapter 4 in this volume) are relevant for grounded theory studies.

In Western cultures, the interview format is familiar from television shows, professional consultations and other encounters. In the study with older Chinese people, we found that by describing Phase 2 data collection as 'conversations' rather than interviews, we achieved better recruitment and improved data. Initially older Chinese people perceived 'interviews' to be threatening and were reluctant to divulge their views for fear of being wrong and challenging the interviewer.

Group discussions

Group interviews are rather like other types of interviews in that the researcher directs the questioning and responses are made to the interviewer. They are not the same as focus-group interviews because participants are not encouraged to engage with each other by challenging, debating and arguing about issues. They are commonly used in group settings, like schools, and are a cost-effective way to collect data from many participants.

Focus groups

In focus group interviews, the purpose is to encourage interaction between the participants so that a range of views may be elicited and discussion is generated. Decisions must be made at the outset whether focus group participants should be similar or not and whether they should be strangers or already known to each other. These are likely to relate to the research question, topic area and sampling strategy and should take account of cultural norms and gender and power relationships. For example, in some cultures women may feel uncomfortable discussing sexual health problems in mixed gender groups. Focus groups are generally run by a facilitator, whose role is to introduce topics, encourage participation and address participant confidentiality, comfort and safety issues, while an observer has the role of recording the nature and type of participation by group members. The number of participants may vary from 6 to 12 depending upon the topic and group. There needs to be a balance between the desire to have a range of views represented and the difficulties of managing a large group and making sense of the resultant audio-recording. It may be preferable to have smaller groups if topics are likely to be very personal or elicit strong emotions, such as with bereaved people. For more on focus group interviewing, see Cronin (2008) and Millward (2012).

In the study of older Chinese people, we conducted focus groups with participants who were already known to each other as members of Chinese community groups. This had the advantage of providing access to older Chinese people (a normally 'hidden' population) and, as they were familiar with the community settings and other members, they appeared to be relaxed and generally willing to participate and talk freely. However, their experience of other group sessions had been in the context of health education talks and, despite careful explanations of the purpose of the research (both written and verbal), some participants expected to be told about cancer services rather than volunteering their views. In Phase 2, we selected the vignette method of prompts for interviewing, which involves presenting participants with a fictional or real-life 'case' or scenario relevant to the research topic/question, as it allows people to discuss sensitive topics such as cancer and dying in relation to a third person. It also facilitates comparison as well as revealing how choices and preferences are expressed. In practice, many participants preferred to tell their own stories and describe experiences of cancer in friends and family members.

Timing of data collection

In a grounded theory study, data collection and analysis are concurrent activities. Typically, an initial period of data collection is followed by preliminary open coding (explained below), from which the research focus may be refined and research questions modified. This in turn requires changes to data collection protocols and sampling. Grounded theory research involves reciprocal periods of data collection, analysis, reflection, theory development and theory testing in spiral patterns of activity which are unlike formal linear experimental designs. These are hard to capture in written accounts of the method such as this chapter and in submissions for ethical review boards that are typically more familiar with more structured linear approaches.

Theoretical sampling

Grounded theory, along with other types of qualitative research, does not rely on notions of statistical representativeness to make claims about the generalizability and authenticity of the findings. At the beginning of grounded theory fieldwork, samples are selected purposively because it is believed that they can contribute to the topic under investigation. This is different from 'convenience' samples which consist of people who are most readily available and willing to participate. Purposive samples should be selected on the basis of criteria which must be explicitly stated when reporting the results. At the outset, it is important to define the characteristics of the sample that are assumed to provide data of relevance to the research topic.

During the process of data collection, as the research question becomes refined, the sampling strategy is modified to include participants who may contribute different perspectives or experiences. This continues across the study as the researcher returns to data collection, seeking out participants whose data can illuminate, extend or challenge constructs that are discerned in the data. This is referred to as **theoretical sampling**, which is defined as a process of ongoing data collection for the purpose of generating theory, where previous analysis influences decisions about subsequent data to be collected. It is *theoretical* because it is guided by and contributes to the emerging model or theory. Theoretical sampling is an essential characteristic of a complete grounded theory study.

BOX 8.4 — Where to direct theoretical sampling efforts?

Earlier I took Karlsen et al.'s (2014) study of the role played by trusted adults in the spiritual lives of children as an example of an abbreviated form of grounded theory. The researchers' analysis is based on interviews with nine children (four boys and five girls), aged six or seven years, from one non-religious school in south-east England. Seven of the children were White British. Six children were from families with no religious affiliation (and the religious affiliation of another child's family was unknown). The researchers were unable to undertake theoretical sampling due to the practical constraints of the project and so they suggested that their research should be seen as a contribution *towards* a grounded theory on the topic. Their emergent theory showed that the children had little opportunity for negotiating a shared understanding or experience of spirituality with adults and, as a result, either preserved an isolated and secret sense of spirituality or accepted what they observed to be their trusted adults' stance.

If you wanted to extend Karlsen et al.'s emergent theory of the role played by trusted adults in the spiritual lives of children, who would you want to interview? Whose perspectives do you think might add something to their emergent theory?

What makes you think that data from the people whom you have identified could extend the emergent theory? Remember that you always need to provide a clear and convincing rationale for each of your research decisions.

For example, in the study of older Chinese people, we sought to recruit older Chinese people (defined as over 50 years of age) resident in two areas of the UK, one city with a large 'China town' and one area without, as we believed these social differences could reflect cultural identification and support. While we started by accessing those people who used Chinese community groups, we extended data collection in the interview phase to those who chose *not* to use these groups. The research team also debated whether to include second generation 'born in Britain' Chinese people because they were more likely to be more fully integrated into Western culture and to be English-speaking. We purposively sought a hetero- geneous sample of older Chinese people who varied in terms of gender, places of origin (for example, Hong Kong, mainland China, Malaysia) and socio-economic status.

The status of the data

It is important to consider the status afforded to the responses of participants and the impli- cations which are drawn from talk, and the purposes of the analysis of talk from differing perspectives. I will start by differentiating between two major conceptual approaches in qualitative methods of analysis:

- Those approaches that are concerned with inferring *meaning* from data and draw infer- ences about what people think, feel and do. These can be characterized as 'experiential' approaches. They include methods of analysis such as thematic analysis, framework anal- ysis, grounded theory analysis, interpretative phenomenological analysis and narrative analysis.

- Those approaches that are concerned with how talk is *used* in social situations and that do not make inferences about how people feel or think. These can be characterized as 'discursive' approaches. They include methods such as discourse analysis, conversation analysis and analysis of institutional interaction.

The conventional status afforded to interview data, for example, when using grounded theory analysis, is that responses are construed as evidence of what people think and feel and how they *understand* their world. These insights are assumed to have stability over time and are inferred as being characteristic of that individual. Grounded theorists feel able to draw conclusions about the state of mind of individuals on the basis of their talk. They are interested in exploring the influence of previous experiences and personal understandings on the emotional and cognitive reactions displayed in talk. Thus, from this perspective, talk is seen as representing the contents of people's minds and providing direct access to thoughts and emotions. Descriptions are taken to represent a 'real' account of experiences and are seen as indicative of feelings *at the time* of the experience, although it is clear that the interview presents a retrospective account of experiences. The social situation of the interview is regarded as largely unproblematic.

In comparison, discursive approaches regard interview responses as evidence about how people *use* language to construct that particular situation at that particular time (although these approaches can be wary of interview data and prefer naturally-occurring data) (see Chapter 10 in this volume). Discursive approaches make no assumptions about consistency of responses in other situations, no inferences about how people think or feel, and explain talk as representing a repertoire of ways that people have of dealing with questions in social situations, such as in research interviews.

In the study of older Chinese people, we accepted the utterances of participants as indicative of their knowledge, attitudes and beliefs about cancer and end-of-life issues. This was a stance that we brought into the research. To use a term explained in Chapter 2 in this volume, it was the basic epistemological assumption that shaped how we regarded the data.

BITE-SIZED SUMMARY

3

Data for grounded theory analysis can be drawn from various sources but individual and focus group interviews are the most frequently-used ways of generating data. One distinctive feature of grounded theory research is that it does not proceed in a linear way with the collection of data being completed and then followed by data analysis. Instead there are reciprocal periods of data collection, analysis, reflection, theory development and theory testing, with each feeding into the others. Theoretical sampling is part of this and involves a process of ongoing data collection for the generation of theory, with the direction of sampling being determined by the analysis of previously-gathered data. Before starting analysis (and ideally before starting the research process), the researcher should commit to a particular stance towards the status of the data and what the researcher believes they can say from the data. In other words, they need to commit to a particular epistemological perspective for their research.

Data preparation

Transcription

Prior to undertaking any type of qualitative analysis, 'raw' spoken data need to be transformed into a textual format. Typically, this involves the transcription of audio recordings into written text. This is the first stage of the analysis and critical decisions need to be made at this point about the style of transcription to be used. In grounded theory analysis, it is usual to transcribe both the speech of the researcher and the participant but not usual or necessary to transcribe prosodic, paralinguistic or extra-linguistic elements such as pauses, intakes of breath and changes in volume and speed (as some discourse analysts and all conversation analysts would do, for example).

Novice researchers may wish to undertake the transcription of at least a few interviews themselves because this allows them to develop an intimate familiarity with the data and to identify some potential analytic lines of inquiry. Transcription may be a laborious process but it gives the researcher a chance to become intimately familiar with the detail and texture of the data. If the majority of transcription is done by clerical workers, it is necessary to listen to all the audio-recordings and carefully check through the transcripts for errors and omissions. Rennie (2000) maintains that there should be continuity in data collection and analysis. He argues that the person undertaking the interviews will already have an understanding of the text and analysis of elements of the text will be influenced by knowledge of the whole interview and its social context. In the study of older Chinese people, interviews were first transcribed into Chinese and then translated into English. Careful checking of the transcripts was done using the original audio-recordings and the research team discussed problematic and unclear words in the translation. Box 8.5 provides an excerpt from an interview to demonstrate the type of transcription conducted.

BOX 8.5 ▶ An excerpt from an interview and possible open codes

Transcript	Open codes
(conducted in Mandarin, translated into English)	
Ms Sing:	
This … this congee, I think when patients are weak it is easier to be absorbed.	'nature of food'
Interviewer:	
Yes, easier.	
Ms Sing:	
Right, easier to be absorbed. So for patients, medicine is important but food therapy is also important. You should let her eat whatever her condition allows her to eat. I think we have lots of food therapy in Chinese culture; this is one of the strengths of our Chinese culture. Also, I said earlier I mentioned to have a community centre and the problem nowadays, people	'beliefs about digestion' 'food therapy' 'Chinese culture'

(Continued)

take too much medicine. These medicines are chemicals and they stay in your tummy and you don't know what they would do to you.	'too much medicine' medicine – problems
So if you have this community centre the doctors or nurses can give you a check up regularly and monitor your medicines. If you have taken the medicines for a long period they would see if you really need them at all. Or you might need to change to another type of medicine that might cause fewer side effects.	'check-up on medicine use' medicine-problems
Interviewer: Right, right, that is important.	
Ms Sing: Right, but there are many old people who do not understand what drugs they are taking and they just swallow them in confusion.	medicine – old people

Notes:

- Last names are used as a mark of respect with older Chinese people and we have used a pseudonym here.

- 'Congee' is a type of soup.

An alternative position in grounded theory is that analysis should be directly conducted from the spoken word rather than from transcripts because this allows access to the prosodic and paralinguistic features of the data. For example, irony is difficult to 'capture' in written transcripts because the tone of voice or an accompanying giggle may indicate the intention of the speaker that is not directly evident from the words alone. There are also disagreements about the use of punctuation in transcripts and how the text is presented. Coffey and Atkinson (1996) argue that parsing text into clauses retains more of the emotional resonance of the spoken words. This type of transcription gives the written text a poetic appearance. In conclusion, transformation of spoken language into written text should be regarded as the first stage in the interpretative process.

Use of software to assist analysis

Grounded theory analysis requires researchers to manage large volumes of textual data. It is therefore essential to establish consistent and reliable systems to handle data, whether data are to be stored and processed electronically or in hard copy form. This ensures that, during analysis, data can be retrieved when required and also provides an audit trail (part of the process of establishing the quality of an analysis). To this end, novice researchers should consider the use of qualitative data analysis software if they have a reasonably large data set and/or if more than one person is going to be involved in the process of analysis. There are many different software packages (for example, NVivo: see Silver and Lewins, 2014), with some specially designed to facilitate grounded theory analysis. They have the advantage of facilitating the manipulation, indexing and retrieval of data but do not alter the need for an intensive engagement with the data during the intellectual process of coding and interpretation. The disadvantage of some packages is that they are labour intensive to learn and also in terms of their input and coding requirements and may inadvertently serve to structure data analysis in prescribed ways (for example, as hierarchical or linear models).

Data analysis

As highlighted earlier, there are numerous versions of grounded theory analysis and many lively debates about what constitutes the 'correct' procedures. The account offered here draws heavily on the procedures described by Bartlett and Payne (1997) which are derived from the position taken by Strauss and Corbin (1990). They are summarized in Table 8.1 and offer a possible way to conduct data analysis. Novice researchers should use the analytic procedures which are most congruent with their philosophical and epistemological stance. However, there are key features of analysis which are typical of grounded theory and they will be emphasized in the following account.

Table 8.1 Procedures for a grounded theory analysis (based on Bartlett and Payne, 1997)

Activity	Comments
Collect data	Any source of textual data may be used but semi-structured interviews or observations are the most common.
Transcribe data	Full transcriptions of interviewee and interviewer talk.
Develop initial categories – open coding	Categories are developed from the data by open coding of the transcripts. 'Open coding' means identifying and labelling meaningful units of text, which might be a word, phrase, sentence or larger section of text.
Saturate categories	'Saturation' means gathering examples of meaningful units of text from interview transcripts until no new examples emerge of the categories that have been identified through the analysis.
Defining categories	Once the categories have been saturated, formal definitions in terms of the properties and dimensions of each category may be generated.

Table 8.1 (Continued)

Activity	Comments
Theoretical sampling	From the categories which have emerged from the first sample of data, theoretically relevant samples are chosen to help test and develop categories further.
Axial coding – the development and testing of relationships between categories	During axial coding, possible relationships between categories are hypothesized and tested against the data obtained through ongoing theoretical sampling.
Theoretical integration	A core category (or, in some cases, more than one main category) is identified and related to all the other subsidiary categories to determine its explanatory power. Links with existing theory are established and developed.
Grounding the theory	The emergent theory is grounded by returning to the data and validating it against actual segments of text. A search for deviant cases may be used to test the emergent theory.
Filling in gaps	Finally, any missing detail in the theory is filled in by the further collection of relevant data.

Initial coding and the constant comparison technique

The initial coding of text is done after careful and repeated readings of the material. Meaningful units are identified, highlighted and labelled. These units may be words, phrases, sentences or larger segments of text. The labels are referred to as **categories** (but as 'codes' in some other qualitative research approaches). Strauss and Corbin (1990) describe this as **open coding** and suggest asking repeated questions of the data at this stage. Glaser (1992) describes this as substantive coding and recommends that labels are closely dependent upon the data, perhaps even using the words of participants if appropriate (referred to as *in vivo* categories).

There are dilemmas for researchers in how conceptually concrete or abstract to make their initial codes. There is a danger that a very concrete approach to initial coding results in numerous codes for small units of text which are very close to the data but do little more than repeat the text (Rennie, 2000). Alternatively, the rigorous questioning proposed by Strauss and Corbin (1990) may mean that analysis is very protracted and that conceptual categories are introduced early in the analysis, thereby shaping the analysis according to the theoretical influences of the researcher rather than staying true to the data. Whichever approach is taken, the aim of initial coding is to capture the detail, variation and complexity of the source data.

As more data are accumulated, further instances of the same and new meaningful units are coded in each transcript. This results in numerous categories and subcategories. The same data may be coded under more than one category. It is normal for categories to be initially descriptive and to become more analytical during the process of analysis. The researcher will become aware that certain categories occur frequently in the data and that coding of new data yields fewer and eventually no new examples. This is described as **saturation**. It serves as an indication when initial coding and data collection can cease.

Glaser and Strauss's (1967: 1) original version of grounded theory emphasized the use of 'a general method of comparative analysis'. This is commonly described as the **constant comparison** technique: as segments of text are identified, they are examined against previous categories for similarities and differences. This process means that coding may need to be revised and categories re-labelled, merged or split to take account of new insights. This may require previously coded transcripts to be revisited and recoded. This is characterized by Henwood and Pigeon (1994) as a 'flip-flop' between data and conceptualization.

Novice researchers need to develop a systematic way to index categories and track the segments of text that provide the instances of these categories. This was traditionally done by physically cutting and pasting chunks of transcript but it is now more usually managed with a word-processing program or with qualitative data analysis software. Once categories appear to be saturated, concise and meaningful definitions of the properties and dimensions of each category should be written. In Table 8.2, an example is given of how a section of transcript that had been open coded (see Box 8.5) was further revised in the light of other data to produce more conceptually refined codes.

Table 8.2 An example of the constant comparison process

Excerpt	Open codes	Revised codes
Right, easier to be absorbed. So for patients, medicine is important but food therapy is also important. You should let her eat whatever her condition allows her to eat. I think we have lots of food therapy in Chinese culture. This is one of the strengths of our Chinese culture. Also, I said earlier I mentioned to have a community centre and the problem nowadays, people take too much medicine. These medicines are chemicals and they stay in your tummy and you don't know what they would do to you.	'beliefs about digestion' 'food therapy' 'too much medicine' 'medicine – problems'	food as an essential therapeutic tool ambivalence towards Western medicine

Theoretical sampling and axial coding

During the intermediate period of analysis, further data collection is undertaken. It is usual at this stage to move into theoretical sampling of further participants who are selected because they are assumed to illuminate or test the emerging theory. Strauss and Corbin (1990) describe a process of **axial coding** in which the numerous categories generated during their method of initial coding are refined and reduced. The analytic work required during axial coding involves examination of each category to discover linkages, relationships, redundancy and new patterns. They advocate the use of a coding paradigm that is designed to sensitize the researcher to higher order features such as 'process'. This may require the reformulation of some of the categories as greater insight is achieved and conceptual abstraction moves the categories further from a descriptive account of the data. This is called **theoretical coding**. Strauss and Corbin incorporate hypothesis testing into the method of producing a grounded theory (for example, by repeatedly proposing statements that account for the findings and examining if they can be substantiated from the data), while Glaser emphasizes this more in the final phase. Glaser's (1978, 1992) version appears to focus more closely on coding emerging from the data, with more abstract analysis occurring in the later stages.

Data synthesis

Throughout the whole process of analysis, researchers are encouraged to write memos (see Box 8.6 for an example). These are ways to capture the thought processes of the researcher. In research teams they are also useful ways to share insights and justify how analytic decisions are made. Memo writing functions as an audit trail which may be helpful in tracking analytic processes. Memo writing is regarded as essential and many specialist qualitative analysis software programs have the facility to display memos alongside categories. During later stages of theory development, there is an active interplay between memo writing, data analysis and data questioning. The researcher works pro-actively with the data and with the initial and subsequent categories to achieve steadily more analytic insights. This may also involve further refinement of the research question.

| BOX 8.6 | An example of an analytic memo |

The role of food in health and illness

When talking about the use of foods in illness, the participants seemed to divide their discussion into the foods that were believed to prevent cancer and foods to be avoided and the special anti-cancer 'therapeutic' foods. It is evident in the data that older Chinese people in our sample believe that the body in illness has lost its normal balance and generally this is attributed to the presence of toxins. So the role of foods in illness seems to be about getting rid of the toxins and to replenish the body with the lost elements required in balancing the body and thereby strengthening it.

Development of new theory

In the final stage of analysis, careful scrutiny of the categories will result in the identification of a **core category** that has major explanatory power. The aim of this stage is to organize and integrate the remaining categories in conceptually meaningful ways (see Box 8.7, for an example). Practically, it may be helpful to work with visual images of categories so they can be arranged and rearranged to develop an understanding of patterns that emerge to form theory. Strauss and Corbin (1990) describe this process as selective coding, while Glaser (1992) refers to it as theoretical coding. During this process, links are made with existing theory which may further develop the emergent theory. This is described as **theoretical sensitivity**. Grounded theories tend to be specific to the context from which they are derived but should have explanatory potential and be more than merely descriptive accounts of the data.

There are differences in Strauss's and Glaser's views on what constitutes a good theory. Strauss and Corbin (1990) emphasize the need for a complex, detailed account while Glaser (1992) emphasizes parsimony and its potential modifiability in presenting theory. In my view, a grounded theory should offer a coherent account to explain the topic under investigation. This may be clustered around a core category or a number of linked themes but should not comprise a diverse collection of interesting but largely unrelated themes. This may mean that researchers need to be selective in their emphasis.

BOX 8.7	**An example showing links between existing theory and coding**

Existing theory and policy related to cancer diagnostic information

Current communication practices in cancer care emphasize the full and open discussion of diagnosis and prognosis with the patient at a pace and style compatible with their wishes (National Institute for Clinical Excellence, 2004). However, actual communication practices are probably more conditional than fully open (Hagerty et al., 2005). Trends in the UK have highlighted the autonomy of the patient in health care decision making (Fallowfield, 2001). There are assumptions in the literature that Chinese people favour disclosure of a cancer diagnosis to family members rather than the patient (Rowlands, 2005). Our research indicated there were various preferences about the disclosure of a cancer diagnosis. Some of the participants expressed a wish to be told of the diagnosis while a minority would not want to be told. There were quite a few participants who were non-committal. While great importance was attached to family life and obligation, there was also a sense in which

(Continued)

people still wanted to be fully informed themselves. Overall, there was a preference that disclosure should be given to both the patient and family members together.

Links to data and coding

Main category: preferences for disclosure

Participants were asked about their own preferences for disclosure of cancer and nearly two thirds of them said they would want to be told of the diagnosis. The following are examples of subcategories in the initial open coding:

- Needing to make arrangements

  'And some people are frightened by the thought of death, but then on the other hand if death is unavoidable through your cancer then it would be nice for the sufferer to be able to put things in order.' (Woman, interview 27)

- To prepare mentally

  'If it was myself, I would want to know. Then I would mentally prepare myself.' (Woman, interview 16)

- To know the cause of death

  'So you would know what you died of.' (Man, interview 23)

Testing of emerging theory

Having developed new theory, the researcher needs to return to the data to validate it against segments of text. In this process, there is a continuation of the rigorous constant comparison process described previously. It may also be appropriate to collect small amounts of new data specifically to test aspects of the theory, perhaps by returning to the same participants or new people selected purposively. In addition, a search for deviant cases will help to assess the limits of the theory. According to Glaser and Strauss (1967: 6), 'generating a theory from data means that most hypotheses and concepts not only come from the data, but are systematically worked out in relation to the data during the course of the research'. Early formulations of the grounded theory method emphasized the need to derive hypotheses from the new theory which may lead to further qualitative or quantitative research.

How to assess the quality of a grounded theory analysis

There are a number of criteria for judging the quality of qualitative research generally (for example Elliott et al., 1999; Yardley, 2000; see also Chapter 2 in this volume). None are perfect and some have been the focus of lively debate (see Reicher, 2000). Much will depend upon the version of grounded theory espoused by the researcher and his/her epistemological position. However, some suggestions are offered below.

Goodness of fit

In the original version, Glaser and Strauss (1967) emphasized the requirements of 'goodness of fit' and 'work'. By **goodness of fit**, they meant that categories must be applicable to the data and not 'forced'; the term 'work' referred to the emergent theory which must explain the behaviours under investigation. Glaser's subsequent critique of Strauss was largely about the 'forcing' of analysis caused by the use of a coding paradigm which he thought no longer allowed theory to emerge or be 'discovered'. In addition, grounded theory should be accessible. According to Glaser and Strauss (1967: 3), 'The theory must also be readily understandable to sociologists of any view point, to students and to significant laymen'. Of course, for grounded theory analysis conducted within psychology, we should replace 'sociologists' with 'psychologists'.

Many of the analytic procedures of grounded theory are designed to ensure robustness. According to Rennie (2000), in Glaser's version there is a distinction between verification and validation. Validation of the theory involves procedures within the method while verification comes from hypotheses derived from the theory and subsequently tested using quantitative methods. In comparison, Strauss and Corbin (1990) argue for the inclusion of hypothesis testing *within* the analytic method.

External validation

A number of strategies may be used which seek to confirm the quality of the analysis with reference to the views of others. Triangulation has been proposed to support the claims made (Foss and Ellefsen, 2002). This refers to exploring the same phenomenon from different vantage points, on the assumption that similar findings from each perspective indicate that the research has presented a valid picture. Triangulation may take a number of forms such as methodological triangulation, theoretical triangulation or respondent validation but it should not be regarded as a panacea. Respondent validation involves returning the emerging theory to participants to obtain their views on its credibility. In my view, this often just generates more data from differing perspectives rather than establishing the validity of one particular perspective. Likewise, triangulation suggests that it is possible to obtain validation of theory by collecting data from more than one source, either using different techniques of data collection or by combining different theoretical positions. Heath and Cowley (2004) caution against combining Glaserian and Straussian versions of grounded theory within a single study. A team approach to analysis may offer support to novice researchers but there is a danger that in trying to establish consensus, individual insights are lost. Rennie (2000) is critical of all these approaches to validation because he considers them to be inherently positivist, providing a spurious 'objectivity'. They rely on the notion of a single reality against which the emerging theory can be assessed.

In the study of older Chinese people, initial open coding was conducted independently by team members on the first five focus group transcripts and, from that, consensus was reached on categories. The actual coding of transcripts was then undertaken by the researcher who collected the data. Repeated discussions of problematic categories and revisions occurred throughout the analysis.

Reflexivity

Reflexivity refers to the acknowledgement by the researcher of the role played by their interpretative framework (including theoretical commitments, personal understandings and personal experiences) in creating their analytic account. Procedures central to the grounded theory method such as constant comparison and the writing of **memos** promote a critical awareness of the role of the researcher and their cognitive processes. The recognition of one's theoretical and disciplinary background should be attempted before undertaking data collection to ensure that the research agenda is open to new insights from the participants. Likewise, the techniques of **open coding** that draw on participants' own words for category labels help to prevent premature closure of the developing theory. Grounded theorists do not claim that it is possible to 'bracket' presuppositions as in phenomenology; instead researchers are generally acknowledged to be co-producers of the data, for example during interviews and during interpretation of the data and development of theory.

BOX 8.8 | **Working with reflexivity**

Imagine that you were part of the team conducting the grounded theory study of older Chinese people's beliefs and perceptions regarding cancer and its treatment and their preferences about end-of-life care (refer back to Box 8.2 to remind yourself about the details of that study).

Think about your cognitive and emotional responses to the research topic and to the group whose perspectives were being studied.

- What sort of responses are you aware of?

- What expectations might you have had about what the participants would say?

- Where do you think your responses and expectations come from?

- How might these responses and expectations have influenced how you approached the analysis of the data?

Your expectations could be seen as an informal theory that you hold about the research topic – a personal theory that could shape the grounded theory that you develop in helpful or unhelpful ways.

- How could you have ensured that your personal theory made a helpful contribution to the development of your grounded theory?

Writing up and presentation

The literary ability to construct an argument is needed in writing up qualitative research. Generally the presentation of results is much less formulaic than in experimental reports but the methods used and the processes undertaken during the analysis need to be made explicit to readers.

In presenting a grounded theory, it is important to explain the process of analysis (as in any methodological account) and demonstrate how the core category and subcategories are derived from the data. The new theory is then presented with sufficient detail of the constituents of the core category to be understandable, together with the relationship of the core category to other categories. Graphical representations of conceptual categories and their linkages may be helpful for readers. In addition the research report should provide excerpts of data such as text, images, field notes or transcriptions upon which the analysis is based. Novice researchers should be explicit in how they have selected the supporting excerpts to defend against the criticism that they have just found a few 'juicy quotations'. Excerpts should be clearly labelled with identifiers that allow readers to know that more than a single participant has been cited in support of a claim. In writing up qualitative research, a compromise is required between providing sufficient data for readers to draw alternative conclusions and enabling them to see how the interpretations have been arrived at, and an overly long account.

A useful exemplar of a written-up grounded theory study is presented in Appendix 2 (Report 3) in the present volume. Readers should also consult the journal articles suggested in the 'Further reading' section at the end of this chapter which demonstrate how grounded theory research might be presented.

BITE-SIZED SUMMARY

4

When data have been prepared (which usually involves transcription), the analytic process can begin. Initial or 'open' coding aims to generate categories that collectively capture the detail, variation and complexity of the data. Constant comparison is undertaken: this involves considering segments of data in terms of their similarities to and differences from existing categories which are amended as necessary.

Further data may be generated at this stage through theoretical sampling. The categories generated through initial coding are examined to discover linkages, relationships, redundancy and new patterns. This axial coding produces a more refined and reduced set of categories. As the analysis unfolds, more conceptually abstract categories are developed and an emergent theory takes shape from the interplay of memo writing, data analysis and data questioning. A core category is identified which integrates the categories and has major explanatory power. The emergent theory is further developed as links are made with existing theory and it is carefully tested against the data. The 'goodness of fit' between the theory and the data that gave rise to it is a key indicator of the quality of any grounded theory. The theory should then be written up in a way that is clear and that demonstrates its origins in the data set.

BOX 8.9 **Coding practice**

In Appendix 1 in this volume, you will find transcripts of two interviews from a study that looked at how ex-soldiers renegotiate identity after leaving the army. Select one of these transcripts and apply open coding to at least the first four pages, keeping the research question in mind. The more data you can work with, the better. You may be able to engage in constant comparison as you generate categories. It is difficult to undertake meaningful axial coding when working with only a short data extract. Nonetheless, see if you can discern any links between the categories that you develop.

When you have completed your coding, think about what this experience has taught you about the initial stages of the coding process in grounded theory analysis. What were the most insightful and most challenging aspects? How closely did your experience match the descriptions that I gave of the coding process in this chapter?

If you are reading this chapter as part of a course in qualitative research, invite other classmates to code the data as well and compare the codes that you have produced. What are the differences and similarities between your sets of codes? It is unlikely that you will all have produced the same codes. Think about why you might have generated different codes.

In Chapter 9 in this volume, Sheila Hawker and Christine Kerr offer their reflections on the process of analysing the interviews with the two ex-soldiers, using grounded theory analysis.

CHAPTER SUMMARY

This chapter has presented and discussed the origins, principles and practicalities of grounded theory analysis, drawing upon one study to exemplify the analytic process. Undertaking a grounded theory analysis can be challenging, exciting, frustrating and enjoyable. In an ideal world, it is important to be well prepared, well equipped and adequately funded and to design your research carefully, setting goals and targets using a realistic time frame. Of course, you need also to be flexible in accommodating the unexpected and be open to new experiences, discoveries and ways of seeing the world. Finally, good research is rigorously conducted and accurately recorded. Grounded theory requires intellectual engagement, innovation, theoretical sensitivity, reflexivity and the ability to write. I hope that this chapter will inspire and guide your research.

Further reading

Charmaz's (2014) *Constructing Grounded Theory* is an engagingly written book which presents one version of grounded theory procedures in a concise and explicit style. This book would be of value to both novices and experts. It should be read alongside articles that report grounded theory studies in clear ways so that you can see how researchers have applied the principles of grounded theory analysis and how they write up their work.

In Appendix 2 in this volume, you will find Sque and Payne's report on their grounded theory research which considered how families of deceased people decided whether to donate their loved one's organs for transplantation. For a longer version of this report, see Sque and Payne (1996). Two more recent examples of grounded theory research on health-related topics are the studies by Basinger et al. (2015) on how college students who are living away from their family home cope when a family member is diagnosed with or treated for cancer, and by Marks et al. (2015) on how health-care professionals who work with children and adolescents with chronic fatigue syndrome/myalgic encephalomyelitis understand the condition. Remember, though, what I said earlier about some researchers claiming to have used grounded theory analysis but actually only using its coding procedures without trying to generate new theory. If you want to find examples of grounded theory analysis to enhance your learning about the approach, stick to instances where the researchers have generated new theory.

9

DOING GROUNDED THEORY

Sheila Hawker and Christine Kerr

This chapter presents a grounded theory analysis of data on two ex-soldiers' experiences of leaving the army. It describes how researchers become immersed in the data through familiarization with the context and the content of the interviews. In this exercise, two interview transcripts were interrogated through the use of open codes and categories that facilitated the identification of patterns, relationships, similarities and differences both within and across the two accounts. As concepts emerged, categories were grouped together and the two transcripts were subjected to further interrogation. A working hypothesis was generated and outlined, which is ready to be tested by additional interviews. Suggestions are made about future participants and the process of theoretical sampling is described. Finally, the strengths and weaknesses of using a grounded theory approach in this context are considered.

Introduction

Grounded theory is a systematic method of data analysis and theory development. **Constant comparison** of data is the key component of this method. Textual data, usually in the form of interview transcripts and often accompanied by field notes and observations, are systematically examined in order to uncover the subjective realities of participants through thorough scrutiny of their accounts. The aim of grounded theory analysis is to identify the social processes that produce the phenomenon being studied and to use these insights, derived from the data, to generate new theory that explains that phenomenon. Put simply, cases that have the same outcomes are examined to see which conditions they have in common, thereby revealing potential causes. Cases that are similar on many dimensions but have different outcomes are also compared to see where the main causal differences might lie.

For the purposes of the analytic exercise presented in this chapter, the grounded theory method was simplified and is presented here as a series of phases (see Figure 6.1). However, it must be stressed that grounded theory analysis is an iterative and recursive process; while each phase informs the next, all phases are revisited as the research project progresses. As theory emerges, the researcher will return to the data and select new participants to extend and test it (a process referred to as **theoretical sampling**). Sheila Payne presents a more detailed account of the principles and practicalities of grounded theory analysis in Chapter 8 in this volume. Here we shall focus on how these were applied to two transcripts of interviews conducted as part of a qualitative study on ex-soldiers' experiences of leaving the army and their post-army lives (see Appendix 1 in this volume).

Many researchers use specialist software packages when analysing qualitative data. There are clear advantages to this in terms of managing data, recording **codes** and concepts, the construction of a **code book**, searching and sifting codes, and grouping them into **categories**. The qualitative software analysis package NVivo was used for this exercise (Silver and Lewins, 2014). However, before any data were entered into the analysis package, we spent time reading and re-reading the two transcripts in order to familiarize ourselves with these data. In a real study, there would be continuity in data collection and analysis. We would either have conducted these interviews personally or at least have had access to the recordings and field notes in order to familiarize ourselves with both the content and the context of the data (Rennie, 2000). Similarly, while a general description of the focus of the project was available to us (see the Preface to Appendix 1 in this volume), a researcher would normally be familiar with the exact nature and context of a project's particular research question(s) before approaching the data analysis – allowing for the fact that research questions can be revised in grounded theory work as the research unfolds.

Whether or not a literature review should be carried out in advance when applying grounded theory is debatable but in this case neither of us was familiar with the academic literature on ex-service personnel. To this extent, we were truly 'naïve' researchers. The two interviews used here are semi-structured and this type of interview is often better suited to the later phases of grounded theory analysis. It is more usual to start with less structured interviews to explore the research topic before the analysis is further refined.

A researcher must be reflexive about her/his own role in data collection and analysis. It is notable here that the interviewer himself is an ex-serviceman, which is reflected in his choice of words during the interviews – for example, 'civvy street' – and the participants were aware of his service background. This factor should be noted as it may have intimated or encouraged shared understandings between the interviewer and the participants, thereby influencing the content of the interviews. So although coding the transcripts may at first appear to be the main activity in a grounded theory analysis, it should be recognized that analysis begins from the very start of the project. Familiarization with the research question, the context of the interviews, the interview data and reflection upon the role of the researcher are all integral parts of a grounded theory analysis.

As explained above, under normal circumstances, a researcher would have more contextual data than we had available here. The researchers would also have had more time and space to explore these data. If this were a real study, we would probably have spent weeks analysing the first batch of data as coding generally only becomes more rapid and efficient as a

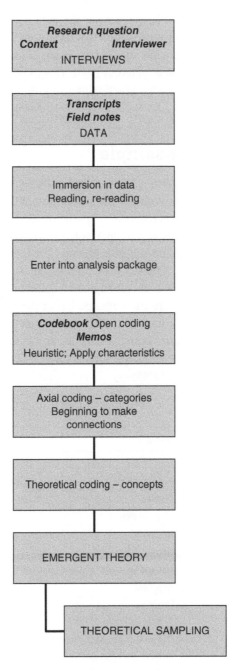

Figure 9.1 Phases of grounded theory analysis

study progresses. It is difficult to outline the iterative process of grounded theory in a straightforward and accessible way within the confines of a short chapter. To combat this problem, we will focus on only one small part of our coding and analysis and explain it in depth.

As readers are probably quite distanced from the data under discussion, we suggest that, before proceeding, you should thoroughly familiarize yourselves with the two transcripts, think about what you notice while reading them and consider what words you could use as 'shorthand' to represent any ideas you may have. This experimentation is an important part of the exercise because explaining the practicalities of grounded theory analysis without being familiar with the data is a little like explaining how to swim without being in the water.

Characteristics of the sample

It is important to record the characteristics of the sample as it grows. This allows the analyst to examine responses from different groups of people and to note and record similarities and differences; it also informs further recruitment of participants. It must be emphasized that this categorization is not aimed at finding a representative sample. The purpose is to delve into the breadth of experiences around the phenomenon being investigated. By recording these details, any strong bias in the sample is also highlighted. The advantage of an analysis software package is that these attributes can readily be assigned to each transcript so that data can be sifted and sorted under the various headings. Using the information we have about the ex-soldiers Brian and David, we have drafted a preliminary chart for this exercise (see Table 9.1). Additional variables would normally be added as a study progresses so, as well as informing future sampling, recording information in this way will aid familiarization with the data and the eventual writing up of the study.

Table 9.1 Attributes of the sample

Variable	David	Brian
Gender	Male	Male
Age	Not known	Not known
Marital status	Married	Married
Children	Has children	Has children
Length of service	Not known	Not known
How long since leaving the army	Not known	'several years'
Rank on entry	Not known	Not known
Rank on exit	Sergeant	Sergeant
Job in army	Driver	Not known
Current employment	School caretaker	'training'
Reason for joining army	"to get away because I didn't have a trade"	Not known
Reason for leaving army	'Options for change'	Health

The basic characteristics of grounded theory research have been outlined. It involves the close and systematic examination of textual data to identify participants' subjective realities and the social processes that produce the phenomenon being studied. The insights gained are used to generate new theory to explain that phenomenon. We have noted the importance of researchers being very familiar with the research question, the context of the interviews and the data before starting analysis. There is also a need for researchers to reflect upon their role in the research process and to keep records of the characteristics of participants. We are now ready to begin the formal part of the analytic process – although remember that grounded theory research is iterative, with the researcher moving from data collection to analysis and back to data collection.

BITE-SIZED SUMMARY
....
1

Open coding

When the researcher is thoroughly familiar with the initial data that have been collected, it is time to begin the **open coding** of the first interview transcript. This process of coding in grounded theory analysis is clearly described by Sheila Payne in Chapter 8. The purpose of coding is to continue systematically the process of 'noticing'. The application of code words to sections of data – be they single words, phrases, sentences or complete paragraphs – constitutes the naming of phenomena which facilitates collecting, sorting and thinking about things in the data. Each code acts as a label to highlight items that have been noticed in the accounts. Some codes will be objective or concrete and serve to echo what is contained in the text, while other codes will be more abstract or heuristic, reflecting the analyst's ideas as each line of the data is studied for information relating to the research question. The actual names of the codes are decided by the individual researcher who records the meanings of the code words she/he has assigned. This allows for consistency between coding sessions (coding is mentally demanding and so there is a limit to how much coding you can do in one go) and to facilitate comparisons with others who might be coding the same piece of data. Some codes will be *in vivo*, consisting of words or phrases used by the interviewees themselves, thereby reflecting the realities of the participants. For instance, two *in vivo* codes that we produced for the exercise were 'locked the gate' (David, line 98) and 'used up' (David, line 119). These are expressions taken directly from the transcripts. The complete list of code words and the meanings assigned to them constitute a code book for the project – another task greatly simplified by the use of a software package.

When we began to code Brian's and David's accounts for the first time, we utilized a great many codes and assigned meanings which varied from the very objective 'age' ('the age of the participant at interview') to the more heuristic 'the army as carer' ('holistic care of soldiers as part of the army package – examples: housing, health'). We noted that there were many similarities between the two accounts: both participants are male, married and have children (codes included 'gender', 'marital status' and 'children'); both participants appeared to value what being in the army afforded them (codes included 'duty', 'self-esteem', 'education' and 'social life'); both men expressed a sense of loss when they left (codes included 'abandonment', 'loss' and 'locked out'); both expressed some resentment at the way the army had treated them at the time of their leaving (codes included 'bitterness', 'on your own', 'used up' and 'best years') but both Brian and David had maintained some association with the army (codes included 'links', 'transition', 'social life' and 'ex-soldier'). In a normal study, all of the issues we identified would be interrogated further by contrasting, comparing, sifting and sorting all of the codes we applied to the text. For the purposes of this exercise, we are going to focus upon just one cluster of codes relating to the issue of army standards and the way these are reported to impact upon civilian life.

The study from which this exercise originates was concerned with the re-negotiation of identity after leaving the army. With this focus in mind, we coded the data extract below with the following codes: 'terminology', 'us and them', 'army education' and 'standards'. It would appear that Brian viewed service personnel and civilians very differently and believed his army training had instilled more commitment, a sense of duty and higher standards than those of many civilians. Interestingly, the terminology he used ('we', 'they') could suggest that he still viewed himself as part of the army rather than as a civilian.

4	**Brian:** I think I've learned in the forces and the thing is you learn these
5	things in the army without realizing it a lot of the time, so that when you
6	come out and start comparing yourself to the people working alongside
7	you, you find that you've got a much greater sense of urgency. You tend
8	to pay more attention to detail, you don't bother about the time so much,
9	you don't clock on or clock off. If the job takes twice as long as it should,
10	you just work on as necessary. We seem to be much more flexible, much
11	more adaptable to situations, and it's all stuff I've learned in the forces and
12	the experience I've had where you need to be adaptable, where the
13	situation might change. You've already learned to adapt to new situations
14	– and that comes through all the time. When I look around I see that all of
15	the time, lack of attention to detail, how they just skimp over things, and
16	no attitude. You know, we do our best all of the time.

When we compared David's account with Brian's, we could see there were similarities. Like Brian, David intimated that, as an ex-soldier, he had higher standards than civilians and was prepared to spend extra time and do a job efficiently. Consequently, the codes attached to the data extract below were similar to those used for Brian's extract, including 'standards', 'discipline', 'terminology' and 'us and them'.

240   ... when I used to come back at night, I used
241   to park all the wagons up so all the bumpers were level. Funny as it
242   may seem, they had them parked all over the car park. It made it harder
243   to get out. They couldn't see the fact that by lining them all up it was
244   easy to get them out. Um, it was other little things like your paperwork.
245   Keep your paperwork in order – it makes it easy. I think that side of
246   life used to hinder me because all I would do was spend an extra ten
247   minutes. All they wanted to do was in, out and go.

However, we noted that the terminology used by the two participants differed slightly. Although David also talked of 'they' when he referred to civilians, he used the term 'I' rather than 'we' when he made comparisons with the way he performed at work. This could suggest that he was more distanced from the army than Brian and we would add a memo to this effect here. The use of **memos** is a key element of grounded theory. Memos are recorded throughout the analysis in parallel with data collection, familiarization, note-taking and coding. Essentially a memo is a note or reminder to oneself about an idea, a code or property, an observation about a relationship between codes or a thought about future possible questions or participants. Making memos at all phases of the research project, from the design to the final analysis, informs the gradual build-up of theory. Memos guide the researcher to examine the data from different angles rather than simply focusing upon whatever is immediately obvious. In this case, our memo would have speculated about why David might have been more distanced from the army than Brian. Had Brian been in the army for longer than David? Had David been out of the army for longer than Brian?

Table 9.2 shows some of the open or free codes that were generated around the issue of army and civilian standards and shows how they were collapsed into groups or categories containing codes with similar qualities as the analysis proceeded. The categories tend to be more abstract than the open codes and again the meanings assigned to them by the researchers are recorded.

At this stage, the categories are arbitrary and the open codes can be grouped into more than one category. Again it must be emphasized that codes and categories will change and adapt throughout the analysis as ideas and linkages emerge. It is important to keep track of these processes and record thoughts and emergent ideas in memos. Systematic tracking of the process of analysis is an integral part of the **theoretical sensitivity** that grounded theory researchers must have if insights and ideas are to be developed into a theory that is truly grounded in the data. We cannot over-emphasize the importance of this. Remember that the key criterion for evaluating any grounded theory is **'goodness of fit'** – that is, the extent to which the theory accords with the data that generated it – and so a researcher needs to be able to identify exactly how every aspect of the theory that is produced arose from the data. A complete record of the analytic process is therefore essential.

Table 9.2 Code groupings

Code words	Categories	Axial coding	Emergent theory
Education			
Socialization			
Duty	Army standards		
Discipline			
Standards			
Self-esteem			
Status			
Terminology	Self-identity		
Difference			
Ex-soldier		Army added value	'Once a soldier, never again
Links			a civilian'
Preparation			
Adjustment			
Job search	Period of transition		
Ex-soldier			
Outside			
Links			
Problems in civvy street			
Links	Us and them		
Terminology			

So open coding is not a linear process. It involves the creation of puzzle pieces which are fitted together, only to be disassembled and reassembled into different pictures. Our account of the analysis now moves into the next stage where we continued to look for types, sequences, processes, patterns and relationships within and across accounts.

BITE-SIZED SUMMARY

2

Researchers who are doing grounded theory analysis for the first time sometimes feel unsure about how to begin the analytic process. They may be uncertain about what exactly coding involves and what codes look like. We have reflected on our open coding of the interview transcripts and have presented some of the initial codes that we produced from the data. It should be clear that our codes are closely tied to the data – which is especially important in grounded theory work. We have noted the importance of writing memos throughout the analytic process because these are essential resources in building a grounded theory and in satisfying a fundamental criterion for good grounded theory research.

Axial coding

Axial coding refers to the way in which categories are now further refined through examination, comparison and thinking about them in relation to each other. At this stage, developed categories are now reassembled into major categories or axial codes which reflect the working hypotheses or propositions that the analyst has induced through the systematic examination and questioning of the data.

Returning to our analytic process, the categories in Table 9.2 – 'army standards', 'self-identity', 'period of transition' and 'us and them' – were considered again and related back to each participant. The transcripts suggested that both ex-soldiers believed that in some way the army had made them different from civilians in terms of their work practices. In fact they went further and suggested that they were more committed, more efficient and better organized than many civilian workers. They claimed that their ways were superior and that this can cause problems for them in civilian life because other workers did not work in the same way. So now these grouped codes or categories can be related together under the new major category 'army added value'. We now need to ask what constitutes this 'added value'. These accounts suggested that an eye for detail, organization, commitment and discipline were some of the contributing factors.

Major categories can be tested against the data in order to confirm or refute them. To test the emergent axial code 'army added value', we returned to the transcripts to look for more examples and any counter-examples of this phenomenon and code them accordingly (see lines 49–60 in David's transcript and lines 70–78 and 259–262 in Brian's transcript for further examples). However it was also clear that in some instances the participants' army training and army standards had not been viewed as having provided added value and had caused problems for the two men when other (civilian) workers resented or were not comfortable with their ways of working. See below for an example:

```
230    Brian: … A lot of my work, I train people
231    up … my work is training and I've had to adapt my training style to be more
232    civilian friendly than in the military because it was…people used to say,
233    'Well, we come to you and you don't teach us – you shout at us', which
234    was – all I was doing was projecting my voice so that people would hear
235    me at the back but I've had to adapt it in such a way that people are more
236    happy with it and it's slightly less structured than what it was when I was
237    in the forces – a bit more casual.
```

The study is trying to understand the process of re-negotiating identity on leaving the army. From the transcripts, we understood that army socialization meant that ex-soldiers may be left with skills and a demeanour that could be somewhat redundant in civilian life or were not valued in the same way as they were in the army. However, it would seem from these two accounts that ex-service personnel may still be likely to value these ways and be reluctant to discard them.

Now we can add more factors and density to the analysis. Further insight is gained and more questions are raised through examining the codes and categories, thinking about the axial coding and asking further questions of the data. How do ex-servicemen deal with these conflicts? Do they try to change? The excerpt above indicated that Brian had to adapt and change his demeanour in order to be more accepted by civilians. It was also clear from his account that he spent much of his working life in the company of other ex-service personnel. Has this made the transition easier for him? Has it been easier for him than for David? Both men were reluctant to leave the army. Does this make a difference?

Theoretical coding

Theoretical coding, which is also known as selective coding, is the final phase of analysis. The aim here is to draw together the codes and categories, reformulate important categories in a conceptual way and move towards an overarching theory or explanation that can be applied to all accounts and will also explain conflicting data. When researchers reach the stage where one category is mentioned with high frequency and is well connected to other categories, it is safe to adopt this as the **core category** (although more than one core category may emerge). This core category then acts as the thread or the story line of the research and integrates all aspects of the emerging theory. The ideas that have been presented as significant by the participants will be clearly represented within this explanatory core concept. This point in the analysis is referred to as **theoretical integration**.

Considering the limited data that were available to us in this exercise, it was obviously impossible for us to come to any conclusions, report findings or safely adopt a core category for this study. However, for the purposes of the exercise, we are proposing that 'once a soldier, never again a civilian' could be considered a working hypothesis for a core category that has the potential to develop into a possible theory. From the data, it seemed apparent that, although these participants had left the army and were now technically civilians, they had been socialized into army ways of being and thinking and could not completely revert back to civilian life. They considered themselves to be different from civilians; no longer soldiers, they were now ex-soldiers rather than civilians. As stated earlier, we have focused upon and drawn out just one cluster of codes so this is necessarily a very early and tentative speculation.

What next?

In order to test this working hypothesis or proposition, we need to apply it to further data. This involves theoretical sampling. Participants would now be selected according to their ability to shed further light on our research problem and test how useful our developing theory is for explaining the similarities and differences in these additional accounts.

The potential core category of 'once a soldier, never again a civilian' should be tested with other ex-army personnel to see whether they feel the same as Brian and David did. Interviews with further participants would allow us to examine whether the transition to civilian life was different for them in any way. Do other ex-soldiers compare themselves favourably to civilians in terms of work practices? It would be important to find out whether participants of different gender, army rank or those with longer or shorter periods of service than Brian and David expressed similar views to them. Does length of service make a difference in terms of ease of transition to civilian life? Do all ex-service personnel miss the social life that Brian and David reported as part of army life? How have they coped with that? Have they all maintained some link with the army? What we would be seeking at this stage are confirming but especially disconfirming cases in order to test the limits of the theory being developed.

The emergent theory should be tested against new data until **saturation** is reached. By this, we do not only mean that certain issues or themes are being raised repeatedly. Saturation is reached when the theory that has emerged can fully explain all variations in the data. When saturation will happen cannot be predicted as each grounded theory study is unique in terms of the process, the recognition of emergent theory and the number of participants required for this to happen.

We have traced the phases of analysis that follow initial open coding and have examined axial coding and theoretical coding. Theoretical coding allows for the identification of a core category that acts as the thread of the analysis and forms the centre of the emerging theory. We have suggested a potential core concept from our analysis of the two ex-soldiers' interview transcripts but this needs to be tested through theoretical sampling.

BITE-SIZED SUMMARY
· · · · · · · · · · · · · · ·
3

BOX 9.1 ▸ Reflecting on your coding practice

In Box 8.9 in Chapter 8 in this volume, you were invited to code at least four pages of one of the transcripts in Appendix 1 that we have analysed.

- If you did that, how similar or different was your coding compared to our engagement with the same parts of the transcript?

- From what you have read in the present chapter, is there anything different that you would do if you were doing your coding again?

Practising and reflecting on your practice is really the only way of refining your skill in grounded theory analysis – and indeed in any qualitative research approach.

Strengths and weaknesses of the approach

Grounded theory is data driven. It allows researchers the freedom to develop their theory through the thorough and systematic examination of empirical material. The approach aids the understanding of complex behaviours and their meanings through the exploration of the social processes which produce them. This makes grounded theory particularly useful in situations where little is known about a topic or where a new approach to a familiar area is required. Importantly, grounded theory has its own source of rigour. There is a continuing search for evidence that can disconfirm the emerging theory. It is driven by the data in such a way that the final shape of the theory is likely to provide a good 'fit' to the situation in a way that also makes sense to the participants involved in the study (Glaser, 1992).

However, grounded theory is not the most straightforward approach to qualitative inquiry and should not be chosen lightly. As the data are fragmented through coding and categorizing, the researcher risks losing sight of the totality as expressed by the participants. It is an approach that requires procedures to be repeated and recorded systematically yet also demands imagination and insight. Most importantly, the iterative nature of grounded theory makes it a time-consuming method with no clearly predictable end point. In the competitive world of academic research, writing successful research proposals and completing projects on time are of paramount importance. Grounded theory can make it difficult for a researcher to provide advance details of a sample, calculate costs, gain ethical approval and predict the length of a project.

CHAPTER SUMMARY

The exercise that we have reported in this chapter was limited by the data and information available to us as well as by the confines of space and time. What we have tried to demonstrate is the way ideas emerge through immersion in both the content and the context of the data, through coding and categorizing and through repeated testing. The key to grounded theory is constant comparison. Segments of data are compared with existing data-based categories until theory emerges and it is this emergent theory that informs the selection and recruitment of subsequent participants. Grounded theory is a method of systematic inquiry. We emphasize the importance of recording all ideas, codes, meanings, categories and discrepancies to ensure rigour and validity through a clear 'decision trail' which begins at the outset of the study and ends with the final theory.

Further reading

We echo Sheila Payne's recommendation of Charmaz's (2014) *Constructing Grounded Theory in Chapter 8 in this volume*. That book is very well written and goes a long way towards demystifying grounded theory for those who are relatively new to the approach, although it is important to remember that she presents one particular version of grounded theory. Urquhart's (2013) *Grounded Theory for Qualitative Research: A Practical Guide* is also ideal for the novice who may have lots of 'How?' questions as it guides researchers in the practical aspects of using grounded theory analysis.

These should be read alongside articles which report grounded theory studies. For example, see Hallam et al.'s (2008) research on how people with acquired profound hearing loss and their families adapt to the challenges involved, and Loopstra et al.'s (2015) study of how parents assess acute pain in young children. In Appendix 2 in this volume, you will also find Sque and Payne's report on their grounded theory research which considered how families of deceased people decided whether to donate their loved one's organs for transplantation.

10

DISCOURSE ANALYSIS

Adrian Coyle

This chapter provides an overview of key considerations in discourse analysis. This approach to research is based on a particular perspective on the social world, referred to as social constructionism. The assumptions that make up that perspective are outlined and three forms of discourse analysis within psychology are described. We then move into the practicalities of discourse analysis, starting with a consideration of discourse analytic research questions and sampling requirements. Suggestions are offered about what a researcher might usefully attend to when applying discourse analysis to a data set. Finally, questions about the quality and usefulness of discourse analytic research are considered.

Introduction

Discourse analysis is an approach to research within psychology that grew out of the 'turn to language' among some psychologists in the 1980s. From the 1950s, scholars in other disciplines, such as philosophy, sociology and linguistics, developed a view of language which challenged the traditional notion that language provides a set of clear resources to label internal states and external reality. Instead they argued that language is social and productive: it constructs versions of reality and performs social actions. This view shifts the focus from individual language users and their motivations and towards what language *does* in social interactions. Psychology remained largely unaffected by this development and instead focused much of its attention on individual cognition. The 1980s saw some psychologists pick up the view of language as social action that had developed in other disciplines and use this to ask critical questions about the fundamental assumptions upon which much psychological theory and research were built.

A milestone in this process was the publication in 1987 of *Discourse and Social Psychology: Beyond Attitudes and Behaviour* by Jonathan Potter and Margaret Wetherell. This book called for a radical reworking of the issues that social psychology had traditionally addressed. Psychologists in general have long worked with language and text in the form of spoken responses within interview settings and written responses to questionnaire items. The question then arises as to what status we should give to this material. It is often assumed that language is a neutral, transparent medium, describing events or revealing underlying psychological processes in a more or less direct, unproblematic way. Psychologists recognize that people may distort reality when they use language to present themselves in a favourable light or because of memory biases. Yet it is assumed that these can be eradicated or at least minimized if we carefully refine the ways in which we generate and collect data.

Discourse analysis has adopted a very different, thoroughly social understanding of the nature of language, drawn from the developments in other disciplines outlined above. This can make it difficult to provide an accessible introduction to the approach. To a psychology student whose research socialization has been focused on the use of experiments, surveys and statistics to study cognitive operations, discourse analysis can seem as though it involves a different language altogether – and one that is dauntingly complex. I want to point out from the outset, though, that discourse analysis is not an arcane academic pursuit. Any speech or text that critically considers the implications of language use for socially important matters can be seen as doing a basic form of discourse analysis.

To take one example, in the summer of 2015, the British media gave extensive coverage to the presence of several thousand refugees, asylum seekers and economic migrants from various troubled areas of the world who were camped in and around Calais in northern France. Many made attempts to enter the United Kingdom by stowing away on lorries, ferries, cars and trains travelling through the port of Calais or the Eurotunnel terminal there. Key figures in the British government made statements about the situation which elicited criticism from various sources, focused on the social implications of the language that was used. A notable example concerned a term used by the British Prime Minister, David Cameron. Here is how the story was reported by *The Guardian* newspaper:

> Rights groups have rounded on David Cameron, saying his description of migrants in Calais as a 'swarm of people' trying to reach Britain was dehumanising.

> The prime minister's words brought into focus the emotive language used by politicians and the media about the migrants in makeshift camps in the French port town.

> Speaking during a visit to Vietnam, Cameron told ITV News attempts to enter the UK had increased because 'you have got a swarm of people coming across the Mediterranean, seeking a better life, wanting to come to Britain because Britain has got jobs, it's got a growing economy, it's an incredible place to live'.

He added: 'But we need to protect our borders by working hand in glove with our neighbours, the French, and that is exactly what we are doing.'

A British official later denied Cameron's words had dehumanised the migrants.

The Refugee Council was first to condemn Cameron's language.

The charity's head of advocacy, Dr Lisa Doyle, said: 'It's extremely disappointing to hear the prime minister using such irresponsible, dehumanising language to describe the desperate men, women and children fleeing for their lives across the Mediterranean Sea.

'This sort of rhetoric is extremely inflammatory and comes at a time when the government should be focused on working with its European counterparts to respond calmly and compassionately to this dreadful humanitarian crisis.' [ ]

Harriet Harman, Labour's interim leader, said the prime minister 'should remember he is talking about people, not insects. I think it's a very worrying turn that he appears to be wanting to be divisive and set people against, whip people up against, the migrants in Calais.'[1]

In this extract, we see two people being invoked who draw critical attention to the functions performed by the use of the term 'swarm' to refer to the refugees or 'migrants'. They are said to describe this language as 'dehumanising', reducing 'desperate men, women and children' to the level of 'insects' ('swarm' is normally used in a literal sense to refer to a large number of insects, especially when they are in motion). The commentators attend to the social functions of using this term, presenting it as arousing strong emotions among those who hear it ('inflammatory') and as mobilizing public sentiment against the refugees. We can also consider how the extract as a whole works up and reinforces the functions attributed to David Cameron's language. His words are said to have 'brought into focus the emotive language used by politicians and the media' on the issue. Here his words are presented as representing and distilling a body of similar 'emotive' language that had been used by others around that time (with similar functions inferred). The possibility of this language being dehumanizing is acknowledged and deflected by a 'British official' in the extract. However, this attempt at deflection is outweighed across the article by the invocation of a series of commentators who present the language as divisive as dehumanizing.

In this extract, we can see people being represented as attending to the social function of a particular use of language, which is an important aspect of what discourse analysis involves. The extract itself (and the longer article from which it is drawn) can be seen as doing discourse analysis in that it advances and reinforces a particular interpretation of

---

[1]http://www.theguardian.com/uk-news/2015/jul/30/david-cameron-migrant-swarm-language-condemned The empty square brackets in the extract indicate where some text from the original article has been omitted.

the social function of the language that was used through the way in which it assembles and organizes the interpretations of selected commentators. And, in our examination of the article, the functions of the language used in it and the way in which those functions are achieved, we have also now done some discourse analysis – and a rather complicated form of it, given that we have analysed text (the extract) that is itself analysing text (the words of David Cameron).

Now that you have been initiated into the practice of discourse analysis, we can expand upon the assumptions about language and about our social and psychological worlds on which discourse analysis rests. It is not possible to get very far with discourse analysis unless you really understand these assumptions. If the ideas that are put forward in the next sections are hard to follow, you may find it easier to understand them when you see them applied to data in Chapter 11 and Report 4 (Appendix 2) in this volume. Hence it may be wise to read the present chapter and then turn to those resources before re-reading this chapter. After that, things should start to fall into place.

Discourse analysis and social constructionism

Within the approach to psychology that underlies discourse analysis, language is represented not as reflecting psychological and social reality but as *constructing* it. In other words, the language that we use is not treated as if it reflects some objective truths that exist 'out there' and that can be accessed if we use the appropriate scientific methods. Instead, language in the form of discourses is seen as constituting the building blocks of 'social reality' (note that it is common practice to use inverted commas to draw attention to the constructed nature of taken-for-granted 'things'). The analysis of discourse emphasizes how social reality is built up or constructed through language and it aims to gain 'a better understanding of social life and social interaction from our study of social texts' (Potter and Wetherell, 1987: 7).

Discourse analysis can therefore be classed as a **social constructionist** approach to research. In broad terms, the social constructionist perspective adopts a critical stance towards the taken-for-granted ways in which we understand the world and ourselves, such as the assumption that the categories we use to interpret the world correspond to 'real', 'objective' entities (Burr, 2015). These ways of understanding are seen as having been built up through social processes, especially through linguistic interactions, and are culturally and historically specific (see Box 10.1 for an example).

Most people will concede this to some extent when they think about situations in which we deliberately create a purposeful version of events. For example, when applying for a job, we tend to include on the application form material that shows us in the best possible light. Anything that indicates the sorts of strengths that we want to claim will be emphasized and anything that might weaken our application will be glossed over or, if possible, omitted altogether. In that situation, we are using language to build up a particular version of ourselves that is oriented towards specific ends, that is, securing an interview and ultimately securing the job.

BOX 10.1 — The social construction of sexuality categories

The categories 'gay man', 'lesbian' and 'bisexual' are now a taken-for-granted part of how we talk about sexualities. It is easy to forget that defining people in terms of their consistent, frequent or occasional preference for sexual partners of the same gender as themselves only began in the eighteenth century. Prior to this, there were terms that referred to sexual activity involving people of the same gender but these terms did not denote a particular kind of person. Furthermore, the ways in which these behaviours were socially organized, regulated and responded to varied across cultures. The term 'homosexual' was not coined until the mid-nineteenth century with the increasing medicalization of sexuality. Terms such as 'gay man', 'lesbian' and 'bisexual' were only adopted in the 1960s and 1970s in line with the political concerns of the gay liberation and women's movements (for analyses of the social construction of 'the homosexual' up to that point, see Plummer, 1981). And with the postmodern trend within 'queer theory', concepts of 'the gay man' and 'the lesbian' were later subjected to critical scrutiny (Sedgwick, 1990). Furthermore, the category of 'heterosexual' and the sorts of behaviours and relations associated with it have also changed over time (for example, see Anderson and McCormack's, 2015, research on intimate contact and touch among young heterosexual men). This example illustrates a fundamental contention of social constructionism: there is nothing fixed or inevitable about what may appear to be common-sense ways of representing the world – they are socially constructed.

However, social constructionism goes much further than this, seeing *all* social categories as constructed through language, even those that appear grounded in seemingly fixed qualities. For example, it might be imagined that sex categories of male and female are determined and distinguished through biological considerations. Yet, the existence of intersex people (people whose biological sex cannot be clearly classified as either male or female) shows that this is not the case. The way in which intersex people have been treated by medicine indicates just how much is at stake when people's bodies challenge the social construction of sex categories as an either/or matter (Reis, 2009).

Social constructionism represents what is called the **epistemology** of discourse analysis. Epistemology is a philosophical term that refers to the assumptions we make about what knowledge is, how we generate knowledge, what we know and how we know what we know. It is often discussed alongside **ontology**, which refers to the assumptions we make about the nature of being, existence or reality (and discussions often slip between the two).

All research approaches and methods are based on a set of epistemological assumptions. The emphasis on language as a constructive tool is one of the core assumptions of discourse analysis. The language user is viewed as selecting from the range of linguistic resources available to them (words, phrases, metaphors, clichés, etc.) and using these resources to construct a version of events, although not necessarily in an intentional way. The person may not recognize that they are constructing something when they speak or write but this simply highlights the extent to which the constructive use of language is a fundamental, taken-for-granted aspect of social life – one that we may not even be aware of.

It is important to grasp a major implication that follows from this social constructionist epistemology for psychologists who employ discourse analysis. Unlike most other research approaches in psychology, discourse analysis does not use people's language as a means of gaining access to the 'reality' of their psychological and social worlds. Instead, discourse analysis examines how people use language to construct versions of their worlds (including their psychology) and what is gained socially from these constructions. Its social constructionist commitments make discourse analysis much more than a method: it is a particular way of understanding the social world and so is better thought of as a research perspective or approach.

Within psychology, discourse analysis grew out of the 'turn to language' by some psychologists in the 1980s. It is grounded in a set of assumptions about knowledge that are referred to as social constructionism. As a social constructionist approach, discourse analysis queries the idea that the categories we use to interpret the world correspond to 'real', 'objective' entities. Instead discourse analysts regard language as *constructing* psychological and social realities. In their research, discourse analysts examine how people use language to construct versions of their worlds and the social functions that are performed by these constructions.

BITE-SIZED SUMMARY

1

Defining 'discourse'

So far, I have been referring to 'discourse' analysis but have not yet defined what we mean by 'discourse'. Various meanings have been ascribed to the term. Drawing out the common features, **discourses** can be defined as sets of (written or spoken) linguistic material that have a degree of coherence in their content and organization and that perform constructive functions in broadly defined social contexts. Different discourses can be invoked to construct any object, person, event or situation in a variety of ways. Some discourses are standard resources for sense-making in particular cultures (see Box 10.2). Incidentally, it is worth noting that, in their classic text, Potter and Wetherell (1987) preferred the term 'interpretative repertoires' rather than 'discourses' because they said the idea of 'repertoire' implies flexibility in the ways in which the linguistic components of the repertoire can be put together. This term is still used in some forms of discourse analysis within psychology.

> **BOX 10.2** **Liberal individualism as a culturally hegemonic discourse**

One standard discourse used in many different social contexts in the Western world is the discourse of liberal individualism. Within this discourse, the public sphere is constructed as populated by autonomous individuals who have rights not to be unduly interfered with by society (Marquand, 1991).

Consider how a father might justify his decision to pay for his daughter to be educated at a private school (for which fees are paid) rather than at a local state school. He might say that it is his right as a parent to do whatever he thinks necessary to obtain the best education for his daughter in order to improve her chances of success in later life. He might explain that the high quality facilities and small class sizes offered by private schools increase the likelihood of her obtaining a good education. This justification is constructed within a discourse of liberal individualism. Claims about the 'right to choose' are based upon a liberal assumption that the individual's choices should be tolerated and respected (usually provided they are legal), even if, in making those choices, the individual does not contribute to or even undermines the common good. So a friend might challenge the father by saying that, by opting out of state education, he absolves himself from the need to lobby for and contribute to improvements in his local state school, leaving this to those parents who cannot pay for private education. In such a discussion, the father who speaks from within a discourse of liberal individualism, emphasizing his right to do the best for his daughter, may seem reasonable and may 'win out' because he is using a standard discourse for making sense of our actions and one that seems entirely reasonable because it is so commonplace. The term that is sometimes applied to such dominant, powerful discourses is 'hegemonic'. The friend who argues against it by stressing the importance of the collective may end up being dismissed as 'politically motivated'.

Approaches to discourse analysis

Discourse analysis assumes that linguistic material has an **action orientation**: language is used to perform particular social actions or functions such as justifying, questioning and accusing. Key tasks that discourse analysts set themselves within this action-oriented approach are (a) to identify what functions are being performed by the linguistic material that is being analysed; (b) to consider how these functions are performed and what resources are available to perform these functions. This entails a close and careful inspection of qualitative textual data. There are different approaches to the study of discourse within psychology. In this section, we consider the main approaches.

Discursive psychology

The approach known as **discursive psychology** was developed principally by Jonathan Potter and Derek Edwards (Edwards and Potter, 1992; Potter, 1996 – for a history, see Wiggins and Potter, 2008). Discursive psychologists tend to be concerned with the detail of talk. In this, they adopt and adapt approaches drawn from conversation analysis (see Atkinson and Heritage, 1984). Discursive psychology views language as a form of social action, addresses the social functions of talk and considers how these functions are achieved. It is particularly attentive to the ways in which 'factual' accounts and descriptions (which might be interpreted by other research approaches as straightforward 'objective' representations of internal or external psychological and/or social realities) are made to appear as such (that is, 'factual').

The identification of 'discourses' tends not to be part of discursive psychology. Its concerns are more localized, focused on the data under study, rather than moving beyond the data and seeking the sort of broad patterns associated with the term 'discourses'. Discursive psychologists are interested in discursive practices – what people *do* with language – and how people negotiate meaning through linguistic interactions in everyday settings and institutional contexts. An example of discursive psychological research that has examined talk in an everyday setting is provided by Hepburn and Potter's (2011) analysis of video-recordings of family meal times involving pre-school children. By closely examining the language of the parents and children, they showed how threats were done in this context by the parents when the children failed to conform to behavioural requirements (for example, by not eating their food) and how the children responded to the threats. Through the insights that were gained, the research challenges the way in which social psychology has traditionally understood and studied social influence; it presents discursive psychology as an alternative.

An example of a study on talk in an institutional context is provided by Hepburn and Wiggins' (2005) analysis of transcripts of telephone calls to a helpline run by the UK National Society for the Prevention of Cruelty to Children (NSPCC). They focused on parts of the calls that included discussions about body size, weight or food issues. Their analysis shed light on how body size can be made relevant in talk to hold people accountable for their actions – in this case, childcare practices. The concerns of the research in these examples are recognizably psychological – social influence and children's well-being. However these are not seen as located within individuals' heads but as thoroughly social, as worked up through linguistic interaction.

Foucauldian discourse analysis

Discursive psychology has been represented as politically limited by some researchers who are more concerned with issues such as identity and selfhood, ideology, power relations and social change. This perspective has been termed **Foucauldian discourse analysis** because it is said to owe a particular debt to the work and/or commitments of the philosopher Michel Foucault. This form of discourse analysis arose from the work of Ian Parker, Erica Burman and Wendy Hollway (for example, Burman and Parker, 1993a; Hollway, 1989; Parker, 1992). Writers within Foucauldian discourse analysis see the world as having a structural reality, which they usually describe in terms of power relations; these are viewed as underpinning how we understand and talk about the world (Burr, 2015). The Foucauldian approach holds that discourses 'facilitate and limit, enable and constrain what can be said, by whom, where and when' (Willig, 2013: 130). Hence, dominant, hegemonic discourses privilege versions of social reality that accord with and reinforce existing social structures and the networks of power relations associated with them. Analysts study the availability of **discursive resources** within a culture and the implications that this carries for those living within that culture.

To take an example, Spohrer (2011) drew upon Foucauldian ideas in her discourse analysis of how 'aspiration' is constructed in policy debates about how young people can be encouraged to participate in education and employment in the UK. Her analysis of government reports, discussion papers and speeches found that the debate on 'aspiration' constructs young people from disadvantaged backgrounds as lacking in aspiration and deficient; translates social structural problems of inequality into individual, psychologized problems; and constructs disadvantaged young people as being responsible for promoting their own economic status through aspiring to achieve. Although this research was not conducted by a psychologist, it is concerned with how psychological discourse is used to construct young people in problematic ways. Much discourse analytic work shares this quality: it is *about* psychology or, more specifically, about psychological discourse.

One feature of discourse analytic research that is associated with Foucauldian discourse analysis is **positioning**. This comes from the work of Bronwyn Davies and Rom Harré (1990) and represents one discursive interpretation of the social psychological concept of identity. When an individual is constructed through discourse, they are accorded a particular **subject position** within that discourse, which brings with it a set of images, metaphors and obligations concerning the kind of response that can be made. For example, within a bio-medical discourse, people who are ill are placed in the subject position of 'the patient', with its obligation to act as a passive recipient of care from those who are placed in the subject position of 'medical experts'. In their linguistic response to that positioning, the individual can accept it (and fulfil the obligations of their position) or they can resist it. Of course, the person can also position themselves within a discourse and their audience can accept or reject this positioning. Any individual may assume some positions fairly consistently within their talk while other positions are more temporary, giving rise to variability. By adopting, rejecting or negotiating the subject positions offered within a discourse, the user of that discourse is constructed as a subject. As Davies and Harré (1999: 35) commented, the question of 'who one is [ ] is always an open question with a shifting answer depending upon the positions made available within one's own and others' discursive practices'.

An example of an analysis of positioning is provided by Willig (2011) who used Foucauldian discourse analysis to reflect critically on constructions of cancer and associated subject positions. Unusually, her data were reflections on her own experiences after receiving a cancer diagnosis. She identified two main constructions which she termed the 'cultural imperative to "think positively"' and the construction of 'cancer as a moral concern'. The 'think positively' imperative was said to impose the requirement that the person with cancer demonstrate a belief that things will turn out well and all problems will

---

BOX 10.3 | **Positioning in action**

Below is a short extract from a conversation between two men in their early twenties called Will and Pete. They are in the second year of their degree course. They are not close friends but have met up several times to work on a shared project for their degree. Pete has had a disability since birth and uses a wheelchair; Will is non-disabled. The conversation from which this extract is taken occurred over coffee after they had finished discussing their shared project.

Will: I don't mean to be patronising but I think it's remarkable the way you handle it [disability], you really seem to be on top of it and determined to make the best of it and look for the positive.

Pete: I don't think so at all, you just have to get on with it and keep the show on the road as much as you can, it's a lot more difficult than other people think sometimes.

- What positioning can you see going on or being negotiated in the extract?

- What other data would you need to allow you to draw more confident conclusions about positioning here?

- Thinking of the positions that you have discerned, what discourses or constructions might they be associated with? Any answers that you provide will have to be quite speculative because you have only been given a very short data extract to work with.

be resolved, that they 'fight' their cancer and do not accept it as it is. These can be seen as subject positions within the 'think positively' discourse. The 'cancer as a moral concern' discourse constructed cancer as having been brought about by the self and lifestyle choices and as a sign of some sort of moral failure. This was seen to place the person with cancer in the subject position of having to accept responsibility and adopt a more committed approach to their health and well-being.

Critical discursive psychology and critical discourse analysis

In addition to the two approaches outlined so far, a third approach has emerged which attends both to the detail of linguistic interaction in a particular context and to broader patterns in collective linguistic sense-making. This has been termed **critical discursive psychology**. It aims to combine the foci adopted by discursive psychology and Foucauldian discourse analysis and thereby create a rich, extensive analysis.

The tenets of critical discursive psychology were expounded by Margaret Wetherell (1998) and were initially applied in her work on masculinities with Nigel Edley (for example, Edley and Wetherell, 1999). In a more recent example, Jingree and Finlay (2013) used critical discursive psychology to examine expressions of dissatisfaction and complaint about social care services by people with learning disabilities during research interviews. Critical discursive psychology can also be seen in action in the study by Simon Goodman and Lottie Rowe in Appendix 2 (Report 4) in this volume, in which they consider how opposition towards Gypsies is debated in internet discussion forums.

A final approach that is worth noting is **critical discourse analysis**. This overlaps with Foucauldian discourse analysis in that it is concerned with how the abuse of social power, dominance and inequality are enacted, reproduced and resisted in text and talk in social and political settings. It is a form of discourse analysis that is more commonly encountered outside psychology than within. For an overview of this approach, see Wodak and Meyer (2009).

BITE-SIZED SUMMARY

2

Discourses can be defined as sets of linguistic material that have a degree of coherence in their content and organization and that perform constructive functions in broadly defined social contexts. Dominant, powerful discourses are described as 'hegemonic'. Three approaches to discourse analysis within psychology have been described: discursive psychology, Foucauldian discourse analysis and critical discursive psychology. The different emphases and foci of these approaches were described and illustrated. Critical discourse analysis was also noted but this is more usually applied in other disciplines.

Discourse analytic research questions

Although discourse analysis has been used to investigate a wide variety of research topics, it is only appropriate for the exploration of particular types of research questions. Many research questions from elsewhere in psychology are based on a logic of factors and outcomes, whereas discourse analytic research questions focus on construction, rhetoric, ideology and action.

Potter (2003) identified four foci in discourse analytic research questions (see Table 10.1; see also Box 11.1 in Chapter 11 in this volume). With these critical and analytic foci, it is not surprising that discourse analysis has been taken up with enthusiasm by those who wish to give psychology a radical, political edge. Some analysts choose to focus on discourses which reproduce social relations of dominance and oppression and/or which include oppressive aspects that are often glossed over. Discourse analysis can be used to indicate that alternative discourses could be developed and promoted in their place. Yet it is important to acknowledge that the supplanting of oppressive discourses is a complex and lengthy process and there is no way of predicting with confidence what the social implications of discursive change might be.

Table 10.1 Four foci in discourse analytic research questions (Potter, 2003)

Foci of research questions	Examples
How specific actions and practices are linguistically done in particular settings.	Kurz et al. (2010) examined how politicians from the major Australian political parties invoked and managed the issue of 'climate change' in parliamentary debates, public speeches, media interviews and press releases in the run-up to the 2007 general election there.
How particular accounts of things are constructed and made to seem factual and objective or how seemingly factual accounts are challenged.	Horton-Salway (2007) examined how medics and members of myalgic encephalomyelitis (ME) support groups construct relevant illness categories. In her analysis, she showed how support group members sought to establish the genuineness (or factual-ness) of their condition by contrasting themselves with those whom they constructed as having less serious conditions but as having 'jumped on the bandwagon' (of ME).
Psychological practice: this involves re-framing psychological concepts in discursive terms.	Liebert and Gavey (2009) interviewed professionals who had a stake in supporting the use of a particular class of drugs for treating depression. The research question asked how, in their talk, these professionals managed the dilemma created by research evidence that these drugs can be harmful. Participants were found to use language that minimized the significance of risks, emphasized notions of benefit and/or questioned the validity of risks.
Exploitation, prejudice and ideology: this involves examining how racism, sexism, ageism, homophobia and other oppressions are expressed, justified or rendered invisible.	Wetherell and Potter's (1992) extensive study of racist language and practice in New Zealand is a classic example of this type of research. This was extended by Lyons et al.'s (2011) study of how young adults in New Zealand talked about and understood immigration, immigrants and cultural diversity, and the functions and implications of these understandings for power relations, race relations and the construction of immigrant groups.

Sampling text

In order to conduct an analysis of discourse, researchers need access to texts in which they can discern discourses, the linguistic resources offered by those discourses and the uses to which these resources are put by speakers or writers. All spoken and written material can be conceptualized as a text and subjected to discourse analysis.

There has been some debate among researchers about the most appropriate types of data for discourse analysis. Potter (1997) has argued that 'naturally occurring' data (that is, data that would have been available anyway if the researcher had not been present) are preferable to interview data (see also Potter and Hepburn, 2005). His reasoning is that research interviews are contrived contexts and the data generated there tell us more about the demands of the interview context, which interviewees are assumed to orient towards, than anything else. 'Naturally occurring' data include transcripts of telephone conversations, articles from newspapers and magazines, transcripts of television programmes, web pages, discussions on internet forums and song lyrics. The examples of discursive psychology research by Hepburn and Wiggins (2005) and Hepburn and Potter (2011) that were given earlier used naturally occurring data, as did Spohrer (2011) in her study which applied Foucauldian discourse analysis and the study reported by Goodman and Rowe in Appendix 2 (this volume) which used critical discursive psychology. Other researchers have defended the use of interview data in discourse analytic work and have argued that the different agendas of interviewers and interviewees can be a focus for interesting analysis (for example, see Griffin, 2007) or have argued that a distinction between 'natural' and 'contrived' data does not really stand up to scrutiny (Speer, 2002). In practice, discourse analytic studies have used a wide range of data sources.

Within traditional approaches to sampling in psychological research, the emphasis is placed upon securing as large and representative a sample as possible. Within discourse analysis, if interview material is used as a source of data, there is no necessity to sample discourse from a large number of people. If newspaper reports of a particular event are to be used, it is not necessary to collect all reports from all newspapers on that event. The analysis stage of qualitative data is almost always more laborious and time-consuming than the analysis of structured data so researchers must beware of ending up with an unmanageable amount of unstructured data to sift through. What is important is to gather enough text to discern the variety of discursive forms that are commonly used when speaking or writing about the research topic. This may be possible from an analysis of relatively few interview transcripts or newspaper reports, especially where common discursive forms are under consideration. In this case, larger samples of data add to the analytic task without adding significantly to the analytic outcome. Where an analysis is purely exploratory and the analyst has little idea in advance of what the analytic focus might be, larger samples of data are required.

Recordings of talk in interaction (whether 'naturally occurring' or in interviews) needs to be transcribed before analysis. Accurate transcription of recordings is a lengthy process which is made even more laborious if the transcriber wishes to include every 'um' and 'uh' uttered by the speakers and to measure pauses in speech production. This sort of detailed approach is less often seen in discourse analysis than in conversation analysis, although it is good methodological practice to produce as detailed a transcription as you can. For more on transcription, see Box 11.2 in Chapter 11 in this volume.

How do you *do* discourse analysis? Some pointers towards practice

Whilst it is relatively easy to present the central theoretical tenets of discourse analysis, spec-ifying exactly how you go about *doing* discourse analysis is a different matter because there is no clear, agreed set of formal procedures. It has been contended that the key to analysing discourse is scholarship and the development of an analytic mentality rather than adherence to a rigorous methodology (Billig, 1988). The emphasis is placed upon the careful reading and interpretation of texts, with interpretations being backed by reference to linguistic evi-dence in the data. The first step is said to be the suspension of belief in what is normally taken for granted in language use (Potter and Wetherell, 1987). This involves seeing linguistic practices not as simply reflecting underlying psychological and social realities but as con-structing and legitimating a version of events.

However, I cannot help feeling that a more systematic methodological approach would be helpful to someone who is undertaking discourse analysis for the first time, especially given the uncertainties and challenges that have been reported by novice discourse analysts (see Harper et al., 2008). It is all very well to suggest that to conduct discourse analysis, you need to develop 'a sensitivity to the way in which language is used', especially to the 'inferential and interactional aspects of talk' (Widdicombe, 1993: 97). Yet, it is unclear exactly how this sensitivity is developed and systematized. In an attempt to provide some pointers, Potter and Wetherell (1987) provided a loose ten-stage approach, with two stages devoted to the analytic process. Wiggins and Potter (2008) have suggested that doing dis-cursive psychology involves working through a specified range of activities in no particular order (with one exception: see below). Willig (2013) has outlined six stages of Foucauldian discourse analysis which can be seen in Table 10.2. These stages will not be elaborated here because Chris Walton applies them to data in Chapter 11 in this volume and provides a clear, evaluative account of how they worked in practice.

While certain foci are particularly characteristic of individual approaches to dis-course analysis, some key analytic concerns are shared across approaches. Wiggins and Potter (2008) suggest that, in doing discursive psychology, you should start by coding the data. This is an ideal starting point regardless of the approach to discourse analysis you are using. If the research focus has been specified in advance, you should identify instances of the research focus within the data at this point. For example, in the study by Liebert and Gavey (2009) that was outlined in Table 10.1, the research question focused on how professionals who advocated the use of a particular class of drugs managed the dilemma created by research evidence that these drugs can be harmful. The initial focus for coding

Table 10.2 Willig's (2013) stages of Foucauldian discourse analysis

Stages	Analytic questions associated with each stage
1. Discursive constructions	In what ways are the discursive objects (the phenomena of interest to the research) constructed?
2. Discourses	In which wider discourses are the discursive constructions of the objects located?
3. Action orientation	What is gained from constructing the discursive objects in this way at this point in the text? What are the functions of these constructions? How do they relate to other constructions in the surrounding text?
4. Positionings	What subject positions are offered to the speaker(s) or writer(s) and others by the discourses that are invoked in the text?
5. Practice	In what ways do the discursive constructions and the subject positions offered within them open up or close down opportunities for action?
6. Subjectivity	What consequences follow from taking up the subject positions that have been discerned for speakers' or writers' subjective experience? In other words, what can be felt, thought and experienced by the speakers or writers from within those subject positions?

would be responses to the raising of the research evidence in the interviews. Do participants treat this as dilemmatic – as interactionally troubling? How do you know? How do they respond linguistically? Seeking answers to these questions in the data will generate some initial codes. It is worth being as inclusive as possible and noting what appear to be borderline instances of the research focus. This makes it possible to discern less obvious but nonetheless fruitful lines of inquiry.

The coding process is more complex if the research focus has not been determined in advance. In this case, it is necessary to read and re-read the text, looking for recurrent discursive patterns shared by the accounts under analysis. This is what Chris Walton and I had to do when we undertook the discourse analytic part of a multi-method study of public 'attitudes' towards new genetic technologies in the UK (or, from a discourse analytic perspective, social constructions of these technologies) (Shepherd et al., 2007). The research focus on public 'attitudes' was so broad that we had to adopt an open, inclusive approach to the coding of data drawn from the media and focus group interviews. As the coding progressed, we discerned patterns in how new genetic technologies were being constructed in the data set. For example, the idea of these technologies 'interfering with nature' was a recurrent feature. We then coded in a more specific way, looking for other instances of these patterns which would expand our sense of how they operated in the data while at the same time remaining open to the identification of new patterns. Widdicombe's (1993) notion of sensitivity to the way in which language is used becomes important at this stage. Impressions about which discourses are being invoked and which constructions are being advanced in the text are developed and reformulated in light of whether the linguistic evidence needed to support them is available. It is important that the analyst should remain open to alternative readings of the text and to the need to reject preliminary impressions that are not supported by the text.

Note that, with a large data set, it may be worth using appropriate software to help organize and code the data, such as NVivo (Silver and Lewins, 2014), as we did in the research on new genetic technologies. If you are coding spoken data that you have transcribed, it is worth listening to the original recordings as well as reading the transcripts because this will allow you to hear how language was used in context and to develop more nuanced codes.

A useful strategy for the next stage of analysis involves reading the text mindful of what its functions might be. Remember that any text is held to have an action orientation and is oriented towards fulfilling certain functions, so the question is 'What functions is this text fulfilling and how is it fulfilling them?' The formulation of hypotheses about the purposes and consequences of language use is central to discourse analysis. However, identifying the functions of language is often not a straightforward process because these functions may not be explicit. For example, when someone asks you to do something, they may phrase it not as an order or command ('Do the washing up') but as a question to which the expected answer is 'Yes' ('Would you like to do the washing up?').

In seeking to identify discursive functions, a useful starting point is the discursive context. It can be difficult to identify function from limited sections of a text. A variety of functions may be performed and revisited throughout a text, so it is necessary to be familiar with what precedes and follows a particular extract in order to obtain clues about its functions. Although Foucauldian discourse analysts also emphasize context, they attach a specific meaning to the term. Parker and Burman (1993) have stated that the analyst needs to be aware of broader contextual concerns such as cultural trends and political and social issues to which the text alludes.

To take an example, in the study of constructions of new genetic technologies, some views were expressed in the focus groups that closed down the possibility of further discussion on the issue for the speaker and at times for the other participants interacting with that individual. One such 'bottom-line' resource in discussions of cloning technologies was the invocation of the status of the embryo as human life (Shepherd et al., 2007: 386–7). For example:

Megan: That's absolutely fine if they take your own stem cells but taking embryonic stem cells I don't think is right, [ ] they're experimenting on embryos at the moment to extract their stem cells and then the thing dies basically

Amy: Not fully grown embryos

Megan: It's still human life, isn't it?

By looking at what happened in the data after these invocations, we could see that participants did not continue to contest the substance of the argument being made by the person who invoked the status of the embryo as human life. In the extract above, Amy does so ('Not fully grown embryos') but does not persist after Megan explicitly states her conviction that embryos are 'human life'. Our knowledge of other cultural debates involving the status of the human embryo, such as debates on the ethics of abortion, suggested why this invocation functioned successfully as a bottom-line resource – because to continue to challenge the argument that was being made could have steered the discussion onto highly controversial, personal and interactionally difficult terrain.

Another analytic strategy that may be helpful is to examine a text in a situated way, mindful of what version of events it may be designed to counteract. Any version of events is but one of a number of possible versions and therefore must be constructed as more per-suasive than these alternative versions if it is to prevail. Sometimes alternative versions will be explicitly mentioned and counteracted in a text (for example, in a transcript of court pro-ceedings) but on other occasions they will be implicit. If analysts are sensitized to what these alternative versions might be, they may be well placed to analyse how the text addresses the function of legitimating the version that is being promoted.

In analysing function, it is useful to become acquainted with the ways in which various features of talk and written text are described in the discourse analytic (and conver-sation analytic) literature. These discursive features frequently perform specific functions. Therefore, if analysts are able to identify these features, they can examine the text mindful of the functions that these features typically perform. For example, the use of terms such as 'always', 'never', 'nobody' or 'everyone' may represent what have been called 'extreme case formulations' (Pomerantz, 1986). These take whatever position is being advocated in the text to its extreme and thereby help to make this position more persuasive. When people provide lists of things in talk, these lists routinely consist of three parts or elements (Jefferson, 1990). In conversation, 'three-part lists' signal the end of a specific point in the speaker's argument but, in other texts, they work up the persuasiveness of an account by cre-ating a sense of comprehensiveness. For those interested in becoming acquainted with these technical features of discourse, Potter (1996) outlined a wide range but the best strategy is to examine studies that have used discourse analytic and conversation analytic approaches.

According to Potter and Wetherell (1987), one way of identifying the functions of texts is through the study of variability in any text. The fact that talk or writing varies might seem a common-sense statement. If we were analysing talk or writing from different people about a particular phenomenon, we would expect variations related to whether individuals eval-uated the phenomenon positively or negatively. However, variation also occurs *within* an individual's talk/writing, depending upon the purposes of the talk/writing. The same applies to talk within groups: a group might negotiate an agreed outlook on something at one point and then qualify or completely change that outlook at another point. Variability in formal writing may be harder to discern than in free-flowing talk because the writer is likely to have had a chance to review their words before publishing them. This does not apply so much to text from internet discussion forums where contributors tend to write more responsively, and variability can often be readily found within individual contributors' writing.

> ## BOX 10.4   Considering some textual features
>
> Go back to the extract at the start of this chapter from *The Guardian*'s article on David Cameron's language about refugees. Re-read what I said there about the functions of the language in the extract.
>
> - Find examples of extreme case formulations and three-part lists in the extract.
>
> - How do these features contribute to the functions being performed by the text?
>
> - Can you discern any other functions that they might also perform here?

It has been claimed that, in their search for individual consistency, mainstream approaches to psychology have sought to minimize or explain away intra-individual variation (Potter and Wetherell, 1987). Discourse analysis, in contrast, actively seeks it out. If we accept that variability in a text arises from the different functions that the text may be fulfilling at different points, the nature of the variation can provide clues to what these functions are. To take an example from the study on responses to new genetic technologies, in one focus group the participants negotiated a clear consensus at an early stage that the development of genetically modified foods was something negative – an instance of 'interfering with nature' that could have unanticipated adverse effects on health and the environment. As the discussion progressed, participants continued to invoke this 'nature' discourse as they spoke about other emergent genetic technologies. In this, they occupied subject positions as 'environmental guardians' and 'informed commentators who can see the bigger picture'. The function of their talk seemed at least partly oriented towards the construction and enactment of a collective view of the group as right-thinking in the sense of being concerned for the welfare of the planet and humanity.

However, quite late in the discussion, one participant, who had not contributed previously, said that she was a single mother who had to feed her family on a tight budget and she did not care whether foodstuffs were genetically modified as long as they were cheap and affordable. The talk that followed this intervention saw the discussion draw back from the initial consensus and shift towards a concerted consideration of situations in which the production and consumption of genetically modified foods would be acceptable. In this, participants spoke from 'balanced' and 'inclusive' subject positions. Here the function of their talk seemed to be oriented towards accommodating the dissident speaker and other potentially dissident views while hanging on to as much as possible of the construction of the group as 'right-thinking'. Their initial concern for an abstract notion of humanity now had to accommodate the expressed and imagined priorities of *specific* humans!

If we were adopting a different research approach and were trying to find participants' 'real attitudes' from the data, we would have to choose between the early definitively expressed view and the later qualified view. Using discourse analysis, we are interested in the construction and negotiation of versions of things rather than individuals' attitudes and so our analysis would fully incorporate both views *and* the turning point afforded by one speaker's intervention. The variability in the data here would be explained in terms of what we might call the interactional business of the talk and the subject positions adopted.

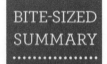

BITE-SIZED SUMMARY

3

Discourse analytic research addresses particular types of research questions. These focus on how the phenomena of interest to the research (including psychological practice) are constructed through language; how actions and practices are done in language; and how types of oppression operate through language. Any spoken or written materials (referred to as 'texts') can be suitable as data for discourse analytic research. The key consideration in sampling is to gather enough text to discern the variety of discursive forms that are commonly used when speaking or writing about the research topic. It can be difficult to specify exactly how to do discourse analysis but some writers have identified stages in the process or foci for analysis. These include an initial coding phase followed by the identification of the functions being performed by the text and how those functions are performed. This can be done by examining relevant parts of the text in context; considering what versions of events particular parts of the text may be oriented towards counteracting; identifying textual features that frequently perform specific functions; and attending to variability within the text.

Quality and usefulness of discourse analytic research

It might sometimes seem as if discourse analysts are overly complicating straightforward uses of speech and writing and are reading too much into their data. In Chapter 11 in this volume, Chris Walton reports on how his research group felt unsettled at having to draw so much upon their subjective understandings when analysing positioning. Yet discourse analysts are not free to put forward whatever interpretations they want: they have to be mindful of whether their interpretations satisfy criteria for a 'good analysis'.

There has been some debate about what those criteria might be for discourse analysis and for qualitative research more generally (see Chapter 2 in this volume). Discussions about the evaluation of psychological research tend to focus on concerns about reliability and validity. These criteria are based on the assumption of 'scientific objectivity' which in turn assumes that the researcher and those who are researched are independent of each other. With discourse analysis, this cannot be the case. Analysts who demonstrate the socially constructed nature of other people's talk and writing cannot make an exception for their own talk and writing. Like the people whose language they are analysing, analysts construct a purposeful account of their texts, drawing upon their available linguistic resources and ideological frameworks. In my own discourse analytic research, factors such as my training as a social psychologist, my familiarity with existing work relevant to the research topics, my political outlook and my personal commitments all influence the **interpretative framework** that I bring to bear on the analyses. Acknowledging this and reflecting upon it is termed **reflexivity**. It should not be seen as undermining the analysis because no one can adopt a perspective-less, 'objective' stance on the world. Instead, it should be seen as part of a process of making research more accountable, more transparent and easier to evaluate.

This reflexivity bridges the chasm that more traditional research approaches create between the researcher and the researched and makes it impossible to assess an analysis of discourse using traditional evaluative criteria. In Chapter 11 (Box 11.6), Chris Walton identifies more suitable criteria for evaluating discourse analytic research and invites you to apply them. The most basic criterion though is whether an analysis is persuasively grounded in relevant data. Researchers should demonstrate how analytic conclusions were reached with reference to the data and should illustrate all interpretations with sufficient relevant data. Readers can then judge for themselves whether the interpretations are credible. They can offer alternative readings of the text so that, through debate, coherent and persuasive interpretations can be achieved.

A fundamental concern that has been expressed about discourse analysis from its early days is that it is far removed from 'real-life' issues and threatens psychologists' aspirations to influence practices and policies outside the research domain. If we accept that 'Language (organized into *discourses*) ... has an immense power to shape the way that people ... experience and behave in the world' (Burman and Parker, 1993b: 1, emphasis in original), discourse analysis *does* have considerable practical potential. Willig (1999) produced an edited volume entitled *Applied Discourse Analysis* which demonstrated how discourse analysis can inform social and psychological interventions on issues such as smoking, sex education and psychiatric medication. Since then, others have developed this case for the practical value of the insights produced by discourse analysis (for example, see Hepburn and Wiggins, 2007) and have routinely oriented to the implications of discourse analytic work for practice in diverse domains (for example, see Hepburn, 2006, on how her analysis of calls to an NSPCC helpline was found useful by call takers).

> ### BOX 10.5 — Reflecting upon discourse analysis
>
> Consider the questions below. If possible, check your responses with others who have also studied or used discourse analysis. This will help clarify and develop your understanding of the approach.
>
> - In light of your reading about other qualitative approaches to psychological research, what do you think are the main ways in which discourse analysis overlaps with them and differs from them?
>
> - Think of research questions for which discourse analysis would *not* be appropriate. What is it about these questions that makes them unsuitable for exploration through discourse analysis?
>
> - What might be the main obstacles to using discourse analysis alongside other research approaches to explore a particular research question?
>
> - If you are a student and were using discourse analysis in a dissertation, how would you convince classmates who used other approaches that your research was as potentially 'useful' as theirs?

CHAPTER SUMMARY

This chapter has presented the principles and practicalities of discourse analysis, illustrated by examples from my own discourse analytic work and the research of others. Although I have provided some useful pointers about how discourse analysis might be undertaken, I also hope that readers have gained a clear sense of how discourse analysis cannot be treated merely as an analytic technique. Researchers who choose to use discourse analysis also choose to employ a range of assumptions about the social world and should ensure that their contextualization of their study (for example, in a literature review), research questions, analyses and discussion of the implications of the research fit with these assumptions. In conclusion, it is fair to say that, while discourse analysis is perhaps not a research approach for the faint-hearted, nonetheless for those who can work with text in a sustained, detailed way and who relish the idea of asking critical questions about taken-for-granted dimensions of social life, it can prove extremely rewarding. Moreover, as Abell and Walton (2010) have indicated, even if you do not sign up to the whole discourse analytic enterprise, you can take its insights about language as a site where psychological life is produced and played out and you can usefully integrate these into other forms of psychological research. A pluralistic approach to qualitative research offers one way of doing this (see Chapter 14 in this volume for more on this).

Further reading

Potter and Wetherell's (1987) very readable and broad-ranging text *Discourse and Social Psychology: Beyond Attitudes and Behaviour* remains the obvious starting point for anyone interested in discourse analysis, together with Burr's (2015) extensive and accessible book on *Social Constructionism*. The volumes by Wetherell et al. (2001a, 2001b) and Potter (2007a, 2007b, 2007c) are invaluable to novice analysts as they focus on the process of analysis within different traditions and present a wide range of examples. Willig's (1999) *Applied Discourse Analysis: Social and Psychological Interventions* provides examples of how different versions of discourse analysis can inform interventions on a range of practical issues.

Articles that offer interesting examples of discourse analysis with practical relevance are those by Hepburn and Wiggins (2005), in which they present their analysis of transcripts of telephone calls to an NSPCC helpline, and by Jingree and Finlay (2008), in which they examine how support staff working with people with learning disabilities talk about choice and control for service users. In Appendix 2 in this volume, readers will find Goodman and Rowe's discourse analytic report on arguments about racism in discussion forums about Gypsies. For a longer version of this report, see Goodman and Rowe (2014). Readers who are interested in other analyses that Simon Goodman has undertaken on talk about racism and prejudice may wish to consult Goodman and Burke's (2010) analysis of discussions about whether it is racist to oppose asylum seeking. Their analysis links back to the observations with which we began this chapter on the newspaper article about David Cameron's language about refugees.

11

DOING DISCOURSE ANALYSIS

Chris Walton

This chapter presents one researcher's account of how a research group applied Foucauldian discourse analysis to transcripts of two interviews with ex-soldiers which offered accounts of being in and leaving the army and of post-army life. The chapter begins by identifying the discursive objects that were the primary foci of the analysis and then provides an account of how the various stages of the analytic process were negotiated and what they produced. Consideration is given to alternative research questions that could have been asked of the data and the different transcription formats that may be used in discourse analytic research. Comparisons are offered with other forms of discourse analysis and questions are raised about some aspects of Foucauldian discourse analysis.

Introduction

After conducting discourse analysis with accounts of leaving the army, the group of researchers that I had worked with reflected on what we had learned. We concluded that 'doing discourse analysis' was not really about following the steps of a particular method. Instead it was more concerned with developing confidence in how we used analytic concepts and working out how to report our analysis in ways that were consistent with the theories and epistemological positions of discourse analysis. In other words, doing discourse analysis seemed to us to be about achieving a familiarity with and a fluency in the use of the analytic concepts relevant to the various forms of discourse analysis.

To begin the chapter with such a statement might be off-putting to readers who are looking for a step-by-step account of 'how to do discourse analysis' based upon our experiences. Do not fear! This chapter *will* provide a step-by-step account of our analytic work but

I have deliberately begun with our reflections on the process of doing discourse analysis to emphasize that this sort of **reflexivity** was central to our performance of discourse analysis. In Chapter 8, Sheila Payne described reflexivity as the acknowledgement by the researcher of the role they play in creating their analytic account (see also the coverage of researchers' 'speaking positions' in Chapter 2). Whilst I will provide an account of the step-by-step workings of our analysis, I will, in parallel, also offer an account of our reflexive concerns about the work that we were doing at each step. Also, I need to point out that, while I am offering an account of the analyses and reflections of an analytic group, this is very much *my* account of the analytic process. Other group members may have represented the analytic process in a different way and emphasized different considerations.

The following analysis focuses on 12 researchers' work on two transcripts of interviews with ex-soldiers (see Appendix 1 in this volume) over a period of two days (approximately 16 hours of working time in total). In keeping with the focus of the research that generated the data, we chose a form of analysis that would produce findings that might be applied to the real-life problems faced by ex-soldiers in their transition to civilian life. The approach that we chose was **Foucauldian discourse analysis** (Willig, 2013), which provides for discussion of subjectivity and possibilities for practice (see Box 10.2 in Chapter 10 in this volume for an outline of the stages of Foucauldian discourse analysis). That said, in common with Willig (2013), we recognized that, in working towards engaging with practice and subjectivity, we would be working through levels of analysis shared by other forms of discourse analysis. For example, identifying the various ways in which the phenomena of interest to the research are constructed is common to all forms of discourse analysis, while a focus on the action orientation of talk is a primary feature of the discursive psychology approach (Edwards and Potter, 1992) and the identification of **discourses** is common to the critical discursive psychology approach (Wetherell, 1998) and to other forms of discourse analysis (see Chapter 10). Consequently, the descriptions of the various stages of our analysis are relevant to readers who are thinking about pursuing forms of discourse analysis other than a Foucauldian approach. However, whether we ever actually managed to produce a Foucauldian discourse analysis of the interview transcripts is debatable. This concern will be oriented to at the end of the chapter.

The research questions

Before we read the two interviews with ex-soldiers that were to be our data, as a group we tried to outline what our analytic interests were. We tried to formulate research questions that would guide our readings of the interviews and be compatible with the theoretical underpinnings of discourse analysis. This is always a useful starting point for doing a discourse analysis and indeed for doing any sort of qualitative analysis. The interviews were taken from a study concerned with ex-soldiers' experiences of leaving the army and the challenges this presented for them in terms of changes to their identity or sense of self. Therefore, the research questions that seemed sensible to us and that fitted with a discourse analytic focus on construction and function were:

- How did David and Brian construct the experience of leaving the army?

- How did they construct their army and post-army identities?

- What functions were served by these identities?

These questions, we felt, provided us with three discursive objects that would guide our initial readings. **Discursive objects** are the phenomena of interest to a research study. The study seeks to explore how these phenomena are constructed in talk, writing and/or other forms of text. In this case, our discursive objects are 'the experience of leaving the army', the 'army identity' and the 'post-army identity'. We hoped that a focus on these discursive objects and the functions they served within the interview and in wider contexts would allow us to move through the stages of discourse analysis.

BOX 11.1	What makes a discourse analytic research question?

As you can see from the other qualitative methods covered in this book, the types of questions asked by researchers using one or other qualitative approaches or methods vary in their focus. These differences are a direct consequence of the different episte-mological positions underlying each of the methods (that is, the assumptions a method makes about the bases or possibilities for knowledge). At the simplest level, research questions vary according to whether the method adopts a realist or constructionist **epistemology**; that is, whether the method admits the possibility of examining what people *really* think, feel or experience or whether it limits the analysis to how people *talk about* their thoughts, feelings or experiences. Thus one possible discourse analytic research question that could be applied to these data would be 'How do men construct their experiences of leaving the army and its impact on their identity?' This question focuses on how the research participants create accounts of their experiences without assuming that these accounts map onto the men's thoughts, feelings and experiences. If you are mostly interested in studying people's thoughts, feelings and experiences in your research and if you assume that you can get access to these through analysing qualitative data, you should use a research method that shares your concerns and your assumption – but not discourse analysis.

What other research questions could you ask of the data in Appendix 1 from a discourse analytic perspective? Remember that the focus of these questions should be on the processes (how) and resources (discourses) through which people perform social actions (functions).

For more on discourse analytic research questions, see Chapter 10 (Table 10.1) in this volume.

One of the observations that emerged from our initial readings – reported here because of the implications that it had for our final analysis and therefore for the presentation of that analysis in this chapter – concerned the differences between the two interviewees: Brian and David seemed to talk about their experience of leaving the army in different ways. On the basis of these initial impressions, we decided to treat Brian's and David's interviews as case studies. Consequently, at each stage, the analysis will move between the two interviews. Whilst this approach was an effective strategy for working with just two texts, the group agreed that it would not work so well for a larger data set. In such an analysis the focus would likely be on identifying consistencies and inconsistencies in how people talked across the data set, in the way certain objects were constructed, in the discourses that were drawn upon and in the functions they served. It should also be noted that, at each stage, the analysis presented here is partial; this chapter is intended only to provide an illustrative rather than exhaustive analysis of the interviews.

BOX 11.2 — Levels of transcription and types of analysis

The question of the level at which to transcribe the interviews was resolved for us because the interviews were given to us already transcribed. Similarly, transcription is not an issue for researchers who subject existing textual materials to discourse analysis, such as magazine or newspaper articles, websites or material from online discussion forums. However, for researchers setting out to do discourse analysis on interactional data such as interviews, focus groups and naturalistic recordings (for example, of discussions in professional meetings or phone calls to helplines), the issue of the level of transcription is an important one. The researcher chooses a more or less detailed level

(Continued)

of transcription depending on whether they are primarily interested in the structure or the content of talk.

For example, conversation analysts are primarily interested in the structure of talk. They typically use the detailed transcription notation system developed by Gail Jefferson (Atkinson and Heritage, 1984). This notation system allows the analyst to include such things as rising and falling levels of pitch and the precise location of the starts and ends of speakers' turns in a conversation. Each of these features might help the researcher in determining the meaning of an utterance or the orderliness of an interaction. If, however, a researcher intends to adopt a more Foucauldian discourse analytic approach, they are likely to be less concerned with the structural details of the production of talk, such as pauses and overlaps. Instead they will be more concerned with identifying broader-level features of a text, such as discourses, which can be identified from a less detailed transcript. Whatever level of detail you adopt in your transcription, you should take extreme care to reproduce the data as accurately as possible.

BITE-SIZED SUMMARY
1

In the opening parts of this chapter, we have considered the vital preparatory work needed for a discourse analytic study. This concerns the development of appropriate research questions – that is, questions that ask about the processes and resources through which people perform social actions. The research questions provide discursive objects that the researcher can focus on when they engage with data. If data need to be transcribed, the level of specificity that is needed depends on the form of discourse analysis that is being used. From the outset, we emphasized the importance of reflexivity in discourse analysis – the discussion by the researcher of the role they play in creating their analysis.

Discursive constructions

Having identified the discursive objects, the first step in the analysis was to identify how each of these three discursive objects was constructed. Even this first step seemed to require a move into the new and unusual. We were not really interested in Brian and David as individuals or in the 'reality' of their experiences. Instead, we were trying only to focus on the words and phrases that they used when they talked about or *constructed* the experience of leaving the army and their respective army and post-army identities. The categories, rights, obligations and activities that people draw upon when talking about or constructing a particular discursive object are referred to as **discursive resources**. Our task was to identify the discursive resources that were used by Brian and David in the interviews as they constructed their experience and identities and to develop a sense of how these resources fitted together.

Given that we were using the concept of 'identity', it is worth noting how identity is conceptualized within discourse analytic approaches and how this compares with more traditional social psychological approaches. For example, in social identity theory (Tajfel and Turner, 1986), an individual's identity, the way they might think, feel and act, is supposed to be based upon and made relevant by their relatively stable membership of any number of social groups. An individual's identity might be supposed from what we might know about them – for example, their sex, age, ethnicity or sexuality. In contrast, within discourse analytic approaches, identity is highly dynamic (see the discussion of 'positioning' in Chapter 10). It is both a social construction and a social accomplishment managed and achieved through speakers' orientations to interactional concerns. In this sense, identity is a participant's resource, constructed and mobilized in a 'bottom-up' manner rather than being imposed on them by the researcher in a 'top-down' way. In this analysis, identity will be treated as both a topic within talk (the social construction) and an effect of talk (the social accomplishment). Identities, in this case the army and post-army identities, are constructed by the interviewees out of sets of discursive resources: for example, the social categories of which the interviewees claim membership or which they apply to others and the normative behaviours that are culturally associated with members of those categories.

The army identity

David

David drew upon a wide range of discursive resources when talking about his army identity, something he did quite explicitly and which made our job easier. Most obviously, his army identity was constructed in terms of being 'a member of a team' (repeated in lines 17–18). Team membership carried with it moral implications such as 'being honest to your mates' (repeated in lines 66–68) and was potentially extendable such that it could include not only 'your mates' but the army as a whole: 'I was a driver and, without us drivers, no-one would get their goods' (lines 28–29). David's army identity was also constructed through the use of particular categories such as 'driver' (line 28), 'Sergeant' (line 93) and 'soldier' (line 321). These categories are located within the logistical and hierarchical structures of the army and confer upon their members certain rights and responsibilities.

Other less explicit discursive constructions of David's army identity include the emphasizing of independent capabilities and the importance of orderliness: 'I can make my breakfast, I can make my dinner, I can sew, I can iron, I can wash' (lines 208–209), 'I like things in lines. I like things in neat packages' (lines 238–239) and 'Keep your paperwork in order' (line 245). Thus, for David, the army identity was simultaneously defined in terms of collectivistic (being a part of a matrix of interdependency) and individualistic (being independent) attributes.

Brian

Brian's army identity was rarely explicitly the topic of talk. Instead it was implicit in his constructions of differences between his own working practices and those of his civilian colleagues. Out of these contrasts, there seemed to emerge a clear construction of a 'typical' army identity with which Brian appeared to self-identify. This was most clearly evidenced by his use of first person plural pronouns: 'We seem to be much more flexible' (line 10) and 'we do our best all of the time' (line 16). The latter quotation was noticed as containing an extreme case formulation (Pomerantz, 1986) – a rhetorical feature that increases the persuasiveness of an account, in this case highlighting the contrast between the working practices and ethics of military or ex-military and civilian personnel.

As with David, we noted in Brian's talk that the hierarchical rank structure of the army seemed to be central to a valued individual identity, particularly through its role in constituting and ordering social identities: 'You've got an identity there and you feel good about yourself' (lines 287–288), 'you had a much more definite identity which other people could relate to' (lines 323–324) and 'I think that's because I had a definite label [sergeant]' (line 339). Appearance and the wearing of a uniform were also key discursive resources in the construction of the army identity: 'in the military you can tell just by looking at someone where they are in the pecking order [ ] and so you can temper what you say to them and how you say it to them' (lines 184–186).[1]

The post-army identity
David

The centrality of team membership to David's army identity contrasted sharply with his constructions of a post-army identity. David, who at the time of the interview held the post of school caretaker, reported that 'you're not a team member within the school because you're not a teacher' (lines 48–49). The absence of team membership in civilian life seemed

---

[1]Empty square brackets indicate where material has been omitted from a quotation. Three dots indicate a pause (untimed) in the speaker's talk.

to be central to David's post-army identity. Indeed, David explicitly constructed 'civilians' as having 'different ideas of being in teams' (line 58) and that this was another source of dissatisfaction: 'That's the difficult part, I find' (line 60). This construction of the differing concepts of teams between the army and civilian life and its implications for David's identity seemed to be summed up in the segment of reported speech in lines 42–43: "'Well, that's it. David, you did a good job, we miss him, fine, get someone else in.'" In contrast to his army identity, David's post-army identity was constructed in terms of an absence of 'real' team membership and his being under-valued in those 'teams' to which others might ascribe him membership.

Other notable discursive resources constitutive of David's post-army identity included the emphasis that he placed on appearance and the contrasting effects that it had in army and civilian contexts: 'Now I walk out the door in my overalls and I think, "Well, yeah, that's it." You try to give an appearance of someone who's been trained and disciplined but it's not the same, it's not the same. You don't have the same effect as anywhere else' (lines 321–324). This quotation seemed to us to work up the importance that is assigned to appearance in the army, specifically the wearing of a uniform and the relational effects of that uniform. David describes these effects as the consequences of the meanings that uniforms hold within military contexts (such as the location of the wearer within the rank structure). In talking about his post-army identity, David constructed an absence of the function of appearance in constituting social identities.

Brian

Again Brian's account differed from David's simply because he constructed his post-army identity as not dissimilar to his army identity, at least in terms of its implications for his sense of self-worth: 'And since I've been out, it's almost the same I think – not much has changed there really' (lines 288–289). This is not to say that Brian constructed his post-army identity as identical to his army identity. Indeed, features of his army identity were invoked as potential sources of tension and conflict within civilian contexts: 'I came across as aggressive, abrupt, arrogant ... [ ] but I was just sort of being what I was doing really and in the military environment that was ... it wouldn't even have been picked up on' (lines 220–223). We recognized that this quotation contained a three-part list (Jefferson, 1990), another rhetorical device that works up the persuasiveness of an account by creating a sense of comprehensiveness. However, Brian did not construct such tensions as intractable nor as requiring a wholesale transformation between his army and post-army identities. Instead, it seemed to us that Brian's post-army identity was constructed as a minimally reworked, 'civilianized' version of his army identity: 'I've had to adapt my training style to be more civilian friendly' (lines 231–232). It was this apparent adaptability and flexibility, which Brian had previously constructed as part of his army identity, that really seemed to mark the difference between Brian's and David's interviews.

Identifying discursive resources

As we noted earlier, when people talk about or construct a particular discursive object, they draw upon a wide array of categories, rights, obligations and activities. When doing this constructive work, people also draw upon certain practices to make one 'description' more persuasive than another possible description that is often left implicit. Discursive resources include such categories as 'soldier' and the characteristics that are ascribed to members of that category. The persuasiveness of a description may be worked up through a practice such as an extreme case formulation (Pomerantz, 1986) – for example, 'we do our best all of the time'. It is, however, important to note that such practices can be used by people in relation to a wide range of topics and discursive objects. They are not therefore features of talk that are constitutive of a 'discourse' (see below). In contrast, the constructed relationships between categories, activities, rights and obligations and the way these might structure relations between members of particular categories and therefore constitute social orders are the very stuff of 'discourses'.

Taking 'civvy street' as a discursive object of interest, study the transcripts in Appendix 1 in this volume and try to find the categories and attributes that Brian and David draw upon to construct it. Remember: be careful to differentiate those resources specific to 'civvy street' from those practices that function to make the account persuasive.

We have now moved into the analytic work and have engaged in the first stage of Foucauldian discourse analysis. In this we considered how the discursive objects were constructed by Brian and David through their talk in the interviews – how they constructed the experience of leaving the army and their respective army and post-army identities. Characteristic ways of conceptualizing identity within discourse analysis were noted – as a topic within talk and as an effect of talk. Our analyses drew out the ways in which David and Brian constructed army identity and post-army identity and the relation between these.

Discourses

This stage of the analysis required us to try to organize and categorize the various discursive resources drawn upon in relation to each of the discursive objects, namely the army identity, the post-army identity and the experience of leaving the army. This process of organization and categorization would result in the identification of the discourses that we believed to be at play within the transcripts. To invoke Adrian Coyle's definition of the term in Chapter 10, discourses can be thought of as sets of linguistic material that have a degree of coherence in their content and organization and that perform constructive functions. The use of the concept of 'discourse' or 'discourses' (or, to use the term preferred by Potter and Wetherell, 1987, an 'interpretative repertoire') is associated with Foucauldian discourse analysis but not with discursive psychology which has a more localized focus (see Chapter 10 for more on the different approaches to discursive work). Foucauldian discourse analysis explicitly aims to identify broad patterns in language use. In doing this, it generates analyses that draw in analytic concepts such as discourses that extend beyond the data that are being studied. Discursive psychology, on the other hand, generates analyses that are micro-textual, closely linked to and not moving beyond the data being studied. In our efforts to identify regularities and patterns, we tried to be attentive to similarities and differences between the discursive resources from which Brian and David fashioned their respective army and post-army identities.

The first discourse that we settled upon was a 'collectivistic discourse'. This discourse seemed to be prominent in David's accounts of his army identity and his post-army identity. Within it we felt that we could locate all David's constructions of the importance and value of teamwork and team membership within the army, and the constructed contrasts with civilian life. Further, we felt the collectivistic discourse, with its emphasis on collective aims, could encapsulate David's constructed lack of purpose on leaving the army.

The second discourse that we discerned was an 'individualistic discourse'. Though David and, to a lesser extent, Brian drew upon a collectivistic discourse in the construction of their army identity, they both drew upon discursive resources that emphasized individual capabilities, agency, dedication, adaptability, performance and, perhaps most significantly, the importance of individual status and recognition of status through the hierarchical structure of the army. Just as the collectivistic discourse was pre-eminent in David's interview, so it seemed to us, the individualistic discourse was pre-eminent in Brian's.

Whilst the collectivistic and individualistic discourses allowed us to categorize most of the discursive constructions of David's and Brian's army and post-army identities, there were a number of constructions that did not fit neatly into either. At this point we reminded ourselves that there could be any number of discourses at play within the interviews and realised that this need not be a problem. The use of the category 'civilians' by David, Brian and the interviewer, Arnie, to refer to a group with shared characteristics, which stand in contrast to those of the army, seemed also to be part of a 'military discourse' – 'military' because the very concept of the military rests on its distinction and the distinction of its members from 'civilian' and 'civilians'. Finally, we decided that such discursive constructions as 'civilianized' could be located within an 'assimilationist discourse'. Within this discourse, operating successfully in a particular group or culture was contingent on the wholesale adoption of the behavioural norms of that group or culture, which required the abandonment of any previously held norms.

As a group, we were more comfortable with some of our categorizations than with others. We agreed that, perhaps given more time and a larger data set, our organization of the discursive resources as constituting particular discourses might have been different. Similarly, we acknowledged that another group of readers might have identified different discursive resources and categorized them differently. However, these were the resources that we had identified and categorized and these were the discourses that we had found most persuasive in our group discussions and deliberations. In a world of infinite readings, we reasoned that persuasiveness and closeness to the data counted for a great deal.

BOX 11.4 — **Identifying discourses**

The discourses that we identified were the result of our analysis and our discussion. There is no guarantee that anyone else would come up with the exact same set of discourses or that they would have labelled them in the same way we did.

Study the transcripts in Appendix 1 in this volume. Given the same research questions and discursive objects, would you have arrived at the same conclusions that we did? Would you have given the same labels to these sets of discursive resources?

Look back over the discursive resources that we identified as constructing the army and post-army identities and look for any resources we might have missed. Try to think of other ways in which these resources might be grouped. Think about the commonalities within and between those collections of resources. Are there other ways of characterizing those commonalities and differences? You can also do this for the 'civvy street' resources you identified in the exercise in Box 11.3.

As we were doing the analysis, we recognized that, by categorizing certain discursive resources as belonging to a collectivistic discourse and others as belonging to an individualistic discourse, we were drawing upon terms and concepts that had existing meanings within social psychology. As concepts, collectivism and individualism have typically been applied at a cultural level, as dimensions along which cultural differences might be understood (Triandis, 1996). Collectivism and individualism applied at the individual level, as dimensions of personality, have been conceptualized as 'allocentrism' and 'idiocentrism' (Triandis et al., 1985). Our analysis and our argument that Brian and David both drew upon discourses of collectivism and individualism could, therefore, be read as an account of what allocentrism and idiocentrism might look like in practice. However, the important distinction is that, within a discourse analytic approach, the evident use of these discourses would not be assumed to be a consequence of some underlying personality tendency – a position that is bolstered by the fact that both David and, to a lesser extent, Brian drew upon *both* the collectivistic *and* individualistic discourses. Within the non-discursive, personality-based approach of Triandis et al. (1985) and based on the evidence presented in this analysis, Brian and David would have to be viewed as being simultaneously idiocentric *and* allocentric.

Action orientation

The analytic stages of considering the action orientation of the data and considering positioning within the data were the cause of much uncertainty. Willig (2013) presents these as the third and fourth stages in Foucauldian discourse analysis. The action orientation stage is meant to attend to the interactional functions (for example, attributing responsibility) that are performed by particular discursive constructions within a text. In other words, the focus is on the social action that the discursive constructions orient towards in the text. The positionings stage is said to be concerned with the **subject position**s that are offered to the speaker and others by the discourses that are invoked in talk. The example of a subject position presented in Chapter 10 (taken from Willig, 2013) is that of 'the patient' within a bio-medical discourse which comes with the obligation to act as a passive recipient of care from those who are placed in the subject position of 'medical experts'. However, we saw positioning (and responses to positioning) as oriented to interactional functions within the data. In other words, we saw positioning as necessarily having an action orientation and so we had difficulty in treating a consideration of action orientation and a consideration of positioning as discrete stages in analysis. We suspect that Willig (2013) separated these for the sake of clarity but, in practice, they may be best thought of as aspects of the same stage of analysis.

Given that Arnie had used broadly similar questions in each interview and given the analytic focus on the discursive object of the experience of leaving the army, we decided to focus on David's and Brian's responses to Arnie's invitation to recount their experience of and feelings about the transition from army to civilian life (lines 76–78 in David's interview and lines 54–58 in Brian's interview). Again, it should be remembered that the analysis presented below is not exhaustive and is intended only to illustrate this particular stage of the discourse analytic process.

David

In lines 89 to 114, David constructed leaving the army as having immediate relational, psychological, physical and social effects. The immediate relational effects of leaving the army were worked up through the use of reported speech and the titles that it contained: 'someone's saying "ID card – thank you, Mr Jones". And that hit you, you know. Someone's actually calling you "Mister". No one's calling me "Sergeant" any more' (lines 91–93). David's relational identity constituted through the army's rank structure was constructed as immediately and casually extinguished through the simple use of titles. The consequences of this were subsequently constructed in a three-part list of responses: 'That was funny. That was a shock. That's when you knew' (lines 93–94). This list also seemed to us to construct a 'psychological' process of 'realization', from the initial acknowledgement of oddness of the use of 'Mister' as a form of address ('funny'), to an affective response to the use of 'Mister' ('shocked') and finally to a cognitive understanding of the implications of the use of 'Mister' ('you knew').

The immediate physical and social effects were constructed in terms of the negation of David's rights of access to physical spaces and resources: 'it's like they're throwing you outside and locked the gate' (lines 97–98) and 'you can't pick up the phone and get hold of the old housing people any more' (lines 101–102). This exclusion from spaces and services was also constructed as provoking affective responses: 'That was painful' (line 99) and 'it's a funny feeling' (line 103). These constructions of the numerous and various effects of leaving the army all seemed to us have the action orientation of working up, within the research interview, the experience of transition as immediate and total – a sudden transition from interdependence to independence, from inclusion to exclusion and from group membership to individual isolation.

Brian

Where David focused on the experience of leaving the army as an historical event recounted in narrative form, Brian focused only on one aspect of the transition from army to civilian life, that of finding a job: 'obviously I was totally preoccupied in trying to find a job' (lines 60–61). By his focus on his constructed need to find employment, Brian could be interpreted as delimiting the effects of leaving the army; the only effect of leaving the army is that it forced a change of job. Such a move may be interpreted as having the action orientation of minimizing the experience of leaving the army and of directing discussion away from, glossing over or even denying the existence of any other more personal effects that the transition might have had.

Lines 60 to 99 could be seen as having the action orientation of managing and attributing responsibility for the problems that Brian reportedly encountered in finding work and in working in 'civvy street'. The issue of finding work was dealt with in lines 60 to 70. This section seemed to have two defining characteristics: the practices of normalization and extrematization (constructing something as a routine, regular activity and as involving extreme effort). Normalization was apparent in the three-part list of activities that comprised lines 62 to 64: 'I was sending loads and loads of applications off and I was getting loads and loads of interviews and I was going to the interviews and getting down to the last two or three people.' Extrematization was apparent in the repeated phrase 'loads and loads' in these lines. Combined, these two features work up the sense that, by his agency – the repeated 'I was' clearly establishes Brian as the agent in this sequence – Brian came close to getting a good many jobs. One of the significant contributions of discursive psychology has been in demonstrating how much and how often talk has the action orientation of managing matters of responsibility and blame or 'accountability' in the immediate interactional context. In this case Brian's talk about his job-seeking efforts has the action orientation of managing and specifically limiting his accountability for not immediately finding employment.

BOX 11.5 — **Determining action orientation**

The concept of 'action orientation' is an interesting one within discourse analysis. Determining 'action orientation' is most easily understood as attempting to answer the question, 'What is this speaker doing here?' The answers that you might generate to that question may be oriented to one or more of the various levels of context across which the text is assumed to operate. That is to say, what a speaker says may be oriented to some matter in the local interactional context of, in this case, the interview and/or to some more macro-level context such as a matter of ideology. Within discourse analysis, it need not be one or the other: speakers are interpreted as orienting to local and more distal contexts simultaneously.

Look at how David answers Arnie's question about the experience of making the transition to civilian life (lines 76–129). David draws on a lot of resources and practices, such as reported speech, in this answer. Try to identify parts of the answer that seem concerned with David's immediate status in the interview (for example, how he manages his potential blameworthiness for his reported negative experience) and those parts that are concerned with more general issues (such as an evaluation of the army's support for ex-servicemen). You may find it helpful to start from how David justifies his account of the experience as an anti-climax.

Positioning

As was indicated earlier, according to positioning theory, one of the things that discourses do is provide subject positions for the users of those discourses. In this sense, discourses do not only constitute the objects of talk (what is being talked about) but they also constitute subjects (those who are doing the talking). In constituting subjects, a discourse is also theorized as locating those subjects within the structure of rights and duties for those who use that discourse. As the concept of subject positions within a Foucauldian discourse analytic framework follows from the concept of discourses, our analysis of Brian's and David's positioning has to be based on our identification and interpretation of the discourses at play in the interviews, more so than any previous stage of the analysis. As such, the persuasiveness of our analysis of the subject positions afforded to speakers and the functions they served depends upon our individual and collective competence and confidence as members of a particular culture in identifying and understanding those discourses.

For some members of the group, this was a profoundly unsettling step, seeming to represent a move away from the textual evidence of the data and placing too great a reliance on our subjective understandings and our cultural competence. This unease about using our subjectivities may be felt by inexperienced qualitative researchers regardless of the method they are using because the task does not fit comfortably with what most of us have been taught about psychology as an 'objective' science. The uncertainty and unease associated with this step in the analysis was reduced somewhat by the fact that we were able to check our interpretations and their persuasiveness with the other members of the group.

Following from the relative prominence of the collectivistic and individualistic discourses within the interviews, we tried to think about the kind of subject positions that they respectively afforded David and Brian and what the consequences of these positions were. In doing this, we found it helpful to frame the task as questions: 'What did the collectivistic discourse do for David?', 'What did the individualistic discourse do for Brian?'

By drawing primarily upon the collectivistic discourse, David was afforded a subject position from which he could contrast his army and post-army identities and thereby construct a sense of dissatisfaction with civilian life. In turn, this contrast provides the basis for the assimilation discourse, a discourse that clearly demarcates cultural differences with consequent threats to an individual's social identity. Furthermore, the subject position constituted by the collectivistic discourse, with its emphasis on interdependence, provided for the purposelessness that David ascribed to civilian life. Occupying a subject position constituted by the collectivistic discourse but without collective aims, David was robbed of individual purpose and denied value in his civilian life.

In contrast, by consistently drawing upon an individualistic discourse, Brian occupied a subject position that provided for continuity between his army and post-army identities. Consequently Brian's interview was marked by an absence of the experience of leaving the army as a negative event. Indeed the individualistic discourse constituted a subject position from which Brian could unproblematically construct himself as valued more in his civilian work context than he was in the military context.

Practice and subjectivities

One of the things that really struck us about doing discourse analysis was the amount of time that it takes. Hence, we were not able to engage fully with the stages of practice and subjectivity (which Willig, 2013, presents as separate stages of analysis) within the time frame that we had allowed for the analytic work. Consequently the discussion of how the analysis might have developed through these two stages is speculative.

BOX 11.6 — Evaluating discourse analytic research

In Chapter 2 in this volume, Adrian Coyle considered criteria that have been proposed for evaluating qualitative research. In light of the uncertainty that members of our group had about moving from talking about discourses to talking about subject positions and the emphasis this placed on their status as competent members of a culture, this seems a good point to reflect on the criteria by which we might evaluate qualitative research and thereby hopefully gain greater confidence in our analyses.

Of the evaluative criteria proposed by Yardley (2000), those most pertinent at this stage are 'sensitivity to context', 'rigour and transparency' and 'coherence'. These criteria may roughly be expressed in terms of the following questions:

- Have we/you recognized all the various contexts within which the data may be interpreted – from the interactional context of the interview to the wider cultural context?

- Have we/you generated a thorough and clearly evidenced and reported analysis?

- Do our/your analyses answer the research questions and are they consistent with the philosophical perspective underlying discourse analysis?

Apply these questions either to the analysis we have presented above or to the analyses you have done in response to the exercises in the previous boxes in this chapter. For example, is the analysis sufficiently sensitive to the self-presentational work that Brian and David might have been engaged in when being interviewed on what is a highly personal topic?

Be critical: ask whether the analysis really does meet the criteria specified in the questions. Think about what we/you might have missed. This might be in the data itself, in the way that we/you have understood the data or in the way that we/you have presented the analysis. Be aware of the epistemological position underlying discourse analysis. Do we/you slip into 'realist talk' at any point (something that is hard to avoid even for experienced discourse analysts)? In other words, do we/you ever start to treat what Brian or David say as reflecting what they 'really' think or feel?

Willig (2013: 132) describes the focus on practice within Foucauldian discourse analysis as following from the idea that 'discursive constructions and the subject positions contained within them open up or close down opportunities for action. By constructing particular versions of the world, and by positioning subjects within them in particular ways, discourses limit what can be said and done.' This idea presented us, as novice analysts, with a theoretical conundrum that we were not entirely able to resolve. This conundrum centred on the status that could be accorded to 'practice' or 'what can be done'. Our concern arose from our understanding that, within discursive approaches, talk and texts are not assumed to reflect 'practice' or 'what can be done' unproblematically. Talk of 'practice' or 'what can or cannot be done' is just that, *talk*, and its functions are limited to the interactional context within which it occurs. What we seemed to be striving for was some way of linking the discourses within the interviews and the constructions of action and practice that they supported to the world beyond. After some discussion, we recognized or remembered that talk *is* action and that what Brian and David did within the interviews could be theorized as practice and therefore was constrained and constituted by the discourses that they drew upon. However, this line of argument would again limit our discussion of practice to Brian's and David's interviews. Ultimately we decided that, whilst we could appreciate how discourses as culturally available resources could be identified as serving particular functions within texts and as opening up or closing down various possibilities, we were not sufficiently confident (on account of our limited data, analysis and experience) to extrapolate what possibilities for practice were opened up or closed down by the discourses that we had identified.

Similar concerns and dilemmas arose when we considered the final stage of a Foucauldian discourse analysis: subjectivities. Willig (2013: 130) argues that discourses 'make available certain ways-of-seeing the world and certain ways-of-being in the world' and that a focus on subjectivities involves a concern with what can be felt, thought and experienced from within various subject positions. Theorizing the possibilities of feeling, thought and experience that might follow from discourses of collectivism and individualism seemed to us to be very similar to theorizing the possibilities for practice – and riven with the same epistemological dilemmas. Certainly, the discourse of collectivism could be interpreted as providing for David's *feelings* of abandonment, exclusion, isolation and even bereavement. Yet what status should we, as discourse analysts, ascribe to those feelings, given that they are present only in talk and we do not necessarily assume that talk reflects an underlying reality of thoughts and feelings? That David reports experiencing these feelings is explicit in the text and their action orientation has been engaged with earlier. The question that we faced was whether the potential for *really experiencing* such feelings could be a consequence of the forced abandonment of the use of a collectivistic discourse in the construction of self-identity.

We decided that the answer to this question depended primarily upon whether we, as analysts, adopted a strongly social constructionist or a critical realist epistemological position (see Chapter 2 in this volume). At best we were only able to conclude that there was some scope to view the content of the interviews as demonstrating the constitution of David's and Brian's subjectivities in a very partial way.

Our initial analytic observations were extended and deepened as we proceeded (or tried to proceed) through the remaining stages of Foucauldian discourse analysis. We considered the discourses that David and Brian drew upon in their talk: collectivistic, individualistic, military and assimilationist discourses. We examined the action orientation of David's and Brian's talk. David's talk appeared to construct the experience of moving from army to post-army life as an immediate and total transition. Brian's talk was oriented more specifically towards managing responsibility for his reported problems in finding work after leaving the army. Next we identified the subject positions that were offered by the discourses that David and Brian invoked. The collectivistic discourse provided David with a position from which he could contrast his army and post-army identities and construct a sense of dissatisfaction and purposelessness in his civilian life. The individualistic discourse enabled Brian to occupy a subject position that provided for continuity between his army and post-army identities. Applying these stages generated much critical reflection on what we were called upon to do as discourse analysts and on how far we could move beyond the data, particularly in relation to the final stages of analysis about practice and subjectivity.

BITE-SIZED
SUMMARY
....

3

Reflections

As ought to be apparent from the preceding speculations about how our analysis might proceed to the levels of practice and subjectivity, one of our main concerns was how far from the data we could or should move. As novice analysts at the time, perhaps we lacked the theoretical sophistication and confidence to support building links between our idiographic analysis of just two interviews on the topic of leaving the army with the practicalities of leaving the army and the experiences faced by the many ex-servicemen and women that are *out there*.

A second concern was one of responsibility to Brian and David and, beyond this data set, to anyone whose texts may be subjected to discourse analysis. By focusing on the way that they constructed their accounts, by identifying the discourses that they drew upon and that structured their experiences, were we in some way not taking the reality of those experiences seriously enough? In focusing on the language that they drew upon, were we diverting attention away from the materiality of their experiences? Also we were concerned that, in doing discourse analysis, in representing their accounts in such an obscure and potentially unrecognizable way, were we failing to meet some kind of implicit agreement as social researchers to report their experiences in a way that they would recognize and agree with?

Third, though we made efforts to create dialogues between our discursive analysis and existing social psychological literature on such matters as identity, collectivism, individualism, allocentrism and idiocentrism, we remained uncertain as to how to do this effectively and in ways that would be consistent either with a social constructionist or critical realist position. We were convinced that such dialogues are possible and necessary if discourse analytic work is to enter effectively into mainstream social psychology. The work of Frost, Nolas and colleagues in developing a 'pluralistic' approach to qualitative research (Frost and Nolas, 2011; Frost et al., 2010) may provide pointers to a way forward (see Chapter 14 in this volume for more on a pluralistic approach). In our case, though, we felt that our uncertainty about how to create such dialogues was a consequence of our failure as a group to determine clearly the epistemological position from which we were operating (see Chapter 2 where Adrian Coyle stresses the importance of this).

The resolution to such concerns, we were forced to conclude, might only come with greater knowledge of the history and philosophy underlying the various discourse analytic approaches, further experience of the approach and greater confidence born of some sorts of external validation or challenge. Whether we succeeded in doing Foucauldian discourse analysis and whether we could count ourselves as discourse analysts would depend upon our having the confidence to write and publish this analysis or some other piece of discourse analytic work and invite the scrutiny of our peers – which is exactly what we have done in this chapter.

CHAPTER SUMMARY

This chapter has offered an account of Foucauldian discourse analytic practice, applying the various stages of analysis to a discrete data set. The account has constructed certain stages as more challenging than others, with difficulties attributed to the constraints of the analytic context but also to the apparent requirements of some stages to move beyond what some analysts regarded as a credible evidence base and also to make inferences about the 'real world'. I hope that researchers who are inexperienced in discourse analysis will find this account useful in identifying one way through the discourse analytic process and raising some important matters for further consideration. However, I wish to emphasize that, in developing skill in discourse analysis, there is really no alternative to 'getting your hands dirty' – trying to apply the principles of discourse analysis to text and obtaining feedback from experienced others. Also, as with Chapter 10 in this volume, I would remind readers that this chapter, like any text, is itself open to discourse analysis so you may wish to use this text as data for your first steps into discourse analysis or to refine your existing analytic skills.

Further reading

Articles by Schegloff (1997) and Wetherell (1998) provide some insight into the tensions between forms of discourse analysis and other approaches to the study of discourse. Merino and Tileagă (2011) offer an interesting contemporary example of discourse analytic research.

12

NARRATIVE ANALYSIS

Brett Smith

This chapter introduces narrative analysis as a way of engaging with storied data. There is a rich and often complex theoretical background to narrative analysis. Some key assumptions are first unpacked, highlighting the philosophical underpinnings of narrative research. The approach to narrative described in this chapter derives from narrative constructionism. This assumes that stories do more than simply reflect or recount experience: they *act* in people's lives in ways that matter deeply. The chapter then distinguishes between two broad standpoints for approaching analysis, those of 'story analyst' and 'storyteller', before going on to describe how to conduct one particular form of narrative analysis – a dialogical narrative analysis. Reflections, examples and practical exercises are provided throughout to help readers get to grips with the theory and method of narrative analysis.

Introduction

In recent years, a growing number of psychologists have turned to narrative analysis as a useful way to understand human life (for example, Crossley, 2000; Esin et al., 2014; Josselson and Lieblich, 1993; McAdams, 2013; Medved et al., 2013; Sarbin, 1986; Smith, 2013a). But what are the philosophical and methodological commitments that are foundational to a narrative analysis? What is a narrative analysis and what differentiates it from other qualitative analyses? Why use a narrative analysis? And how might you go about doing a narrative analysis? In this chapter I respond to these questions (Nick Caddick addresses the 'How?' question in an extended way in Chapter 13 in this volume). The responses offered should not be seen as the final or definitive word on narrative analysis. This is because there are differing theoretical positions among narrative researchers (Schiff, 2013; Sparkes and Smith, 2008), diverse definitions of narrative (Frank, 2012; Riessman, 2008), and various types of narrative analysis (Gubrium and Holstein, 2009; Holstein and Gubrium, 2012a; Lieblich et al., 1998; Spector-Mersel, 2014; Stephens and Breheny, 2013). Given this, my aspirations here are modest and choices about what to include are necessarily selective. I hope, however, that the chapter will not only be a useful 'hands on' resource for appreciating and doing a narrative analysis but will also help readers to engage further with and think about the wide range of narrative work being produced.

Before proceeding, it is important to acknowledge that engaging with a narrative analysis can be a difficult process. For example, on many occasions I have felt confused and anxious when thinking about which type of narrative analysis to use from the various options available. Feelings of bewilderment have often also swirled through my body when trying to understand the different methodological or theoretical positions advanced by scholars. Because a narrative analysis lacks a prescribed, step-by-step, linear procedure (a point I return to later), I felt unconfident and worried when I first started thinking about how to do analytic work with stories. I am not alone here. Numerous conversations over the years with both students and well-established, esteemed academics have revealed that there are many other people who have also experienced bewilderment and anxiety when it comes to narrative research.

I say this not to put readers off. My point – and my hope – in acknowledging this is threefold. First, when getting started, it can be comforting to know that it is not unusual to feel anxious or have some self-doubt about making sense of data through narrative analysis. Second, doing excellent qualitative research of any kind is not easy – nor should it be. This is because qualitative research is more than a technique or a procedure that can be learned quickly. As with the other qualitative approaches covered in this volume, it is a craft and way of being that requires something called 'phronesis', which means 'practical wisdom'. The key to developing this lies not just in reading book chapters or engaging with exemplars in action or attending professional workshops but actually *doing* analysis and learning through experience. Third, whilst a narrative analysis can be hard work, it can also be enormous fun and highly rewarding. Rich psychological insights can be produced and exciting possibilities generated.

Philosophical assumptions and theoretical commitments

To practise a narrative analysis, the philosophical assumptions that underpin it need to be considered. This might seem rather dry and abstract but try to stick with it for now because it is important to have a good sense of these assumptions in order to undertake narrative analysis in a truly informed way. Later in this chapter and especially in Chapter 13, you will see how these assumptions play out in practical terms in narrative analyses.

As described here, narrative analysis is underpinned by **ontological relativism** and **epistemological constructionism** (Smith, 2013a). The former refers to the assumption that, whilst it is accepted that physical things exist, psycho-social phenomena are multiple, created and dependent on us, as opposed to existing independently of human conceptions and interpretations. The latter means that knowledge is constructed and fallible. In addition to these philosophical assumptions, the theoretical assumptions – methodology – that inform a narrative analysis also need to be outlined. This is because, as Holstein and Gubrium (2012b: 5) have noted, 'Methods of analysis do not emerge out of thin air. They are informed by, and extend out of, particular theoretical sensibilities'. Or, as Schiff (2013: 256) put it, rather than divorcing theoretical commitments from methods (as often happens with other approaches), 'narrative psychology requires a fit between theory and method'.

Various theoretical approaches exist for practising a narrative analysis. One is called **narrative constructivism** (Sparkes and Smith, 2008). This is similar to what Schiff (2013) termed a 'cognitive-personality approach' to narrative. Narrative constructivism is an individualistic approach that conceptualizes narrative as a cognitive structure or process that is to be found inside the mind. Narrative is a 'thing' that people 'have' and something their minds do to structure and represent experience, identity, others and the world. In constructivism, then, narrative is an internalized form: when someone tells a story, the story they tell is seen as providing a more-or-less transparent window into their mind, experience and identity.

Another approach that one might adopt to inform how an analysis is practised is **narrative constructionism** (Esin et al., 2014; Sparkes and Smith, 2008). This is the approach taken in this chapter. It is similar to the interpretive and socio-cultural approaches to narrative described by Schiff (2013). In contrast to narrative constructivism (with a 'v'), narrative constructionism is a socio-cultural-oriented approach that conceptualizes human beings as meaning-makers who use narratives to interpret, direct and communicate life and to configure and constitute their experience and their sense of who they are. These narratives are passed down from people's social and cultural worlds.

Narrative constructionism has several key characteristics. Drawing on the work of various scholars (for example, Bochner and Riggs, 2014; Brockmeier, 2012; Frank, 2006, 2010a; Freeman, 2011, 2014; Gubrium and Holstein, 2009; Hydén, 2014; Phoenix and Orr, 2014; Tamboukou et al., 2014), these characteristics include the following. The first important point is that narratives are the resources from which people construct their personal stories and understand the stories they hear. To unpack what this means, a subtle distinction between story and narrative is needed. A story is a specific tale that people tell. In contrast, a narrative is a resource that culture and social relations make available to us and, in turn, we use to help construct our stories. Thus people tell stories, not narratives. Narratives are the crucial resources that provide people with a template – a scaffolding of sorts – from which to build and structure their own stories as well as understand the stories they hear or see in action. It is difficult to sustain a consistent difference in usage because the words 'story' and 'narrative' overlap so frequently. Nonetheless, the distinction and the implications it holds are important.

The distinction reminds us that a narrative is 'not in itself a story, and stories can be collected into types of narrative' (Frank, 2010a: 200). Five important implications follow from this. Firstly, people may tell stories that are very personal but these stories do not spring from their minds nor are they made up by the people themselves. Instead they are constructed from the narratives that surround the storytellers. Secondly, people's stories and their understandings of the stories they hear are not pristine reflections of the experiences depicted in the stories nor are they transparent windows into psychological phenomena or derived from their private minds. This is because when a person tells a story, they draw on the 'menu' of **narrative resources** that culture and social relations make available. One example of a narrative resource would be what Frank (2012) termed 'the medical restitution narrative' that follows the plotline of 'Yesterday I was healthy, today I'm sick, but tomorrow I'll be healthy again'. This is a dominant illness narrative that many people use to construct personal stories of their own illnesses. Thus, the stories people tell are constructed from resources that emerge from outside them and these stories need to be considered as culturally and relationally constructed, as partly manifested in types of narratives that surround them within culture and relationships rather than inside their minds.

Thirdly, narratives are not only resources for telling personal stories but are, in Frank's (2010a) terms, also actors. What this means is that a narrative, far from being passive, has the capacity to *do* things: narratives *act*. What narratives crucially do is help constitute our sense of self and identities, create and frame our subjective experiences and emotions, bring meaning to our lives, and shape what becomes experience through ordering events, teaching people what to pay attention to and showing us how to respond to those kinds of things (Frank, 2010a). In such ways, as Mayer suggested, the psychological function of narrative goes deep:

BOX 12.1	Where do narratives come from?

Getting to grips with narratives as 'cultural resources' that culture and society somehow 'make available' to us can be a difficult and confusing process. To help with this, make a list of your ten favourite movies and consider the way the plot develops in each of them. How many movies, for instance, draw on the 'romance narrative' of the 'gritty underdog' who rises up against the odds to achieve victory? Or how many draw on a 'redemption plot' where the hero or heroine endures some kind of calamity but manages to turn around their fortunes and win back favour, love or money? Considering the broad genre of these movie plots (comedy/romance/tragedy) can also help us to understand the resources used to tell stories.

Stories imbue our experience with 'meaning'. Events become meaningful to the extent that they can be fit into or evoke some larger narrative about ourselves or our world. Stories establish our identity. Our sense of self depends on our ability to cast ourselves as the main actor in our autobiographical narrative. It is impossible to say who we are without telling a story. And, finally, stories motivate our actions. When we act we are often to a great extent enacting, we are acting out the story as the script demands, acting in ways that are meaningful in the context of some story and that are true to our character's identity. (2014: 7)

Narrative is a practical medium and the primary medium for action. In other words, people use stories to do things. In narrative constructionism, the emphasis on narratives as resources and actors has its complement in an equal emphasis on people as acting beings (Frank, 2010a). Narratives are crucial resources and do things on us but we are not condemned to live out the narrative resources that are passed on through culture or passively do what a narrative teaches us to do. People in relationships also act and here stories are crucial. Within relationships, stories are a key medium for action. On the one hand, a person can act by choosing to tell a story, selecting what particular type of story to tell and artfully composing the story they tell in relation to the context, past responses from people, the expectations of a listener, and so on. On the other hand, the stories we personally tell are often not passive. They are also a medium for doing things on, with and for people—whether that is to motivate, to explain oneself, to enrol others in a cause, to connect to or disconnect from a group, to make people sad, happy, fearful or angry or, for example, simply to entertain. Thus people are acted on but are also acting, embodied beings.

Fourthly, whilst people's narrative resources are often stable, storytellers should remain unfinalized. What this means, in light of ideas from Bakhtin (1984) and Frank (2010a), is that when a person tells stories there is always the possibility that they and their story can change over time. As long as they are alive, the storyteller has not yet uttered her or his final or last word.

Fifthly, narratives are embodied. Stories are told with, in, through, on and out of bodies. As Hydén explains:

> telling and listening to stories is an activity that is accomplished through the use of bodies. Both telling and listening to stories involve bodily processes: the body and its parts are used as communicative instruments and as resources for structuring and interpreting stories. (2014: 139)

For example, people tell stories with other bodies, co-creating stories in the process. Bodies are also present in stories and in storytelling. Hands, eyes or the voice are often used when telling stories to communicate and clarify meaning. We sometimes use bodily experiences, such as felt bodily sensations towards a person, an event or action (people might call this 'gut feelings'), to inform the stories we tell and listen to within relationships.

The philosophical assumptions and theoretical commitments that underpin narrative analysis have been described. Particular attention has been paid to narrative constructionism and its key characteristics. These include a distinction between narratives and stories, and an understanding of narratives as acting, as performing psychological functions for those who invoke them and those who hear them, and as resources for action.

BITE-SIZED
SUMMARY
. . . .

1

What is a narrative analysis?

After considering the assumptions and commitments that underpin narrative analysis, we now turn to the fundamental question of what narrative analysis is. Narrative analysis is an umbrella term for a family of methods that share a focus on stories (Riessman, 2008). This is a useful understanding from which to start. It captures the distinguishing feature of a narrative analysis and its centre of gravity, that is, a focus on the story. But if we are to appreciate and do some justice to the complexities surrounding the 'What is it?' question, narrative analysis needs to be unpacked further. One way of doing this is to consider the different standpoints towards narrative and the specific types of analysis that fall under the stances that characterize the family of narrative analytic methods.

The different standpoints towards narrative research include a **'story analyst'** and **'storyteller'** (Bochner and Riggs, 2014; Smith and Sparkes, 2006). Examples of the types of analyses that each standpoint might use are highlighted in Table 12.1. A dotted line is used to separate the standpoints in order to highlight that, despite the differences between storytellers and story analysts, a researcher does not have to pledge allegiance to one standpoint only and see the other as a family enemy. Each stance approaches

Table 12.1 Narrative analysis as a story analyst and storyteller

Story analyst	Storyteller
Thematic narrative analysis: The focus is on the content within the whole story – what is said, that is, what topically and thematically surfaces in the realm of a story's content (for example, see Riessman, 2008; Sparkes and Smith, 2014).	**Autoethnography:** The focus is on creating evocative stories about the researcher's lived experience, relating the personal to the cultural (for example, see Ellis, 2004; Short et al., 2013).
Rhetorical narrative analysis: The focus is on identifying what oppositions (for example, good and bad therapy) and enthymemes (for example, incomplete or probable arguments) are in stories (for example, see Feldman et al., 2004).	**Poetic representation:** The focus is on transforming data in a poem-like composition (for example, see Richardson, 2000; Sparkes and Smith, 2014).

Table 12.1 (Continued)

Story analyst	Storyteller
Structural narrative analysis: The focus is on the 'telling' of the story, that is, how people's stories are put together. This can include an examination of the linguistic phenomena used, the story's overall sequential composition or the narrative resources used to organize and structure stories (for example, see Lieblich et al., 1998; Riessman, 2008; Sparkes and Smith, 2014).	**Creative non-fiction:** The focus is on creating a story that is grounded in research findings and composed using the techniques of fiction (for example, see Smith et al., 2013).
Interactional narrative analysis: The focus is on the interactional activity through which stories are constructed. This approach examines how stories are constructed during interactions that occur either in everyday life (*in situ*) or within researcher-created contexts (such as interviews) and interactions (for example, see Bamberg and Georgakopoulou, 2008; Gubrium and Holstein, 2009).	**Ethnodrama:** The focus is on producing a written play script based on stories collected and interpreted (for example, see Saldaña, 2011; Sparkes and Smith, 2014).
Personal narrative analysis: The focus is on the internalized and evolving life stories of individuals (for example, see Crossley, 2000; McAdams, 2013).	**Ethnotheatre:** The focus is on turning a written play script into an actual theatrical production. The play becomes another layer of analysis (for example, see Saldaña, 2011; Sparkes and Smith, 2014).
Visual narrative analysis: The focus is on how and when the image was made and who created it, what is included (and excluded) in the image itself, how component parts are arranged, the use of colour and technologies, and people's responses to an image (for example, see Griffin, 2010; Riessman, 2008).	**Visual representations:** The focus is on presenting stories as forms of analysis in visual form (for example, photographs, drawings or short films) (for example, see Parsons and Lavery, 2012; and the work by Phoenix at http://vimeo.com/43182928).
Performance narrative analysis: The focus is on what is spoken and how and, notably, who a story is directed to, when and why, that is, for what purpose (for example, see Riessman, 2008; Smith et al., 2009).	**Musical performance:** The focus is on using music as way of analysing data and communicating findings (for example, see Sparkes and Smith, 2014).
Dialogical narrative analysis: The focus is on what is told in the story and how, and what stories do – what happens as a result of telling that story (its effects) (for example, see Frank, 2010a, 2012; Phoenix and Smith, 2011; Smith, 2013; Sparkes et al., 2012).	**Digital narratives:** The focus is on using the internet and/or web-based resources (such as Facebook) to construct a digital story (sometimes with participants) that is analytical (see Bundon, http://elk.library.ubc.ca/bitstream/handle/2429/45647/ubc_2014_spring_bundon_andrea.pdf?sequence=1; Page and Thomas, 2011).

narrative from different angles and each serves certain purposes. Thus, for particular purposes, on some occasions a researcher might choose to operate as a storyteller. On other occasions, for certain purposes, they might shift standpoints and decide to operate as a story analyst.

When adopting the standpoint of story analyst, the researcher places narratives under analysis and communicates results in the form of a realist tale to produce an analytical account of narratives (Bochner and Riggs, 2014). 'Narrative-under-analysis' refers to the practice of using one or more specific types of narrative analysis, such as a thematic or structural narrative analysis, to scrutinize, think about and theoretically interpret certain elements of a story. The research conducted is *on* narratives where narratives are the object of study and, in analysis, are placed under scrutiny. A 'realist tale' is the most common way of communicating qualitative research. It has three key characteristics (Sparkes and Smith, 2014). Firstly, the researcher/author is almost completely absent from most segments of the finished text. There is no use of the first person and no reflections upon the author's role in constructing the report. This is termed 'experiential authority'. Secondly, the researcher/author presents extensive and closely edited storied data to reveal what is known as the participant's point of view. Thirdly, illustrated through empirical data, the researcher/author tells a theoretical account of the story to provide an explanation of it. This is known as 'interpretive omnipotence'. What the researcher as author then ends up with is an abstract tale of narratives rather than a story itself.

In contrast, when operating as a storyteller, analysis *is* the story and the story is communicated in the form of a creative analytical practice to produce a tale *as* a story. Rather than writing about or commenting on participants' stories, this is where the researcher actually retells those stories in one form or another in order to share key aspects of participants' experiences. In this case, the end product would read more 'like a story' than a traditional research report as realist tale. To say that analysis is the story is to emphasize that, rather than putting a story under analysis and doing research *on* narratives, the story in its own right is analytical and theoretical; it does the job of analysis because analysis happens in a story (Bochner and Riggs, 2014; Ellis, 2004). Given this, storytellers do not transform the story into another (theoretical) language. They use the stories they gather and present these to the audience/reader as a form of theory and analysis. They recast data to produce a story and the story is a theory. To help do this, rather than tell a story and represent results through a realist tale, they use a creative analytical practice (CAP). As described by Richardson (2000), CAP is an umbrella term for research that is cast into evocative and highly accessible forms, such as autoethnography (a personal story of the researcher's own experience) and creative non-fiction (a genre in which research findings are conveyed in the form of a 'fictional' tale that is grounded in empirical data). Accordingly, rather than produce a research report about narratives as story analysts do, what the storyteller ends up with is an analytical report as a written, visual or performed story itself.

Why choose to use a narrative analysis? Developing a rationale

No matter what kind of qualitative analysis you choose to use, whether that is interpretative phenomenological analysis (IPA), thematic analysis, grounded theory, discourse analysis or narrative analysis (see Chapters 4–13 in this volume), all choices must be made in informed, principled and disciplined ways (Coffey and Atkinson, 1996; Sparkes and Smith, 2014). Choosing an approach to analysis just because it is fashionable, commonly used within your field, relatively easy to do or likely to produce publishable work is not appropriate (although any of these reasons can be one consideration among others in choosing an analytical approach). One useful way to go about making informed analytical choices is to consider the various differences between a narrative analysis and some other kinds of qualitative analysis (see Chapter 14 for comparative reflections on the approaches covered in this volume). These include the following (some have been alluded to earlier).

First, narrative analysis focuses on one specific genre of discourse, that is, a story. Other qualitative approaches and analyses are interested in all genres of talk and text. Second, through some form of intense coding, most qualitative analyses break data apart, including any stories contained in the data. In contrast, when doing a narrative analysis, the researcher is wary of '**over-coding**' the data. Over-coding is where many different codes are assigned in order to break the story down into much smaller, more 'manageable' chunks. In contrast, the aim in narrative analysis is to keep the story intact in order to preserve and examine the wealth of storied detail contained in it. Third, narrative analysis differs from some other forms of analysis, such as IPA, in that there is a strong emphasis on human lives as culturally and relationally constructed, including our experiences.

A fourth subtle difference between a narrative analysis and other qualitative analyses lies in the focus on the 'whats' (for example, what the story is about) and 'hows' of talk (for example, how the story is structured). In IPA, grounded theory and some versions of thematic analysis, the interest is not so much on the hows but rather on what is said in terms of the content (what Clarke and Braun describe as 'semantic meaning': see Chapter 6 in this volume). In contrast, in the various forms of discourse analysis, the focus is on the hows of talk, with the whats being under-emphasized or ignored (see Chapter 10 in this volume). Narrative analytic methods focus on both the whats and hows of talk (Gubrium and Holstein, 2009). As Gibbs (2008: 71) argued, 'The analysis of narratives and biography adds a new dimension to qualitative research. It focuses not just on what people said and the things and the events they describe but on how they said it, why they said it and what they felt and experienced.'

Another useful way to go about making informed analytical choices is to consider the strengths and weaknesses of a particular approach to analysis. Grounded in the theoretical premises outlined earlier, a narrative analysis has the following strengths. First, it can honour the fidelity of lives in and across time. Stories are our crucial equipment for making sense of, organizing, rewriting and communicating our past, present and possible futures. Unlike in other forms of discourse, like a list, account or chronicle, stories involve a specific mode of temporality in which there is a tacking back and forth between events in question and the evolving whole to which they contribute. For example, somebody transitioning out of the army might recall events from their past in a new or different light now they have moved into civilian life, and their changing interpretation of those past events may shape their understanding of the present and how they move forward into the future (see Nick Caddick's analysis in Chapter 13 in this volume). Thus, by focusing on stories, a narrative analysis provides rich insight into the subjectivity of our past actions, present behaviours and future intentions, discerning new meaning and significance in an unfolding plot. It can enable researchers to chart the movement of human lives over time (Phoenix et al., 2007).

Second, a narrative analysis can reveal the relational and cultural fabric of human lives in and across time; how other people and the culture we live in are woven into and shape our lives and stories. As Schiff (2013: 250) argued, 'narrative psychology has a special role to play in the understanding of persons in social and cultural context, which distinguish it from mainstream psychology'.

Third, stories are singularly good resources for communicating the experiences, emotions and meanings that people attach within relationships and culture to events, behaviours, actions, embodiment and so on. Because of this, an analysis of these stories can provide a rich understanding of human experiences, emotions and the constant reaching for meaning in culture. None of this is to claim that a story transparently represents or simply mimics personal experience, emotions and meanings. Rather, it is to hold onto a dual recognition. It is to recognize that stories available within social relations and culture shape what becomes experience, emotion and meaning. At the same time, narrative analysis recognizes that people often depend on and defend what they experience as internal bodily feelings and their interior lives (Frank, 2006). Stories are important here. For example, even though stories are shaped by culture, people feel a sense of ownership over 'their' stories because they are living them, in their bodies, day after day. Stories help us communicate this felt sense that we have – a bodily feeling – of being the 'author' and originator of our own experiences (Burkitt, 2014).

Fourth, a narrative analysis can reveal not just what a story is about and how it is structured but also, as an actor and form of action, its functions. In so doing, it can enable researchers to understand how well people are served by their stories – how stories take care of people, cause them trouble or become dangerous. For example, the 'restitution narrative' that was mentioned earlier can sometimes be 'dangerous' if a person fails to get better and the story no longer fits with their experiences. The story thus sets the person up for a fall and we might say that this story has worked 'on' that person. Considering the function of stories can help in understanding how narratives shape human conduct, what people accomplish with stories, what narratives do on people and with what effects.

Fifth, a narrative analysis can help us understand how the body itself is woven into stories and how it is simultaneously lived and experienced as a physical thing while at the same time being shaped by the stories we hear and retell. Sixth, it can produce compelling and complex theoretical knowledge. Seventh, particularly when operating as a storyteller, a narrative analysis can produce research that is accessible to wide audiences and is highly effective for knowledge translation (Smith et al., 2015). Eighth, narrative analysis recognizes the 'unfinalizability' of people (Frank, 2010a). Because people can and do change, this recognition is both ethical and an empirically faithful account of human life.

Like all approaches to qualitative analysis, narrative analysis is not perfect. It holds the following difficulties and weaknesses. First, sometimes it can be difficult to identify actual stories for analysis. This might be because one story can ebb seamlessly into another.

Alternatively, a speaker can hop from one subject to another, producing stories that are not discrete or self-contained. Or, some stories are so thin, that is, skeletal and highly truncated, that identifying a story becomes difficult.

Second, for some (for example, Atkinson, 2010), narrative analytic work often suffers from 'narrative exceptionalism'. This refers to the belief that narrative is an especially distinctive form of behaviour. There is no reason to endow narratives with any qualities different from any other spoken discourse or unspoken activity. Others (for example, Bochner and Riggs, 2014; Frank, 2010b) offer a defence of narrative exceptionalism because they believe that narrative is distinctive among human capacities and distinctively fundamental for human flourishing. For example, Frank argues:

> Stories enjoy an exceptional place in human lives, first, because stories are the means and medium through which humans learn who they are, what their relation is to those around them (who counts as family, as community, and as enemies), and what sort of actions they are expected to perform under which circumstances. Stories teach which actions are good and which are bad; without stories, there would be no sense of action as ethical. (2010b: 665)

Third, because a narrative analysis privileges stories and sees them as often exceptional, if one is not careful, human experience and the person can fade into the background. For example, the researcher may come to see the story itself as the totality of their participants' experiences and forget that there is still a person out there walking around and doing other things besides telling stories. Fourth, narrative analysts tend to make sense of stories collected from a singular interview (as Nick Caddick has tried to do in Chapter 13 in order to produce an analysis that is comparable to those offered in the other 'Doing' chapters in this volume). This in-and-out-the-door approach is common in general in qualitative research, including work done using IPA, thematic analysis and grounded theory. It is not 'bad' or 'wrong'; excellent data can be generated. But researchers need to go about making sense of such data with a good measure of interpretive humility. Only so much can be said about people's lives from a one-shot interview.

BITE-SIZED SUMMARY 2

The core question of what constitutes a narrative analysis has been examined. Two basic standpoints towards narrative research have been identified and explored: 'story analyst' and 'storyteller' standpoints. The differences between a narrative analysis and other kinds of qualitative analysis have been discussed so that readers can make informed decisions about whether to use narrative analysis for particular research projects. The strengths and weaknesses of narrative analysis have also been examined to help inform these decisions more fully.

How to do narrative analysis: a guide

We now turn to the question of how to do narrative analysis. What follows is a set of guidelines through which a constructionist narrative approach might proceed. Drawing on Frank (2010a, 2012), the analysis described here is a **dialogical narrative analysis** (DNA). A DNA examines how a story is put together in terms of the narrative resources that are artfully used. It also 'studies the mirroring between what is told in the story – the story's content – and what happens as a result of telling that story – its effects' (Frank, 2010a: 71–2). Thus, in a DNA, stories are examined not simply for what is said or the narrative resources used to help structure storytelling. It extends analytic interest to what stories do. Before describing how a DNA might be done, we need to start with a few qualifications.

As highlighted in Table 12.1, there are many different types of narrative analysis that a researcher might use for different purposes. For example, if a researcher aims to focus on how an interviewer and interviewee perform a story together and why something is said in the interview context, a performance narrative analysis would be a useful option. If one seeks to focus on what the content of stories is, a thematic narrative analysis would be a sensible choice. However, if one wishes to combine aspects of the previous two analytic orientations but in addition ask 'What as actors do stories do and how well are people served by their stories?', a DNA is an appropriate choice.

As well as a focus on stories, another common thread that binds many narrative analyses together relates to how method is understood. There are at least two different ways to understand method. Neither is superior to the other; each serves different purposes. One understanding has come to dominate much qualitative research. We might term this a prescriptive (Frank, 2010a) or codified model (Chamberlain, 2011). Here method is largely understood as a prescribed set of steps or procedures that the analysis should follow. IPA, thematic analysis and grounded theory largely embody this understanding of method (see Chapters 4, 6 and 8 in this volume). In a codified model, a method is relatively easy to learn and do. Despite that, the codification of methods can lead to researchers producing 'what the method suggests they should' (Chamberlain, 2011: 50). This model is sometimes held up by journal editors, journal reviewers, university research project/thesis examiners and ethics committees as the most rigorous way to conduct qualitative analyses.

Yet, as Frank (2010a) reminds us, there has always been another tradition in which method has guidelines but is not prescriptive. In other words, another legitimate understanding of method is as a heuristic guide – a guide to interpretation. This understanding has a long history in the social and human sciences. Many narrative analyses adopt this understanding – and for good reason. According to Frank (2010a: 73, emphasis in original), 'Too many methods seem to prevent thought from *moving*'. Without a set sequence of rules or steps that one must follow, narrative analysis encourages movement of thought. For Frank (2010a: 73), 'Analytic or interpretive thought that is moving is more likely to allow and recognise movement in the thought being interpreted'. Movement of thought can take the analyst in unexpected and fertile directions, breathing fresh life into moribund concepts, encouraging theoretical curiosity and provoking new ways of seeing in the process. In my own experience, (see, for example, Smith, 2013a) practising method as a heuristic guide has enabled me to consider new stories that participants might tell about disability which had until now not been highlighted in the literature. Thus, the lack of prescriptive procedures can mean that engaging in an analysis is daunting but there are many virtues that go with understanding and practising method in this way. There may be no definitive rules to follow but guidelines do allow analytical competence to be worked up systematically and rigorously.

Drawing on Frank (2010a, 2012), what follows is a guide for doing a DNA which represents an attempt to help aspiring narrative analysts to steer a way through the analytic process. This guide consists of various analytic strategies. These are mostly presented as a set of questions that are grounded in the theoretical assumptions outlined earlier and that orient a DNA. The rationale for approaching analysis as a method of questioning is based on several observations. For Frank (2010a: 72), 'Some methods are more useful for the questions they offer than for any procedures they prescribe'. Questions do more than act as a guide for how to move along in the analytic process. Approaching data with a set of carefully considered questions in mind and examining the data with the aid of these questions can help to get thought moving. It can spur imagination and inspiration that, in turn, can lead to insight and understanding.

BITE-SIZED SUMMARY

3

An understanding of method as a heuristic guide – in contrast to the more common-place understanding of method as procedural guidelines – has been introduced. The differences between these two approaches to method have been outlined and the benefits of seeing method as a heuristic guide have been identified, paving the way for an introduction to the method of dialogical narrative analysis.

The analytic process

The contour of the guide for doing a DNA can be viewed as cyclical and iterative as opposed to linear and fixed. The researcher engages in the process of moving forward through each strategy outlined in the guide but can move back and forth between each, circling backward and forward sometimes, even jumping between strategies as well as appreciating that some will have different utility with respect to different stories. Thus, following Frank (2012: 44), some 'will be most useful for thinking about why they do not apply to a story. Others can open up what was unnoticed about the story.'

Getting the story

- *Deciding what is a story and/or narrative.* Many definitions of a story and narrative exist but, to analyse stories, a researcher needs to decide what is a story and if they see it as different from a narrative. These were differentiated earlier in this chapter but, to reiterate, a story is a tale that people tell. 'Story' is a complex genre that routinely contains characters (for example, people or animals), expresses a point of view (for example, 'I think people in the army are different to civilians': see Chapter 13) and a plot (for example, a structure that connects events over time, which has a complicating action where some event disrupts the initial state affairs, and a resolution, that is, an overarching consequence or explanation for why something happened). To help decide what is a story, a researcher can also use their experiences: often we know a story when we hear one.

- *Collect big and/or small stories.* It may be stating the obvious but, to analyse stories, a researcher needs stories! Whilst interviews are commonly used to collect stories, autobiographies, letters, diaries, vignettes, the media (for example, newspapers), ethnographic fieldwork notes, the internet (for example, blogs), visual material (for example, photographs) and conversations in everyday life can all be good sources of stories – big stories, small stories and everything in between (Freeman, 2011; Phoenix and Sparkes, 2009). 'Big stories' are long stories that entail a considerable amount of reflection on an experience or event, a significant part of a life, or the whole of it. In contrast, 'small stories' refer to fleeting conversations told during interaction about mundane things and everyday occurrences.[1]

- *Transcribe data.* If collecting stories from interviews, for instance, you should transcribe the data verbatim as soon as possible after collecting it. Transcription is much more than a technical exercise. It is a constructive process in which analytical thoughts can emerge and 'percolate'. Thus, not only should a researcher carefully decide on what to include and how to present the transcribed data; they should also think of transcription as part of the analytic process. You should jot down notes as you transcribe. For instance, ask yourself what types of stories might be emerging, which ones seem crucial and how particular stories unfold.

- *Writing.* Write continuously throughout the research project. Writing is not a 'mopping activity', something to be done just at the end of the research to communicate the results. Writing is a form of analysis because analysis happens in the process of writing (Richardson, 2000; Sparkes and Smith, 2014). As you jot down notes, write memos, edit your report and so on through the entire research process, you can progressively discover ideas, what counts and how stories 'hang together'. Think of writing as an iterative and

---

[1]There is some debate over small and big stories (for example, see Bamberg, 2011; Freeman, 2011). For example, small stories are often depicted as naturalistic data – that is, data that are neither elicited by nor affected by the actions of researchers – whilst big stories are often thought of as data constructed by researchers and participants in contexts such as interviews. This said, small stories can and do occur in contexts like interviews and big stories can and do occur in everyday life. Thus, rather than thinking of a small story as belonging just to everyday life and big stories as belonging solely to an interview context, researchers might consider making use of both kinds of stories in whatever context they are constructed (Sools, 2013).

inductive process of hearing stories speak to the research aims, representing those stories and theoretical thoughts in writing, revising your selection of stories and theory as you develop your arguments, and revising the writing as those stories and theory require (Frank, 2012). But, of course, writing has to start somewhere. To get analysis moving, to open it up, the following strategies are offered.

Getting to grips with stories

- *Indwelling*. Like familiarization or immersion within other types of analysis (for example, thematic analysis: see Chapter 6 in this volume), 'indwelling' involves reading the data (for example, an interview transcript) several times whilst, if possible, listening to any recording and jotting down initial impressions. But, according to Maykut and Morehouse (1994: 25) it also 'means to live within ... understanding the person's point of view from an empathetic rather than a sympathetic position'. As part of this, rather than thinking of the person as a vessel from which to extract information, the researcher orients themselves to the participant as someone who is a storyteller and who shares a story with another person or other people.

- *Identify stories*. Identify the story or stories in the actual data (for example, in the transcript). To help with this, look out for new beginnings in talk where there are marked shifts in content. The researcher might also try to look for where each line might be seen to begin and end. Once a collection of lines is established, a story may come into view. Another strategy is to look for classic elements of story structure in the text: Is there an orientation or setting introduced? Is there a complicating action and a resolution? Is there a coda (a summary or concluding event) that returns to the present? To help with this, look for phrases like 'It all started with . . .' because these can signal an opening to a story, and declarations such as 'So that's why I left' because these can highlight the end of the story. Finally, try to get a feel for stories being developed across the interview/transcript as a whole.

- *Identify narrative themes and thematic relationships*. The focus here is on 'what' is said; that is, the content of the story. A **narrative theme** is a pattern that runs through a story or set of stories. To search for and identify themes in a manner that keeps the story or stories intact, look for patterns within the stories by closely reading the text. To help with identifying patterns, the researcher can ask, 'What is the common theme(s) or thread(s) in each story?', 'What occurs repeatedly within the whole story?' As you systematically work through the text, identify theme materials by highlighting key sentences in different colours, underlining key phrases in the text and/or circling key words. In addition, in the margins of the transcript, field notes or other data source, write extended phrases (in four or five words) that summarize the manifest (apparent) and latent (underlying) meanings of the data. Do not think of this process as a typical sort of coding which, in other qualitative approaches, usually involves coding line by line and summarizing data in a code of one, two or three words. As we noted earlier, this can result in over-coding which can break the text down too much for a narrative analysis to work; the researcher is left with a set of codes, not a story. Thus, rather than over-code by coding the data line by line, think of the process as '**theme-ing**' the data.

- *Identify the structure.* The focus here is on 'how' the story is put together. To help with identifying the structure, consider (a) the direction(s) of the story (for example, decline and then progress) and depict this in a graph (see Figure 12.1 for a useful illustration of this); (b) the use of terms that point to structure (for example, when the participant refers to experiencing a 'crossroads'); (c) the participant's reflections on specific phases or chapters in their life (for example, 'It was then that I realised I had to fight to recover from my illness'); (d) the use of evaluative comments (for example, 'My life has gone downhill since I retired from the army'); (e) tone and changes in tone within the story (for example, pessimistic and later optimistic); (f) the objectives or 'wants' of the characters involved (for example, after spinal cord injury Jon wants to walk again); the conflicts or obstacles they face as they try to achieve their objectives (for example, doctors say that medicine has not yet found a cure for spinal injury); tactics or strategies they employ to reach their objectives (for example, going to the gym to keep muscles healthy for when a cure does come); their attitudes towards others and towards given circumstances (for example, optimistic about walking); the particular emotions they experience through-out (for example, sadness and a sense of loss); and/or their 'subtexts' or underlying and unspoken thoughts (for example, scared about a cure not happening).

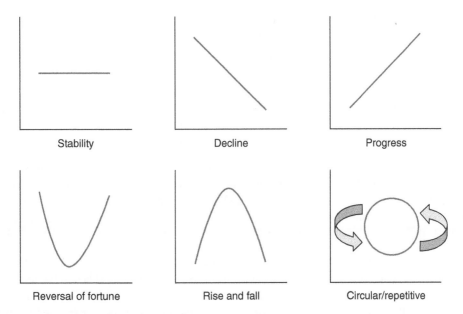

| Stability | Decline | Progress |
| Reversal of fortune | Rise and fall | Circular/repetitive |

Figure 12.1 Visualizing story structure (based on Gergen and Gergen, 1983): the x axis represents time while the y axis represents the trajectory of the narrative

> ## Practise getting to grips with stories
>
> Think about an autobiography that you have read recently (or choose an interesting one to read). Try to identify the types of story the narrator is telling about his or her life. What are the main themes? What is the structure of the narrative?

Opening up analytical dialogue further

Following Frank (2010a, 2012) and Sparkes and Smith (2012), when reading the data, thinking with it and travelling with the stories in their everyday lives, a researcher might next ask the following questions. Some questions can open up what was unnoticed about the story; the usefulness of others will arise from thinking about why they do not apply to a story. Each set of questions and each response to them will not always be applicable for inclusion in the final research report but asking each question can enhance understandings of the story. In addition, when asking each question, a researcher can think with the story as a whole. It can be useful to write a paragraph or two in response to each question or group of questions, revising and editing as needed.

- *Resource questions*. What resources does the storyteller draw upon to shape their experiences? What narrative resources shape how their story is told? Not everyone can simply access any narrative resource they wish and people cannot simply tell any story they choose about their lives and expect to be believed. Who, then, has access to which resources? Who is under what constraints in the resources they use? To understand the resources being used, it might be useful also to ask what other resources might lead to different stories. What might be preventing those alternative resources from being mobilized? How does the story reiterate, borrow or counter these narratives?

- *Circulation questions*. Understanding who your participants tell their stories to in everyday life can reveal useful insights into who those stories are intended for and how they may have been constructed with that intended audience in mind. Who, then, tells which stories to whom? Who would immediately understand that story and who would not understand it? Are there some people to whom the storyteller would not tell that story, and why not?

- *Connection questions*. The stories we tell to others can appeal to or repel those others. To whom does a person's story connect them? Who is placed outside this connection? How might groups be formed through sharing a common understanding of a certain story? Who does the story render external or 'other' to the group? Who is excluded from the 'we' who share the story? Who does the storyteller speak against? Who does the storyteller want to hear the story and who might they be afraid to hear it?

- *Identity questions.* What stories give people a sense of who they are? How do these stories do this? How do people tell stories to explore who they might become, and if not, why?

- *Body questions.* Stories are told not only about our bodies but using – and out of – our bodies. We often get a sense or a feeling within our bodies of what stories are good, virtuous and worth listening to or acting on, and which are bad, loathsome or best ignored. What stories do the participant and the researcher hold close to their hearts? How do these stories enable and constrain the ways we understand participants' experiences? What stories evoke fear in our bodies? What is our body telling us about the story, the storyteller and what it means to live well? How does your body respond to the story and what might that tell you about the story that was told? For an example in action, see Sparkes and Smith (2012).

- *Function questions.* As an actor or form of action, what does each story do for and on the person? That is, how might the story a person tells be useful to them, help them live a good life and do things 'for' them, and how might it lead them down dangerous roads and do things 'on' them? What does this story do for and on other people? How does a story shape a person's conduct, affecting what they do and do not do?

The process of doing a dialogical narrative analysis has been described. Some key elements of the process – not linear 'phases' or 'stages' – have been identified including indwelling, identifying stories, identifying narrative themes and thematic relationships, identifying structure and asking **dialogical questions**.

BITE-SIZED
SUMMARY
· · · · · · · · · · · · · · ·
4

Pulling the analysis together

This can be done in numerous ways. For example, a researcher might choose to move from a story analyst to a storyteller. Drawing upon a creative analytical practice like creative non-fiction, they might synthesize the results of a dialogical narrative analysis (DNA) in and as a story. The researcher might also produce a traditional realist tale in which the story – and its effects – are described systematically and explained to the reader (see, for example, the way Nick Caddick presents his analysis in Chapter 13 in this volume). Here a researcher might blend the results generated from the strategies around a set of interacting and interplaying themes that capture the content of stories and their functional dynamics or they might begin with a particular analytic interest and then organize the stories around it. Alternatively, as in the work of Frank (2010a) and Phoenix and Orr (2014), there can be a focus on pulling the results together to build a typology of narratives. This analytical move of identifying different types of narratives that people draw on to construct their stories is summarized as follows.

Build a typology

This can be done by reading through each result from the phases and then bringing these together – clustering them – into a set of narratives that constitute various 'ideal types' (that is, clearly defined narratives that are different from other ideal types and express something unique about participants' experiences). As an example, consider the two ideal types identified in Chapter 13 as belonging to the two different stories told by the participants. Each story identified as belonging to a particular ideal type should capture not just content and/or structure but also functions – what it can do. To help with this process the researcher can (a) translate the stories into images and then imagine these impacting on people and consider the consequences; (b) create time to think about the story, tell the story slowly to themselves, wait and listen to it and reflect some more without rushing the thinking process along; and (c) structure their writing around each type, revising and editing along the way to help 'discover' further the types of narratives used. After identifying the types of stories people tell, name each in a way that captures the essence of each narrative, for example a 'quest' narrative that speaks of life as an adventure or a 'chaos' narrative that speaks of life as an endless series of destructive events or a meaningless and empty vacuum. It can be useful after this to revisit the data to ensure the typology being built is grounded in the stories collected. The researcher may then need to revise the typology and names of the narratives.

Represent the results

Structure the report around the typology (for example, see the paper by Smith and Sparkes (2004) which is structured around a typology of three ideal types). The report can take the form of a realist tale but, given the commitment to 'unfinalizability', any ending of a DNA as represented in a realist tale is necessarily provisional. This does not mean that the results or end report are tentative. Rather, whilst all reports need to close for practical reasons, participants in most studies are still alive and, rather than giving their last word, can tell new stories in which they may become someone different (Frank, 2010a).

BOX 12.3 — **Understanding your story**

As an exercise in getting to grips with narrative analysis, consider the stories you tell about your own life. To do this, pair up with a classmate and take turns to interview each other (while audio-recording the interview). Begin simply with the question 'Tell me about your life' and proceed to ask your partner questions about their life, what their hopes and dreams are, what their greatest achievement is, their worst fear, their biggest disappointment and who are they close to. Take your time and be open. Then transcribe the interview that features your own story and conduct a narrative analysis of it, following the approach set out in this chapter. What dialogical questions might help you gain a deeper understanding of your own story? Where might your story be leading you and what might it be doing both on and for you? Coming to know your own story better will also make you better placed to hear others' stories as different or similar to your own and will help you consider how your own story might influence your interpretation of other people's lives.

CHAPTER SUMMARY

This chapter has described one way of going about practising a narrative analysis. It has highlighted the epistemological, ontological and theoretical commitments that inform how a narrative analysis can be practised. What a narrative analysis 'is' was described by highlighting its focus on story, two different analytic standpoints and various specific types of analysis that each stance gravitates towards in order to make sense of and communicate stories. A rationale for why a narrative analysis might be chosen was offered, grounded in a set of distinguishing features, strengths and weaknesses. The chapter then moved from a focus on 'what' and 'why' questions to 'how' a narrative analysis might be conducted. A series of analytic strategies that form a guide was highlighted. It is hoped that the example of a narrative analysis that follows in Chapter 13 will be useful as a resource from which to learn more about narrative analysis in practice.

Further reading

The paper by Smith and Sparkes (2011) provides a detailed discussion of how stories 'do' things by describing how different people might respond to a 'chaos' narrative. The paper by Douglas and Carless (2015) offers an example of research produced from the storyteller standpoint using the creative analytical practice of performance ethnography/ethnodrama. Finally, Frank's (2010a) book *Letting Stories Breathe* may be considered essential reading for anyone with a serious interest in analysing stories.

13

DOING NARRATIVE ANALYSIS

Nick Caddick

This chapter demonstrates how one version of narrative analysis – dialogical narrative analysis (DNA) – might be conducted. Adopting the methodology described by Brett Smith in Chapter 12 in this volume, I show how DNA can be put into practice to analyse interview data on the topic of transition from the army into civilian life. I demonstrate how to identify stories and themes/ structures within them and how key analytical concerns of DNA, such as asking dialogical questions and considering what stories *do* both for and to people, might be addressed. The worked example shows how two people can tell very different stories about a particular experience (in this case, transition) and what the consequences of these different stories are for their lives.

Introduction

Dialogical narrative analysis (DNA; see Frank, 2012, and Chapter 12 in this volume) is a comparatively recent addition to the range of analytical approaches that focus upon narrative and storytelling. There are currently no guides available that demonstrate how you might go about doing a DNA. My aim in this chapter is therefore to show, rather than tell, how DNA might be practised using the example of stories told by two ex-servicemen about their experiences of transitioning out of the army into civilian life (see Appendix 1 in this volume for the interview transcripts that were used in the analysis). The analytical process that I present is, however, not intended as a 'recipe' or 'template' for doing DNA because DNA does not prescribe any step-by-step approach. The method is deliberately flexible to allow for movement of thought rather than providing a codified or procedural basis for producing research findings. For me, this is what makes it so exciting – although I concede that this lack of definite procedural steps can make it seem daunting for someone attempting narrative analysis for the first time. This chapter should be read as one example of how DNA can be performed, showcasing simply the types of analytical concerns that make up a DNA (for another example, see Report 5 in Appendix 2 in this volume). The analytical steps taken to explore people's stories (in particular the types of dialogical questions asked in an analysis) will vary depending on considerations such as the research topic and questions, source(s) of data and the researcher's relationship with the participants/storytellers themselves.

In order to situate myself in relation to the stories told by David and Brian, I will first outline my 'speaking position' as a researcher to give readers a sense of what I brought to the analysis and what may have shaped the way I engaged with the interview transcripts (for more on researchers and speaking positions, see Chapter 2 in this volume). My doctoral research, in which I used DNA, has explored the effects of surfing in the lives of combat veterans experiencing post-traumatic stress disorder (the research presented in Appendix 2, Report 5 is drawn from that work). I therefore have some familiarity with the types of stories told by ex-servicemen like David and Brian. Whilst neither David nor Brian showed any indication of psychological distress based on their military experiences, their stories of transition and identity renegotiation resonate with some of the difficulties that the participants in my research faced upon leaving the forces (that is, in addition to their trauma and suffering). Accordingly, whilst I have attempted to analyse Brian's and David's stories 'on their own terms' as much as possible, it is perhaps inevitable that my understanding of other veterans' lives and experiences influenced how I approached Brian's and David's stories and my eventual interpretation of them. For example, I am familiar with stories like David's whereby veterans encountered the bewilderment of 'civvy street' when their military service had ended. By contrast, Brian's story was less familiar to me and taught me that the military can provide people with narrative resources that help them transition smoothly into a civilian environment.

Before I begin my demonstration of DNA, a brief comment on terminology is warranted. The terms **'story'** and **'narrative'** are often used interchangeably in the literature on narrative. This is partly because the meaning of these terms overlaps and a distinction is often difficult to sustain. In this chapter, though, I follow the broad distinction outlined by Brett Smith in Chapter 12 of viewing stories as the specific tales people tell of their lives whilst narratives are the broader 'story templates' and cultural structures/resources that people use to construct their individual stories. With this point in mind, I now present my analysis of David's and Brian's stories starting with my initial thoughts and readings of the transcripts. I then outline how I identified the types of stories they told, along with the main themes and structure of the stories. Next, I describe the process of working with dialogical questions to explore the two ex-servicemen's stories. Finally, I conclude with some reflections on the process of doing DNA.

Orienting to David's and Brian's stories

I began the analysis by immersing myself in the stories of David and Brian, that is, by reading and closely re-reading the interview transcripts which I understood as stories told by the two men about their transition out of the army. I quickly noticed that the interview data were more structured and the interviewer was more actively involved than would normally be the case in data generated specifically for narrative analysis. Typically narrative analysis relies on data generated from sources where participants are given the opportunity to develop lengthy stories about their experiences with minimal interruption. These include interviews but also visual narratives, diaries, internet blogs and particularly autobiographical work. Nevertheless, I found it useful to think of the transcripts themselves as stories with a beginning, middle and end, which Brian and David developed gradually in response to the interviewer's questions. After an initial reading of the transcripts, I re-read them with two broad questions in mind that formed my research questions for conducting the analysis. The first, following the original study's aims (see Appendix 1 in this volume), was 'How did David and Brian experience their transition from the army to civilian life?' The second question, helping me focus on stories, was 'What stories helped David and Brian make sense of their transition experiences?' This is a typical question for narrative analysis and distinguishes it from other qualitative approaches. I then proceeded to equip myself to develop themes from the data by highlighting the portions of the transcripts that I felt spoke to these questions and recording in the margins initial ideas about the kinds of stories Brian and David were telling. As I am unable to demonstrate this specific process within the confines of this chapter, I provide a brief reflection in Box 13.1 that explains how '**theme-ing**' the data relates to other aspects of doing DNA.

BOX 13.1	The iterative process of doing a dialogical narrative analysis

DNA usually unfolds as an iterative process of data generation and data analysis: these proceed in tandem rather than sequentially (see Chapter 8 on grounded theory for another approach in which data generation and data analysis occur at the same time). For example, as I read the transcripts of interviews conducted early in a study, I may begin formulating analytical ideas about participants' stories that will inform the questions I ask in future interviews. The answers to these might lead me in new, unanticipated directions. By 'theme-ing' the transcripts, I identify patterns and structural elements of stories that I can later compare with other participants' stories and look for similarities and differences in their experiences. Asking dialogical questions (see below) is an important part of this process. For example, asking early on what people's stories are doing for and to them may help develop an understanding of these stories that shapes how the analysis unfolds. For this chapter, I have clearly been unable to engage fully in this iterative process as I did not collect the data myself and did not have access to the larger data set. My analysis of Brian's and David's stories is therefore limited to what I have been able to discern about these stories from studying the transcripts and reflecting on the stories they told.

Identifying stories

What struck me most when reading David's and Brian's stories was the difference between their overall transition experiences. Whereas Brian seemed to have tactfully navigated his transition to civilian life with a degree of ease and efficiency, David wandered in a meaningless void in which his life as a civilian lacked the sense of purpose and direction previously granted him by his army career. Upon my initial reading of the transcripts, I was unsure how to make sense of this difference. Why was it that Brian had managed to find a way of being in civilian life that suited him and enabled him to carry on living a 'good life' whilst David seemed condemned to a life of apathy and banality without the army? To begin exploring this conundrum, I started looking for the stories that shaped their individual transition experiences and through which they made sense of their lives before, during and after leaving the army.

Clues to the story David constructed about his life in the army are given right at the start of his interview (other 'clues' or 'tips' on identifying stories can be found in Chapter 12). In response to the first question about whether the army influenced his sense of self (lines 1–13), David initiates a story about growing from boyhood to manhood in the army. For example, we learn that as a 'nipper', David lacked confidence and that he joined the army to get away because he 'didn't have a trade' and had 'no or very little education'. I interpreted this as a 'lowly beginnings' narrative in which the central character (David) uses the army as a springboard for escaping his humble circumstances and pursuing something noble, worthwhile or virtuous perhaps. In the army, he became something that transcended his early life destiny. The story of transformation is continued in his response to the next question (lines 15–23):

Arnie: What aspects, if any, of being a soldier were important to you?

David: I was a member of a team and I was an important member of a team and I was recognized as doing something for my country. You know, I was prepared to go. If they say, 'Right, David, Kuwait has been attacked, you know, I was ready to go'. Yeah. It wasn't a case of 'Woah, it's their country, it's nothing to do with us'. If the boss wanted to send me, then away I go. That was important to me. It's like, as I say, I had an identity and I belonged to somewhere.

David's comments here suggest that his personal life story became caught up in the broader political narrative of the army and its role in society as protector/enforcer (for example, in the liberation of Kuwait as part of the first Gulf War in 1991). David was an important cog in a much larger machine that performed a vital social function. His role within the team provided his life with a sense of meaning and purpose and constituted an organizing principle for his life story. Furthermore, the values he considered noble and worthwhile (including honesty, discipline and obedience to authority) and which he sought to embody as part of his journey from lowly beginnings towards a higher state of virtue were derived from his place within the collective organization of the army. Throughout this chapter, I will unpack the implications of David's story about his military career for his transition to civilian life.

By contrast, Brian's story contains no evidence of the 'lowly beginnings' narrative that shaped David's experience. Brian provided no information about his upbringing or his reasons for joining the army, perhaps constructing his past as relatively inconsequential for his present story (that is, omitting his background from the narrative – Spector-Mersel, 2011). The 'type' of narrative that structured his experiences in the army is less readily apparent from his interview transcript. As such, I found it interesting to consider what story he was *not* telling. Unlike David, Brian's personal story did not seem to be encompassed by the broader societal 'master narrative' of the army and its place within society. Accordingly, whilst a sense of belonging to the larger collective was clearly important to Brian, there is no indication that he depended upon this identification with the collective to provide his life with meaning and value in quite the same way as David did. This is not to suggest that the army was unimportant to Brian's life story; on the contrary, it was instrumental in shaping the kind of person he became. Rather, his story was less about what military people are part of and more about what they are or what they do. He described the character role of 'soldier' and all that this entails, for example being flexible and adaptable, having a sense of urgency and attention to detail and being disciplined, hard-working and reliable. The story he told was about demonstrating his appropriation of this character role by progressing through the rank structure of the army. Once again, I will unpack the implications of Brian's story for his transition experiences as the chapter unfolds.

Based on my reading of the transcripts, both David and Brian encountered a kind of 'narrative problem'; that is, neither of them wanted to leave the army when they did and both had to find ways of continuing their life stories after a major chapter of those stories (that is, their military careers) had ended. Having identified the stories that David and Brian told about their military lives, I began to explore how they each responded to this problem by considering the themes and structure embedded within their stories of transition to civilian life.

BITE-SIZED SUMMARY 1

Initial aspects of dialogical narrative analysis have been outlined and engaged with. This began with a brief consideration of my 'speaking position' as a researcher and analyst in relation to the data on two ex-servicemen's stories of the transition from army to civilian life. Dialogical questions were suggested that were appropriate to the data, would help to understand the storied nature of the data and would give shape to the analysis. Key stories were discerned within David's and Brian's interview transcripts. I also pointed to the analytical value of noting the absence of stories that a speaker could have used.

Identifying themes and structure

A number of key themes were repeatedly emphasized by both men throughout their stories of transition to the civilian world. One theme common to Brian's and David's stories was a sense of difference and superiority over civilians in terms of working practices. As Brian commented: 'I've noticed that the way ex-military guys manage their staff is much better than the way a civilian-trained person does' (lines 70–72). Both men portrayed themselves as direct, decisive, disciplined and willing to do things 'properly' whereas civilians in comparison were portrayed as lazy, unruly and interested in doing only the minimum amount of work required. This theme, in turn, relates to the broader notion of high standards and traditional values that permeated every aspect of military life and that were seemingly absent or not recognized in civilian life. Such values and standards formed key components of both men's stories which shaped how they experienced their transition from the army into civilian life, albeit in different ways.

Highlighting the differences in their transition experiences, Brian's and David's stories each embodied a separate core theme in response to the problem of transition. The major theme in David's story is that of loss. David woefully and regretfully tells of losing his place in the organization that gave his life meaning and purpose and of feeling worthless and alone in civilian life. His despair is evident in his response to being asked whether he feels he is still in an important job: '[Sigh] People like to tell me I've got that now but I know I haven't got that now' (lines 35–36). He believes that nobody now cares about the values and standards that previously afforded him status and recognition within the army and that constituted his idea of striving for a noble and worthwhile life. Consequently his story of transition was marked by loss, apathy and regret. In contrast, the major theme in Brian's story is that of adaptability. Brian described one of the key attributes of soldiers as their flexibility and ability to adapt to new situations: 'the forces learned me how to adapt to new situations and this was just another situation to adapt to' (lines 216–218). He repeatedly emphasized how he was able to adapt his capabilities and his ways of relating to others to suit his new job and situation in civilian life. Brian was able to uphold his values and standards by changing his expression of them which, he admitted, was not always easy but ultimately it enabled him to continue his identification with army life during and after transition. His story of transition was thus marked by a sense of agency, adaptability and personal control.

In addition to themes, the structure of Brian's and David's stories reveals valuable information about their transition experiences (see Chapter 12 for further advice on identifying structure). David's transition story was structured by a narrative of decline: life once was good, meaningful and worthwhile and now it is bad, meaningless and worthless. David began to structure his story as a decline when he described leaving the army as disappointingly anti-climactic: 'No one's calling me "Sergeant" any more. That was funny. That was a shock. That's when you knew. And then that's it – you walk out and no one's prepared you for that' (lines 92–95). He then continued to develop the structural element of decline by making repeated references to the 'void' of civilian life and by telling of everything he missed about the army. Brian's story, on the other hand, embodies a more stable narrative trajectory: a transition has occurred, yet life carries on pretty much as it always has. This structure of stability is evident in the following comments where Brian compared his feelings towards himself before and after transition:

> when I was in the forces, you feel good about yourself anyway. You've got an identity there and you feel good about yourself. And since I've been out, it's almost the same I think – not much has changed there really. Obviously what I do now is different but I don't think I've changed a great deal. I still try to maintain my ideals and the principles that I had from before, which is perhaps why, every now and again, I've caused a few ructions because I've still tried to maintain and perhaps enforce my ideals on other people perhaps. (Lines 286–293)

In both cases, the narrative structure of David's and Brian's stories highlighted important features of their lived experiences of transition as the catalyst for a descent into despair or as a relatively seamless continuation of a prior life story. By considering how stories are told – that is, their narrative structure – we thus come to a fuller understanding of the experiences these stories not only recount but also help to bring about. To appreciate story structure, it can help to depict the trajectory of a person's story in graphical form. See Figure 13.1 for an example of this in relation to Brian's and David's stories.

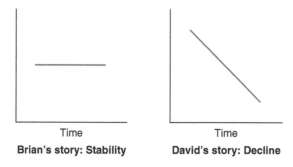

Time   Time

Brian's story: Stability   **David's story: Decline**

Figure 13.1 Brian's and David's narrative trajectories: the x axis represents time while the y axis represents the trajectory of the narrative

BITE-SIZED SUMMARY
....
2

Key themes that were evident in Brian's and David's stories have been identified alongside the basic structure of their stories. Identifying themes (what is said) and structure (how it is said) provides valuable analytical information about stories that can help you understand participants' experiences. You can also use this information as the basis for asking more complex dialogical questions (see below).

> ## BOX 13.2 Presenting the analysis
>
> In this chapter, I have chosen to present my analysis under headings drawn from the account of the analytic process offered in Chapter 12 in order to illustrate that process. In doing so, I would like to point out that a narrative analysis would not typically be presented in this way. An example of how narrative analysis may be presented and represented in textual form can be found in Appendix 2 (Report 5). In addition, there are many different ways to present a narrative analysis and no strict guidelines on how this should be done. For example, the analysis might be structured under several subheadings that relate to different thematic or structural components of the stories identified, with each of these discussed in detail in the results section of a paper (for example, Smith, 2013a). Alternatively, the results of the analysis might be split into just two or three sections with the first describing the stories told by participants and subsequent sections detailing the effects of these stories in the participants' lives (for example, Caddick, Smith and Phoenix, 2015a). Further still, the analysis itself may be represented as a story, presented as an undivided whole with the purpose of showing rather than telling or explaining the significance of the data (for example, Smith, 2013b). As such, there is a variety of possibilities for presenting a DNA and plenty of room for creativity in deciding how to format the analysis.

Identifying the social, cultural and relational dynamics of stories: asking dialogical questions

Up until this point in the analysis, it might appear as though Brian's and David's stories were personal tales they had spun around their experiences retrospectively in order to make meaning of their lives. To adopt such a view, however, would be to miss the social, cultural and relational dynamics that shaped not only the type of stories they told about their transition experiences but also the way they told them, their reasons for telling them and the consequences of telling these particular stories for their personal and social lives. Asking dialogical questions are a crucial means of opening up the social, cultural and relational dynamics of stories. This aspect of DNA can be complicated to get to grips with; further advice can be found in Chapter 12. In this section, I will explore three dialogical questions that enabled me to open up Brian's and David's stories and I will consider how these dynamic influences affected their storied lives. The process of asking dialogical questions is summarized in Table 13.1.

Table 13.1 Asking dialogical questions

Type of question	Example	Purpose
Identity questions	How is the storyteller's identity shaped by the story they are telling?	To help us understand the ways in which people's identities develop according to the stories they tell about themselves.
Resource questions	What narrative resources does the storyteller borrow from the wider stock of cultural narratives in order to tell their story?	Stories are never simply one's 'own' and can never be fully original. All stories that people tell draw upon narrative structures that culture and society make available (for example, a 'rags to riches' plotline). Asking resource questions helps us understand how people are able to tell the stories they tell and where these stories come from.
Connection/ affiliation questions	Who does this person's story connect them to/disconnect them from?	The process of telling stories about oneself is a thoroughly social one. Even if the story is told inside a person's mind, there will still be an 'imagined audience' that will be important to shaping the story. Certain stories may be approved or disapproved of by certain people or groups, connecting us to these people or disconnecting us from them. Understanding who shares a person's story and who is opposed to it gives us valuable information about the social process of storytelling.

Identity questions

Identity was a clear focus of the original interviews conducted by Arnie Reed (see the preface to Appendix 1 in this volume), so it makes sense to start with identity questions. Narrative theorists often view personal identity as a social performance, constituted through stories (Smith and Sparkes, 2008). In other words, people not only *tell* stories to explore who they are; they *live*, *enact* and *perform* them in social life (Frank, 2010a; Smith and Sparkes, 2008). From this perspective, identity can only be maintained as long as there are opportunities for performing that identity in a way that will be recognized by oneself and others as a socially 'valid' performance. It is clear from Brian's and David's interviews that they both sought to enact similar stories in civilian life that focused on their continued performance of the character role of 'soldier'. For both men, this meant continually striving to embody the values and ideals (for example, discipline, honesty and reliability) that shaped their respective stories of military life. For David, however, losing his place in the collective organization that validated his expression of these ideals – and constituted his way of living a good and virtuous life – resulted in him losing the opportunity to enact his preferred identity. For example, one way of enacting his military identity was by taking pride in his appearance and uniform as a reflection of virtue and discipline. As a school caretaker, opportunities to do this were limited:

> I miss walking out the door and making sure I'm all right. I'm proud to be a soldier. Now I walk out the door in my overalls and I think, 'Well, yeah, that's it'. You try to give an appearance of someone who's been trained and disciplined but it's not the same, it's not the same. You don't have the same effect as anywhere else. (Lines 319–324)

Unlike David, Brian was seemingly able to continue his identity performance as 'soldier' in his new role in civilian life. Brian's story focused on being 'ex-forces' – on the type of person he became and still was through military service and training. He did not require continued membership in the armed forces to validate his identity performance, merely that others recognized him for it. As Brian put it, 'people know I'm ex-forces whether I tell them or not' (lines 433–434). His embodied performance of being a soldier was thus validated by others: 'It's just that they pick up on the way I act, the way I behave and the way I speak as well – they pick on it straight away and they know' (lines 436–438). For Brian, having others validate his social identity performance enabled him to sustain his military identity despite now being technically classed as a civilian: 'So, although I feel I have quite adjusted to civilian life, um, really I'm still an ex-serviceman. I'm not a civilian as such' (lines 441–443).

As David's and Brian's stories show, the process of creating and maintaining identity through storytelling does not take place in a social vacuum. Rather, it is an inherently relational or dialogical activity, depending on others to support, validate and sometimes contest these performances. DNA thus enables us to consider how people's identities are created and transformed through a social process of telling and enacting stories about ourselves.

> **Narrative identity** has been introduced and described as relational – that is, a social process that evolves along with other people in the storyteller's life. Asking 'identity questions' helps us to understand how people tell stories to make sense of who they are and who they might become.
>
> BITE-SIZED SUMMARY
>
> 3

Resource questions

Narrative resources are the plots or storylines that society and culture make available to us, from which we selectively draw to construct the stories we tell. Gaining 'access' to such resources is important and may depend on certain characteristics or experiences that make it possible for a person to narrate particular stories about themselves (for example, one's status as a current or former soldier in the British army). Not surprisingly, the majority of the narrative resources used by Brian and David to tell stories about their lives were provided to them by the army. Yet the availability of resources for telling stories about their post-army lives seemed to differ between David and Brian. For Brian, the ability to maintain close links with other ex-forces personnel was an important resource that enabled him to continue his storied performance of 'being ex-forces' and have that performance validated by significant others. This was evident in the way he talks about his first job as a civilian:

> I treated my first move into civilian life, especially the job, as another posting really and it worked quite well because the first job I went to...I was working in a small department of about ten people and six of those were ex-forces and they were all from my old regiment and some I knew from before anyway so really it was very similar to another posting, just another job. (Lines 191–196)

Narrative resources are linked to narrative identity in that resources are required for sustaining identity performances. Brian managed to keep alive some of the army's narrative resources by maintaining links with other ex-military personnel, thereby establishing a sense of continuity between his former military identity and his current position in civilian life. Furthermore, Brian was able creatively to adapt the narrative resources given to him by the army (for example, the 'adaptability' and 'flexibility' of good soldiers) to suit his new role in society. By emphasizing the adaptability of soldiers, he not only reinforced his identity performance but also found a useful story to guide him through the experience of transition.

David, on the other hand, found that the narrative resources he depended on for narrating his story had been stripped away by his experience of leaving the army. Being part of a team was an important resource that no longer existed for David once he was forced to leave. Furthermore, upon leaving, he was made to surrender everything that connected him to his story including his uniform, his title as 'Sergeant' and his access to army locations and relationships. Accordingly, all of the props that had supported his story of transformation from lowly beginnings to being an important part of a much larger story were removed, leaving him feeling empty and without an alternative story to fall back on. As David's words suggested, when he walked out the gate on his last day he was confronted immediately with this unsettling emptiness: 'you walk out and there's nothing – there's that void. It's just like an open space, an empty space' (lines 127–129). David went on to describe how unprepared he felt for leaving the army, which may be one reason why he experienced a great 'void' in civilian life. In Frank's (2013) terms, there was no 'narrative map' to guide him in civilian life; his previous map – his sense of direction in life – was constituted solely by his place within the organizational structure of the army.

DNA enables us to appreciate that people's stories are not theirs alone and that they necessarily borrow from the broader narrative resources supplied by culture, society and various institutions (such as the military) in order to tell stories. People then exercise a degree of agency and choice in adapting and applying these resources to their personal stories, although they do this within certain material and discursive limits. For example, whilst Brian and David, theoretically speaking, had access to the same set of narrative resources in the army, David's ability to rework these resources in civilian life was limited both by the story he was previously caught up in and by a lack of opportunity for enacting a military identity in the school where he worked post-transition. Brian, on the other hand, seemed well positioned to carry the army's narrative resources with him into his civilian work environment through the story he told and the connections he subsequently made. Below, I discuss how connections with others are both cultivated and inhibited through stories.

Connection/affiliation questions

The stories we tell can connect us to others who may share our story and our perspective on things. They may also disconnect us from other people who contest or oppose our stories. Illustrating the relational focus of DNA, an important question to ask is who the storyteller is connected to or alienated from by the stories they tell. Both David and Brian recounted instances in which their stories of military life – including their continued efforts to embody the ideals that shaped these stories – complicated their relationships with their civilian counterparts. David, for example, described how 'being an ex-soldier' hindered his efforts to integrate himself into civilian working practices while previously working as a truck driver:

> Where it hinders me is the fact that I like things in lines. I like things in neat packages and so when I go – like when I was driving the truck, when I used to come back at night, I used to park all the wagons up so all the bumpers were level. Funny as it may seem, they had them parked all over the car park. It made it harder to get out. (Lines 238–243)

Likewise, for Brian, continuing his storied performance of 'being ex-forces' seemed to alienate him from civilian colleagues:

> I was going about it [the job] differently to how everyone else did. Everyone else did what was expected and I was going that extra sort of mile every time and I found that was causing a lot of problems because I was doing it and no one else was. (Lines 83–86)

The values that David and Brian were invested in and which shaped their stories were not shared by others and set up boundaries between them and their civilian counterparts. Fortunately perhaps for Brian, he was able to find others who shared his stories of 'being ex-forces' and who appreciated the military values he continued to display:

> it was quite helpful to speak to them and find out what was going on. Just coming out and being a bit of the new boy there and it is a slightly different environment but that ... I felt, I think things would have been different if I hadn't gone for that job first off and been surrounded by ex-forces people, especially some of the guys I'd known from before

as well, or if ... and even ones I didn't know, we had mutual friends with other people we knew between us, so that worked out really well. (Lines 203–210)

Working with other ex-forces people seemed to facilitate Brian's transition to civilian life by connecting him with others who knew what he was about and who embodied a similar 'character type' as former soldiers. Thus, whilst Brian's military identity and stories often disconnected him from civilian relationships, they helped him forge bonds with other ex-forces personnel which, in turn, helped smooth his experience of transition to the civilian world. By asking such connection/affiliation questions, DNA helps us to understand storytelling as a thoroughly social process that influences not only the teller but other people in the teller's social worlds.

Synthesizing the results

After opening up Brian's and David's stories through the use of dialogical questions, I returned to thinking about their stories as a whole in order to synthesize the results.

BOX 13.3 | **Thinking with stories**

Thinking *with* stories rather than just *about* them can be useful when conducting a DNA. Thinking about a story involves abstractly scrutinizing it, dissecting it and theorizing it from a disciplinary perspective in order to develop theoretical abstractions. Thinking *with* stories, on the other hand, involves trying to understand the story from the point of view of the teller. Imagine yourself telling that story and what it might feel like. This is similar to adopting an 'emic' perspective, as described by Sparkes and Smith (2014), in which the researcher endeavours to 'enter into' the phenomenon being investigated (something that echoes the phenomenological commitment found in interpretative phenomenological analysis – see Chapter 4 in this volume). Doing so requires patience and thoughtfulness but is worth the extra effort as it can enable the researcher to understand participants' stories on a deeper level. It is also important when working with dialogical questions. For example, by developing a deeper appreciation of participants' stories – by getting inside the story and feeling its nuances – the researcher may get a feel for the most important concerns from the storyteller's perspective and thus for what questions should be asked that speak to those concerns and that may help to open up the analysis.

> The notion of 'dialogical questions' has been introduced as a key analytical concern of DNA. Asking dialogical questions helps to unravel the social, cultural and relational dynamics of stories; that is, the ways in which stories are shaped by broader cultural narratives and how other people are often strongly influential in shaping the way in which we tell stories about ourselves, who we tell these stories to and why, and how they are told. There are many kinds of questions you can ask in relation to your data to open up the analysis: you are not limited to those presented in this chapter (see Chapter 12 for further examples of dialogical questions).
>
> **BITE-SIZED SUMMARY**
> ················
> **4**

This is similar to the process of typology building and pulling the analysis together as described by Brett Smith in Chapter 12. At this stage in my analytical process, I wondered whether Brian's and David's stories might represent different 'ideal types' as narratives of transition from the army to civilian life. As part of this process, I considered naming their stories in a way that would capture the overall content and storytelling in Brian's and David's interview transcripts. Put rather crudely, we might call Brian's story a narrative of 'adaptation' to civilian life whereas David told a story of 'un-adaptation' or 'mal-adaptation'. Brian's story of transition and identity renegotiation positioned him as having made a successful transition into civilian life. Drawing on the notion of soldiers as adaptable to new situations, he characterized his transition as successful and appeared to be content with life. Whilst he evidently missed his time in the forces, particularly the social side of army life, he had found ways of replacing what he missed and therefore experienced his current life as a 'good compromise'. By contrast, David's transition story depicted him as 'un-adapted' to civilian life. He experienced the civilian world as an alien landscape where people played by different rules and the things that mattered – and still matter – to him about army life were not valued by the people around him. He appeared unhappy with his lot in life and was beginning to question its purpose. The two men's stories thus appear radically different and may be said to constitute opposing 'ideal types' of transition narrative.

Identifying function

DNA conceives of stories as 'actors' in people's lives. This means stories do things for and to people that make a difference to their lives and affect them in both good and dangerous ways. An important component of any dialogical narrative analysis is thus likely to be identifying what effects the story is having in a person's life. David's and Brian's transition narratives affected their lives in distinct ways. For David, being unable to continue his story of personal transformation in which he became a respected member of an important team meant that he was destined for an unhappy and apparently meaningless life as a civilian. His story led to what Freeman (2009) termed **'narrative foreclosure'**; that is, the story he had been telling about his military life had ended and there was no way of moving creatively into the future. The future, then, seemed to hold nothing more than an endless repetition of an empty and meaningless present, a situation of despair encapsulated in David's comments about his current job: 'This is me for the rest of my life' (line 223). As such, his story had effectively ended and there appeared to be no way of opening up a new chapter. His story thus worked *on* him in ways that prevented him from exploring future possibilities and living a productive and meaningful life.

Brian's story seemed to affect him in a rather more positive way. By cultivating a sense of continuity in identity and narrative resources, his story of 'adaptability' enabled him to transition amicably into civilian life, despite him not wanting to leave the army or being totally ready for the transition. Unlike in David's case, Brian's life story seemed to move smoothly into a new chapter. His story thus worked for him by enabling him to adjust to life without the army, helping him also to address the 'narrative problem' that I identified earlier of continuing his life story after the ending of a major chapter. The different effects of David's and Brian's stories may be suitably summed up in the following responses:

Arnie: Um, do you think you've adjusted to civilian life?
David: No. No. I would say that in one easy answer there. (Lines 392–394)

Arnie: Looking back, would you have done anything differently? Or not?
Brian: No, I don't think so. No, everything's worked out as I would have hoped. Yeah. (Lines 452–455)

As 'actors' in their lives, Brian's and David's stories thus demonstrate the importance of narratives in understanding the effects of transition and identity renegotiation for ex-forces personnel.

Reflections

DNA involves thinking about how people and their stories co-exist. In DNA, stories are conceptualized as dynamic, relational and constitutive forces in people's lives. From this perspective, the world may be viewed as something akin to a web of story-mediated interaction between different social actors. This said, one challenge when doing DNA is to avoid seeing everything as the product of a story and thus reducing all forms of human action to narrative. Not everything is narrative and, as such, it is important when doing narrative analysis not to force all that a participant says or does into story-shaped explanations. I hope to have avoided this temptation in this chapter whilst also demonstrating the fruitfulness of DNA in terms of illuminating people's subjective lives and experiences. As a final thought, I wish to point out that any DNA must necessarily remain unfinalized. David and Brian are (presumably) still out there in the midst of stories that are continually unfolding to this day. Much might have changed in the years since the original interviews were conducted and David and Brian may well have moved on to tell vastly different stories about their experiences of civilian life. Indeed, what was once true of their transition experiences may no longer be so, as meanings often change with the passage of time and experiences are always reinterpreted from the vantage point of the present. DNA therefore invites us to study people's stories – and the effects of their stories – whilst all the time remembering that, when the analysis is over, the story goes on.

BOX 13.4 — **Practise identifying stories, themes and structure**

The following extract is taken from an interview with a combat veteran named Samuel (a pseudonym), which was conducted as part of the project reported by Caddick, Smith and Phoenix (2015a) and summarized in Appendix 2 (Report 5) in this volume. Samuel is a member of a UK-based veterans' surfing charity who has recently relocated himself to another part of the country and has also been treated for alcoholism. The charity of which he is a member was set up to help veterans dealing with post-traumatic stress disorder (PTSD), although Samuel himself was not officially diagnosed with PTSD. Samuel suffered multiple problems including relationship breakdown and a descent into alcoholism following ten years' service in the military. The interview from which this extract is taken was conducted after Samuel had been a regular member of the surfing charity for two years.

Read the extract and begin to consider what type of story Samuel begins to construct in response to the first question and what extra detail is given in response to the second. Think about the key themes that are evident in the extract and what the structure of the story might be. Consider, for example, what the trajectory of Samuel's life story is that is revealed in his responses. If you want to stretch your understanding of narrative analysis, consider what dialogical questions you might ask to gain further insight into this extract.

(Continued)

Nick: So where do you think your life is going at the moment?

Samuel: Forwards probably, yeah – yeah, I mean it all just seems really pos-
         itive at the moment, I know I've got friends around me. I've made
         more friends here in a couple of years than I had back home in a
         lifetime and sometimes – you know, what I'd count as real friends,
         alright – it might be ten, but that's still ... I think ten good friends is
         quite a lot to be honest. Yeah – and I think that is just kind of – that's
         moving forward but it's not moving forwards too fast, I'm just taking
         things steady, enjoying what's happening, but also making – I think
         learning that stuff, I think – I thought there was nothing you could tell
         me about anything and now I realized that I actually knew sod all. So
         I've just opened my ears a bit and kind of learnt a bit and I'm just
         enjoying it and it feels like an adventure at the minute of life – do you
         know what I mean? And I just feel quite lucky that I've got a second
         chance at it because I think a couple of years ago, I might not had,
         it might have been different, so yeah.

Nick: OK, and what do you think your biggest challenge is in life at the
         moment?

Samuel: Erm, my biggest challenge is – my biggest challenge is quite often
         like, the smallest ones in some ways. You know, my biggest chal-
         lenges are when I'm feeling that I'm having a real bad time – and
         sometimes the biggest challenge is picking the phone up and talk-
         ing to someone, being – I think being honest with people about
         how I'm feeling. It's so easy for me to say I'm alright when I know
         I'm not and I need to talk about something, making that first step
         into it, I find really hard. Opening the door to getting some help or
         advice I find really difficult and it doesn't seem to get any easier with
         practice either. And relationships are still challenging I think. But
         again – I think I was lucky in rehab in that I think I got quite an insight
         into myself – maybe into how I've done things badly in the past. You
         know, I can see where I've gone wrong, so I've got no real excuse
         to keep repeating it, if I do it's kind of like my choice – it's up to me
         if I wanna keep ... I've reached a point now where I can say 'Well,

I know that's not gonna work, do I really wanna do it again?' – and sometimes doing it again is actually the easy option. You know – keep screwing up, keep treating people badly, sometimes in the short term is the easy solution, so sometimes doing the right thing is sometimes the challenge, yeah.

CHAPTER SUMMARY

In this chapter I provided an example of the process of conducting a dialogical narrative analysis. I began by identifying the key stories that David and Brian used to construct their experiences of transition from military life. I then highlighted the themes and narrative structure of these stories, including loss and narrative decline in David's story compared with adaptability and narrative stability in Brian's. Following this, I demonstrated one of the key analytical features of DNA by posing dialogical questions in relation to the data. Exploring these questions highlighted how narrative identity, narrative resources and connection/affiliation between the storyteller and other people were important aspects of David's and Brian's stories that powerfully shaped their transition experiences with various consequences for and on their lives.

Further reading

The full version of the article summarized in Report 5 (see Appendix 2) provides an example of a dialogical narrative analysis study (see Caddick, Smith and Phoenix, 2015a). Two further papers from the same project also provide examples of DNA in action by exploring 'collective stories' and peer relationships among combat veterans (Caddick, Phoenix and Smith, 2015b) and processes of masculinity, health and help-seeking among combat veterans (Caddick, Smith and Phoenix, 2015c). Frank's (2012) chapter in the book *Varieties of Narrative Analysis* provides a theoretically sophisticated and detailed overview of the method of dialogical narrative analysis.

14

ANALYSING QUALITATIVE DATA: COMPARATIVE REFLECTIONS

Evanthia Lyons

This chapter offers comparative reflections on the employment of the five approaches to the analysis of the data presented in Appendix 1, concentrating on the analytic foci, matters of epistemology and the 'value' of the outcomes. The major similarities and differences between the five approaches are highlighted. Particular attention is paid to how each of the approaches conceptualizes and deals with the way researchers should use existing psychological knowledge and their personal experiences and speaking positions in the process of conducting qualitative research. The chapter also discusses the goals of psychological inquiry and the question of what are the most appropriate criteria for evaluating research carried out within each approach. Finally, it considers the relative usefulness and appropriateness of adopting a mixed methods or a pluralistic approach to research.

Introduction

In Chapter 1, I noted that, when we were developing the concept for this book, Adrian Coyle and I had two main goals. Firstly, we wanted to provide the reader with a sense of how the theoretical and epistemological positions underlying different approaches to qualitative research influence the research process and how (relatively) novice researchers experienced their attempts to apply the 'experts'' descriptions of the analytic process to a common data set. We believed this would make explicit the uncertainties and dilemmas that are often faced by qualitative researchers and would also provide examples of how such issues are dealt with in practice. Secondly, we were keen to provide the reader with a comparative context so that the reasons for and the implications of choosing to employ one approach rather than another would become clear. As was also discussed in Chapter 2, more recently, some researchers have argued for the value of engaging with the same data set from different epistemological and methodological perspectives (Frost et al., 2010; Mason, 2006; Moran-Ellis et al., 2006; Shaw and Frost, 2015).

This chapter highlights some of the differences and similarities between the five analytic approaches that we focus on in this volume: interpretative phenomenological analysis (IPA), thematic analysis, grounded theory, discourse analysis and narrative analysis. In particular, the chapter summarizes the epistemological assumptions underlying each approach and discusses the implications of these differences for some central concerns of qualitative research, namely the role of the researcher in the research process, what the appropriate goals of psychological inquiry are and what criteria are most appropriate for evaluating qualitative research. Some of these questions have been raised more or less explicitly in other contributions to this book. I want to extend the discussion by first summarizing and comparing the position each approach takes on these issues and by drawing on the experiences of the researchers who analysed the common data. Also, I will consider the reasons for which we may choose to adopt a mixed-method or pluralistic approach to our research and the implications of such a choice for the conceptual coherence of the research. In addition, I will discuss the political implications of the choices we make in the research process, especially in relation to how we conceptualize the relationship between ourselves, as the researcher, and the participants.

The chapter starts by summarizing and comparing the epistemological underpinnings of each of the approaches as these assumptions have implications for how each approach deals with these issues. It then turns to how each approach sees the role of the researcher. Within qualitative research, the researcher is seen as an important part of the process of knowledge production, bringing to it their own understandings, conceptual orientations and a stock of cultural knowledge. Qualitative researchers are therefore expected to reflect on their actions and reactions during all stages of the research process. These reflections can become part of the data and play a role in the interpretation of the data. I have focused my discussion on two particular aspects of the researcher's role. First, how should the researcher use their own biographical experiences and existing theoretical knowledge in the analytic and/or interpretative stages of the research? Second, what are the political implications of the relative speaking position of the researcher and the participants?

I then examine the goals of psychological inquiry as stated by each of the five approaches and discuss how far each approach strives to produce **description**, prediction and/or **explanation** or to offer a **social critique** of the status quo. Finally, I discuss what criteria are most appropriate for evaluating research carried out within each approach in relation to three aspects: technical proficiency, theory development and application.

Comparing the epistemological underpinnings of the five analytic approaches

The main differing epistemological stances that research can take have been described by Adrian Coyle in Chapter 2. The importance of the epistemological underpinnings of the research approach you choose to employ in a project has, we hope, also been illustrated in both the 'theoretical' and 'analytic' chapters in this volume. The epistemological basis of each approach influences the research questions you pose, the status you give to your data, how you conceptualize your role as a researcher and what conclusions you can draw from your data.

There are different ways of conceptualizing the epistemological positions underlying different approaches to analysing qualitative data. One of the earlier useful descriptions was given by Henwood and Pidgeon (1994) who identified three main strands of psychological inquiry. The first strand is based on an empiricist epistemological position: the main methodological principle is that of a discovery of valid representations by using inductive reasoning and it evaluates qualitative research by using criteria analogous to reliability and validity. The second strand is based on contextualism. The main methodological principle involved here is the construction of intersubjective meaning and the usefulness of qualitative research is argued on the basis of generating new theory which is firmly grounded in participants' own meanings in concrete contexts. The third strand is based on constructivism and its main methodological principle is that of interpretative analysis. This strand focuses on 'the reflexive functions of language, which construct representations of "objects" in the world and which have material discursive effects' (Henwood, 1996: 31).

Reicher (2000) distinguishes between experiential approaches and discursive approaches. The former refer to approaches which are concerned with understanding how people experience and make sense of their world whereas the latter are concerned with how language is used to construct particular versions of reality. Madill et al. (2000) conceptualize the differences in epistemological positions of qualitative research in terms of a continuum where on one end is what they call a **naïve realist** position and on the other is a **radical constructionist** position. Somewhere in between these is a **contextual constructionist** position. Naïve realism in its simplest form assumes that reality can be discovered by the use of appropriate methods. However, other forms of realism recognize that knowledge is not objective (or, in the case of **critical realism,** that knowledge of reality cannot be achieved with certainty). This places them closer to the contextual constructionist position which assumes that all knowledge is context specific and influenced by the perspective of the perceiver. Radical constructionist epistemologies reject the idea that data reflect reality and focus on how reality is constructed through language.

Any attempt to place the five approaches we focused on in this volume – as they are theoretically described and then put into practice by researchers in the analytic chapters – in any of these classification systems quickly leads to the realization that these classifications are somewhat oversimplified. For example, it can be argued that IPA, grounded theory and narrative analysis fall under the category of experiential epistemologies whereas discourse analysis would be classified under the discursive category. Or if we were to adopt Madill et al.'s (2000) epistemological continuum, grounded theory would be closer to the realist end of the continuum, IPA and narrative analysis would be nearer to the contextual constructionist point and discourse analysis would be near the radical constructionist end of the continuum. However, if we look more closely at the assumptions that these methodologies are based on and how they are applied in practice, we can see that some of them do not fall clearly under one or another category. Furthermore, thematic analysis is described as a 'method' rather than a 'methodology' and researchers are invited to make a choice of an epistemological position before they apply thematic analysis to their data set. The important issue for users of thematic analysis is that they conceptualize and undertake all the stages of the analysis and research process in a manner which is consistent with their chosen epistemological position rather than which epistemology they choose to employ (see Chapters 6 and 7 in this volume, and Braun and Clarke, 2012, 2013).

For instance, the version of grounded theory discussed by Sheila Payne in Chapter 8 is based on a realist epistemology in that, following Glaser and Strauss (1967), it assumes that participants' perceptions of an event or a social situation directly reflect reality. At the same time, it emphasizes the need to understand the meanings participants attach to particular events and that the resulting theories and knowledge ought to be situated in particular contexts. So, in that respect, the version of grounded theory put forward in Chapter 8 shares some epistemological assumptions with both realist and contextual constructionist approaches.

IPA is based on a phenomenological approach (see Chapter 4) or a 'contextual constructionist' epistemology (Madill et al., 2000). The assumption is that language reflects the experiences of and the meanings participants attach to particular events and social situations, although Jonathan Smith (1993; Smith et al., 2009; Willig, 2013) acknowledges that the process of accessing participants' experiences and meanings is not a simple one: it requires the researcher to *interpret* the data. Brett Smith, in Chapter 12, argues that narrative analysis can be based on either an epistemology of narrative constructivism which sees narratives as cognitive structures inside people's minds or narrative constructionism which conceptualizes narratives as cultural resources available to individuals in their attempt to make sense of their lives. In his chapter, Smith focuses on this latter approach to narrative analysis which is closer to the social constructionist end of the epistemological continuum rather than the phenomenological end. Discourse analysis is regarded as being based on a radical constructionist epistemology which challenges the taken-for-granted ways we categorize and make sense of the world around us. It sees language as constructing categories and events rather than reflecting 'reality'. However, in Chapter 11, Chris Walton has paid particular attention to Foucauldian discourse analysis which emphasizes not only the constitutive role of language but also that the discourses open to a speaker are shaped by the social structures and power relationships within which he or she is located. This suggests a commitment to at least some aspects of reality lying outside language.

In this volume, we have chosen to present five qualitative analytic approaches and how they can be applied to a data set separately. We did this deliberately so that it is easier for the reader to engage with them and get useful insights into how each one of them can be used effectively, what kind of research questions can be addressed and the sort of data account likely to be generated. This implies that a researcher can choose what approach of data analysis to adopt on the basis of their chosen epistemological position and/or the research questions they seek to address. However, as I mentioned earlier, there is a debate amongst qualitative researchers about the relative value of adopting a pluralistic approach to research (Frost et al., 2010; Mason, 2006; Moran-Ellis et al., 2006; see also Chapter 2 in this volume).

A pluralistic approach (using different qualitative methodologies in the same project) or a mixed method approach (using both quantitative and qualitative approaches) can lead to a more comprehensive understanding of the data set and can encourage **reflexivity** if used in a principled way. It encourages researchers to understand better how their own position in the research process and/or in relation to the topic of research may be implicated in the interpretation of the data (Shaw and Frost, 2015). The discussions around the relative appropriateness and value of employing a pluralistic approach to research moves the question of how to choose a particular method/methodology for analysing our data beyond either an almost ideological allegiance to a particular epistemology or a pragmatic stance focused on what method suits the research topic/question best. (That sort of pragmatic stance makes the whole choice rather circular as our epistemology informs to a large extent what research questions we address.) It leads to an engagement with the issue of what aspects of the data we should most usefully try to account for in the context of a particular project and how the adoption of a particular epistemological standpoint might influence our interactions with our participants, the quality and aspects of the data disclosed to us and the consequences of reporting on these data for various audiences. Furthermore, the answers to these questions may lead to the adoption of diverse approaches in the same research project (see, for example, Dewe and Coyle, 2014). Clarke et al. (2015) presented a meta-study of ten studies that applied more than one qualitative method to a single data set. They concluded that 'analytical pluralism enables researchers to produce rich, varied understandings of phenomena, and opens up multiple possibilities of interpretation because it avoids privileging any particular approach or framework over another' (Clarke et al., 2015: 16). However, they also emphasized that qualitative analytical pluralism highlights the need for the researcher to think very carefully about how their epistemological and ontological positions, theory, method and findings link together and how the data accounts generated by using different analytic approaches can be integrated in a systematic and coherent way.

I have put forward some useful ways of conceptualizing different epistemological stances underlying the methodological approaches included in this book. The difficulty of placing each of the five approaches into any of these classifications has been shown, as some approaches are either based on more than one epistemological position or have been explicitly defined as methods rather than methodologies and therefore distinguished from particular epistemologies. Whichever epistemological stance you need to base your method of data analysis on, the important thing is to do so explicitly and use it in a principled and consistent way. I have also discussed two of the main advantages of adopting a mixed methods or a pluralistic approach to research: obtaining more insights from a data set or a fuller understanding of your research topic and opening ways to reflexivity.

BITE-SIZED
SUMMARY
....

1

The role of the researcher

Taking into account the researcher's theoretical knowledge and biographical experiences

One of the main implications of the epistemology underlying the methodological approach you choose to employ is the role you, as a researcher, are expected to play in the research process and how you are supposed to use and engage with the theoretical knowledge and biographical experiences you bring into that process. How researchers' theoretical and biographical backgrounds can be drawn into the research is evidenced in the analytic chapters where most authors discussed their uneasiness at privileging one interpretation over another either because members of their analytic team with different backgrounds put emphasis on other aspects of the data or used different theoretical concepts to make sense of the data.

Within the grounded theory approach as it is presented in this volume, which is based on a realist epistemology, the researcher is expected to generate a theory that accounts as accurately as possible for the data. However it is important to note that other versions of grounded theory would acknowledge the interpretation and social constructionist aspects of the analytic process (Charmaz, 2014; Rennie, 2000). Irrespective of the researcher's social positioning and/or previous relevant experience and/or the particular views they hold, a skilled researcher is expected to be able to discover and present the actors' meanings and understandings of the phenomenon under investigation in a particular context. In analysing the transcripts of the ex-servicemen in Chapter 9, Sheila Hawker and Christine Kerr refer to the process of coding as the process of 'noticing'. They wanted to emphasize the importance of systematically thinking about your data and that codes and links between codes are there in the data to be noticed – to be discovered. They also remind us that one of the key evaluative criteria of grounded theory research is 'goodness of fit' between data and the emergent theory. The relative appropriateness of the evaluative criteria outlined in Chapter 2 for each approach will be discussed later in this chapter. What is important here is to note the distance placed between the data and the researcher in the analysis stage of the research.

Adopting a phenomenological (Giorgi and Giorgi, 2008) and hermeneutic philosophy (Palmer, 1969; Ricoeur, 1970), IPA acknowledges that, in trying to explore the meanings and experiences of participants, the researcher engages in an *interpretative* activity. The researcher is trying to make sense of the participants' own struggle to make sense of their world. The researcher's pre-existing knowledge and conceptions are therefore actively implicated in the analytic process as the researcher tries to describe and account for participants' experiences. The role of the researcher is twofold. First, they strive to put themselves in the place of the participant and second they ask critical questions of the participants' words, being aware that there is no straightforward and direct relationship between what people express and their experience (see Chapter 4). A superficial reading of this process may lead someone to wonder whether here IPA shares with radical constructionist approaches the assumption that speakers construct their realities and experiences to fulfil certain functions in either the micro-conversational context or the macro-ideological context. However, there is a difference between IPA and discursive approaches in that IPA assumes that the researcher can access motives and understandings that the participant is either not aware of or finds difficult to express, whereas discursive approaches do not attribute motives to participants and do not take their words to reflect experiences that participants may or may not be aware of. Rather they examine the accounts that people offer of their experiences and consider what particular conversational and/or ideological functions are achieved through these accounts.

Narrative analysis, as discussed in Chapters 12 and 13 in this volume, sees the role of the researcher both as a 'storyteller' and a 'story analyst'. In dialogical narrative analysis, the approach described in this volume, the task of the researcher is seen as both describing and interpreting the data. It assumes that drawing on her or his own experiences, the researcher is able to make sense of the personal and cultural meanings that participants use in written or oral texts to describe their experiences. Furthermore, the researcher adopts an active and creative role in interpreting the data and creating a coherent and persuasive account of the data.

Discourse analytic approaches see the role of the researcher as constructing or authoring an account of the data (see Chapters 10 and 11). Based on the assumption that language is constitutive of reality rather than reflecting it, discourse analytic approaches do not give theories or analytic accounts a special status. The latter are seen as particular constructions of events, as are the data under investigation. The researcher is therefore expected to be reflexive.

The thematic analysis approach, as outlined by Clarke and Braun in Chapter 6, portrays the researcher as a 'sculptor' whose efforts focus on applying certain analytic procedures systematically to construct a plausible and useful account of the data. This approach explicitly acknowledges that the analysis is the result of the active engagement of a researcher with the data, bringing to bear their specific skills, background knowledge and theoretical concerns. Given the flexibility that thematic analysis affords the researcher, how much distance a researcher can or should put between them and the data will depend on the specific epistemological standpoint they wish to adopt.

This summary has demonstrated that all approaches acknowledge that the psychological knowledge and experiences of the researcher are inextricably interlinked with the research process. However, as I have already hinted, they differ in their recommendations as to how we should respond to this issue.

Advocates of earlier versions of a grounded theory approach have argued that this 'baggage' is something that the researcher needs to try to put aside when starting their research (Glaser and Strauss, 1967). However, we can question to what extent it is possible to be aware of all our beliefs and background knowledge that may be relevant to the way we conduct a piece of research. If we were able to be aware of them, to what extent can we put them out of our minds? If we were to do this, how can we define the parameters of the phenomenon we are investigating and/or what areas/domains we should ask questions about? Other researchers in this area accept that such an approach is utopian and argue that what researchers should do is to make explicit at the start of the project any beliefs and experiences which may influence the way they conduct their research (see Pidgeon, 1996; also Chapter 8 in this volume). For example, Charmaz (1990, 2014) suggested that qualitative researchers need to have a perspective from which they actively seek to build their analyses, without merely applying it to new data. Such a perspective includes the substantive interests that guide the questions to be asked, the researcher's philosophical stance, the school of thought that provides a store of sensitizing concepts and the researcher's personal experiences, priorities and values.

IPA invites the researcher simultaneously to put aside their own experiences so that they can enter the life world of the participants and also to actively use their background knowledge in order to interpret the experiences that participants express. Similarly, narrative analysis assumes that the researcher can access the cultural meanings which surround the participants' narratives and use those to analyse the data and provide the researcher's account. Thematic analysis also acknowledges that the researchers' skills, knowledge and experiences will inform the outcome of data analysis. Although this conceptualization of the role that the researchers' own understandings and knowledge may play in the research appears, perhaps, more plausible, none of the approaches described above satisfactorily theorizes how the researcher's 'baggage' is implicated in the research. They do not tell us how to incorporate our own insights into the final account of the data that we produce when the analysis has been completed (Willig, 2013).

On the other hand from a discourse analytic perspective, a researcher can only offer their own *construction* of the research data rather than discover 'facts' or witness participants' 'experiences'. The researcher therefore needs to ask questions about the possible implications of the particular accounts they produce for the discursive and material contexts in which the data and research audiences are located.

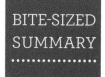

BITE-SIZED
SUMMARY
....
2

How the role of the researcher is conceptualized within each methodological approach is informed by the underpinning epistemological stance that the research adopts. Most approaches recognize that researchers bring their own skills, theoretical and personal knowledge into the analytic process but vary in terms of whether they claim that you can (or to what extent they recommend you try to) bracket these during the analysis and/or make them explicit and transparent when you construct your account of the data.

Representing 'the Other'

One frequent source of anxiety for qualitative researchers is the issue of how we represent participants. This is a concern which may arise for several reasons. Firstly, this issue may relate to the quest for authenticity: the researcher may wish to ensure that they do not 'mis-represent' the accounts and experiences of participants. Does a researcher have to be an 'insider' or an 'outsider' to the group they study in order to be able to understand fully the experiences of the participants (Dwyer and Buckle, 2009; Mullings, 1999)? Secondly, this is an issue that may have political implications, particularly when participants have different experiences from ourselves and belong to groups which are not given opportunities to voice their experiences and claim their rights (Kitzinger and Wilkinson, 1996). Thirdly, many researchers acknowledge that their own positioning (that is, how they are located and locate themselves in terms of categories such as gender, class, ethnicity, religion, institutional context and personal relations) and that of their participants are an inextricable part of the research process and the co-construction of knowledge. However, it has been recognized that the binary conceptualization of positionality as insider versus outsider is over-simplistic as the experiences of researchers' and participants' selves are more unstable, multi-layered and relative than these simple categories allow (Hopkins, 2009; Suffla et al., 2015, Yuval-Davis, 2013)

Analysing the transcripts of interviews with the ex-soldiers (see Appendix 1) using grounded theory in Chapter 9, Sheila Hawker and Christine Kerr have pointed out that one of their concerns was that they did not have enough contextual knowledge of how the data were collected and the background of the participants. They were, therefore, anxious to emphasize that they could not have full confidence in their interpretation of the data. In this case, they were anxious that the emergent themes and theory may not be grounded in the 'right' interpretation of the participants' words. In other words, they were concerned that their interpretation and conclusions may 'mis-represent' the participants' accounts.

In Chapter 5, when reporting the attempts of the IPA group to analyse the account provided by the ex-soldier David, Lesley Storey commented on the anxiety of the group that the use of particular theoretical constructs to make sense of David's world would distance their interpretation from and 'mis-represent' his experiences. She also discussed the difficulties that may arise from identifying too closely with the participant during the analytic process.

This, she felt, might result in researchers forcing 'the data to conform to *their* experiences'. Equally, if the researcher negatively dis-identifies with the interviewee, she argued, it 'can make it difficult to empathize (or at least sympathize) with the interviewee and thus attain the sort of "insider" perspective on the research topic to which IPA aspires'. The researchers were keen to understand the world of the interviewee through his own eyes and not to judge him or represent him in ways that he would either not recognize or perhaps not agree with.

Constructing an account of applying Foucauldian discourse analysis to the interview transcripts, Chris Walton acknowledged that the focus of the analytic group was not on understanding the experiences of David and Brian (see Chapter 11). Instead, their analysis focused on 'the words and phrases that they used when they talked about or *constructed* the experience of leaving the army and their respective army and post-army identities'. In this sense, the discourses the group identified as used by David and Brian to construct their identities were instrumental in representing or re-constructing them in particular ways.

Similarly, Gareth Terry (Chapter 7) and Nick Caddick (Chapter 13), who analysed the interview transcripts using thematic analysis and dialogical narrative analysis, placed emphasis on showing how their accounts were grounded in the data rather than the political consequences of their accounts for the people who generated the data. Terry described in some detail the steps he took to ensure that the codes and themes he included in the analysis were grounded in the data, as well as how he put them together to generate the final account of his analysis. Caddick focused on identifying the stories that the storytellers (the interviewees) used to talk about their transition from their army to their civilian lives and what functions these narratives had for their identities and lives. He did not express concerns for the authenticity of his account other than to caution that the stories and narratives he identified may change as the stories of the participants continue to unfold over time. Perhaps this is because dialogical narrative analysis acknowledges that there are no right or wrong narratives; there are just stories and narratives that a researcher constructs and identifies using appropriate analytic procedures. We could question, though, whether researchers can access cultural meanings and narratives of groups other than their own or of a different time. Such cultural meanings are likely to be accessed using written or oral accounts by privileged or educated groups who are able to produce dominant versions of history, thus ignoring the experiences of more disadvantaged groups.

In all five analytic chapters, it becomes apparent that the researchers are constantly pre-occupied with the question of how the final report of their analysis will have implications for how their participants are represented (see also Victoria Uwannah's reflections on different aspects of the same issue in Chapter 2, Box 2.2). Irrespective of the approach to data analysis adopted, the authors emphasize the importance of producing an account of the data set which is 'grounded' in the raw data. In this respect, they strive to establish the credibility of their particular versions of David's and/or Brian's accounts by showing that the researchers' accounts are not arbitrary: they are based on empirical evidence. This is not to say, however, that any of the analytic approaches presented in this volume would see the interpretation of empirical evidence as either a neutral or an objective process. As was noted above, all five approaches acknowledge that researchers engage in an interpretation or a (de-/re-) construction of the data and that this process is conceptualized within each of the five approaches to a greater or lesser extent as being subjective and political. Most of these acknowledge that the final analytic account would comprise particular versions of David's and Brian's worlds that would represent/construct David and Brian in particular ways. Furthermore this acknowledgement gives rise to different concerns depending on the epistemological basis of each approach.

Two main factors may influence this process: first, the use of existing theory and psychological jargon; and, second, the way the researcher constructs themselves. Thus, based on a realist epistemology, the version of grounded theory presented in Chapter 8 raises questions about the extent to which the researcher understands the contextual meanings attached to particular events by the participants and therefore the extent to which the emergent theory represents the participants in the same way that participants make sense of themselves.

Based on a phenomenological approach, IPA raises questions about the extent to which the researcher is able to enter the inner world of the participants and interpret the data in a way that elicits the 'real experiences' of the participants. Again the concern here is with ensuring the relevance and perhaps the recognizability of the accounts to the participants. Within the version of narrative analysis presented in Chapter 12, questions arise regarding the validity and privileging of the researcher's narrative over the participant's narrative. Finally, based on a radical social constructionist epistemology, discourse analysis is concerned with how the researcher's speaking positions may influence how participants are constructed though the analysis. Irrespective of the particular epistemological stance chosen by a researcher who uses a thematic analysis approach, the issue of showing how their account is grounded in the data is always of central concern.

How we represent others becomes particularly important when participants belong to groups that are often constructed as '**Other**' in particular cultures. For example, feminist researchers have argued that women have been traditionally constructed as 'Other' (Kitzinger and Wilkinson, 1996; Ussher, 1991). People with mental illness, lesbians and gay men, bisexuals and transgendered people, economically disadvantaged people, people with HIV/AIDS, non-White people and people with disabilities have also been constructed as 'Other': they are defined in opposition to the norms of 'mentally healthy', heterosexual, cisgendered, privileged middle-class, White and able-bodied people (see, for example, Ansara and Hegarty, 2012; Coyle, 1996; Fowler and Hardesty, 1994; Marks, 1996).

The issue here is whether we should speak for these groups in order to empower them and have their voices expressed via our reports with the hope of shaping social change or whether such attempts are presumptuous and reinforce the denial of a voice to the 'Other'. This dilemma is aptly summarized in the following two quotations: 'We must take on the whole world; we cannot afford "no go areas" of the imagination; we cannot afford to refuse an opinion on any subject' (Livia, 1996: 36); 'No one should ever "speak for" or assume another's voice … it becomes a form of colonisation' (Sinister Wisdom Collective, 1990: 4)

> ### BOX 14.1 — Who is the 'Other'?

An example of how apparent 'sameness' is not always reflected in the eyes of the researcher and the participants is discussed by Ranti Oguntokun (1998). Oguntokun studied the experiences of Black African refugee women in the UK and describes how she began her research assuming that, being a Black African woman herself, she and her participants would not be 'Other' to each other. As she said:

> I assumed that a shared skin colour, shared continental origins and a shared immigrant status would give me the right to represent these women's experiences with legitimacy and authenticity as an 'insider', avoiding the errors that culturally and ethnically dissimilar researchers may make. (p. 526)

However, she goes on to discuss how she soon realized that she could not continue to claim similarities between her own experiences of feelings of displacement and homesickness and those of her participants, most of whom had fled war-torn areas and endured terrible hardships. Moreover, her participants did not allow her to make such claims either. One woman, who was a refugee from Somaliland, said to her:

> I do not talk to other people about Somali because it is too much. You cannot understand. You do not have war in your country, no? It is too bad, you yourself will weep for Somali. (p. 527)

Oguntokun's reflections provide us with a striking example of how apparent 'sameness' can become illusory in the context of diverse experiences between members of 'the same group' and the dilemmas faced by researchers who want to represent people who are different from them. In responding to this, Oguntokun (1998) acknowledged the differences between herself and the participants and endeavoured to produce an account which was knowledgeable about and sympathetic to the experiences of the Black African refugee women, positioning her not within the group but knowledgeably alongside the group members.

Kitzinger and Wilkinson (1996) have identified four different ways that feminist researchers suggest that we, as researchers, should deal with the issue of 'Othering'. Firstly, some have argued that we can only speak for ourselves – that is, we can only conduct research with groups whose experiences we share. Secondly, it has been claimed that we should speak of Otherness only to celebrate it. However, this carries a risk of idealizing the 'Other'. Thirdly, another strand of thought suggests the way we should deal with the issue of Otherness is to try to destabilize the relationship between self and 'Other'. This may mean that we try to reverse the established power relationships by having members of less powerful groups (for example, a Black researcher) researching the more powerful (for example, White people).

One of the assumptions underlying the debate about the implications of researching the 'Other' is that there is a simple way of grouping people or placing them in particular social categories. For instance, in my work with young people from ethnic minority communities, I often have to write about the experiences of women of South Asian origin. Do they constitute an 'Other'? My participants and I belong to different ethnic and age groups but we can also be categorized as women and as immigrants (as I come from Cyprus). I often find that I interview women who are of a lower socio-economic status to me but we can both recite experiences of discrimination. Which group membership should be the one that defines us in ways that determine whether I and my participants are 'Other' to each other or people from the same group? People belong to multiple groups and it will be both very impractical and reductionist if we were to argue that we can only research and speak for people who have the same profile of group memberships as us. Furthermore, as researchers we need to be very careful in assuming that, because our participants belong to a particular group, they necessarily define or construct their identities in terms of these memberships (Camp et al., 2002; Finlay and Lyons, 2000; Lyons et al., 2006). Discussing her work on 'bordering', Yuval-Davis (2013) also argued for the need to avoid prioritization of any social divisions such as class or gender.

From a critical, radical social constructionist perspective, it is also important to note that representing the 'Other' is not merely a descriptive process. The way we represent the 'Other' does not reflect the experiences of the 'Other'; it also constitutes us and the 'Other' in particular ways. Alcoff (1994, 2006) argues that we need to evaluate instances of speaking for others by asking questions about the reasons why we wish to speak about the 'Other', the relevance of who we are and the experiences we carry for what we say about the 'Other' and the effects of what we say on the discursive and material context.

I have chosen to devote significant space to discussing this issue as I think it is important to raise questions about the political and value implications of our research. In books such as this, which are concerned with the intellectual and technical debates about how we conduct research, it is easy to think inadvertently of the research process as socially and politically neutral and be overly concerned with the rigour of our methodological skills to the detriment of considering the intended and unintended consequences of our practices. I hope this discussion raises your awareness of the need to question vigilantly the political and social implications of our research endeavours.

BOX
14.2

Practices enabling critical engagement with the self–'Other' relationship

There are a number of different strategies you can employ to adopt a critical and reflexive approach to speaking for an 'Other'. For example:

- Ask the participants to evaluate the validity of your account of them.
- Listen to how the participants speak of 'your group' so that your own perspective is problematized and its relativity exposed.
- Listen to how other members of the powerful group (your group) speak about members of the group to which the participants belong (the 'Other').
- Try to provide opportunities to create a dialogue between you and the participants so that no account is privileged.

Some of these are easier to achieve than others. The important point is to employ strategies to interrupt the process of privileging the account of the powerful group to which we as social scientists often belong. For a fuller discussion, see Fine (1994), Kitzinger and Wilkinson (1996) and Suffla et al. (2015).

This section focused our discussion first on how the different analytic approaches conceptualize the role of the researcher. Depending on the epistemological underpinnings of each approach, the researcher has been conceptualized as an observer rather than being at the centre of the research process. I have also highlighted the importance of considering the relative positioning of the researcher and the participants at the different stages of research from the design of the research to the interpretation of the data.

BITE-SIZED
SUMMARY
. . . .
3

Evaluating the five analytic approaches

In this section, I would like to address the different ways we can evaluate research conducted within each of the five approaches presented in this book. In Chapter 2, Adrian Coyle pointed out that there are some evaluative criteria that seem to recur in the literature on qualitative research methods. These have to do with ensuring that the contexts in which the participants are located are adequately described, that the analytic process is presented in a transparent and detailed way, that there is a reflexive account of how the researcher's 'speaking position' might have influenced the research at its various stages and that interpretations are grounded in research data. He also focused on the practical implications of the research. Examining the evaluative criteria that qualitative researchers have put forward (see, for example, Elliott et al., 1999; Meyrick, 2006; Yardley, 2000), it seems that these relate to either the rigour and quality of the research activity or the usefulness of the research outcomes. The usefulness of the research is often seen as its potential contribution to theory development and/or its applicability to real-life situations.

Coyle suggested that there is no consensus amongst qualitative researchers as to the most appropriate criteria for evaluating qualitative research and that this may not be surprising given the variety of qualitative research methods. I want to extend this discussion by focusing on the evaluative criteria appropriate to each of the five methods considered in this book. What constitutes an appropriate criterion depends on what the method claims to attempt to achieve but we can also evaluate a particular method from an epistemological perspective different to that on which it is based. Therefore, before considering the dimensions along which we can evaluate research carried out within the five methods, it is useful to revisit the goals of psychological inquiry as stated by each method and which stem from the epistemological stance they take.

Within grounded theory, the aim is often to develop inductive theory which is closely derived from the data. The emergent theory must be able to explain the data elicited from all the participants, even the cases which provide conflicting data. The aim is to generate a theory that explains the social and psychological processes under study and understands the local network of causal relationships which may result in particular events and how the participants made sense of them. Researchers using grounded theory look for possible and plausible mechanisms by which one event/variable leads to another and examine the complexity of the networks of actions and processes in concrete contexts.

Whilst the aim of grounded theory is to derive an explanatory theory on the basis of data, IPA is mainly concerned with providing a detailed description of the participants' lived experiences. *Why* the participants experience their world in particular ways is only a secondary concern to an IPA researcher. Similarly, narrative analysis is more concerned with detailed description than explanation. Moreover, the focus is on analysing individual experience and meanings in depth rather than looking for commonalities between different people.

Within discourse analysis, the goal of psychological inquiry is to offer a critical interrogation of the status quo by destabilizing taken-for-granted ways of categorizing the world. Discursive psychology examines the social functions performed by particular discursive resources in talk and text. Foucauldian discourse analysis sometimes goes a step further by trying to theorize about the social structures and power relationships which make certain discursive resources available and the implications for the subjectivities of those who use them. In this sense, Foucauldian discourse analysis can provide a theory of how historically some discourses have come to be the way they are or how they are grounded in particular structures and institutions (for example, see Parker, 1992).

Given the flexibility that thematic analysis affords the researcher in terms of the epistemological stance they can adopt, the goal could be either a description of experiences rather than a theoretical explanation of how and why participants construct their world in particular ways or, similar to discourse analysis, a linguistic deconstruction of participant meanings and exploration of the functions that they serve. Narrative analysis as discussed in this volume will have goals aligned to description or will offer a social deconstruction and/or critique of the cultural narratives used by participants to make sense of their world.

Given the differences in what each of the focal research methods strives to achieve, it is appropriate that we use different criteria to evaluate them (although some criteria are relevant to all, such as the need to evidence interpretations by quoting relevant data). For example, a grounded theory study within a realist epistemology that aims to generate a theory is best evaluated by demonstrating that methods of data collection and the analytic processes captured the 'real' experiences and meanings of the participants. This can be demonstrated by being transparent about the analytic process and sometimes going back to participants to check the validity of the researcher's analysis (although this raises questions about how differences between the researcher's interpretations and the participants' interpretations are dealt with). Furthermore, the validity of interpretations can be assessed by a method of triangulation (see Moran-Ellis et al., 2006) – that is, the validity of the analysis can be demonstrated by the extent that two or more researchers reach the same conclusions.

Within discourse analysis, discursive psychology is concerned with how language constructs particular objects and phenomena and most often aims to challenge the taken-for-granted ways of constructing the world rather than explaining under what conditions certain behaviours would occur. In contrast, Foucauldian discourse analysis is concerned with the influence of social structures, institutions and power relationships on the availability of particular discourses and in turn the possibilities for action that particular discourses afford. In this respect, Foucauldian discourse analysis is more concerned with explaining under what conditions certain discourses would be taken up. However, given that both approaches are based on a radical social constructionist epistemology, it would be inappropriate to evaluate them in terms of the extent to which they accurately represent 'reality'. Rather they should be judged in terms of the rigour and quality of the analysis. For example, Antaki et al. (2003) have discussed six shortcomings with the way that many researchers who engage in discourse analysis treat talk and textual data: a) under-analysis through summary; b) under-analysis through taking sides; c) under-analysis through over-quotation or through isolated quotation;

d) the circular identification of discourses and mental constructs; e) false survey; and f) analysis that consists in simply spotting features in the text.

However, the question of whether psychology should be concerned with the development of theories or just the description of social and psychological phenomena is worthy of our consideration. One answer would be that the state of psychological knowledge is such that we cannot claim that we can strive for explanation since we have not yet described our target phenomena adequately. Another answer could be that psychologists should aim to develop explanatory theories if they are to be involved in finding solutions to real-life problems or in bringing about social change.

This last-mentioned argument is linked to a key issue of research evaluation, namely the degree to which we think the research is useful. Consideration of this evaluative criterion raises a number of questions, such as what the research should be useful for and for whom it should be useful. We have already raised the issue of whether research should necessarily always contribute to the development of theory but should research also need to be readily applicable to real-life situations in order to be considered useful? And who should the researcher provide useful information to? Should researchers aim to conduct research that would be useful to the participants, those funding the research or other potential users of the research findings?

Many researchers, especially those who espouse a social constructionist approach, have levelled criticisms at the notion that psychological knowledge can and ought to be readily applicable to real-life situations. Willig (1999) identified three different types of critique directed at attempts to apply psychological knowledge to real-world situations. Firstly, it has been argued that, by claiming that particular applications are based on 'scientific' and 'objective' knowledge, the stakeholders of a particular application legitimize their activity and therefore prevent others from raising questions about how, why and in whose interests psychological theories are being applied. She calls this the 'ideology of application critique'. Secondly, Willig refers to the critique levelled by Cromby and Standen (1996), who argue that those with power, such as governments, use psychological research findings to justify particular policies which they pursue for political or economic reasons. This is often called the 'abuse/power critique'. Thirdly, she cited Widdicombe's (1995) argument against critical psychologists putting forward recommendations for interventions on the basis that such recommendations tend to disempower rather than empower oppressed groups by reifying particular meanings and discourses attached to them. However, Willig (1999) argues persuasively that discourse analysis can contribute to social and political practice by offering a social critique of the status quo, empowering oppressed groups and guiding reform.

Whether we endeavour to produce research that could address real-life problems or whether we strive to provide a rich and interesting description of a social or psychological phenomenon and what criteria we think should be applied to evaluate our research are all questions and dilemmas that can only be resolved in the context of a specific project. What is important is that we as researchers take the time to think about the potential usefulness or otherwise of the research we engage in.

> ### BOX 14.3 — Choosing a qualitative research approach to adopt

Think of a research topic you want to explore; for example, 1) the impact of recent economic crises in the Western world on relatively disadvantaged groups or 2) the relative engagement of young people with social media or 3) stigma and obesity. You can choose one of the three topics outlined here or another which is of interest to you.

Now consider the following questions with regard to your chosen research topic from the perspective of *two* of the research approaches we discussed above (IPA, thematic analysis, grounded theory, discourse analysis and narrative analysis). You may want to do this by yourself and write down the answers or, if you have the opportunity, it will be useful to consider the answers to the questions below in discussion with other students or colleagues. This exercise will help in better understanding why we may choose to adopt one or more approaches, as opposed to others, to study these topics.

First, here are some questions to make explicit the epistemological position you feel comfortable with.

1 What assumptions does each of the two approaches you are considering make about the data you can obtain? What status, for example, do they give to the views of the participants? What do they claim that the role of the researcher could/should be?

   What other questions do you need to ask yourself in order to be explicit about the epistemological position you will want to adopt?

Now consider the implications of adopting a particular research approach for the questions you can ask about the research topic.

2 What would be appropriate research questions to ask if you adopt each of these approaches? Which research questions do you think will be likely to produce the most useful or interesting answers? Why?

Having formulated some research questions, take the time to reflect on what, in addition to the epistemology you chose, might have influenced the way you formulated your research questions.

3 What existing literature might have influenced the way you phrased your research questions? What, if any, personal beliefs or experiences relevant to the research topic

(Continued)

might have influenced the way you phrased your research questions? How would each research approach that you are considering adopting encourage the researcher to deal with a) existing theoretical and empirical evidence and b) their personal beliefs and experiences?

Thinking of the value of the expected outcomes of the research,

4   What would be the most appropriate criteria to use to evaluate the quality of the work you will produce? Do you think you will be able to describe your participants' experiences and views? Or do you think you will be able not only to describe these but also to explain why and/or how these have come to be the way they are? Will your findings/ the account of the data you produce be useful? To whom and why?

Before you make a final decision about which approach to adopt, identify two or three additional questions you need to consider in order to make an informed decision.

BITE-SIZED SUMMARY
· · · · · · · · · · · · · ·
4

Different evaluative criteria would be appropriate for data accounts generated by different analytic approaches. These should be chosen on the basis of what type of knowledge (for example, a descriptive or an explanatory account or a social critique of the research topic) the researcher aimed to produce, which in turn is informed by the epistemological stance adopted by the researcher. In addition, the notion of, the usefulness of research, as an evaluative criterion has been discussed.

CONCLUDING REMARKS

In this book, we aimed to equip the reader with the conceptual and methodological tools to navigate the uncertain waters of qualitative research in psychology. Qualitative research offers exciting opportunities for studying the complexities, contradictions and ambivalences of our emotionally charged, social and psychological worlds in depth. We hope we have managed to enthuse and encourage you to embark on research into issues that are socially and politically important and especially those that matter to you.

We endeavoured to provide answers to some of the questions that you might have had about conducting qualitative research or that might arise as you embark upon the qualitative research process. We hope that we have raised as many questions as we have answered. Hopefully you will grapple with some of these and arrive at your own answers which can contribute to the further development of qualitative research methods. Producing knowledge should after all be a collaborative endeavour!

Further reading

For those interested in studying further the complexities of the relationship between epistemology and method, Michael Smith's (2005) book *Philosophy and Methodology in the Social Sciences* provides an excellent discussion of these issues. For those interested in the debates surrounding the relationship between research and real-life applications, especially on the applicability of discourse analytic research, Carla Willig's (1999) *Applied Discourse Analysis: Social and Psychological Interventions* provides useful reading. Finally, for those who are interested in reflecting further on the political implications of how we represent the 'Other', Sue Wilkinson and Celia Kitzinger's (1996) edited volume on *Representing the Other* provides useful insights and examples of how researchers working with different groups of participants dealt with such issues. For a more in-depth consideration of the conceptualization of the 'insider–outsider' debate, Linda Alcoff's (2006) book *Visible Identities: Race, Gender and the Self* is a useful resource.

The article on issues of representing the 'Other' by Oguntokun (1998) provides a very useful discussion of the implications of the perceived positioning of the researcher and her participants. Frost et al.'s (2010) article on the value of pluralism in qualitative research is worth reading to further your understanding of the advantages and difficulties of adopting a pluralistic analytic approach.

APPENDICES

APPENDICES

APPENDIX 1

Data Set

PREFACE

Arnie Reed

The research project from which the data used by the various analytic groups and individual researchers in this book is drawn was a qualitative study of ex-soldiers' accounts of renegotiating identity after leaving the army, which I undertook as part of my doctoral training in counselling psychology at the University of Surrey. The study is intimately tied up with my own history. It might therefore be helpful to contextualize the research by outlining some pertinent aspects of my history which provided the impetus for the work.

Having served as a soldier for 26 years, the army is a context with which I have some familiarity. However, at the time of my discharge from the army, I knew nothing about the process or experience of leaving it. I had moved from one army posting to another, gaining experience as a soldier, while at the same time civilian life became more and more distant from me. After leaving the army, my attempt to adapt to civilian life saw me trying to immerse myself in this new and sometimes strange life context and to 'make it work'. In doing so, I tried to distance myself from my previous military service – to stop being a soldier and become a civilian. It soon became clear, however, that it is not at all an easy or straightforward process to set aside 26 years of your life: the wonder is that I ever thought it might be.

The culmination of this growing realization coincided with my signing up for a doctoral training programme in counselling psychology at the University of Surrey. Here, I was given the opportunity to research a single topic for three years, exploring it from diverse theoretical and methodological vantage points. Although I considered several research options, I suspect it was inevitable that I would be drawn to something that I knew best – namely the army – and, paradoxically, to something I knew little of, apart from my own isolated experiences of it – namely the process of leaving the army. The thought of 're-entering' the army through association with other ex-soldiers in my research was both exciting and challenging. How had other soldiers coped after discharge? How would I feel after being reminded of aspects of army life that I still missed? Would my own sometimes difficult and negative feelings be re-awakened? How had other soldiers fared during their own experience of leaving the army and would they be prepared to share these experiences with me?

I conducted first a qualitative research project and then a quantitative one, exploring how ex-soldiers experience and talk about the transition from army to civilian life once they retire. My particular focus was on the implications of this experience for their sense of self, which led me to use identity process theory to inform my qualitative work and to structure my quantitative research (Breakwell, 1986, 1996; Jaspal & Breakwell, 2014). However, this theory was used with a lightness of touch in my qualitative work: it did not play an obvious role in the shaping of the interview schedule and never drove the analysis but simply informed it, being invoked only after the data were analysed as far as possible on their own terms.

For the qualitative study, I recruited ten ex-servicemen firstly through advertising in a local newspaper in a garrison town in south-east England and then through 'snowballing' from the initial sample that had been recruited in this way (that is, having participants nominate others who might wish to take part). The men were aged between 40 and 48, with a mean age of 43.5 years. All were White and married. They had spent between ten and 24 years in the army, with the mean duration of service being 20.5 years. They had left the army between one and ten years prior to the research interview, with the mean length of time since discharge being 5.6 years. On discharge, one participant had held the rank of major, four had been warrant officers, three had been sergeants and two had been corporals. In terms of their occupational status at the time of the interviews, two were in professional jobs, three were classed as technicians or associate professionals, two were craft workers and three held elementary occupations.

I interviewed each man using a semi-structured interview schedule. I recorded the interviews on audiotape and transcribed them (changing the names of participants and amending any other identifying information in order to preserve confidentiality; three dots in the transcripts indicate where the participants paused) before subjecting them to qualitative analysis. This was a fascinating process, especially the challenge of sometimes trying to bracket my own experiences lest they end up overly shaping my interpretations while at the same time figuring out how to use my personal experiences to enrich the analysis. It became clear that my own experiences were both similar and dissimilar to those of the participants. Some participants had experienced greater difficulties than others in the transition to civilian life; some apparently had experienced few or none. Despite my concerns that this group might not want to engage in this research, it appeared that – perhaps because I was positioned as 'one of them' or 'one of us' – the majority really wanted to talk about their experiences and feelings during and after their own transition. Although I harboured doubts and concerns about conducting this research, the whole experience was a positive and useful one for me, helping to validate and accommodate my own experiences. Additionally, being allowed to enter the world of this extraordinary group of people and to share their range of rich experiences left me feeling privileged and humbled – and for that I will always be grateful.

I was delighted to be asked to allow part of the qualitative data set to be used by the analytic groups and individual researchers in this book and have been fascinated to see and compare the outcomes of their analyses as they applied interpretative phenomenological analysis, thematic analysis, grounded theory, discourse analysis and narrative analysis to the transcripts. Although I have decided not to reveal which specific method of analysis I used in my qualitative research, my reflections in this preface probably make it clear to readers that I did not use discourse analysis.

Time has dimmed my memory of the challenges, frustrations and anxieties involved in trying to make sense of my data (the study was conducted in 2000) so that now what I most clearly recall are the thrilling moments of breakthrough and clarity. My hope is that readers who decide to use the transcripts to practise and refine their own qualitative analytic skills will experience some of those high points too.

Interview transcript: David

1   **Arnie:** In what ways, if any, do you think your sense of yourself has
2   been influenced by being in the army?
3
4   **David:** It gave me more confidence. As a nipper when I first joined
5   the army, I wasn't confident at all. I think I joined the army to see how
6   I could do it for one thing. Number two – I joined to get away because
7   I didn't have a trade. I had no or very little education. The education I
8   did have behind me wasn't up to much, so I needed a job where I could
9   go in and have some money in my pocket. And, as you know, in them
10   days, they were 'Yeah, if you want a job my son, come this way' and
11   that was it. But it definitely gave me confidence – confidence to go
12   out. As we said, once I left the army, I could find a job
13   anywhere … within reason.
14
15   **Arnie:** What aspects, if any, of being a soldier were important to you?
16
17   **David:** I was a member of a team and I was an important member of a
18   team and I was recognized as doing something for my country. You
19   know, I was prepared to go. If they say, 'Right, David, Kuwait has
20   been attacked, you know, I was ready to go'. Yeah. It wasn't a case of
21   'Woah, it's their country, it's nothing to do with us.' If the boss wanted
22   to send me, then away I go. That was important to me. It's like, as I
23   say, I had an identity and I belonged to somewhere.
24
25   **Arnie:** You had an identity – could you talk a little bit more about
26   having an identity?
27
28   **David:** Yeah, I was, I was part of a team. I was a driver and, without
29   us drivers, no one would get their goods, so we were important and I
30   was proud of that. Uh, so that side of the identity was important to me,
31   you know – we were important in doing a job.
32
33   **Arnie:** Do you have that now?
34
35   **David:** [Sigh] People like to tell me I've got that now but I know I
36   haven't got that now. You know, I'm in the school [working as a
37   caretaker] and they say, 'Oh, without the caretaker this wouldn't
38   happen and this wouldn't happen. You know where everything is – we
39   don't.' True. Yeah, you know. If I was to have a week off, it would
40   start falling down because people don't know where everything is. But
41   in the same vein, if I happened to walk out of there and if I was to get
42   run over by a bus, you know, it would be case of, 'Well, that's it.

43   David, you did a good job, we miss him, fine, get someone else in'.
44
45   **Arnie:** It seems to be a little different for you from being a team
46   member within the school and being a team member in the army.
47
48   **David:** You're not a team member within the school because you're
49   not a teacher. The teachers all sort of get round their … I sometimes
50   wonder why the kids of today act like they are and I can understand by
51   the standards of some of the teachers. They can't do simple things.
52   Like, at the end of the day before the class is dismissed, the teacher
53   could say 'Right, we are going to pick bits of litter up'. They don't do
54   that. They just leave it off, you know, as if to say, 'Ah, it's only the
55   caretaker and his staff – they'll do it'. It annoys me because being part
56   of a team as we should be, as we were in the army, you know, we
57   would have all helped right from the top all the way down. Civilians
58   have different ideas of being in teams. They go as far as what's good
59   for themselves and then, 'Right, that's it', and that to me is not being
60   part of a team. That's the difficult part, I find.
61
62   **Arnie:** I'd like you to think and talk about whether or not your values
63   and personal beliefs have anything to do with your training as a soldier
64   or experiences in the army.
65
66   **David:** I would say a great percentage of them, yes. As in, as in being
67   honest to your mates – yeah – which, you know … if you're not honest
68   to your mates, then God, you were in the dog house, right up to your
69   neck in the dark and murky stuff. Um, discipline. Yeah, I think I
70   learned a great majority of them being in the army. Ah, I wouldn't say
71   I could have learned them at home because my mother died when I
72   was young, when I was little, you know, um, so being brought up by
73   my grandmother, right, I don't think she had a great deal of time so, so
74   yeah, I think I got a lot of them from being in the army.
75
76   **Arnie:** People tend to experience events like this sort of transition into
77   civilian life in their own unique way. I'd like to hear how you
78   experienced it and what your feelings were.
79
80   **David:** About leaving? It was an anti-climax. It was a … I don't know
81   what I expected but I didn't expect to just … You sort of stood in front
82   of this officer who reeled off a load of crap because, you know, the
83   officer I was stood in front of didn't like me anyway. We never saw
84   eye to eye from the day I got there because he knew I was only there
85   for 18 months because of 'Options for Change' [plans for reducing the
86   size of the army in the light of the end of the 'Cold War']. The unit I
87   was at was closing down so they had to send me somewhere. Um and,

88 you know, so he came out of his office and reeled off 'Oh, we've really
89 enjoyed having you' and all this … and I thought, 'You lying git'. But
90 then you just walked out of his office and the next thing you know,
91 someone's saying 'ID card – thank you, Mr Jones'. And that hit you,
92 you know. Someone's actually calling you 'Mister'. No one's calling
93 me 'Sergeant' any more. That was funny. That was a shock. That's
94 when you knew. And then that's it – you walk out and no one's
95 prepared you for that. I just … Once you're out that gate, that's it. I
96 know I can't even get back into the camp where, not ten minutes ago, I
97 was a serving sergeant. I can't get back in. You know, you … it's like
98 they're throwing you outside and locked the gate, you know, and that's
99 it – you're on your own. That was painful. And then having to sort of
100 fend your way through the world like … If something falls off your
101 house, you can't pick up the phone and get hold of the old housing
102 people any more – you've got to deal with it. In fact, there's no great
103 problem in that but it's a funny feeling. You know, 'Bloody hell, I've
104 got to deal with that now'. Yeah. Um, and going around and, you
105 know, like we were saying, you walk round and you walk down the
106 street and you see ghosts. You know, you walk down streets where you
107 walked down as a serving soldier and you can see all these ghosts,
108 people you've met, you know. Or, come out of this shop and you
109 expect all the lads to come staggering down the road drunk as skunks
110 or something like that and they don't and I still see them today, you
111 know. I can sit down in [named garrison town where he lives] and
112 yeah, the mind goes back to the times and you think, 'Yeah but there's
113 no one there any more' and, you know … you think, 'Jesus, you never
114 expected it to be like that'. You thought that maybe there's someone
115 you could talk to but there isn't. Even, you know, when they say you
116 can go to SSAFA [Soldiers, Sailors and Air Force Association – a
117 charitable organization that offers help to ex-service people] and all
118 that, even they sort of put you on the back burner once you're a
119 civilian because they think 'Yeah, that's it, you've used up, you know
120 you've done your bit – off you go'. And you know they don't realize
121 that you've given the best time of your life to them and you give,
122 which I did, I gave 150 per cent to the stage where I got damaged
123 knees and other things and I'm knackered. And so when I came out, I
124 should be out now enjoying myself because my kids have all grown up
125 and I should be now but I can't and you think to yourself, 'Oh Jesus,
126 what have I done?' Would I have done that if I had my time all over
127 again? Yes, even for all I've just said. You know, you walk out and
128 there's nothing – there's that void. It's just like an open space, an
129 empty space.
130
131 **Arnie:** It sounds lonely.
132

133 **David:** If it wasn't for my wife, I think I'd have done something totally
134 crazy. I don't think I'd be around today to be honest if it wasn't for the
135 missus. She was, she was very supportive and I, um, I tended to be a
136 little wild for about a couple of months after I got out, which one does.
137 Uh, it nearly broke the marriage up at one stage. But she stuck with us
138 and here we are. But yeah, it's … it is lonely. I still miss it, I still do. I
139 wish I could get civilianized very quickly.
140
141 **Arnie:** Can you tell me about what it felt like to be thinking about
142 leaving the army and becoming a civilian?
143
144 **David:** I started leaving the army when I was posted back from [a
145 named German town]. Hence that's why I chose, because I had a
146 choice of my unit, and I thought to myself, well a truck driver, that
147 seems like the obvious route to take, being RCT [Royal Corps of
148 Transport]. So I thought if I go for [name of specific army unit], at
149 least they've got the artics [articulated vehicles] there, so I can get out.
150 Although I had a Class 1 licence, I can get experience on them and get
151 the tacco [taccograph] experience, the rules of the road and the driver's
152 hours. Um, I started building up from then. What I aimed to do was get
153 a job first then find somewhere to live. And so I thought, and you
154 know when you have these briefings [army resettlement briefings] and
155 they tell you how hard it is to get a job, which was right in one respect,
156 um, as I think you need a job to get a job in civvy street and so I was
157 gearing up for that all the way through. I was putting favours out and
158 working for firms moonlighting, so I was getting my fingers in quite a
159 few pies. Um, it was the army that wouldn't let me leave. I started
160 gearing up for civvy street.
161
162 **Arnie:** It sounds like you were doing a lot of preparation, practical
163 preparation – was there any mental preparation? Did you think about
164 what it would feel like when you were a civvy?
165
166 **David:** I might have given it one or two thoughts … [indecipherable] …
167 But one thing I could never sort of visualize was civvy street. You
168 know, to me civilians were people that walked around and weren't able
169 to make decisions. That's the feeling you get, you know.
170
171 **Arnie:** Looking back, do you think that you were prepared for civilian
172 life and how being a civilian was going to feel?
173
174 **David:** No.
175

176 **Arnie:** Looking back, do you think there is anything extra that the
177 army might have done to help you adjust to civilian life or did they do
178 enough?
179
180 **David:** Yes, I think the army should allow you to get a feel for civilian
181 life. They should allow you to go and work, um, work experience for
182 instance. In the last six months, they should post you off somewhere
183 and say, 'Right, off you go and we'll see in you in …' – not letting you
184 run wild, having at least to report in once a week or something, um,
185 and let you go and work for somebody. So I think that would have
186 helped a lot. I don't think you can go away on one of these three week
187 [resettlement] courses and, you know, you come back and they think,
188 'Well, he's ready'. You know, I think some of the officers at the top
189 don't realize just how hard it is for someone to get out because I know
190 when they finish, they don't really finish. They go to the officers' clubs
191 and all of those things and they carry on drinking G and Ts for
192 breakfast. They don't think you … [indecipherable] … has to go out and
193 find his work. He doesn't get the money that they're offered in their
194 package, so he's got to go out and find the work, if you can understand
195 what I mean. And it's … you know, it just didn't prepare me at all. Like
196 I said earlier on, you know, one minute I was there and the next minute
197 I was out the gate – I was a civilian, you know. There was no
198 preparation at all.
199
200 **Arnie:** Some researchers believe that when people leave a distinctive
201 environment like the army, there may be an impact on how they see
202 themselves, feel about themselves or on how they behave. I'd like to
203 explore how your sense of being a soldier might or might not have
204 affected how you felt about yourself in civilian life.
205
206 **David:** Yes, I think I understand. You're trained to be disciplined and
207 you're trained to look after yourself. When I say 'look after yourself',
208 not like just combat. I mean by 'looking after yourself', I can make my
209 breakfast, I can make my dinner, I can sew, I can iron, I can wash. Um,
210 I know that there's a lot of civvies out there can't. I was astounded at
211 how many blokes can't iron or sew or can't cook. I just can't believe it,
212 you know. Um, so yeah, that's the thing … that was me.
213
214 **Arnie:** Did you feel differently or the same about yourself in civilian
215 life compared to how you felt about yourself while you were still in the
216 army?
217
218 **David:** Don't feel as … sometimes, not all the times, sometimes I don't

219 feel as though there's a purpose to it. You know, like, going to school
220 [as a school caretaker] and walking along and thinking, 'What the hell
221 am I doing here? Bugger this'. The kids are a bunch of shits, you
222 know. But I've got to do this yet again, today and tomorrow. And you
223 think to yourself, 'This is me for the rest of my life'. I go in there and I
224 just feel, 'Why isn't it like it was in the army?' and hope something
225 will change, yet I get on with it. Um, so I mean the answer to that
226 question is sometimes I feel upset but other times, you know, there's
227 just that void where I just wonder.
228
229 **Arnie:** Can you say something about how, if at all, being an ex-soldier
230 helped you or caused problems for you, or if you feel it made no
231 difference?
232
233 **David:** In civvy street, being an ex-soldier gives you the confidence.
234 Um, I went for an interview for a job. As I said, I've never been out of
235 work. I've had more jobs than I thought I ever would and I think that
236 the simple fact is that when I go on the interviews, I say, 'Right, this is
237 me. This is what you're getting. Take me and I'll be a great team
238 player', and I tell them that. Where it hinders me is the fact that I like
239 things in lines. I like things in neat packages and so when I go – like
240 when I was driving the truck, when I used to come back at night, I used
241 to park all the wagons up so all the bumpers were level. Funny as it
242 may seem, they had them parked all over the car park. It made it harder
243 to get out. They couldn't see the fact that by lining them all up it was
244 easy to get them out. Um, it was other little things like your paperwork.
245 Keep your paperwork in order – it makes it easy. I think that side of
246 life used to hinder me because all I would do was spend an extra ten
247 minutes. All they wanted to do was in, out and go. Um, so yeah, there
248 is a hindrance somewhere way along the line, in some aspects. I think
249 in most aspects it certainly stood me in good stead.
250
251 **Arnie:** Sometimes spouses, relatives or friends can influence how we
252 feel about ourselves, particularly during important changes, such as
253 changing career or lifestyle. I'd like to focus on whether or not the
254 decisions that you made and how you felt might have been influenced
255 by your spouse, relatives, friends and workmates. Can you say
256 something about whether or not you felt supported by your spouse?
257
258 **David:** Supported by ... no, not really. Because the people we knew
259 when we went to live in civvy street were up in [named town], north
260 Wales, so we didn't really know anybody there, so as for support, no,
261 no we didn't get any support from anybody. You just had to go out and
262 try and find your own feet and make lots of mistakes – expensive ones

263   at that.

264

265   **Arnie:** Can you say something about whether or not that lack of

266   support affected how you felt about yourself?

267

268   **David:** There was no one there to give me advice and guide me on

269   things like buying a house. Um, it's all right sitting in a briefing room

270   and someone pointing at a chart and saying, 'Do this and do that'.

271   That's all well and good but, as we know, what you see on paper and

272   what happens on the ground are two different things. Um, we bought a

273   house and it collapsed and we lost everything. I lost all of my money,

274   the lot, in this house in one fell swoop. If I had've been guided, if

275   someone had been there to say, 'Look, this is what you have to look

276   for', if there had been someone up in that area that we could have

277   called on and say, 'Look, I'm buying a house, I've just come out of the

278   army – any chance of coming along and showing me a few pointers?',

279   I think that would've helped. So at least you'd have got the first one

280   over with. I won't be buying another house. I don't want to buy

281   another house ever again. That would have been handy. Um, no, there

282   was no support for me.

283

284   **Arnie:** I wonder if people's feelings or behaviour towards you changed

285   or stayed the same after you became a civilian?

286

287   **David:** Yes I think they did because the people we knew when we

288   were living in [named Welsh town], the people we knew around the

289   area knew me as the soldier from England so they used to come around

290   and we used to have a chat at weekends and all this. But once I got out

291   [left the army], a few of them sort of kept coming round for a while

292   and then all of a sudden they were just gone. They must have thought,

293   'Well that's it, he's got nothing else to offer, the novelty's worn off'. I

294   think people's feelings did change in some respects.

295

296   **Arnie:** Did that have an effect on you or not?

297

298   **David:** No, not really, because I was working permanent nights, so I

299   never used to see them often anyway. Once I got out and I started

300   working properly, no I don't think it did.

301

302   **Arnie:** Working and living in the military environment is different in

303   many ways to civilian life. I was wondering if there are parts of

304   military life which you miss?

305

306   **David:** What, compared to civvy street? I miss the social life, I miss

307 the social life … I miss the programme of events that we used to get in
308 the army.
309
310 **Arnie:** The social programme or …?
311
312 **David:** Both, the social and regimental programmes … in view of my
313 character. Like, we've got days when we're on exercise for a few
314 weeks. Get there and you could plan your life. You knew you were
315 going on exercise and you thought um, you knew that 18 weekends out
316 of the 52 … you knew you were going to kill a few beers and you knew
317 you were going to have a good time. I think you've got over that now.
318 You know you can't plan anything from day to day. I miss the danger,
319 the thrill, the adrenalin rush. You don't get that any more. Um, I miss
320 walking out the door and making sure I'm all right. I'm proud to be a
321 soldier. Now I walk out the door in my overalls and I think, 'Well,
322 yeah, that's it'. You try to give an appearance of someone who's been
323 trained and disciplined but it's not the same, it's not the same. You
324 don't have the same effect as anywhere else.
325
326 **Arnie:** Did you feel you needed to replace things about the army that
327 you missed with something else?
328
329 **David:** Well I tried to join the Association but it's full of old people.
330 The RCT [Royal Corps of Transport] Association, I mean. We joined
331 that but I'm the youngest there by 26 years. You know, um, we went to
332 the Christmas function and it was someone with an organ playing 'Roll
333 out the barrel' and other 1940s music, which is no good to me and our
334 lass. Um, we haven't reached that stage yet. We go back up to [named
335 Welsh town] and we have some friends up there and we go back up
336 there and we have a whale of a time up there – totally go wild. So
337 yeah, that replaces it.
338
339 **Arnie**: You talked about moving around in the house in [named Welsh
340 town] and now you're living in [named garrison town]. What made
341 you come back to [named garrison town]?
342
343 **David:** The house we had up there, um, collapsed and we had to sue a
344 solicitor and get another solicitor to sue the other solicitor and it was
345 quite a hard task, you know. They refused to do it or reluctant, I should
346 say, to do it but we did find one but it cost us a lot of money – money
347 which we didn't have so we had to beg, steal and borrow it. In the end,
348 we lost the house altogether. Um, we had to sell it to pay off some of
349 the debts and this job came up which meant I got a house with the job.
350 Hence, I'm back here. And that's it.
351

352 **Arnie:** You had links then with the [named garrison town] area to
353 know about the job here?
354

355 **David:** Oh yes. The father-in-law was a governor of the school and he
356 told me that there was a job coming up. He didn't actually have any
357 say or input into me getting the job because it was totally down to me,
358 you know. Him being a governor, me coming because we were related
359 – he had to take a step to one side and let me get on with it.
360

361 **Arnie:** When I was preparing for this research I came across material
362 which discussed how people from distinctive jobs might try to lessen
363 the impact of leaving. We've talked about the army resettlement
364 package but I'd like to know a little more from a personal perspective.
365 Did you think about what it might be like when you would've left the
366 army lifestyle and how – how you might feel about that?
367

368 **David:** Well one of the reasons why I think I was moonlighting was to
369 get to know my civilian counterparts and try and get into how they
370 thought and how they worked and how they operated, um, but it was
371 very difficult in some respects. That, uh, as soon as they found out that
372 you were a squaddie – a serving squaddie – working in their firm,
373 some of the drivers – not all of them but some of the drivers – just
374 wouldn't speak to you because you were trying to take over their jobs,
375 which I think, you know ... it's how can I put it, a bit like a Black trying
376 to join the Klu [sic] Klux Klan, you know. You know, we were sort of
377 coming in and we were 'No go', you know. 'You shouldn't be coming
378 in here, you know. You've got a job – what are you doing sort of
379 taking other jobs?', you know. 'There's people out there who are
380 unemployed who want this job', you know. And I'd turn round and
381 say, 'Well, why aren't they here taking the job?' That was hard. It was
382 also giving an insight into how they felt.
383

384 **Arnie:** And that was towards you when you were a soldier?
385

386 **David:** Yeah.
387

388 **Arnie:** But as an ex-soldier it might have been different?
389

390 **David:** Yes, I think it would've been.
391

392 **Arnie:** Um, do you think you've adjusted to civilian life?
393

394 **David:** No. No. I would say that in one easy answer there.
395

396 **Arnie:** Looking back, would you have done anything differently as

397   part of the transition?

398

399   **David:** Yes. I wouldn't have went to [name of army unit]. I would

400   have gone to a TA [Territorial Army] unit, asked for a post as PSI

401   [Permanent Staff Instructor] at a TA unit, knowing that I'd have got

402   extra time off to go and get in there and also um, working with

403   civilians you know, maybe I'd have got a little bit more insight into

404   how they work and how things operate on the other side of the fence.

405

406   **Arnie:** David, that's just about all the questions that I've got. Is there

407   anything on the subject that you want to talk about which we haven't

408   covered?

409

410   **David:** Yeah. I think it's looking at it now in the long term and

411   speaking to other ex-soldiers as well and people who are due to get out,

412   it's that somewhere round the UK there should be a camp or whatever

413   where you could be posted to for six months and then go out and work

414   for the civilians. So you don't have to get paid but you can go out and

415   can get worked in slowly, slowly, slowly and then, at the end of the six

416   months, you'll have a time to be shown possibly how to buy a house.

417   You'd have worked with the civilians, worked in a civilian atmosphere

418   and just totally tried to get yourself civilianized, so when the time does

419   come, you're out and you just slide out instead of fall out.

420

421   **Arnie:** More smooth?

422

423   **David:** Yeah, smoothly. And plus also for the ladies as well, the

424   females as well and the kids because the kids will have gone from

425   pillar to post over that time, so it will obviously give them time to get

426   settled in. And, I don't know about the majority, I don't know what the

427   actual percentage is but it could it be a few anyway, who would be

428   getting out as they are coming to a crucial time in their education and

429   when you just sort of, bang, finished, there's an awful lot of flying

430   around to do. You know, you've got to get yourself a house, you've

431   got to get this, you've got to get that and, you know, the kids are

432   caught in the middle of it. Where that ... if you have a nice sliding slope,

433   you can get them settled, get them in and they can be cracking on with

434   their education. The wives, again, sliding out slowly but surely, getting

435   settled, you know, and so, at the end of the day, you've got a nice

436   transition to civvy street instead of this void and you're sort of

437   wandering around for a few months with your finger up your backside

438   thinking, 'Well, what's this?', you know. 'Where am I?'

439

440   **Arnie:** I'd like you to reflect now just for a moment on the experience

441 of the interview and how's it felt. What have been the positive things

442 and what have been the negative things, perhaps, about taking part.

443

444 **David:** I think one of the positive things is that you're getting it

445 all ... you're getting the questions, you're letting us speak how we feel

446 and not like when you get a lot of these questionnaires – they get you

447 to answer what they want to hear by the way they've put the question.

448 Um, on the negative side, it's, it's very difficult in some respects

449 on ... to describe how you feel. I think that if we'd had a chance to slide

450 over from army to civilian in a nice steady flow, I think that might

451 have been easier. I think because we're just sort of door shut, out you

452 go, you know, you still don't know who you are. And, as my brother-

453 in-law said, it's taken him 11 years to become civilianized – and his

454 wife's still in the forces. Um, but that might have been easier if that

455 makes any sense.

456

457 **Arnie:** It makes perfect sense, yeah. Do you think that taking part in

458 the interview has had any effect or perhaps will have an effect on the

459 way you feel about yourself?

460

461 **David:** No, I think we've sort of ... I think we're still in the army. If

462 you look around the house ... I wouldn't call it ... it's like a married

463 quarter. So, you know, that's drifting away from the question there

464 slightly but ...

465

466 **Arnie:** Well thanks for participating in the interview.

Interview transcript: Brian

1 **Arnie:** In what ways, if any, do you think a sense of yourself has been

2 influenced by being in the army and your experiences in the army?

3

4 **Brian:** I think I've learned in the forces and the thing is you learn these

5 things in the army without realizing it a lot of the time, so that when you

6 come out and start comparing yourself to the people working alongside

7 you, you find that you've got a much greater sense of urgency. You tend

8 to pay more attention to detail, you don't bother about the time so much,

9 you don't clock on or clock off. If the job takes twice as long as it should,

10 you just work on as necessary. We seem to be much more flexible, much

11 more adaptable to situations, and it's all stuff I've learned in the forces and

12 the experience I've had where you need to be adaptable, where the

13 situation might change. You've already learned to adapt to new situations

14 – and that comes through all the time. When I look around I see that all of

15 the time, lack of attention to detail, how they just skimp over things, and
16 no attitude. You know, we do our best all of the time.
17
18 **Arnie:** What aspects, if any, of being a soldier were important to you?
19 When you were in the army, what was important?
20
21 **Brian:** I suppose it was actually being part of something really big, doing
22 a worthwhile job and being able to prove yourself by progressing through
23 the ranks. That was very important to me. To have the opportunity to
24 prove what you can do and how well you can do it.
25
26 **Arnie:** Do you think you've found that in civvy street?
27
28 **Brian:** To some respect but in different ways. The type of job I have now,
29 there is no form of progression through the ranks but that doesn't stop you
30 doing your job well and actually being noticed. But no, there's no real
31 rank structure as such in the job I'm doing at the moment.
32
33 **Arnie:** So how do you feel about working with those differences?
34
35 **Brian:** It's something I've accepted and there's not a problem. I enjoy
36 what I'm doing. One of the main reasons I think I enjoy it is because I've
37 been given a job to do in a given area and I get on and do it. I'm not
38 closely supervised. I belong to a team – there are 16 of us in total and we
39 do come together from time to time and we do help out and work together
40 as we need to but a lot of the time I'm left to my own devices and allowed
41 to make my own decisions rather than having people telling you what to
42 do all of the time.
43
44 **Arnie:** How does that compare with the army?
45
46 **Brian:** Yes, I suppose to a certain extent, I suppose you were
47 guided all of the time but then, as you progress through the ranks, you
48 have more say in what you do and I've always believed that when I was in
49 the forces if someone gave me a goal, how I achieved that goal was up to
50 me, which is exactly the same as what I'm doing now. I'm given an aim
51 and how I achieve it is up to me at the end of the day. No one actually sets
52 out the route which I need to take.
53
54 **Arnie:** People tend to experience events like this sort of transition in their
55 own unique way. I'd like to hear and understand how you experienced it
56 and what your feelings were. So to that end, could you start wherever you
57 want about whatever you want about the whole process of leaving the
58 army and entering civvy street.
59

60 **Brian:** When I first came out, obviously I was totally preoccupied in
61 trying to find a job, finding something to do. That took a while to find a
62 job and I was sending loads and loads of applications off and I was getting
63 loads and loads of interviews and I was going to the interviews and getting
64 down to the last two or three people – no problem at all – but it was
65 obvious from the interviews that when you go to them, the people doing
66 the interviews have preconceived ideas about what the people in the forces
67 are like and their perceptions of military people are totally outdated. And
68 they seem to believe that your style of management means shouting at
69 people and hitting people with big sticks and that's it. They don't believe
70 that we get trained to manage people quietly. And since I've been out, I've
71 noticed that the way ex-military guys manage their staff is much better
72 than the way a civilian-trained person does because the way civilians
73 manage their staff, they see a job – for instance, if their job is to construct
74 a network for telecommunications – that's all they do, just getting the stuff
75 in the ground as cheaply as possible and as quickly as possible. They don't
76 manage the job as a whole – they don't look into the welfare side of life
77 and make sure that their staff are happy. They don't keep that on track –
78 they see it as very narrow. When I was in the forces, you were given a
79 resource which included your guys to do the job and you had to look after
80 that resource, so it was all geared around that you see. But em, once I
81 found a job, I ended up taking probably the first job that was offered to me
82 which wasn't probably a good idea but I didn't want to be out of work and
83 then I found when I was doing the job, I was going about it differently to
84 how everyone else did. Everyone else did what was expected and I was
85 going that extra sort of mile every time and I found that was causing a lot
86 of problems because I was doing it and no one else was. The thing is the
87 job I was doing at the time was an enforcement job and a lot of the time
88 you had to go round and tell people they had to do something in a certain
89 way or they couldn't do something what they was doing and because
90 going round and doing the job which I thought I was doing it as I was
91 supposed to be doing, a lot of complaints were coming back to me at the
92 office of my superiors about the way I was doing the work and um there
93 was a couple of times I was asked 'Well why are you generating all these
94 complaints?' and I said 'Well I'm only doing what I'm supposed to be
95 doing. You've asked me to do this work and I'm actually doing it.'And
96 when they looked into it, they saw, well, that's what I was doing but the
97 other people, if they felt it was going to be confrontational, they just shied
98 away from it and they didn't actually do that part of the job – they just
99 used to let it ride, you see, and find something else to do.
100
101 **Arnie:** It sounds like this was all part of the military overlap which you
102 talked about before – doing your job properly and the military discipline
103 as well.
104

105 **Brian:** And not shying away from confrontation really. If it was going to
106 be confrontational, then try and manage it in a certain way but if it needs
107 to be done, it needs to be done.
108
109 **Arnie:** Can you tell me what it felt like for you when you were
110 considering leaving the army? You've told me that you came out on the
111 redundancy phase. When you started thinking about what it was going to
112 be like being a civilian, can you remember how that felt?
113
114 **Brian:** Well, to be perfectly honest I didn't really want to leave. Although
115 it was my choice, I felt my hand was being forced really. I was making the
116 best of a bad job really. As I said before, part of the reason I came out was
117 partly medical reasons and I felt that, had I stayed in, I wouldn't be able to
118 fulfil my full potential so I decided to come out early and that was making
119 the best of it. But if I had the choice, I would have stayed in. I wouldn't
120 have come out early at all. So yeah, I was a bit ... but other than that, I
121 wasn't particularly bothered. The area we decided to settle, we already had
122 a house here. My children were at school, my wife had a job so really all I
123 had to do was find myself a job and I was quite prepared to do anything if
124 necessary, so I didn't envisage being out of work. When I was applying
125 for jobs, I wasn't just applying for one job, I was reading through the job
126 adverts and thinking, 'Oh I can do that', and so I applied for it. And in
127 total I probably applied for about 20 to 30 different types of jobs because I
128 thought, 'Yeah, I can do that'. And I didn't really have anything set in my
129 mind about what I wanted to do at the time. I just wanted to ... I was
130 coming out, I was going to get a job and take it on from there. I didn't
131 expect to be in the first job all the time and, in the end, it was probably
132 about 18 months to two years I had my first job before I changed. The job
133 I'm doing now I've had for four years now and I'm quite happy to do that
134 and, if I change my work now, I'll probably go for a similar job in a
135 different company.
136
137 **Arnie:** Can you say something about how it felt when you were actually
138 discharged? You've talked a little bit about what you were thinking about
139 when you were thinking about leaving. What did it feel like when you
140 were actually discharged, do you recall?
141
142 **Brian:** No, not really. No. No I don't think ... personally I don't think it had
143 much of an effect or if I worried too much about it but I probably did and
144 my wife seems to think that, when I was in the forces, I was much happier
145 than what I have been since I've been out. But, no, I don't really recall any
146 particular feelings at the time.
147
148 **Arnie:** I'd like to talk about the army resettlement package now – pre-
149 release stuff. I'm aware that the army has got a resettlement package for

150 people leaving the army and I'd like to get an idea of how useful it was for
151 you.
152
153 **Brian:** Well yes, um, the army took me to one side and they gave me
154 training and that's the training I now … is the basis I've used … the basis to
155 get the work I'm doing now. So yes, it was fine, it was adequate. It puts
156 you in the right direction. The only thing is um because I decided to come
157 out a year before I actually left, it wasn't really long enough to put
158 everything into…all the plans I would have like to have gone into, into
159 motion. Really I should have started two or three years in advance rather
160 than try and fit it in one year. You just can't do it – it's too much to do.
161 And the problem is everything you do in the forces, all the experience you
162 gain, it doesn't transfer very well to civilian life so you need to sort of
163 adapt all your skills and qualifications into such a way as civilian
164 employers can actually pick up on it and understand. And that's what I
165 didn't have time to do, you just don't have time to do it in the year. But
166 other than that, yeah, it was great you know.
167
168 **Arnie:** Looking back, do you think that you were prepared for civilian life
169 and how being a civilian was going to feel? You've said that perhaps a
170 year wasn't long enough and you might have liked two or three years to
171 prepare but on the whole do you think you were prepared – and
172 particularly about how being a civilian was going to feel?
173
174 **Brian:** Well, when I first came out, the thing I found most strange was the
175 job I had, I was finishing work about four o'clock in the afternoon. With
176 starting fairly early and finishing about four, I was getting home for about
177 half past four and thinking 'What I do now?' Because before, I'd never get
178 home that early, even when I was based just up the road I used to um … the
179 type of job I was doing – used to be doing that job all day and then you
180 had to do all the admin side and sometimes I didn't get home until about
181 six or seven anyway and I found I had a little more time on my hands and
182 I wasn't quite sure what to do with it. One thing I felt strange was, in the
183 civilian environment, everyone sort of dress and everyone looks the same
184 and in the military you can tell just by looking at someone where they are
185 in the pecking order and where they are and so you can temper what you
186 say to them and how you say it to them. In civilian life in the company,
187 everyone dressed the same, everyone looked the same – you didn't know
188 who you were talking to, whether someone at the same level as you or
189 some of the more senior directors. And I found that very disconcerting
190 until you get to know who the faces are but that was strange. But other
191 than that, I treated my first move into civilian life, especially the job, as
192 another posting really and it worked quite well because the first job I went
193 to … I was working in a small department of about ten people and six of
194 those were ex-forces and they were all from my old regiment and some I

195 knew from before anyway so really it was very similar to another posting,
196 just another job.
197
198 **Arnie:** Did that help, having ex-servicemen around?
199
200 **Brian:** Oh it certainly did help, yeah. Yeah and these guys had been out
201 ranging between um, like a couple of years to probably ten or twelve
202 years. So we had a whole range of experiences and they'd all sort of
203 learned different things and it was quite helpful to speak to them and find
204 out what was going on. Just coming out and being a bit of the new boy
205 there and it is a slightly different environment but that ... I felt, I think
206 things would have been different if I hadn't gone for that job first off and
207 been surrounded by ex-forces people, especially some of the guys I'd
208 known from before as well, or if ... and even ones I didn't know, we had
209 mutual friends with other people we knew between us, so that worked out
210 really well.
211
212 **Arnie:** You've touched on this next thing I was going to ask – and still
213 will. Looking back, do you think that you were mentally prepared for
214 civilian life?
215
216 **Brian:** Yeah. Yeah, I think so and mainly because I believe that the forces
217 learned me how to adapt to new situations and this was just another
218 situation to adapt to and, other than that, it's not been a particular problem.
219 Initially I found it very hard in that way to fit in with civilian workmates
220 because I came across as aggressive, abrupt, arrogant ... which is the way
221 other people would describe me, the type ... but I was just sort of being
222 what I was doing really and in the military environment that was...it
223 wouldn't even have been picked up on. In fact, when I was serving in the
224 military, I was often being pulled up for not being as aggressive as some
225 of my peers. And when I came out, then they were saying, 'Well, you're
226 overly aggressive', which of course I found very strange. But um, I
227 have ... it's several years I've been out now and I've mellowed but even so,
228 people still describe me as being aggressive, overbearing and but um, I've
229 mellowed to such an extent and I suppose you have to ... in such a way
230 to... you have to sort of change your style. A lot of my work, I train people
231 up...my work is training and I've had to adapt my training style to be more
232 civilian friendly than in the military because it was ... people used to say,
233 'Well, we come to you and you don't teach us – you shout at us', which
234 was – all I was doing was projecting my voice so that people would hear
235 me at the back but I've had to adapt it in such a way that people are more
236 happy with it and it's slightly less structured than what it was when I was
237 in the forces – a bit more casual.
238

239 **Arnie:** More civilianized.

240

241 **Brian:** Yeah. Civilians have a preconceived idea of ex-forces anyway and
242 it's based on fact but obviously as it's gone through different people, it's
243 been sort of changed and exaggerated and made bigger and so if you
244 spoke to the average civilian about what a service guy is, they'd probably
245 say, 'Oh he's um, he's very fit and he's aggressive and he's loud', and
246 they're not all like that, but again, so you're losing before you start really.
247 Whenever they wanted someone to head up a sports team or something
248 they'd say, 'Oh, Brian, you're ex-forces you can do that, you know how to
249 do that'. Or when they want someone to take control of a situation, 'Oh,
250 you've done that. You can do that role on these sort of leadership training
251 courses', or anything like that, anything that has a military connotation,
252 'Oh you know what you're doing; you can do that'. So they have
253 preconceived ideas.

254

255 **Arnie:** Mmm. It sounds like they were happy with some of the military
256 qualities that you were bringing to them but unhappy with others.

257

258 **Brian:** Well the thing is, when I first obviously, when I joined my first
259 company I was ... six out of ten of us were ex-military, so they obviously
260 liked military people because they got good value for money from them.
261 They knew the military guys would work hard and they didn't shy away
262 from the work and they did a good job. So, yeah, once they ... and I found
263 even in my other job as well, when I first, the job I'm doing now, I was the
264 first military guy they took on in my department and at one stage we had
265 five people in that department who were ex-military – obviously some
266 have left now – and I find that when you get one guy and if he does a good
267 job, then the company is quite open to bring more people into the same
268 department. And the way it normally works anyway is that you end up
269 then working with people you've know from before because when you
270 know they're going to take military people, then you recommend the
271 people that you know and um, out of the five military guys we had
272 working in my department, three of them I knew from before anyway so ...

273

274 **Arnie:** Again we've touched on some of these issues but I'd like to talk
275 now about the influence of your personal values and beliefs on the
276 transition to becoming a civilian. Some researchers believe that, when
277 people leave a distinctive environment like the army, there may be an
278 impact on how they see themselves, feel about themselves or in how they
279 behave. I'd like to explore how your sense of being a soldier might or
280 might not have affected how you felt about yourself in civilian life and, as
281 I say, you've touched on some of these issues and you can expand on
282 those or you can move onto other areas if you like. Did you feel

283 differently or the same about yourself in civilian life compared to how you
284 felt about yourself while you were in the army?

285

286 **Brian:** No, not really. Because when I was in the forces, you feel good
287 about yourself anyway. You've got an identity there and you feel good
288 about yourself. And since I've been out, it's almost the same I think – not
289 much has changed there really. Obviously what I do now is different but I
290 don't think I've changed a great deal. I still try to maintain my ideals and
291 the principles that I had from before, which is perhaps why, every now
292 and again, I've caused a few ructions because I've still tried to maintain
293 and perhaps enforce my ideals on other people perhaps.

294

295 **Arnie:** Other people's influence, sometimes spouses, relatives or friends,
296 can influence how we feel about ourselves and particularly during
297 important changes like this, such as changing career or lifestyle. I'd like to
298 focus on whether or not the decisions you made and how you felt might
299 have been influenced by a spouse, friends, colleagues. Does that make
300 sense?

301

302 **Brian:** Yeah. No, I don't think ... I suppose I must have been influenced in
303 such a way because the first job I took was fairly local – it was based at
304 [named town] when I lived here. So, and I suppose that must have been
305 influenced by the house we ha- and schooling – my daughter was going to
306 ... so I didn't have to go too far afield. But um, and when I changed my
307 second job, I chose a job even closer to home, so yeah, there must have
308 been some kind of influence there but at the time I wouldn't have probably
309 admitted that I was being influenced or even realized it I suppose.

310

311 **Arnie:** Can you say something about whether or not you felt supported by
312 your wife?

313

314 **Brian:** Oh yeah, yeah. When I decided to come out, my wife was all for it
315 and she said, 'Well if that's what you want to do, then go for it' and she
316 didn't attempt to sway me or influence me in any way really but if I was
317 happy, she was happy.

318

319 **Arnie:** Do you think that people valued you more or less when you were a
320 soldier or as a civilian? Or the same?

321

322 **Brian:** Don't know really. Um, I know ... I suppose I valued myself higher
323 when I was in the forces than now I'm outside because you had a much
324 more definite identity which other people could relate to, even if they had
325 a warped view of what you were doing. So, personally I feel I had greater
326 status when I was serving than now I'm out but, as opposed to people in

327 the company I'm with, I don't suppose there's any difference at all. In
328 fact, I'm probably valued greater by the company I'm working for than I
329 ever was when I was in the forces because of the size of the organization.
330 I'm in a smaller organization here and the job I'm doing is quite key to the
331 company and they need someone ... when I was just one sergeant in the
332 Royal Engineers, there's lots of other sergeants in the Royal Engineers.
333 Now, I am a bigger fish in a smaller pond and so I'm probably valued
334 more by the company than I ever was in the forces, yeah.
335

336 **Arnie:** By the sound of it, your own self-esteem was higher while you
337 were in the army?
338

339 **Brian:** I think that's because I had a definite label I could pin to myself
340 really.
341

342 **Arnie:** A label? Sergeant?
343

344 **Brian:** And obviously it took a lot of time and effort actually to get to that
345 level as well. You know, what I'm doing now, I joined the company as
346 that from day one and, although my job has changed a great deal, I have a
347 lot greater area of responsibility. I have more people to cover and look
348 after now than what I had when I first started but I'm still basically the
349 same – I'm still a health and safety adviser and I was that from day one so
350 it hasn't taken a great deal of effort to actually do that and um, as I
351 progress through the company, I'll be given like more and more
352 responsibilities but I'll only be a health and safety adviser. And so you
353 have to work hard and you have to earn your titles in military life.
354

355 **Arnie:** Has any of what we've talked about so far affected how you felt
356 about yourself?
357

358 **Brian:** No but um, it's probably made me look a lot closer at what I was
359 doing and what I'm doing now and what I was thinking then and now than
360 I ever done before. It's just something you get on and do it really without
361 actually thinking about it a great deal. This has prompted me to think back
362 and think through a few things.
363

364 **Arnie:** I'd like to focus on any parts of military life which you've missed.
365 I was wondering if there were any parts of military life which you miss?
366

367 **Brian:** The main bit really was the social life but I've managed to sort of
368 keep links with that. I still ... I'm an honorary member of the Mess [a place
369 where members of the armed forces have their meals or spend their free
370 time] up at the barracks which I go to every now and again and that's

371 handy because, especially with it being a training establishment, you've
372 got people coming through all the time and it's a good way of meeting up
373 with people that you've not seen for many, many years because everyone
374 comes through there eventually. So that's ideal, so I've managed to retain
375 links up there and other than that, that was probably the only thing that I
376 really ever said I missed. But thinking about some of the answers I've
377 already said, then there's perhaps a few other things in there I've missed
378 as well, such as the status and the esteem and everything else but, um, as I
379 would have said, the most important one was the social side of life which I
380 missed. Work is work really and, although I'm working in different
381 environments with different people now, I've managed to replace one type
382 of work with another type of work and I'm quite happy with that but the
383 social side is a lot different and um, I will keep the links. It's not quite the
384 same, but yeah, it's a good compromise.
385

386 **Arnie:** So it's mostly the social side you miss and you've managed to
387 retain links with that and you enjoy that by the sounds of it. And you
388 touched on other things that you miss and you touched on self-esteem and
389 status and I guess that was linked to the hierarchical situation in the
390 military, that you were a sergeant within that system.
391

392 **Brian:** That's right, yeah.
393

394 **Arnie:** Could you say a little bit more about that? About how you felt and
395 what it feels like now not to be in that situation?
396

397 **Brian:** Well, I think before it was just um, belonging and being part of a
398 system and able to work your way through that system and be able to
399 achieve and now you just … it's not the same. There's no real rank structure
400 the same. No, really the only thing I felt I might miss when I first came out
401 was the … obviously the social side. I knew that I'd miss that, but then I got
402 round that by … as soon as I came out I joined the Mess straight away. That
403 only lasted for 18 months because pressures of work wouldn't allow
404 me to go, to attend the Mess as regularly as I would have liked, so that fell
405 flat after a couple of years. But um, I've since been able to juggle things a
406 bit better and I can fit it in now. And um, initially when I first came out as
407 well, I went straight into the TA. Again that didn't last for long because I
408 was a bit disillusioned with the way the TA was run. Obviously I had one
409 idea of it which it didn't sort of meet up with the reality really. So yeah, I
410 thought I'd sort of miss out on sort of the military life. I thought, 'Well if I
411 can join the TA, it's …' – again it's not quite the army but it's run on
412 similar lines. And I thought that would help ease me into civilian life but
413 again that didn't last particularly long. One was, being working, it was
414 difficult to get there a lot of the time and two um, I was a bit disappointed
415 with the way it was run. It wasn't being run on the same lines as the

416   regular forces and when they started moaning about me not being fully fit
417   because of my eye, I said, 'Well fine, I didn't join the TA for any hassle'. I
418   more joined for the ... having a bit of fun and the social side again but there
419   wasn't a great deal of social side in the TA so I decided, when they made a
420   few waves, I just decided to pack it in and just leave because I had other
421   things to focus on anyway. I had to focus on working on my job and that
422   stuff so I just left.
423

424   **Arnie:** It sounds like it was a little bit of a stepping stone.
425

426   **Brian:** It would have been but that was the aim of doing it in the first
427   place. I thought that would help coming out but, as it happened, I wasn't
428   in there long enough really to get any real benefit from it.
429

430   **Arnie:** Can I ask you to think about whether or not you feel now that
431   you're fully adjusted to civilian life?
432

433   **Brian:** Yes but um people know I'm ex-forces whether or not I tell them
434   or not. Quite often I train people from all round the company and, at the
435   end of the presentation, another ex-serviceman will come and ask me
436   about my military life and I didn't refer to it. It's just that they pick up on
437   the way I act, the way I behave and the way I speak as well – they pick on
438   it straight away and they know, so other ex-servicemen would stop me
439   straight away or other people who've had some involvement – perhaps
440   that their parents had been in the forces or their husband had been in the
441   forces – they recognize it as well and pick up straight away. So, although I
442   feel I have quite adjusted to civilian life, um, really I'm still an ex-
443   serviceman. I'm not a civilian as such.
444

445   **Arnie:** How do you feel when people can readily identify you and
446   approach you in the knowledge that you're an ex-soldier?
447

448   **Brian:** Oh, I suppose it pleases me really I suppose because I've still
449   retained links with this certain part of my life I had, so yeah. It doesn't
450   displease me in any way. It's probably a benefit rather than anything else.
451

452   **Arnie:** Looking back, would you have done anything differently? Or not?
453

454   **Brian:** No, I don't think so. No, everything's worked out as I would have
455   hoped. Yeah.
456

457   **Arnie:** That's all the questions that I've got that I wanted to ask. Is there
458   anything on this subject that you wanted to talk about?
459

460   **Brian:** I don't know, no. I think everything's come out really. Before you

461 came here, I was thinking about what of my experiences would be most
462 useful for other people to hear ...
463
464 **Arnie:** And again you touched on this yourself briefly and I'd like to ask
465 you to reflect for a moment on the experience of this interview. How has it
466 felt? What have been the positive things about taking part and what have
467 been the negative things about taking part?
468
469 **Brian:** Well, I don't think there's any negative things really. On the
470 positive side, it's made me look a little bit closer perhaps how I did feel
471 or... when I did come out and um, perhaps it's made me realize that uh,
472 perhaps there was more of an impact in coming out than what I realized at
473 the time.And perhaps there's more to military life that I missed than
474 perhaps I would have previously admitted to. But other than that ... but one
475 of the positive parts of it was actually now um, after this you've got all the
476 reports together. I will be able to see how everyone feels rather than just
477 myself and see how closely I match other people and whether I'm actually
478 out there alone or whether I'm just the same as everyone else and had
479 similar experiences.
480
481 **Arnie:** So there's part of you which wants to compare yourself to other
482 ex-servicemen and your experiences to other ex-servicemen's experiences.
483
484 **Brian:** Because in the department I work for now, there's another two
485 guys at the moment, ex-forces, both of whom I knew from before when I
486 was serving. One of the guys he also attends the Mess as well and we go
487 up there quite regularly together and the other guy has cut himself off
488 completely from the military and doesn't attend any of these functions and
489 doesn't ... not interested in going back. So obviously there's two different
490 people. There's one who wants to retain the links and another person who
491 wants to forget about it.
492
493 **Arnie:** Do you think that taking part in this interview has had any effect,
494 or will have any effect on the way you feel about yourself? And again
495 you've touched on some of those issues. You said that you think it's given
496 you a little bit more insight into what you really did feel when you were
497 coming out.
498
499 **Brian:** No, I don't think so. Obviously, yes, it's made me a bit closer and I
500 probably have gained something from it but whether I'm actually going to
501 go away and build on that or having a lasting effect, I wouldn't have
502 thought so, no. It's just like ... it's provided some information and that's it
503 really.

APPENDIX 2

Reporting Qualitative Research

PREFACE

Adrian Coyle and Evanthia Lyons

Whether a researcher conducts qualitative or quantitative research, the research process does not end until the study has been written up and presented to a wider audience. This audience may initially be quite a local one in the case of student research, where supervisors and examiners will review the work. However, ultimately the researcher's aim should be to convey their findings to an even wider audience so that, if the study is of sufficient quality, it can add to our knowledge of the research topic, inform debate and, in the case of applied research, shape policy and practice. This entails writing up the research for presentation at conferences and ultimately for publication in academic journals and other relevant outlets. Yet, the process of writing up research can be rather daunting, whether the research is qualitative or quantitative. The researcher may harbour fears about whether their work will withstand public scrutiny. They may be unsure about how best to represent in writing what they have done because relatively little practical guidance is offered in qualitative methodological texts on how to write up qualitative research (for an example of a notable exception, see Holliday, 2007).

We felt that, having taken readers through the principles and practicalities of five qualitative research methods or approaches, something of vital importance would be missing from this book if we did not address the process of writing up qualitative research. We have done this by inviting practitioners of interpretative phenomenological analysis, thematic analysis, grounded theory, discourse analysis and narrative analysis to write reports of studies they have conducted and published as journal articles. Readers can thus gain some insight into how the outcomes of analyses using each method or approach may be presented and can have access to templates for writing up research that may prove useful to those who have not previously written for publication (and to students who are uncertain how best to write up their qualitative research). Each report deals with a fascinating topic (a women's reported experience of anger, lesbian and bisexual women's experiences in relation to social pressure to be thin, the experiences of relatives of organ donors, arguments about racism in internet discussion forums about Gypsies, and the effects of surfing and the natural environment on the well-being of combat veterans) and so has value above its usefulness here as a template for writing up qualitative research.

Of course, readers should also consult other published journal articles that employ each of these methods in order to obtain a sense of the variety of ways in which research using these approaches can be presented. This is important to bear in mind. Just as in the chapters on the five methods, authors have emphasized that there is no definitive way of using their method, so there is no definitive way of organizing the presentation of qualitative research when writing it up. Most academic journals in psychology that carry research reports will expect articles to conform to a general accepted structure, even if that simply takes the form of an introduction, a method section, the presentation of findings and some sort of discussion or conclusion, followed by references. Yet, within that broad framework, there is scope for creativity, especially in the presentation and interpretation of findings. Some non-academic publications (such as publications that are not primarily concerned with research and are aimed at professionals working in applied areas of psychology and related disciplines) may allow even greater scope for the creative reporting of qualitative research.

We felt, however, that straightforward templates would be of limited value because they would only present the finished product without giving a sense of the issues that the authors had to consider in producing their research report. We therefore asked authors to provide reports that featured 'reflective boxes' in which they identified and explained some of the decisions they had made in presenting their research or identified questions that other researchers might usefully consider when writing up their work. Some of the issues raised were general ones that confront the qualitative researcher; others were particular to specific methods or approaches.

We hope that the reports presented in this appendix will assist readers in navigating through the process of writing up qualitative research in order to create engaging stories from their analyses and to bring their work to the attention of audiences that can benefit from it.

REPORT 1

Making Sense of Anger: A Reflective Account of an Interpretative Phenomenological Analysis Study[1]

Virginia Eatough and Jonathan A. Smith

In this report, we present an abridged version of a paper from our study on anger and aggression in women. The paper presents a case study of one woman, different from the person considered in Chapter 4 in this volume, and considers how she uses two long-standing frameworks of meaning to explain her anger and aggressive behaviour: hormones and alcohol. We have edited the paper by leaving out some material that covers very similar ground to that in Chapter 4 – for example, the argument for interpretative phenomenological analysis (IPA) and the description of how analysis was conducted. We have also only been able to present the first half of the results from the paper because of space restrictions. However, we hope that what we have presented here gives you a strong indication of what is involved in writing up an IPA paper. For the complete paper, see Eatough and Smith (2006a).

Introduction

This report considers what it feels like when explanations for one's anger and its behavioural expression begin to break down. The report aims to illustrate the experience of meaning-making and how such meaning-making can be ambiguous, ambivalent and confused. In addition, we will argue that sense-making is always both an individual and social product (Riessman, 1992). Although, inevitably, cultural discourses inform individual meaning-making, this process also involves individual re-experiencing and reinterpreting of the events in one's life. The report demonstrates this dual enterprise by presenting an interpretative analysis of interviews with one female participant.

---

[1]This chapter is closely based on a paper that appeared in the journal *Psychology and Psychotherapy: Theory, Research and Practice* (published by the British Psychological Society) in 2006 (Vol. 79, No. 1, pp.115–35). We are grateful to the British Psychological Society and John Wiley & Sons for granting permission to produce a revised version of the paper in this book.

BOX R1.1	Engaging with the literature

In an IPA study, the 'literature review' is often less extensive than for other approaches. Reference is made to work which helps orient the study but the aim is not to test a hypothesis derived from extant work. It is recognized that issues may arise during the analysis that were unanticipated and that will therefore be picked up by engaging with the appropriate literature in the discussion. What happened in this study was that attributional concerns emerged during analysis and were debated in the discussion. However, we felt we also wanted to help the reader through our analysis by giving a reasonable amount of coverage of the attributional literature in the introduction as well.

Few emotion theorists would doubt that a relationship exists between cognition and emotion and many 'non-cognitive' theories incorporate some sort of cognitive component (Strongman, 2003). Much of the important social psychological research on cognition and emotion has been concerned with appraisal and attribution. Schachter's (1964: 51) two-factor theory of emotion is a cognitive-arousal theory which proposes that 'an emotional state may be considered a function of a state of physiological arousal and of a cognition appropriate to this state of arousal'. Importantly, according to the theory, individuals interpret physiological arousal in light of the circumstances that they believe brought it about. For example, in a romantic context, a pounding heart and trembling hands are interpreted as passionate love (Dutton and Aron, 1974).

Weiner's (1985) attributional theory of emotion proposed that emotions are the outcome of a temporal sequence of different cognitive processes. In the first instance, individuals evaluate the success or failure of an outcome. Second, if the outcome is evaluated negatively, then a cause is looked for. The final step involves classifying the cause according to three attributional dimensions: causal locus (is the cause dispositional or situational?), stability (is the cause transitory or constant?) and, finally, controllability (is the cause under volitional control?). There is evidence that specific emotions are associated with these categorical and dimensional attributions. For example, internal locus and controllability have been related to guilt, whereas controllability and external locus have been related to anger (Neumann, 2000). However, causal attribution models are normative in that they state ideal positions of what people ought to do rather than what people actually do when they think and explain their emotions (Fiske, 2004). Such models have a restricted notion of 'explanation' (Harré, 1981) and what people actually do is typically constructed as deviations and biases.

The claim that attributions exert a causal effect on emotions has been challenged by appraisal theorists (Smith et al., 1993). They argue that attribution is a particular form of knowledge that assists the appraisal process by making inferences about the perceived causes of an event. Causal attributions are not sufficient to bring an emotion into being. On the contrary, the 'facts' of an event must be appraised and evaluated for emotion to arise. From this perspective, emotions are a consequence of evaluations of the personal significance of events and objects and their impact on well-being (Lazarus, 1991). 'Appraisal' is the psychological term for these evaluations and is typically understood as a distinct stage in an information-processing sequence which culminates in the emotional reaction (Parkinson, 1997). However, empirical evidence for a simple causal relationship between appraisal and emotion is weak (see Parkinson, 1997, for detailed discussion of the appraisal–emotion connection).

From the perspective of this report, our concern is that the interpreting, meaning-making person is reduced to the internal cognitive activity of hypothesized causal relationships. This concern is also expressed by some emotion theorists and discursive psychologists. For example, Parkinson and Manstead (1992) suggest that emotional experience is a consequence of our social interactions with other people, our own and other bodies and our physical environment, as well as cognitive evaluation processes. Moreover, emotional events have a temporal dimension and unfold over time. These features are not well captured in vignette studies, which are the usual method for investigating appraisals (Levine, 1996) and rely on simulation or directed imagery tasks (for example, Smith and Lazarus, 1993). The study reported here emphasizes how individuals talk and make sense of their emotions and of being emotional in the very particular context of their unfolding lives.

Method

Participant

The participant is referred to throughout as Marilyn. At the time of the study, Marilyn was 30 years old and living with her partner, John, and their son, Andrew, in a council house in an inner-city location in the Midlands area of England. The area is categorized as extreme in terms of social need and has correspondingly high levels of crime. Marilyn left school at 16 years of age and has worked in a variety of unskilled jobs. Since having Andrew, she has not worked outside the home. All names have been changed to safeguard confidentiality.

BOX R1.2   **'Pen portrait'**

Providing some biographical information about the participants makes them 'come alive' for the reader. The aim is to provide the reader with some holistic sense of the person which contextualizes the analytic material.

Data collection

Marilyn responded to a mail drop in her area asking for volunteers to participate in a study on how women experience and resolve conflict in their lives. After an initial telephone conversation, the first author met Marilyn at her home to discuss participation in the study. This first meeting was an attempt to make Marilyn feel as relaxed and informed as possible by detailing what the study would involve and to address any concerns she might have. This can be referred to as attempting to achieve symmetry between the researcher and participant (Hollway and Jefferson, 2000). Subsequently, an interview schedule was developed and two semi-structured interviews were carried out over a period of three weeks, which resulted in four hours of data. The interviews were conducted by the first author in Marilyn's home and were audio-recorded. There were specific issues we were hoping to address but the primary aim was for Marilyn to tell her story and not simply to be a respondent. The aim was to capture the richness and complexity of Marilyn's meaning-making by being an active listener and by allowing the interview to progress down avenues she opened up rather than those dictated by the interview schedule.

BOX R1.3 — **Adopting a conversational interviewing style**

IPA interviews are participant led and researchers treat participants as experiential experts on the topic under investigation. The aim is to facilitate the giving and making of an account in a sensitive and empathic manner, recognizing that the interview constitutes a human-to-human relationship. Thus, interviews are narrative in style and do not follow a simple question and answer format.

Analysis

Analysis of the data established three higher-order themes that encapsulated Marilyn's lived experiences of anger and conflict. This report presents part of one of these, which is described as a meaning-making theme. It examines how personal and cultural frameworks of meaning mesh with each other and are lived and experienced by the individual person.

Findings

One interrelated aspect of this sense-making theme is presented. The analysis shows how Marilyn invokes cultural frameworks of meaning to explain her anger and aggressive behaviour. The first of these frameworks draws heavily on biological discourses, namely the influence of hormones and alcohol. The analysis demonstrates how Marilyn's attempts to produce a strong and convincing account of these influences are undermined by alternative explanations.

BOX R1.4 ▸ **Selecting analytic themes to report**

When writing for publication and, indeed, often when writing up a student dissertation, it is not usually possible to report detailed analyses in full so the researcher must make a decision about what to include. In part, this might be determined by the focus of the journal or audience you want to reach. Alternatively, the choice might be influenced more by issues of breadth or depth. One question you may wish to ask is whether your aim is to provide a close reading of one particular theme or a less detailed, more expansive account.

'That's all hormones'

Drawing on medicalized discourses that explain behaviour as a consequence of hormones is a culturally powerful way of making sense of one's experiences. Attributing aggressive and violent behaviour to an imbalance in hormones implies a faulty biology and ignores how the individual's material, social and cultural environment also shapes who we are, how we deal with emotional pain and how we manage difficulties in life. A narrative of hormonal influence weaves a potent thread throughout Marilyn's story. In this first extract, Marilyn makes an explicit connection between her hormones and her aggressive behaviour. At the time, she was almost 17 years of age, she very much wanted a baby and her aggression was directed at both her partner at that time and herself:

> I started off with just you know pushing him or hitting him type thing but then it was, it was sort of got worse where I'd start hurting myself as well, like throwing my arms at a mirror and cutting, cutting you know just self-mutilation but not to harm myself. Looking back now it was a cry for help but I mean nobody answered [laughs] basically. And erm I suffered really badly from depression where I had to go on medication. As well as that I had a fertility problem where I had polycystic ovaries … It's awful but I mean that's all hormones as well which explains away a lot of my moods and aggression and that. But I mean I don't know whether it I mean I have got a lot of hang-ups about my family but I think a lot of it is hormonal my aggression and things like that.

This data extract reveals that in addition to being aggressive towards her partner, Marilyn engaged in deliberate self-harming behaviour. For Marilyn, the phenomenological experience of this narrative episode is one of escalation. She moves from relatively harmless acts of physical aggression to those with potentially dangerous and damaging consequences with herself becoming the target. What is interesting here is how Marilyn's hormonal narrative develops throughout our conversation and gains ground as an explanation. In the first instance, Marilyn describes her aggression as a cry for help which went unanswered. This is possibly a relatively new interpretation and is a consequence of the counselling sessions that she has received. Next, Marilyn introduces her depression and fertility condition, the latter setting the scene for Marilyn to make the link between her aggression and hormones. The statement 'that's all hormones' illustrates how Marilyn employs the condition of polycystic ovary syndrome to highlight the pervasive control of hormones over her physical body and possibly her mental state. In the extract, she moves towards stating a blanket, categorical relationship between her hormones and her behaviour. The power of this statement lies in its ability to negate alternative understandings of the anger and aggression events in Marilyn's life and seems to serve as a linguistic climax of this extract. However, there is evidence that she doubts the robustness of her hormonal explanation when she says 'but I mean I don't know whether it I mean I have got a lot of hang ups about my family but I think a lot of it is hormonal my aggression and things like that'. The mention of family difficulties is introduced, then quickly dismissed. The phrase 'explains away' might be ironic, reflecting an awareness on Marilyn's part that she is invoking a 'catch-all' explanation that belies the complexity of what is actually going on.

BOX R1.5 — **Interpretative style**

This section illustrates the style of IPA analysis. We begin with a close attentiveness to and reading of Marilyn's words. However, as we proceed, we are moving from being with Marilyn to thinking about Marilyn in considering her different own reflections on her invocations of the 'hormones' explanation.

'It was the alcohol'

In addition to inferring that the causes of her anger and aggression are hormonal, Marilyn utilizes an equally powerful physiological discourse: alcohol. Describing an incident involving a fight with a partner named Simon, Marilyn says:

It was the alcohol, I do remember I did feel angry, really angry, I mean raged angry but [pause] it was more because I think being humiliated, being shown up, he made me feel stupid in front of my friends do you know what I mean? It's not, I didn't actually think well you're going to have to pay for that but it was that sort of thing. I just don't think I actually thought about the emotional side of it. I just thought right you've shown me up, you're not leaving me alone. I just walked him away, tried to push him away that way but I mean that was really weird that night because I mean like a lot of it was alcohol but I cannot remember a lot of it. It was like a blind rage, it was really and there's been quite a few times that I've been like that without the alcohol, that I really can't recall a lot of what I've done until I've actually looked at the damage. And sat down afterwards and looked at what I've done.

There are several points of interest in this extract. At the outset, Marilyn makes a clear causal statement, which, by the end, is seriously weakened. First, she describes her rage as 'blind' and the end state is of emerging from the fury with little or no memory and of time being lost. Elsewhere we have reported that such intense emotion can be felt without alcohol, something which Marilyn herself comments upon (Eatough and Smith, 2006b). Second, the rage Marilyn feels appears to be fuelled less by alcohol and more by what she experiences as public humiliation, which requires some sort of revenge. Thus it is not simply to do with the effects of intoxication but also to do with issues of integrity and self-worth. Third, 'you're not leaving me alone' can be viewed as a telling statement and it is interesting to speculate on why Marilyn said this to herself. It might simply be that being left alone would increase her mortified feelings or that she no longer had a target for her anger and aggression. However, since leaving home, Marilyn has always been in an intimate relationship. Arguably, these relationships provide evidence that she is a person who is capable of being loved and the unconscious motivation might be to avoid (reliving) the experience of her relationship with her mother. Finally, as with the hormonal accounts, there are cracks beginning to appear in the extract which undermine its strength as an account. At the end of the extract, she acknowledges a certain culpability for her behaviour when she says 'and looked at what I've done'.

BOX R1.6 ▶ Building a narrative account

The final narrative account should be persuasive, illuminating the participants' experience through a mix of interpretative commentary and the participants' own words. It is not possible to say how many excerpts from the data should be presented. However, enough should be provided so that the reader can assess the interpretative claims that are made.

There is also a recognition made in passing that the focus on alcohol allows her to bypass other contributory factors such as feeling hurt and humiliated and how this made her feel about her sense of self.

'I think I got depressed'

In contrast to the simplistic causal accounts of hormones and alcohol, the next extract gives a moving account of the distress Marilyn was experiencing and her specific set of circumstances:

> Paul was the first relationship that when I was sort of violent. Erm, I remember I was happy at first at the beginning of the relationship and then we started living together, we were in a grotty bedsit for a long time. He was working nights, I mean it was, I think I got depressed. And erm I think we'd been together about a year, year and a half and we both wanted a baby erm I remember I was having treatment at the hospital but I was also getting more and more aggressive where I was hitting him. I mean not in the face but in the arms and things like that. Erm I was more verbally abusive and trying to hurt myself more than anything in that relationship where I wanted to cut myself … I think I was in you know like an emotional pain you know, like when your heart aches, I felt heartbroken over something you know, it was probably my mum again and I thought, I think I thought if I hurt myself it wouldn't hurt as much, do you understand what I mean?

Once again, a narrative of escalation is present and Marilyn's emotional pain is felt bodily. At first, Marilyn seems to invoke social or sociological reasons for her aggression (for example, living and working conditions, depression) but these are superseded by more personal reasons. The metaphor of a broken and aching heart is a culturally powerful one and signifies a loss of something precious, be that a person, goal or relationship. This is a much more multi-faceted narrative and differs from the previous ones in that Marilyn's almost casual observation, 'I think it was a cry for help' (see the first extract), is openly acknowledged to have been a time of pain and anguish. Marilyn's loneliness suffuses the account: Paul is physically absent a lot of the time, she is having difficulty becoming pregnant (so is not *with* child) and her pain is such that she wants to hurt herself.

Thus, in the narrative episodes presented above, there are a number of competing explanations. Marilyn draws on the effects of hormones and alcohol as narrative resources to make sense of her anger. These frameworks of meaning are powerful because they satisfy the desire for a simple causal explanation and, at the same time, remove responsibility from her. However, as we have demonstrated, the emphatic statements 'that's all hormones' and 'it was the alcohol' are threatened and begin to break down as Marilyn begins to realize other ways of sense-making.

It is essential that the material and social conditions that make up Marilyn's life world are noted. At the time of her relationship with Paul, she was 16 years of age and, before moving in with him, had slept for several weeks in a van outside his house. Marilyn was not in touch with her mother (and possibly with none of her family), Paul worked nights and her material circumstances were far from ideal. In addition, she found she was unable to conceive and she describes her state of mind at the time as depressed. Finally, there is a move from a general explanation of a cry for help and 'hang-ups about my family' in the first extract towards a more specific, if somewhat hesitant, account involving her mother.

Discussion

BOX R1.7	Placing the analysis in a conceptual context

The discussion is a dialogue between the analytic findings and the existing psychological literature. This dialogue can be critical, drawing attention to how qualitative analyses bring a fresh perspective to our understanding of human beings.

In this section, we build on some of the analytic observations already made by examining them through a theoretical lens. We look at the two long-standing frameworks of meaning that Marilyn makes use of: hormones and alcohol.

We contend that this sort of interpretative analysis illuminates how traditional social cognition perspectives of 'explanation' neglect the experiencing, meaning-making person and what she/he brings to the telling of a life. Paradoxically, the prescriptive and reductive aspects of both approaches are brought to the fore through Marilyn's attempts to understand. The normative and unidirectional causal sequences found in attribution and appraisal research are undermined when faced with the messy and turbulent reality of individual meaning-making.

Marilyn's meaning-making is crumbling and this experience bears little relation to causal attribution models that aim to establish relations of cause and effect. Within the context of the individual life-world, these relations are often difficult to discern and are speculative. We would suggest that attribution approaches, with their reliance on matching cause with effect, are simply unable to explain the complexity of a person's meaning-making. Similarly, cognitive emotion theories, which give the concept of appraisal a central place, neglect meaning-making and the interpersonal communicative function of emotional experience (Parkinson, 1997). Undoubtedly, emotional reactions have an evaluative component but to reduce this simply to a function of cognitive processing is to ignore the experiencing inter-subjective person. For example, elsewhere we have reported how the body plays a crucial role in women's meaning-making around anger (Eatough and Smith, 2006b). The meaning-making activity of the individual sometimes involves rational appraisal but it also entails being imaginative, intuitive and intentional.

Likewise, although we recognize that personal meaning-making is constrained by available cultural discourses and social conventions, individuals struggle and realize them differently in the context of their unique personal and social history. As Rosenwald (1992: 269) rightly states: 'If a life is no more than a story and a story is governed only by the situation in which it is told, then one cannot declare a situation unlivable or a life damaged.' Marilyn's accounts of her lived experiences are illustrative of how her sense of self, her stories and her situations both challenge and embrace understanding through contemporary cultural discourses. The remainder of this section discusses the restrictive nature of these frameworks of meaning. Our view is that causal attribution and rational appraisal theories need to be elaborated upon before they can adequately contribute to an understanding of the sorts of conceptually complex and multi-layered attributions and appraisals that are involved in human meaning-making. Similarly, we argue that individuals' meaning making is constituted, at least in part, by cultural discourses and conventions but is not determined by them.

The analysis demonstrated that Marilyn made associative links between her infertility, her depression and her anger and aggression. This is not surprising given that the influence of hormones on women's behaviour is a culturally powerful discourse that denies women moral agency. In terms of explaining women's anger and aggression, hormonal explanations form one half of a 'mad or bad' dichotomy. Cultural discourses of women's anger construct their experience of this emotion as negative and deviant in terms of their gender. Research suggests that, when women get angry, they feel themselves to be in a no-win situation (Campbell and Muncer, 1987). Lashing out either physically or verbally is experienced as a loss of control and as not conforming to dominant norms of femininity ('bad'). However, if women exercise control and express their anger through crying, they are often perceived as 'hysterical' ('mad'). This is not to say that fluctuating hormonal levels do not have some role in Marilyn's potent feelings of anger and in her aggressive behaviour. There is the fertility problem when she was younger, she had been treated for depression with a tricyclic antidepressant and it is possible that, at the time of the interviews, Marilyn was suffering from post-natal depression. Moreover, it is highly probable that the fertility problem would have influenced Marilyn's menstrual cycle.

However, whether or not hormones are actually an important contributory factor in Marilyn's anger and aggression cannot be ascertained from the interview data. What is important is that she *believes* they do. The analysis illustrates clearly how hormones are a crucial component of Marilyn's meaning-making and the question as to why this is the case can be addressed. Causal explanations that invoke hormones are part of a medicalized discourse, which suggests that there is a solution in the form of treatment to rectify an ostensible imbalance. They work by denying individual moral agency.

Marilyn's adherence to a hormonal account constructs the experience of her anger and aggression as one that renders her passive in the face of forces beyond her control. Equally, it is unsurprising that alcohol plays some sort of role in Marilyn's stories of her anger and aggression. As with hormonal explanations, there is a wealth of empirical evidence that concludes that alcohol consumption often increases levels of aggressive behaviour (Bushman and Cooper, 1990). Alcohol disrupts how individuals process information; researchers call this 'alcohol myopia' (Steele and Josephs, 1990). Nevertheless, despite this evidence, the relationship between the two is oversimplified and overstated in dominant lay and psychological frameworks of meaning. When Marilyn says 'it was the alcohol', she is invoking a simple causal attribution that ignores the wider interpersonal context in which her behaviour takes place. This sort of oversimplification encourages the individual to view her/himself as passive and as having no control because making alcohol responsible is an easier option. Although it does not make the behaviour socially acceptable, it is a socially acknowledged and understood statement that can often go unchallenged. This is in spite of the fact that such causal attributions are never wholly convincing at either the intra-psychic or the interpersonal levels.

The analysis above highlights the contradictions within Marilyn's accounts as she wrestles with the internal and external challenges to her hormonal and alcohol explanations. For example, in the extract in which she offers an explanation of her fight with Simon, the role of alcohol is weakened when it becomes clear that Marilyn's rage is more to do with the experience of public shame that requires redress. In this incident, Marilyn's aggression was not simply a consequence of intoxication levels but also to do with personal worth and integrity. Researchers have demonstrated that aggression is one consequence of threats to the self (Baumeister et al., 1999). Explanations centring on public humiliation or a fear of rejection require a conscious and inwardly reflective scrutiny and point to a sense of self that is experienced as fragile and ruptured. By invoking alcohol, any real attempt to understand what is happening beyond immediate antecedent events is effectively closed down.

SUMMARY

This report has provided an illustration of how an IPA analysis might be presented, while offering continued reflections upon the analytic process. Although it has put forward a case study analysis, the same basic presentational principles apply when formatting an analysis of data from larger samples. We hope that this report, in conjunction with Chapters 4 and 5 on the principles, procedures and practicalities of IPA, will adequately equip readers who are interested in IPA to undertake and write up their own analyses using this method.

References

Baumeister, R.F., Smart, L. and Boden, J.M. (1999) 'Relation of threatened egotism to violence and aggression: The dark side of high self-esteem', in R.F. Baumeister (ed.), *The Self in Social Psychology*. Hove: Psychology Press. pp. 240–79.

Bushman, B.J. and Cooper, H.M. (1990) 'Effects of alcohol on human aggression: An integrative research review', *Psychological Bulletin*, 107(3): 341–54.

Campbell, A. and Muncer, S. (1987) 'Models of anger and aggression in the social talk of women and men', *Journal for the Theory of Social Behaviour*, 17(4): 489–511.

Dutton, D.G. and Aron, A. (1974) 'Some evidence for heightened sexual attraction under conditions of high anxiety', *Journal of Personality and Social Psychology*, 30(4): 510–17.

Eatough, V. and Smith, J.A. (2006a) 'I feel like a scrambled egg in my head: An idiographic case study of meaning making and anger using interpretative phenomenological analysis', *Psychology and Psychotherapy: Theory, Research and Practice*, 79(1): 115–35.

Eatough, V. and Smith, J.A. (2006b) 'I was like a wild wild person: Understanding feelings of anger using interpretative phenomenological analysis', *British Journal of Psychology*, 97(4): 483–98.

Fiske, S. (2004) *Social Beings: A Core Motives Approach to Social Psychology*. Hoboken, NJ: John Wiley & Sons.

Harré, R. (1981) 'Expressive aspects of descriptions of others', in C. Antaki (ed.), *The Psychology of Ordinary Explanations of Social Behaviour*. London: Academic Press. pp. 139–56.

Hollway, W. and Jefferson, T. (2000) *Doing Qualitative Research Differently: Free Association, Narrative and the Interview Method*. London: SAGE.

Lazarus, R.S. (1991) 'Progress on a cognitive-motivational-relational theory of emotion', *American Psychologist*, 46(8): 819–34.

Levine, L.J. (1996) 'The anatomy of disappointment: A naturalistic test of appraisal models of sadness, anger and hope', *Cognition and Emotion*, 10(4): 337–59.

Neumann, R. (2000) 'The causal influences of attributions on emotions: A procedural priming approach', *Psychological Science*, 11(3): 179–82.

Parkinson, B. (1997) 'Untangling the appraisal–emotion connection', *Personality and Social Psychology Review*, 1(1): 62–79.

Parkinson, B. and Manstead, A.S.R. (1992) 'Appraisal as a cause of emotion', in M.S. Clark (ed.), *Review of Personality and Social Psychology, Vol. 13: Emotion*. Newbury Park, CA: SAGE. pp. 122–49.

Riessman, C.K. (1992) 'Making sense of marital violence: One woman's narrative', in G.C. Rosenwald and R.C. Ochberg (eds), *Storied Lives: The Cultural Politics of Self-Understanding*. London: Yale University Press. pp. 231–49.

Rosenwald, G.C. (1992) 'Conclusion: Reflections on narrative self-understanding', in G.C. Rosenwald and R.C. Ochberg (eds), *Storied Lives: The Cultural Politics of Self-Understanding*. London: Yale University Press. pp. 265–89.

Schachter, S. (1964) 'The interaction of cognitive and physiological determinants of emotional state', in L. Berkowitz (ed.), *Mental Social Psychology*, Vol. 1. New York: Academic Press. pp. 49–80.

Smith, C.A., Haynes, K.N., Lazarus, R.S. and Pope, L.K. (1993) 'In search of the "hot" cognitions: Attributions, appraisals and their relation to emotion', *Journal of Personality and Social Psychology*, 65(5): 916–29.

Smith, C.A. and Lazarus, R.S. (1993) 'Appraisal components, core relational themes, and the emotions', *Cognition and Emotion*, 7(3–4): 233–69.

Steele, C.M. and Josephs, R.A. (1990) 'Alcohol myopia: Its prized and dangerous effects', *American Psychologist*, 45(8): 921–33.

Strongman, K.T. (2003) *The Psychology of Emotion: From Everyday Life to Theory*, 5th edn. New York: John Wiley & Sons.

Weiner, B. (1985) 'An attributional theory of achievement motivation and emotion', *Psychological Review*, 92(4): 548–73.

REPORT 2

Are Lesbian and Bisexual Women 'Protected' from Socio-Cultural Pressure to be Thin? A Reflective Account of a Thematic Analysis Study

Caroline Huxley, Victoria Clarke and Emma Halliwell

This reflective report provides another appearance-related example of a thematic analysis study. Whereas the worked example in Chapter 6 focused on gay men's appearance and provided a predominantly latent-level interpretation of the data, this report focuses on lesbian and bisexual women's appearance and provides a more semantic-level interpretation. The study reported here comes from Caroline Huxley's mixed methods PhD research, which was supervised by Victoria Clarke (a sexuality researcher) and Emma Halliwell (a body image researcher) (see Clarke et al., 2012; Huxley, 2013; Huxley and Hayfield, 2012; Huxley et al., 2011). Because thematic analysis is theoretically flexible, it is ideally suited to mixed methods research which often draws upon different epistemological frameworks. In the reflective boxes in the text, Caroline reflects on her experiences of conducting the study and identifies good practice in reporting a thematic analysis study and qualitative research more generally.

Introduction

It is well documented that in Western society women are under social pressure to be considered 'beautiful' by being thin (Grogan, 2008). The media in particular has been criticized for depicting unrealistic and digitally enhanced images of flawlessly thin women as appropriate ideals against which women should compare themselves. However, such ideals are almost impossible for most women to achieve healthily (Tiggemann, 2002) and women's experiences of pressure to attain this ideal are linked to body dissatisfaction, dieting behaviours and eating disorders (for example, Halliwell and Dittmar, 2004).

Less well documented is the heteronormativity of current cultural ideals. The thin but curvaceous body that is very visible in the media (Lyons, 2000) is an expected component of normative heterosexual femininity (Ahern et al., 2011). Two authors have speculated on how such ideals affect lesbian and bisexual women. First, lesbians and possibly bisexual women may be 'protected' from mainstream emphasis on thinness and from subsequent body dissatisfaction because lesbian, gay and bisexual (LGB) communities reject heteronormative ideals and are more accepting of diverse body sizes (Brown, 1987). An alternative perspective states that because lesbian and bisexual women are raised and live in mainstream society (with its emphasis on thinness and heteronormative femininity), they will internalize these beauty ideals and experience body dissatisfaction in the same way as heterosexual women (Dworkin, 1988).

A small body of quantitative research has sought to identify similarities and differences between lesbian and heterosexual women (bisexual women have largely been ignored in the literature to date). Lesbian and heterosexual women have generally reported equivalent levels of awareness of media pressure to be thin (for example, Share and Mintz, 2002). However, there is far less clarity regarding body satisfaction. Recent research has found no differences between lesbian and heterosexual women (for example, Koff et al., 2010), while a meta-analysis of 16 earlier studies found that lesbian women were 'slightly' more satisfied with their bodies than heterosexual women (Morrison et al., 2004). Similarly, some evidence suggests that lesbian women are less likely to engage in dieting behaviours than heterosexual women (for example, Conner et al., 2004), while others have found no such differences (for example, Share and Mintz, 2002). Much of this research is flawed, however, by significant differences in weight and age between lesbian and heterosexual participants, which are not accounted for in the analyses (Morrison et al., 2004), and by the regular omission of bisexual women.

In summary, there is some evidence to suggest that lesbian women may feel 'protected' from heteronormative pressures to be thin. As such pressures are associated with unhealthy consequences such as harmful feelings of body dissatisfaction and disordered eating behaviours (for example, Grogan, 2008), it is important to explore all potential avenues of resistance. However, the findings from quantitative studies are inconsistent and there is no clear indication as to how lesbian and bisexual women's body image concerns are affected by heteronormative social pressures. Qualitative inquiry is valuable in obtaining people's opinions on and understandings of the nature of their experiences (Gonzalez et al., 2013). Therefore, this approach could produce insights that indicate whether (and why) lesbian and bisexual women feel 'protected' from such pressures and how social pressures shape their body concerns and eating behaviours. However, the views of lesbian and bisexual women have rarely been sought. To our knowledge, this is the first such study conducted outside the United States and is the first study to ask these women explicitly to comment on whether LGB communities are 'protective' of their body concerns.

> **BOX R2.1** ▸ **Reviewing the literature**
>
> Unlike some of the other approaches discussed in this book, there are no particular requirements for reviewing the literature in a thematic analysis study. This report provides a fairly conventional literature review that is appropriate to the requirements of the journal in which it was originally published. In general, the aim of a literature review in reports of qualitative research is to contextualize and make a case for the study. This does not necessarily require a comprehensive overview of existing research, unlike in reports of quantitative research (Braun and Clarke, 2013), but it should discuss key literature and relevant theoretical perspectives and concepts.

Method

A semi-structured interview approach was selected to ensure that all participants were asked the same broad questions while simultaneously allowing flexibility so that participants could discuss issues not predetermined by the researchers.

Participants and recruitment

Participants were recruited initially through purposive sampling of the researcher's personal and professional networks. Participants then passed on the study information to their professional contacts, social groups and networks. Fifteen non-heterosexual women living in primarily urban areas of the United Kingdom participated in this study. Participants were given the opportunity to choose their own pseudonym and describe their gender and sexuality in their own words (we use these terms when referring to the women). Eleven participants identified as 'lesbian' or 'gay' and four participants identified as 'bi' or 'bisexual'. Although most participants described their gender as 'female' or 'woman', one bisexual participant was 'undecided' about her gender. Participants ranged in age from 18 to 69 years (the mean age was 34.7 years), although ten women were aged 30 or under. Participants were predominantly middle class (n = 9), highly educated (ten were educated to degree level or higher) and described themselves as White British or White Irish (n = 13; the remaining two participants described themselves as Jewish European).

BOX R2.2 ▶ 'Situating the sample'

In qualitative research it is important to 'situate' the participant sample (Elliott et al., 1999) so that the reader can identify the context and limitations of the research and make judgements about whether the findings are transferrable to other settings. 'Situating the sample' requires the systematic collection of demographic data from participants. It is good practice to ask participants to complete a short 'demographic questionnaire' so that you can collect information about their general characteristics such as their age, sex/gender, race and ethnicity, social class and so on (see Braun and Clarke, 2013), as well as characteristics specific to the study (in this case, information about sexuality was crucial). When constructing my demographic survey, I was mindful that appearance researchers have often defined participants' sexualities using predetermined categories (gay/straight), rather than allowing participants to define and name their sexualities in their own terms. Given evidence of fluidity in sexualities, particularly for women (Diamond, 2008), I avoided the problematic practice of pre-categorizing participants' sexualities by inviting the women to define their sexuality and gender and I used their terms in the report. Enabling participants to describe their characteristics in their own words is particularly important when researching socially marginalized groups who have often been denied a 'voice' in mainstream psychology.

Although the majority of the participants were in their 20s or 30s, four were aged between 47 and 69 years. This broad age range provided diverse perspectives and enabled me to draw inferences about how social pressures affect lesbian and bisexual of women of different ages. For example, the older women in the group were able to reflect on ageing and social pressures to look youthful, which the younger women did not mention.

Although Braun and Clarke (2013) generally recommend a sample of at least six interviews because of the focus on patterned meaning across the data set, there are no further sample size requirements when doing thematic analysis. The sample of 15 interviews in this study is appropriate for a medium-sized thematic analysis interview study.

Procedure

The interview guide was constructed from a review of relevant literature and included questions that focused on how participants felt about their body and how different social environments and the media influenced these feelings. The interviews were conducted in a location chosen by the participant, lasted between 45 and 90 minutes, were digitally recorded and were transcribed verbatim.

BOX R2.3 — **Insider/outsider dynamics**

There is a common assumption that most researchers who study LGB people are themselves LGB-identified and are conducting research from an 'insider' position (Tang, 2006). Because of this assumption, I decided to be open with participants in advance of the interviews that I am a heterosexual woman and therefore an 'outsider' to their experience (see Peel and Coyle, 2004, on heterosexual people in LGB psychology). There are both perceived disadvantages and advantages to being an outsider. One perspective is that an outsider cannot understand or appropriately represent the experiences of their participants because (unlike insider researchers) they do not have the same experiential knowledge (Bridges, 2001). It is also thought to be more difficult for outsider researchers to gain access to and secure the trust of socially marginalized groups such as lesbians and bisexual women (Clarke et al., 2010). In contrast, Hellawell (2006) argued that outsider researchers 'see' things that insiders do not because the outsider position makes it easy to ask 'naive' questions and to achieve the critical distance from participants' accounts necessary for good analysis. Bridges (2001) argued that a 'culturally sensitive' outsider can enhance understandings of the community being researched. As researchers play an active role in the description and presentation of marginalized voices, such as those of lesbians and bisexual women (Tang, 2006), a culturally sensitive standpoint is vital for conducting ethical and non-discriminatory qualitative research.

In addition to acknowledging my heterosexuality in an active way, I attempted to reassure participants that I was trustworthy by noting my adherence to guidance for conducting non-heterosexist research (Clarke et al., 2010). Asher and Asher (1999 argue that explicit disclosure of a culturally sensitive outsider position can encourage openness and trust between heterosexual researchers and non-heterosexual participants. I similarly found that the women appreciated my openness about my heterosexuality and my honesty seemed to help me to build rapport with the participants. There are, however, many subtle ways in which a researcher can be both an insider and an outsider and degrees of both distance and empathy are useful qualities for qualitative researchers (Hellawell, 2006). Although I was an outsider in terms of my sexual identity, I was also – like most of the participants – a young, White, middle-class woman and could empathize with them about mainstream appearance pressures on women.

Data analysis

The women's accounts were analysed using inductive thematic analysis (Braun and Clarke, 2006) within a broadly critical realist or contextualist framework (Willig, 1999). Our approach loosely conforms to the definition of critical realism as a position that affirms the existence of 'reality', both physical and environmental, but at the same time recognizes that its representations are characterized and mediated by culture, language and political interests rooted in factors such as race, gender or social class (Ussher, 1999). In terms of our participants' sense-making, this approach allowed an analysis that takes such accounts at face value or as 'real' without rendering them independent of the historical, cultural or political context in which they take place.

Following Braun and Clarke's (2006) guidelines, the first author read and re-read transcripts from the whole data set before individually coding them. These codes were then organized into initial themes. This initial analysis was reviewed with the second and third authors before being refined and organized into subthemes within overarching themes.

BOX R2.4 ▸ Reflecting on coding and theme generation

I conducted an inductive thematic analysis of the interview data that predominantly focused on semantic meanings (Braun and Clarke, 2006). This approach fitted well with the aims of the interview study which were to explore lesbian and bisexual women's views on and experiences of appearance pressures and to inform the design of subsequent quantitative studies. In terms of the practicalities of coding and analysing the data, I used both hard copies and electronic versions of the interview transcripts: I coded and identified potential initial themes on hard copies and then collated the data electronically. I found the collation of data particularly useful at the review stage when assessing the 'fit' of a theme and whether the participants were addressing the same core concept or issue, which Braun and Clarke (2012) characterize as a theme's 'central organizing concept'. For example, during the initial theme review, I decided that a broad theme of 'appearance pressures' should be separated into 'mainstream pressures' and 'pressures from LGB communities' because the nature of the pressures varied considerably according to the source. I also decided that another initial theme entitled 'prioritizing physical health' was a form of resistance to mainstream appearance norms and should be included within the theme 'critiquing mainstream pressures'. The review process was essential in determining the final structure of the analysis, and for telling a story of the data that captured participants' meanings and was interpretative and analytically organized – in other words, that went beyond simply reporting the data.

Results

Four main themes were identified during the analysis: '"normative" body dissatisfaction', 'mainstream pressures', 'critiquing mainstream pressures' and 'pressures within LGB communities'.

'Normative' body dissatisfaction

Only a small number of women reported being relatively happy with their body size or shape: all the women described at least one aspect of their body that they disliked. Dissatisfaction with the body or with specific body parts primarily focused on size (too large). Such feelings were attributed to all women:

> I hate it if I have to get a [UK dress-size] 12 because I'm normally a 10. That's just women isn't it? (Holly, 69-year-old gay woman)

> My stomach, [like] every female, I would imagine, on the planet, I would like my stomach to be a little bit flatter. (Helen, 30-year-old lesbian)

Participants thought that it was 'natural' and 'normal' for women to be unhappy with their bodies.

Weight loss was described as a boost to self-confidence by a small number of women. A third of women were currently dieting or exercising with the aim of losing weight or getting 'in shape' and three participants had engaged in disordered eating behaviours in the past. These women described how they would severely restrict their food intake and engage in behaviours congruent with a diagnosis of anorexia:

> I would say that I was never anorexic but I would sometimes go for two or three days at a time without eating and ... be proud of myself for that and be trying to lose more weight and wanting to be thinner. (Isabel, 30-year-old bi woman)

Dieting and weight loss behaviours are often self-policed and women may feel disappointed in themselves if they do not meet specific weight-loss targets (Paquette and Raine, 2004). This was reflected in some of the women's comments when weight loss attempts were equated with being 'good':

> I do feel, I think like most women, they always feel, like, sort of half a stone overweight [ ] I'll do it [diet] for a week, I'll be good and healthy and then it'll, you know, go up and down a lot. (Sally, 25-year-old lesbian)

> ## BOX R2.5
>
> ## Weaving together the analytic narrative, data extracts and existing literature
>
> In writing the analysis, I wove together my analytic narrative about the data, data extracts that provided evidence of my analytic observations, and existing literature. Although I use words and phrases like 'a small number', 'several' and 'over half' when reporting themes, I do not usually provide precise numbers. For psychology students well versed in the norms and values of scientific psychology, this might seem problematic and lacking in precision. However, if we keep in mind that a good qualitative interview is only partly determined by the interviewer's pre-planned questions and to a greater or lesser extent will be shaped by the participant's developing interview narrative, then reporting numbers does not really make sense. Writing 'seven women thought X' implies that the other eight women did not think X when it might simply be the case that these eight women did not address this issue in their interviews. Braun and Clarke (2013) recommend that providing precise frequency counts should be confined to the reporting of concrete practices when all participants have been asked about the same issue. For example, in a study exploring women's reasons for keeping or changing their last name upon marriage, it would make sense to report the number of participants who kept their 'maiden' name.
>
> In the report, I used quotations from the interviews illustratively rather than analytically (Braun and Clarke, 2013), which is common in more semantic and contextualist approaches to thematic analysis. I selected data extracts that provided particularly strong examples of the themes. For example, I quoted Laura in the theme 'critiquing mainstream pressures' (see below) to illustrate the analytic commentary about prioritizing physical health over appearance because she specifically used the word 'healthy' and referred to the aesthetics of weight gain.
>
> I also refer to existing literature in the results section, which is unusual in reporting quantitative research but more common in qualitative research reports. When 'writing up' the results, I found I kept wanting to make links with existing literature. This is a good test of whether you should have a combined results and discussion section, as I did (if that is possible within the format of your report) or separate results and discussion sections. In contextualizing my results in relation to the existing literature, I was able to make links between very specific findings (and data extracts) and the wider literature.

The effect that ageing has on the body was mentioned by all participants over the age of 30 years, particularly in terms of failing functionality:

> I'm sort of 50 and I'm going through the menopause [ ] I've got pernicious anaemia and things, so, I feel like my body's just falling apart (Sylvia, 49-year-old lesbian).

However, Sookie (47-year-old bisexual, undecided gender) emphasized that as she aged, she was becoming more accepting of her body, even though it deviated further from cultural ideals:

> When you get older, you don't care as much about your appearance, although your body isn't, you know … it obviously goes downhill a little bit.

Such comments echo Tiggemann's (2004) findings that, as women age, they become less invested in their body as they often prioritize other aspects of their lives, such as their career or motherhood.

Mainstream pressures

All the women experienced mainstream social pressures to be thin and the media idealization of very slim women was frequently referred to in their discussions. For example, Mae (18-year-old bisexual woman) desired to look as 'attractive' as film stars and actresses on television. She was unhappy with her current weight and said that she 'always feels the pressure of losing weight and being thinner'. Several women reported consciously comparing themselves and their body size to media images of thin 'beautiful' women. Although Rachel (62-year-old lesbian) criticized the lack of older women portrayed in the media, she thought that – though not directly comparable – images of young women were 'still a kind of resource or image against which we might measure ourselves'. These comments reflect assertions that media images depicting slenderness as desirable are highly influential in promoting body dissatisfaction in women of all ages (Grogan, 2008).

Women were divided as to their current engagement with mainstream media; under half of the group reported active consumption of mainstream magazines and television. Such media were seen by most participants as heterosexist because of the invisibility of lesbian and bisexual women. Several women commented that media images were mainly aimed at heterosexual women because they often 'play on what is defined as feminine and sexy' (Sally, 25-year-old lesbian), depicting a heteronormative femininity that is not congruent with stereotypical perceptions of 'butch' or androgynous lesbian women (Rothblum, 1994). Despite thinking that they were not specifically targeted, many women felt that media messages regarding body size did have a negative impact on them: 'It's either "This is the new diet" or "Look how thin this person is" and unless you're thin and attractive, you know, you're not worth knowing [ ] That does influence you' (Sally, 25-year-old lesbian). The media was the main focus of discussion around social pressures to be thin.

However, several women also described occasions where male partners or friends made negative comments about their weight. For example, Rachel (62-year-old lesbian) described how her ex-husband referred to her body shape during arguments: 'I think he did use my body shape, er, you know, at times when he wanted to … humiliate me [ ] It was more like a taunt that he could use if we were having a row or something.' Holly (69-year-old gay woman) recalled being teased by a male friend: 'One of them said I was far too big. He used to call me "pear-drop bum". That's when I dieted, that was the reason why.'

A small number of women also thought that their heterosexual friends talked about their body size and appearance more than their non-heterosexual friends. For example, Pat (27-year-old lesbian) recalled how heterosexual friends often discussed their body size/ weight but she 'hadn't ever had a similar conversation with lesbians'.

Such comments suggest that interpersonal pressures often originate from predominantly mainstream (heterosexual) sources. Yet, the source of such comments did not diminish their harmful effect. Jolim (27-year-old lesbian) described how she was bullied because of her weight:

> You're always going to get bullied for being a big girl, doesn't matter if you're gay, straight, bi, anything, you know. People see you as fat, they will call you fat. My weight has always been my, my one prime concern.

Critiquing mainstream pressures

Over half of the women were explicitly critical of mainstream idealization of thinness. These women were particularly angry about the media's emphasis on slimness and, in direct contradiction to comments made by women who were media consumers, actively tried to avoid media exposure wherever possible. These women discussed how unrealistic these ideals were, describing how images were often 'air-brushed' (digitally enhanced). Helen's (30-year-old lesbian) anger towards and avoidance of thin images in the media stemmed from personal experiences of using such images as a motivation to diet and lose weight (in the past, Helen was diagnosed with eating disorders including anorexia):

> It makes me angry that this is going on in the media and nobody's doing anything about it. [ ] Erm, but previously, yes very much so it has affected me and I would, I would often have used, erm, skinny-looking people or athletic-looking people [ ] to help me stay motivated to lose weight, to be thin, to be smaller.

The prioritizing of physical health was presented as a method of resisting the social emphasis on thinness by some women. Desires to be slimmer were expressed in terms of desires to be 'healthy' or a 'healthy weight', while 'overweight' bodies were seen as undesirable because they were 'unhealthy', rather than because they do not conform to cultural appearance ideals:

> I want to be healthy and if I gain weight then I start feeling like I'm getting out of breath running for the bus ... that concerns me, but in terms of the aesthetics I don't really, I don't really care. (Laura, 27-year-old bisexual woman).

These women presented an emphasis on health as a resistance to mainstream idealization of thinness. However, it could be argued that, through the lens of health, these women still subscribed to the social ideal that thin body shapes are desirable because they conflated thinness with healthiness (Gonzalez et al., 2013).

Despite this reported critique of social pressures, there often seemed to be a discrepancy between the women's criticisms of cultural ideals and their feelings about their own bodies. Isabel (30-year-old bi woman) was critical of social pressures to be thin but she acknowledged that, since she was still dissatisfied with her body size, she was not exempt from their influence. Isabel suggested that cultural ideals are so pervasive that everyone is affected, even those who actively attempt to resist them:

> We've all internalized the pressures that society puts on us, whether we like to admit to that or not. Obviously it's nice to feel bigger than your culture and ... societal influences but none of us are really.

This discrepancy between cognitions about social ideals and emotions about personal body size suggests that critical attitudes towards socio-cultural pressures do not necessarily protect women from feelings of body dissatisfaction.

Pressures within LGB communities

None of the women described becoming happier with their body size after 'coming out' and a small number of women felt that LGB communities were actually a source of pressures to be thin. Jolim (27-year-old lesbian) considered herself to be 'overweight' and felt a pressure to lose weight after coming out. This pressure originated from a desire to make a positive impression on other non-heterosexual women. Similarly, Isabel (30-year-old bi woman) described how most of her non-heterosexual friends were thin and she experienced a pressure to maintain her own thinness in order to 'fit in':

> I think that when I first started going out on the scene, most of the lesbians I was hanging out with were quite thin and so I think that, as part of fitting in, I would want to maintain that thin ideal.

In contrast, Tara (23-year-old gay woman) thought that mainstream media was more influential in shaping her body concerns than LGB communities:

> I think I was always more conscious of, like, comparing myself to, erm, you know like, people in magazines as opposed to other gay people really.

Despite these comments, pressures from LGB communities predominantly focused on physical appearance (that is, hair style and clothing choices), which was manipulated in order to be recognised as lesbian/bisexual and used as a method of identifying other non-heterosexual women.

Are lesbian and bisexual women protected from body dissatisfaction?

Support for the argument that non-heterosexual women are 'protected' from mainstream pressures (Brown, 1987) came primarily from a small number of bisexual women who were not currently involved or invested in LGB subcultures. In contrast, the lesbian women (many of whom were currently involved in LGB communities) argued that sexuality is irrelevant and stated that they did not feel 'protected' from social pressures because of an affiliation with lesbian subculture (Dworkin, 1988). Indeed, suggestions that lesbian women might experience less dissatisfaction with their bodies than other women were strongly rebuffed by Tove (39-year-old lesbian):

> I strongly believe that lesbians are under pressure around their body and appearance. I don't think that, erm, they're more relaxed. I think they're ... that the pressures just, just are experienced in different ways.

Such comments are congruent with many of the women's feelings about their own body size/shape. LGB communities were very rarely mentioned during these discussions and were actually referred to as a source of body-related pressure by some participants. This suggests that, for this group of women, such communities do not have a 'protective' influence on their body-related concerns.

Several other participants believed that this discussion was too simplistic. For example, Rachel (62-year-old lesbian) thought that all women experienced the same pressures, regardless of sexuality, but that these pressures differed in severity:

> I think that it's the same kinds of pressures on everyone to look young and ... thin, erm, but I think probably those pressures bear more heavily on straight women.

In terms of the potentially 'protective' nature of LGB communities, Isabel (30-year-old bi woman) described how she felt less pressure to be thin and attractive to men after she had come out as bisexual but increasingly felt pressure to be slender in order to fit in with LGB social space which she perceived as endorsing the thin ideal. Isabel argued that while the source of body-size pressures changed, the nature of such pressures did not.

Discussion

The current analysis accords with some previous research in finding that lesbian and bisexual women are often unhappy with their body size (Myers et al., 1999) and may focus on physical fitness and health rather than thinness as a beauty ideal (Beren et al., 1997; Leavy and Hastings, 2010). These findings support Dworkin's (1988) assertion that all women will experience social pressure to be thin and will feel dissatisfied with their body size/shape. Understandings that body size concerns are 'a "straight woman's" problem' (Pitman, 2000: 59) could actually prevent lesbian or bisexual women from speaking to each other about their own body concerns, reinforcing the notion that lesbian and bisexual women are unconcerned with their body size or with striving towards cultural ideals (Kelly, 2007).

BOX R2.6 — **Drawing out the implications of the research**

In the discussion, we used our analysis to develop arguments and draw conclusions that link back to wider debates about whether lesbian (and bisexual) women are protected from mainstream appearance pressures. In doing so, we demonstrated how the research contributes to existing knowledge.

Thematic analysis is ideally suited to mixed methods research because it is theoretically flexible. This analysis also informed the quantitative components of my PhD research by identifying issues that were important to the participant group, ensuring that I explored issues that were relevant to lesbian and bisexual women themselves, rather than just issues that I assumed to be relevant. Following on from the flaws within existing quantitative research that we identified in the introduction, in the report we made suggestions, based on our analysis, as to how future (quantitative) research could proceed more sensitively.

The current qualitative research highlights the complexity of the social influences that shape lesbian and bisexual women's body image. This complexity suggests that, rather than simply identifying similarities and differences between lesbian and heterosexual women, future quantitative research that is inclusive of bisexual women should explore how different social and personal variables (such as engagement with (heterosexist) media that is exerting pressure about thinness and affiliation to LGB communities) interact to shape different women's body image. Such research could produce a more comprehensive account of how sexual identity might relate to women's body image.

SUMMARY

This report has provided an illustration of how a thematic analysis study might be conducted and presented, with reflections on the analytic and writing processes. Although I conducted a specific type of thematic analysis (inductive and semantic-level) in this research, other forms could be performed and written in much the same way. I hope that this report, alongside Chapters 6 and 7, helps readers to undertake their own thematic analysis and provides a clear sense of what a report of a thematic analysis study might look like.

References

Ahern, A.L., Bennett, K.M., Kelly. M. and Hetherington, M.M. (2011) 'A qualitative exploration of young women's attitudes towards the thin ideal', *Journal of Health Psychology*, 16(1): 70–9.

Asher, N.S. and Asher, K.C. (1999) 'Qualitative methods for an outsider looking in: Lesbian women and body image', in M. Kopala and L.A. Suzuki (eds), *Using Qualitative Methods in Psychology*. Thousand Oaks, CA: SAGE. pp. 135–44.

Beren, S.E., Hayden, H.A., Wilfley, D.E. and Streigel-Moore, R.H. (1997) 'Body dissatisfaction among lesbian college students: The conflict of straddling mainstream and lesbian cultures', *Psychology of Women Quarterly*, 21(3): 431–45.

Braun V. and Clarke V. (2006) 'Using thematic analysis in psychology', *Qualitative Research in Psychology*, 3(2): 77–101.

Braun, V. and Clarke, V. (2012) 'Thematic analysis', in H. Cooper (ed.), *Handbook of Research Methods in Psychology. Vol. 2: Research Designs*. Washington, DC: APA Books. pp. 57–71.

Braun, V. and Clarke, V. (2013) *Successful Qualitative Research: A Practical Guide for Beginners*. London: SAGE.

Bridges, D. (2001) 'The ethics of outsider research', *Journal of Philosophy of Education*, 35(3): 371–86.

Brown, L.S. (1987) 'Lesbians, weight, and eating: New analyses and perspectives', in Boston Lesbian Psychologies Collective (ed.), *Lesbian Psychologies: Explorations and Challenges*. Urbana-Champaign, IL: University of Illinois Press. pp. 294–59.

Clarke, V., Ellis, S.J., Peel, E. and Riggs, D.W. (2010) *Lesbian, Gay, Bisexual, Trans & Queer Psychology: An Introduction*. Cambridge, MA: Cambridge University Press.

Clarke, V., Hayfield, N. and Huxley, C. (2012) 'Lesbian, gay, bisexual and trans appearance and embodiment: A critical review of the psychological literature', *Psychology of Sexualities Section Review*, 3(1): 51–70.

Conner, M., Johnson, C. and Grogan, S. (2004) 'Gender, sexuality, body image and eating behaviours', *Journal of Health Psychology*, 9(4): 505–15.

Diamond, L. (2008) *Sexual Fluidity: Understanding Women's Love and Desire*. Cambridge, MA: Harvard University Press.

Dworkin, S.H. (1988) 'Not in man's image: Lesbians and the cultural oppression of body image', *Women & Therapy*, 8(1–2): 27–39.

Elliott, R., Fischer, C.T. and Rennie, D.L. (1999) 'Evolving guidelines for publication of qualitative research studies in psychology and related fields', *British Journal of Clinical Psychology*, 38(3): 215–29.

Gonzalez, M.L., Mora, M., Penelo, E., Goddard, E., Treasure, J. and Raich, R.M. (2013) 'Qualitative findings in a long-term disordered eating prevention programme follow-up with school-going girls', *Journal of Health Psychology*, 18(4): 587–98.

Grogan, S. (2008) *Body Image: Understanding Body Dissatisfaction in Men, Women and Children*, 2nd edn. London: Routledge.

Halliwell, E. and Dittmar, H. (2004) 'Does size matter? The impact of model's body size on women's body-focused anxiety and advertising effectiveness', *Journal of Social and Clinical Psychology*, 23(1): 104–22.

Hellawell, D. (2006) 'Inside-out: Analysis of the insider–outsider concept as a heuristic device to develop reflexivity in students doing qualitative research', *Teaching in Higher Education*, 11(4): 483–94.

Huxley, C.J. (2013) 'Lesbian and bisexual women's experiences of sexuality-based discrimination and their appearance concerns', *Psychology & Sexuality*, 4(1): 7–15.

Huxley, C.J., Clarke, V. and Halliwell, E. (2011) '"It's a comparison thing isn't it?" Lesbian and bisexual women talk about their body image and relationships', *Psychology of Women Quarterly*, 35(3): 415–27.

Huxley, C.J. and Hayfield, N.J. (2012) 'Individual differences in adjustment and distress: Sexual orientation?', in N. Rumsey and D. Harcourt (eds), *The Oxford Handbook of the Psychology of Appearance*. Oxford: Oxford University Press. pp. 190–202.

Kelly, L. (2007) 'Lesbian body image perceptions: The context of body silence', *Qualitative Health Research*, 17(7): 873–83.

Koff, E., Lucas, M., Migliorini, R. And Grossmith, S. (2010) 'Women and body dissatisfaction: Does sexual orientation make a difference?' *Body Image*, 7(3): 255–8.

Leavy, P. and Hastings, L. (2010) 'Body image and sexual identity: An interview study with lesbian, bisexual and heterosexual college age-women', *Electronic Journal of Human Sexuality*, 13 (http://www.ejhs.org/volume13/bodyimage.htm).

Lyons, A.C. (2000) 'Examining media representations: Benefits for health psychology', *Journal of Health Psychology*, 5(3): 349–58.

Morrison, M.A., Morrison, T.G. and Sager, C.L. (2004) 'Does body satisfaction differ between gay men and lesbian women and heterosexual men and women? A meta-analytic review', *Body Image*, 1(2): 127–38.

Myers, A., Taub, J., Morris, J.F. and Rothblum, E.D. (1999) 'Beauty mandates and the appearance obsession: Are lesbian and bisexual women better off?' *Journal of Lesbian Studies*, 3(4): 15–26.

Paquette, M.-C. and Raine, K. (2004) 'Sociocultural context of women's body image', *Social Science & Medicine*, 59(5): 1047–58.

Peel, E. and Coyle, A. (eds) (2004) 'Special feature: Heterosexual people working in lesbian and gay psychology', *Lesbian & Gay Psychology Review*, 5(2): 54–70.

Pitman, G.E. (2000) 'The influence of race, ethnicity, class, and sexual politics on lesbians' body image', *Journal of Homosexuality*, 40(2): 49–64.

Rothblum, E.D. (1994) 'Lesbians and physical appearance: Which model applies?', in B. Greene and G.M. Herek (eds), *Lesbian and Gay Psychology: Theory, Research, and Clinical Applications.* Thousand Oaks, CA: SAGE. pp. 84–97.

Share, T.L. and Mintz, L.B. (2002) 'Differences between lesbians and heterosexual women in disordered eating and related attitudes', *Journal of Homosexuality*, 42(4): 89–106.

Tang, D.T.S. (2006) 'The research pendulum: Multiple roles and responsibilities as a researcher', *Journal of Lesbian Studies,* 10(3/4): 11–27.

Tiggemann, M. (2002) 'Media influences on body image development', in T.F. Cash and T. Pruzinsky (eds), *Body Image: A Handbook of Theory, Research, and Clinical Practice.* New York: Guilford Press. pp. 91–8.

Tiggemann, M. (2004) 'Body image across the life span: Stability and change', *Body Image*, 1(1): 29–41.

Ussher, J.M. (1999) 'Eclecticism and methodological pluralism: The way forward for feminist research', *Psychology of Women Quarterly*, 23(1): 41–6.

Willig, C. (1999) 'Beyond appearances: A critical realist approach to social constructionist work', in D.J. Nightingale and J. Cromby (eds), *Social Constructionist Psychology: A Critical Analysis of Theory and Practice.* Buckingham: Open University Press. pp. 37–51.

REPORT 3

Critical Care Experiences and Bereavement among Families of Organ Donors: A Reflective Account of a Grounded Theory Study[1]

Magi Sque and Sheila Payne

The purpose of this report is to provide readers with a clear sense of what the outcome of a grounded theory study looks like and how it might be presented when writing a journal article or a student dissertation. The study that this report focuses on explores the experiences of relatives of organ donors. Their experiences were found to revolve around a process of conflict and resolution which we explained in terms of 'dissonant loss'. Throughout the report, text boxes are used at pertinent junctures to highlight important issues in the writing of the journal article upon which the report is based and also some issues specific to the grounded theory process. For the complete journal article, see Sque and Payne (1996).

Introduction

Every year approximately 700,000 individuals die in the UK, yet very few become 'beating heart donors' (that is, donors of major organs). While relatives of potential donors are an important group in the donation process (as their lack of objection is needed before organ retrieval can take place), little is understood about their experiences (Pelletier, 1992).

Empirical investigation into the experiences of donating relatives has been limited both in scope and design. First, the small numbers of donating families, the anonymity that surrounds them and the often wide geographical spread makes access to relatives difficult,

---

[1]This report is an edited version of an article by the authors, entitled 'Dissonant loss: The experiences of donor relatives', which was published in *Social Science & Medicine*, 43(9): 1359–70 (reproduced with permission from Elsevier). The authors wish to thank the participants in the study and Dr Jan Walker for her thoughtful comments on earlier drafts of the article. The research upon which the article was based was supported by the UK Department of Health Nursing Studentship Scheme.

> ### BOX R3.1 ▸ Introduction or background to the study
>
> There is much debate about how much a grounded theorist needs to know about the field they wish to explore. Grounded theory was considered the methodology of choice in this study as little was known about the bereavement experience of families who donated organs of a deceased relative. We could have chosen not to write a detailed literature review and could have included it in the discussion of the findings but we felt that this introduction was essential to make a good case for the study and to show where there were outstanding gaps in the literature and in knowledge about the topic. We also had to take into consideration the particular style of the journal for which we were writing where an elaborated introduction or background was expected.

except by survey methods (for example, Bartucci, 1987; Perez-San-Gregorio et al., 1992) which are limited in their ability to describe the meaning of the experience. Second, the emotive nature of the research and theoretical debates (de Raeve, 1994) that surround the ethics of interviewing any bereaved group make investigation problematic.

La Spina et al. (1993) investigated the psychological mechanisms related to families' decisions to donate by interviewing 20 families between 6 and 12 months after donation. Results indicated that a primary reason for donation was the desire to keep the deceased relative alive through identification with the recipients. This was considered to be a defensive mechanism against the anguish of death. The collapse of this projection, for whatever reason, left the relatives with feelings of guilt that they had somehow lost track of the deceased. These events manifested themselves in depression, anxiety and elaboration of bereavement.

Coupe (1991) addressed the issues of support and perceptions of information given to 17 families at the time the issue of organ donation was raised. Six themes emerged from the study: informing the family, dealing with brain death, organ donation, grief, family needs and facilities, and nursing and medical staff. Organ donation was seen as a difficult subject to raise. However, the request for donation rarely offended the relatives and was often accepted as something the staff 'had to do'. Some families felt that they were given insufficient information about procurement, particularly about how the body would look post-retrieval. The research indicated that individual assessment of families is required to establish when the issue of donation should be raised and who should do it.

Pelletier (1992) used semi-structured interviews with nine relatives of organ donors to appraise what family members identified as the most stressful aspects of the donation process. She identified the most stressful situations as the threat of losing a loved one, the diagnosis of brainstem death, the failure of health professionals to identify the potential organ donor and adjusting to the many changes associated with the loss. Pelletier (1993) further used this donor family sample to extrapolate the emotions experienced and coping strategies used during their stressful situations. During 'the threat to life', a range of emotions such as helplessness, sadness, numbness and panic were reported. Coping strategies involved seeking information, seeking emotional support, keeping the connection (remaining near the relative), escape and avoidance, planned problem solving and exercising control of emotions. Emotions experienced with the confirmation of brain death were disbelief, shock, numbness, anger and sadness. Organ donation was the coping strategy used on this occasion as it provided a mechanism for changing the death into something positive.

Prior to the present study, investigation into donor relatives' experience by qualitative methods had been limited, patchy and incomplete. No investigation had attempted to describe the totality of relatives' organ donation experience or to suggest inductive theory that could explain it. This was the aim of the present study. It was anticipated that such a theory could provide a framework for future investigation through the identification of variables and the generation of hypotheses. It could also suggest pertinent factors necessary in the education of health professionals to ensure appropriate care for donor relatives.

Method

Relatives from 42 donor families were invited by letter to participate in an interview study. Since geographical spread might have been important (due to differences in local practices), families were recruited via three regional transplant co-ordinating centres within England. Relatives were chosen to cover a range of experiences, such as the time since donation and their relationship to the donor. Sixteen families (24 relatives) agreed to participate. A detailed sample profile is provided in Table R3.1.

All the participating families had agreed to multi-organ retrieval. Four donations were spontaneously offered, while 12 were requested. Interviews were carried out in the homes of the participants: these lasted between one and a half to two hours.

In dealing with this sensitive topic, it was important for the researchers to be fully informed about the subject of their exploration. Also, specific preparation for the interviewer role was developed through pilot interviews, carried out with two donor families who had made donations several years previously. These families had both spoken publicly about their experiences. The objective was to explore salient issues and to gain confidence in conducting such an interview.

All the interviews were carried out by the first author (Magi Sque). Following an introduction to the procedure for the interview, participants were asked to tell the story of their experiences. Only after the story was complete did the researcher use the interview guide, developed from the pilot interviews and relevant literature, in further questioning. This guide

---

BOX R3.2	Reflecting on sampling and data collection

While always bearing in mind the constraints imposed by the word limit for articles in a particular journal, one of the most important items that need to be explained is the sample. In a grounded theory, as indicated in the first paragraph below, we wished to capture the widest set of participants' experiences that we could. Hence it was important to show the reader that we had made great efforts by using more than one geographical location, which might have had different support services, different age groups of donors, time since donation and cause of death. Some of these factors are usefully pulled together in Table R3.1. In Chapter 8 in this volume, Sheila Payne has written about over-sensitizing the researcher to the field and we could have chosen not to carry out a pilot study but felt that, because of the sensitive nature of the research and the participant group, plus the questions that the interviewer (Magi Sque) could be asked, as well as her role as a novice researcher, it was appropriate to carry out a pilot study. This strategy did prove invaluable as many difficult issues were often raised during the interviews and Magi was able to give reassurance or was able to suggest referral routes for participants to find answers to their questions or resolve issues. We have therefore stated that a grounded theory *approach* was used rather than classic grounded theory where the researcher would enter the field with little knowledge of the issues that would be likely to arise. It was also important in sensitive research of this nature to be kept informed of the effect interviews had on participants – hence our interview evaluations. Data validation and analysis are briefly reported. This is often a choice one has to make and the debates about data analysis and about checking analyses with participants in grounded theory could run on, so we simply mention the validation process here and that data were analysed in accordance with general principles of grounded theory, which become apparent in the reporting of the findings.

---

was modified throughout the data collection process to incorporate new concepts. Participants were later invited to provide evaluative feedback on their experience of being interviewed.

Analysis of the data was carried out using a grounded theory approach (Strauss and Corbin, 1990). Transcripts were coded for themes which were clustered to form named categories. These categories closely fit the data, as they were derived from the inquiry. Nine participants were asked to review a summary of their interviews to validate the researchers' interpretations.

Table R3.1 Participant sample to show family relationships, age of donor, critical injury and months since donation

Relatives interviewed	Age of donor (years)	Critical injury	Time since donation (months)
Parents	27	Cerebral haemorrhage	5
Parents	25	Cerebral anoxia following cardio-pulmonary resuscitation	7
Parents	20	Head injury from a riding accident	36
Parents	22	Head injury following a road traffic accident	8
Parents	26	Marphan's Syndrome	18
Parents	10	Viral meningitis	16
Mother	22	Cerebral anoxia following an asthma attack	11
Mother	0*	Cerebral anoxia following asphyxiation	11
Father	26	Head injury following a road traffic accident	4
Husband	44	Cerebral haemorrhage	7
Husband	56	Cerebral haemorrhage	8
Husband	48	Cerebral haemorrhage	17
Wife	47	Cerebral haemorrhage	4
Wife	47	Cerebral haemorrhage	18
Wife & mother	22	Head injury following a road traffic accident	7
Wife & daughter-in-law	50	Cerebral haemorrhage	4

* baby 10 weeks old

Results

BOX R3.3   **Reporting the findings**

There are many ways of reporting a grounded theory study and if we were writing this section again, we would entitle it 'Findings' rather than 'Results' (which is how we described it in the original journal article). The term 'Findings' better describes the outcomes of a qualitative investigation, which are not the sort of measurable 'Results' obtained from a quantitative study. We chose to report the findings in three parts starting with the number of categories and the core variable, their titles and Figure R3.1, which shows their configuration.

The second section gives a description of the categories into which explanatory literature is interwoven in accordance with reporting grounded theory. The third part focuses on the theory developed and the literature that lends support to its development.

In describing the categories, we have included illustrative quotations from the interview transcripts as evidence. Choosing quotations can often be problematic for researchers because it can be difficult to decide which quotations are most representative of a specific theme or category. Often there is a conflict about using the most 'startling' quotations that may be particularly memorable or ones that really embrace the substance of the category. Then there is the decision of how many quotations to use. Often there are many good descriptive quotations and the process of elimination can be mentally 'painful' as there is so much you would like to share with the reader. It is also important in reporting grounded theory to give a selection of opposing views if these differ from the main pattern of themes, as is illustrated in this section. However, it must be borne in mind that a journal article relies mainly on the authors' interpretation of events, which should be the substantive part of the findings, with the quotations acting as confirmation of this interpretation. This is how we have tried to report the nature of the categories here.

The analysis of the data produced 11 categories that conceptualized participants' experience. These categories were arranged around the central theme of the research, 'donor relatives' experiences', to form an analytical version of the story, shown in Figure R3.1.

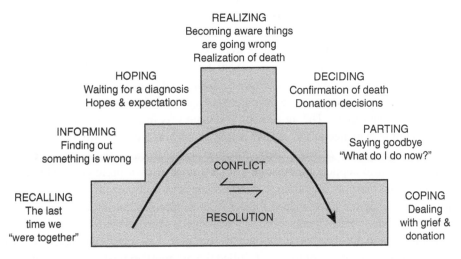

Figure R3.1   A model of donor relatives' experience

The model in Figure R3.1 indicates a sequential relationship of categories that described participants' commonly constructed realities of the donation experience. These were 'the last time we were together'; 'finding out something is wrong'; 'waiting for a diagnosis', 'hopes and expectations'; 'becoming aware things are going wrong', 'realization of death'; 'confirmation of brainstem death', 'donation decisions'; 'saying goodbye'; 'what do I do now?'; and 'dealing with grief and donation'.

There appeared to be particular behaviours through which each phase was acted out by participants. These were: 'recalling', where participants talked about the attributes of their relative and the last occasion they shared together; 'informing', when they were first told something had gone wrong; 'hoping' during the hospital experience; 'realizing' that their relative would not recover; 'deciding' about donation; 'parting' – leaving the relative; and 'coping' with grief and donation. These behaviours were explained through a process of conflict and resolution which pervaded the categories and formed the core variable of participants' experience. A theory of 'dissonant loss' was developed to explain participants' psycho-social concerns during the donation experience, using this core variable. This process of conflict and resolution will now be examined with reference to the categories concerning donation and its outcome.

Deciding – donation decisions

Deciding about donation was often the first time during the period when their relative had been hospitalized that participants were given some control. Up to this point, events had developed around them as they sought to understand and come to terms with their situation. Decisions about donation created further conflicts for participants, such as whether to donate and what to donate.

Participants were approached about donation at various stages during the relative's illness. Nevertheless, they were all consulted following the confirmation of brainstem death. Requests were usually made in an interview with the doctor and the next of kin who had a supporting relative with them. Participants were sympathetic towards requesters, as they had empathy with this sensitive task. Decisions about donation were discussed between significant family members and were mainly consensus decisions. Arbitrators and principal contributors to the decision-making process were the parents or spouses of the deceased relative and final decisions rested with them. The agreement to donate was in these cases made easier when there was tangible evidence of the relative's wishes, such as a donor card. On occasion there was disagreement within families about donation. In these cases the principal contributor made the decision to support the relative's wishes or their own preference. This did cause resentment within families. Deciding to donate sometimes caused conflict for principal contributors as they may not have wished for donation themselves but felt they had to fulfil the wish of their relative. Participants from whom requests were made felt that they probably would not have thought of organ donation and were glad they were approached. They felt it would have been distressing not to have fulfilled the pre-mortem wish of their relative.

Motivation to donate

There appeared to be four major contributing factors about making the decision to donate organs: the wishes of the relative; the attributes of the relative; the realization of the death of the relative; and the confirmation of brainstem death. However, the relative's wishes were of primary importance as the donation was seen to be their gift. A participant, for instance, remembered how she had taken a donor card from her ten-year-old son saying, 'Don't be so silly, you don't want that'. The episode helped her believe that her son, now 22, had intended to help other people after he died and she supported his wife's decision to facilitate the retrieval of his organs.

In some cases, making a decision without the explicit knowledge of the wishes of the deceased was very difficult for participants. The category of 'recalling' – 'the last time we were together' gained importance as the attributes of the relative helped to make the decision:

> We said, well yeah, I think G would like that because she did talk about having a card, only she never got around to having one and being a caring and sharing person that she was, we said yeah we'll do that … she would be more than pleased and proud that we did really.

For more on motivations for donation, see Sque and Payne (1996: 1363–4).

Concerns about donation

Participants had two main concerns about donation: mutilation of the body and the possible suffering the relative might sustain as a result of the operation. It was important to participants that the retrieval of organs was carried out with dignity and propriety. Participants found the knowledge that retrieval was carried out as a regular surgical procedure comforting:

> I thought G was going to be carved up and everything else but it was not so, it was done clinically and I don't think this is ever explained openly … It is done like a surgical operation and there is no fear of the patient being hurt in any shape or form.

There was another type of suffering that was of concern to participants. They felt that the relative had already suffered so much so was it fair to subject them to further indignities by allowing their organs to be removed? A father was concerned about the vulnerability of his child at procurement:

> I wanted to protect her more because I mean, she was very vulnerable, wasn't she? For all intents and purposes she was dead but I did not want her to be cut about. I didn't want her to be injured. You see she was not injured in my eyes because there was no marks. So anything done after that would be an operation and I couldn't comprehend that too much at that particular time. So really that was my reservation – I didn't want her to be hurt.

Conflicts for participants concerning donation were about fulfilling the pre-mortem wishes of their relative and assumptions about contributing to their perceived posthumous suffering.

These concerns were conceivably exacerbated by a poor understanding of brainstem death or affected by the notion of harming the dead. Callahan (1987) highlighted the sentiment that it is possible to 'feel sorry' for the dead person because we do think of the dead as they were ante-mortem. Therefore, it is possible to experience compassion for the dead and to feel genuine moral outrage at broken pre-mortem promises which respect the wishes of the dead. Although the subject of posthumous harm has been debated, Callahan (1987) feels that our empathetic responses to the dead are in part due to our inability to identify with the dead: we are only capable of identifying with pre-mortem states. Feinberg (1985) details these sentiments in that a dead body is a natural symbol of a living person and when a corpse is mutilated it looks very much like one is harming a real person: horror is felt at the mere proposition of such action. This is the way we imagine the dead person and sorrow and outrage can justifiably be felt on their behalf.

However, Callahan (1987) points out that the express wishes of the dead generally merit respect in their own right. This may explain the gratitude that was felt by families who were asked about donation and were able to facilitate this wish for their relative. The question that naturally seems to follow is whether we feel so morally bound when what is willed is wasteful. This could be a painful dilemma for relatives involved in donation requests when the wishes of their loved ones were explicitly opposed to it. Likewise, relatives in this study agonized over the decision to donate if the wishes of the dead were unknown.

Information about donation

While some participants seemed well informed about procurement procedures, others felt that adequate information was not available to support their decisions about donation. For more on this, see Sque and Payne (1996: 1365).

Parting – saying goodbye

Once donation was agreed, participants needed to make decisions about leaving the relative and 'saying goodbye'. This created further conflict and difficulty for participants in equating death with the appearance of the relative when making the decision to leave them:

Interviewer: How did you actually make that decision to go and say goodbye?

Participant: Well, it is very difficult to. All I kept thinking was that I kept saying to my brother-in-law, 'How can you say goodbye to somebody who is still breathing?' I mean, oh God, I kept on saying, 'He's warm, he's still perspiring, he's warm' because to me he wasn't dead really ... because he was still breathing. And I know it was the machine and that but he was too warm.

Except in one case, all the participants in this study chose to leave the hospital soon after the results of the second brainstem test were known and confirmed brainstem death. In no case did hospitals offer participants a full range of options for seeing the relative post-organ retrieval, such as back on the ward, which might have been appropriate for some. This did cause regrets among participants, as they felt that viewing the newly dead would have been more preferable than, in some cases, days later at a funeral home.

In some instances, the nurses offered to inform participants when the retrieval operation had been completed. Some participants found the time waiting for this telephone call and the declaration of cessation of the heartbeat difficult. It did mark a kind of finality but it was an end to any hope of existence for the relative:

> We got the phone call 4.30 Christmas Eve to say they had switched off the ventilator. That was terrible waiting for the phone call. We dreaded the phone to ring. I mean, we knew that he had gone then.

Retrospectively, participants wished that they had had more guidance from hospital staff about options and about the possible effects of choosing how and when they said goodbye.

Parting – what do I do now?

'What do I do now?' was asked of intensive care staff by a father when he was about to leave the hospital. It was the bewildering stage of leaving hospital and dealing with immediate concerns of the hospitalization and its outcome. Families most often felt that once they had left the intensive-care unit, 'A door had closed behind us'. They had very little support from anyone to do with the donation, with one participant saying:

> We sort of felt as if they had the organs and at the moment we had been left.

Hospitals generally did not provide any advice about grief, give any bereavement support contacts or carry out any follow-up. Only in two cases did consultants and transplant co-ordinators suggest participants should get in touch if they had any unanswered questions. Here the needs of some relatives are explained:

> We came away from that hospital with no support, nothing – just a plastic bag with his belongings in, nowhere where you could get in touch with anyone if you needed any counselling … It's like you just walk away empty, you know … If only they could find a nicer way of doing it rather than just writing out a death certificate and sending you away with a plastic bag.

Coping – dealing with grief and donation

The most important thing about grief and donation is that donation does not appear to reduce grief but it changes the emphasis of death to focus on the achievement of the donor and that their kindness and caring are living on. Here a father describes the feelings he had following the death of his son and his donation:

> It's not a reward that you get – it's something that happens as a result of a loved one wishing to give their organs to somebody else. They give their organs to somebody else so that they can have the gift of life and what they give to us is almost not an easy road in grief but a different road through grief – a less harsh road and a less final death because it is a death filled with different emotions. It's filled with the joy of knowing good has come out of his death, as opposed to us having to know that, just, ah, nothing has come out of his death, only pain and sorrow and sadness, and also knowing that it is not only the recipient that receives, it's their family, their friends ... It is a tremendous thing, it ripples out to hundreds of people ... Almost unending the relief and saving of pain that just giving something that is not needed can produce.

Participants reported that the most important thing in providing respite from grief was the ability to talk to others about their bereavement when they needed to. Participants tended to seek out their own social supports but grief was largely managed within the family. A few participants who did not have this internal support sought the help of bereavement organizations, which seemed ill-prepared to be of assistance in this particular circumstance. Families who used bereavement services did not feel that the experiences had been particularly helpful; in one case, the counsellor expressed her objection to organ donation.

Participants received a letter from the transplant co-ordinating units that gave information about organ distribution. Participants found this initial information helpful but desired more information about recipients, as they faced the conflict of part of their relative still living on. This desire for information did not necessarily abate as time went by. In some cases, participants realized that they may not wish to know if the transplant had failed. Others thought this was unimportant as help had at least been offered. Participants put great value on the concept of their relative living on:

> She is not dead and gone sort of thing, you know. She is still out there walking around, which is very pleasing to know ... that her life is still going on, in that context really, life still goes on. She's out there in the big wide world, in four different places at once [laughing] which is unbelievable, unbelievable.

At the time of the interview, although some participants had experienced difficulties with aspects of their bereavement, all remained supportive of their donation decision:

> At the end of the day, it was right, it was the right decision to do, I'm quite happy, I'm quite content, I've got no remorse, no regrets or doubts because I know somebody out there got life.

Donation decisions may have consequences which will affect the rest of donor relatives' lives. Unfortunately, this can only be speculation, as there are no longitudinal studies about donor relatives. However, this study has suggested that, even as time goes by, the effects of the donation are perpetuated in the desire for continuing information about recipients.

Bowlby (1980) proposed that bereaved people generally experience a strong need for continuation of a relationship with the dead person. It is possible that the way the relationship continued to play a central role in participants' lives is manifested in the often intense and sustained yearning for information about recipients because of the attachment participants felt for the part of the donor that 'lived on'. In some instances, this need for information seemed to be influenced by the intensity of the relationship that had existed with the relative.

Theory of dissonant loss: conflict and resolution in the donation experience

This study has suggested that the experience of organ donation can be explained by a theory of 'dissonant loss'. Dissonant loss is defined as 'A bereavement or loss which is characterized by a sense of uncertainty and psychological inconsistency. The loss is assured but the effects of the loss on those involved are unknown.' Dissonance occurs as the loss is encompassed by a series of complex decisions. These decisions are made necessary by the ubiquitous and pervasive elements of conflict and resolution (see Figure R3.2).

The notion that people who hold conflicting or incompatible beliefs are likely to experience dissonance and distress has a long history in psychology (Higgins, 1987). Therefore, the conflict/resolution concept provides an appropriate explanation of the psychosocial influences that families encounter during their donation experience. Conflict is defined in this sense as 'The simultaneously opposing tendencies within the individual or environment which cause discrepancy, discord or dissonance and the distress resulting from these instances'. Within this study, participants described the factors that created resolutions to their conflicts and helped them to move through the phases of the donation process (see Figure R3.2).

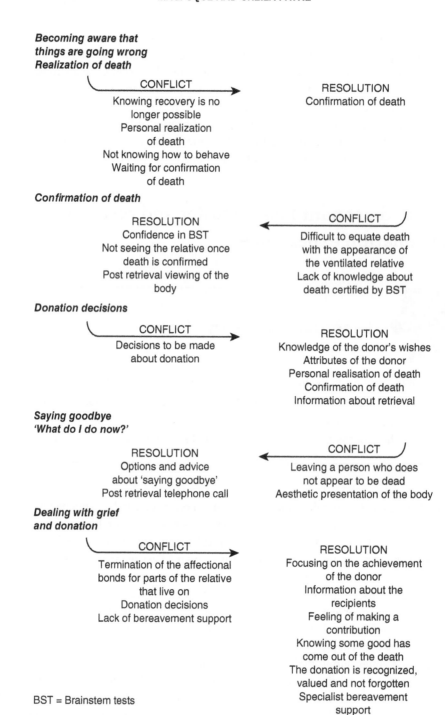

Becoming aware that things are going wrong
Realization of death

CONFLICT
Knowing recovery is no longer possible
Personal realization of death
Not knowing how to behave
Waiting for confirmation of death

RESOLUTION
Confirmation of death

Confirmation of death

RESOLUTION
Confidence in BST
Not seeing the relative once death is confirmed
Post retrieval viewing of the body

CONFLICT
Difficult to equate death with the appearance of the ventilated relative
Lack of knowledge about death certified by BST

Donation decisions

CONFLICT
Decisions to be made about donation

RESOLUTION
Knowledge of the donor's wishes
Attributes of the donor
Personal realisation of death
Confirmation of death
Information about retrieval

Saying goodbye
'What do I do now?'

RESOLUTION
Options and advice about 'saying goodbye'
Post retrieval telephone call

CONFLICT
Leaving a person who does not appear to be dead
Aesthetic presentation of the body

Dealing with grief and donation

CONFLICT
Termination of the affectional bonds for parts of the relative that live on
Donation decisions
Lack of bereavement support

RESOLUTION
Focusing on the achievement of the donor
Information about the recipients
Feeling of making a contribution
Knowing some good has come out of the death
The donation is recognized, valued and not forgotten
Specialist bereavement support

BST = Brainstem tests

Figure R3.2 A theory of dissonant loss

Conflict originated in the contracted and intense emotional period of hospitalization (which has not been reported here but is described by Sque and Payne, 1996: 1361–3). During this time, participants seemed to lose control to the experts, as they were functioning outside of their assumptive world, which includes all we know, our interpretations of the past and expectations of the future (Parkes, 1993). Higgins (1987) described how construct availability or our stored experience of a given situation will influence the possessor's response. Higgins maintains that individuality of response to the situation is due to construct accessibility, which refers to the readiness with which each stored construct is used to process new information.

Since the donors were relatively young, their next of kin were young parents or spouses who were inexperienced with critical injury, death and hospital protocol and without the life experience or information to support their choices. The degree of conflict and uncertainty experienced by participants was exacerbated by a lack of experience and knowledge about the events of donation and organ procurement. It was in this environment that participants were asked to make complex decisions about donation, which had implications for their own emotional well-being and ability to manage their bereavement process.

Conflict in the donation experience existed for participants in two major forms. On the one hand, conflict unfolded as a series of extraneous events over which they had no control, such as the perceived realization of their relative's death. Other conflicts arose as a result of decisions which needed to be made about donation. These decisions did not take place in a vacuous and impartial environment but one that was emotionally provocative. Therefore, conflict may have been experienced more poignantly at this time as participants were persuaded, even against their own convictions, to honour the wishes of the deceased. Participants' decisional conflict was increased when they were asked to accept a non-traditional definition of death – brainstem death – as death (see Sque and Payne, 1996: 1362–3). The implications of brainstem death transcend the usual experience of the lay individual, so there are few role models for participants to emulate in their decision-making.

Decision-making to reduce conflict in the context of organ donation fits the criteria of complex decision-making. Among other features, Orasanu and Connolly (1993) suggest that an important characteristic of a complex decision problem is the uncertainty experienced by those involved in the resolution. Some participants were unsure of the wishes of the deceased and even those who possessed explicit knowledge of their wishes were faced with a number of concerns. Some of these were the mutilation of the body and the perceived continued suffering of the relative during organ procurement. Participants needed to resolve these issues before they gave consent for organ donation. The participants' value system, information sets, relative power, commitment and affective component influenced the outcome.

What were some of the underlying influences that might help us to understand the processes of decision-making by participants? Janis and Mann (1977) point out that, when embarking upon important decisions, individuals become aware of the risk of suffering serious losses from whatever course of action is selected. They will use a number of strategies to cope with this. One of these strategies, 'buck-passing', involves shifting the responsibility for the decision to someone else. Might this be the strategy that donor relatives largely used, by sharing the decision with family members? This seemed likely, as the support they sought would give their decisions legitimacy when they 're-entered' their assumptive world. This may be the reason that these decisions were shared only with close family members. Where participants were aware there might be disapproval from some family members and friends, they kept the donation secret.

The pre-decision situation is generally regarded as one in which the person experiences conflict. The conflict exists because of the simultaneous presence of at least two mutually incompatible tendencies. Janis and Mann's (1977) theory suggests that, to prepare for donation decisions, participants would first gather information about the wishes of the relative and ensure that the preconditions for donation, such as confirmation of brainstem death, had been met. Coupled with this information, they would evaluate the information that they had about procurement and the possible outcomes. Participants relied on medical and nursing staff for this information.

So how did participants make their decisions? Etzioni (1992) argues that choices are made on the basis of emotional involvements and value commitments. Information-processing is often excluded or is a secondary concern. The main context for making decisions lies in moral commitments, affects and social factors such as norms and habits. The importance of emotions and values and the way they fashion choice shows that information and reasoning have limited roles. Also emotions and values affect the information we are able to absorb, the way it is absorbed and our interpretations. Decision-making is not an individualistic event that takes place in isolation within the individual mind but is motivated by values that are culturally embedded. This stands in direct opposition to humans as rational actors. Indeed, as suggested by Whittaker (1990), it would raise the question whether more participants may have consented to organ retrieval than would do so were they not in a state of emotional distress. It appears that participants used decision strategies from Janis and Mann's (1977) rationalist perspective but were also influenced by factors suggested by Etzioni (1992).

Discussion of the method

BOX R3.5	Reflecting on the method

Having integrated the literature with the findings, we *only* discuss the method in the following section. We believe that grounded theory worked very well for this study and, even with a small sample, we were able to provide a potentially useful framework, which has added to knowledge in this area and provided a guide for clinicians who wish to examine their practice.

This study has offered an explanation of donor relatives' experience through the development of the inductive theory of 'dissonant loss'. A grounded theory approach to analysis allowed us, even with a small sample, to derive a theoretical perspective that we believe helps to explain donor relatives' experiences. While caution must be exerted in generalizing the results from a small sample, we believe that the emergent theory suggests a number of potentially useful interpretations.

Making the donation experience explicit may contribute to an understanding of the psychosocial issues involved in donation and transplantation. Increased understanding of this process could provide indicators for the appropriate care of other populations of donor relatives and a theoretical foundation for the education of care professionals. The theory provides a plausible basis for continued research with populations we clearly know little about, such as those relatives who refuse donation. The study has provided supportive evidence for other studies concerning donor relatives (for example, Coupe, 1991; MORI Health Research Unit, 1995; Pelletier, 1992).

One of the main criticisms levelled at qualitative research is that of reproducibility. If this cannot be done, is the work credible? Strauss and Corbin (1990) have made clear that a social phenomenon is not reproducible insofar as being able to match conditions exactly to those of an original study. However, the themes identified in this study are open to support or refutation by other investigators.

Narrative knowledge does place the narrators, researchers and readers in a hermeneutic circle of interpretation, as their own values and interests will affect the meaning of the activity in which they are engaged. Therefore, information about settings, the reflective processes of the researcher and the reciprocal impact of the researcher on the researched does gain a focal importance. The researchers are nurses who are committed to the donation process. This does raise the question about the nature of the information collected and its interpretation. The professional background of the first author (Magi Sque) may have had an impact on the interaction with participants and the development and pursuit of the research agenda. Magi felt that identifying herself as a nurse and researcher was an important element in developing rapport with relatives in this delicate situation. She felt her professional background had prepared her to conduct such interviews with sensitivity and empathy and she was able, as far as it is possible, to gain the co-operation of the participants, who were grateful for the opportunity to express their sorrow and to talk about their deceased relative (for more on this approach, see Coyle and Wright, 1996). As one commented:

> I found the interview very helpful to me. Just to talk to somebody who understands was most welcome. In a roundabout way, it was a sort of therapy.

For some participants, the interviewer's opinion about donation was important as they would not have felt comfortable talking with someone who was opposed to donation. Where this information was not requested, Magi maintained an impartial stance as far as possible. While her professional background could have created some inhibition for participants to confide certain experiences to nurses, we do not believe this to be so, as participants were aware that the researchers were not affiliated with any transplant co-ordinating centre or hospital. This does highlight the issue of interview data validation by participants. While the value of this activity remains questionable (Henwood and Pidgeon, 1995), we feel this exercise allowed us to establish that we had a good grasp of the issues, while the interview evaluations kept us informed about the impact of the interview experience on relatives.

SUMMARY

While there are many theories of loss and separation, there has been no theory which explains the experiences of donor families. Our theory suggests areas where help may be focused. The theory of dissonant loss may usefully be applied to other situations of loss that involve conflicts and complex decision-making. Clearly, there is still a lot we do not yet understand or know about the donation process and its psycho-social effects. Dissonant loss theory may provide a framework for further investigation. We also hope that this presentation of our work and our reflections upon the analytic process will give those who are interested in pursuing grounded theory a clear sense of what the end-product of grounded theory research may look like and how such research might be written up.

References

Bartucci, M.R. (1987) 'Organ donation: A study of the donor family perspective', *Journal of Neuroscience Nursing*, 19(6): 305–9.

Bowlby, J. (1980) *Attachment and Loss 3: Loss, Sadness and Depression*. London: Hogarth Press.

Callahan, J.C. (1987) 'On harming the dead', *Ethics*, 97(2): 341–52.

Coupe, D. (1991) 'A study of relatives', nurses' and doctors' perceptions of the support and information given to the families of potential organ donors'. Unpublished MPhil thesis, University of Wales College of Medicine, Cardiff.

Coyle, A. and Wright, C. (1996) 'Using the counselling interview to collect research data on sensitive topics', *Journal of Health Psychology*, 1(4): 431–40.

de Raeve, L. (1994) 'Ethical issues in palliative care research', *Palliative Medicine*, 8(4): 298–305.

Etzioni, A. (1992) 'Normative-affective factors: Toward a new decision-making model', in M. Zey (ed.), *Decision Making: Alternatives to Rational Choice Models*. Newbury Park, CA: SAGE. pp. 89–111.

Feinberg, J. (1985) *The Moral Limits of the Criminal Law: Volume II – Offence to Others.* New York: Oxford University Press.

Henwood, K. and Pidgeon, N. (1995) 'Grounded theory and psychological research', *The Psychologist,* 8(3): 115–18.

Higgins, E.T. (1987) 'Self-discrepancy: A theory relating self and affect', *Psychological Review,* 94(3): 319–40.

Janis, I.L. and Mann, L. (1977) *Decision-making: A Psychological Analysis of Conflict, Choice and Commitment.* New York: The Free Press.

La Spina, F., Sedda, L., Pizzi, C., Verlato, R., Boselli, L., Candiani, A., Chiaranda, M., Frova, G., Gorgerino, F., Gravame, V., Mapelli, A., Martini, C., Pappalettera, M., Seveso, M. and Sironi, P.G. (1993) 'Donor families' attitudes toward organ donation: The North Italy Transplant Program', *Transplantation Proceedings,* 25(1 Pt 2): 1699–701.

MORI Health Research Unit (1995) *Report of a Two Year Study into Reasons for Relatives' Refusal of Organ Donation.* London: Department of Health.

Orasanu, J. and Connolly, T. (1993) 'The reinvention of decision making', in G.A. Klein, J. Orasanu, R. Calderwood and C.E. Zsambok (eds), *Decision Making in Action: Models and Methods.* Norwood, NJ: Ablex. pp. 3–20.

Parkes, C.M. (1993) 'Bereavement as a psychosocial transition: Processes of adaptation to change' in M.S. Stroebe, W. Stroebe and R.O. Hansson (eds), *Handbook of Bereavement: Theory, Research and Intervention.* Cambridge: Cambridge University Press. pp. 91–101.

Pelletier, M. (1992) 'The organ donor family members' perception of stressful situations during the organ donation experience', *Journal of Advanced Nursing,* 17(1): 90–7.

Pelletier, M. (1993) 'Emotions experienced and coping strategies used by family members of organ donors', *Canadian Journal of Nursing Research,* 25(2): 63–73.

Perez-San-Gregorio, M.A., Blanco-Picabia, A., Murillo-Cabezas, F., Dominguez-Roldan, J.M. and Nunez-Roldan, A. (1992) 'Psychological profile of families of severely traumatized patients: Relationship to organ donation for transplantation', *Transplantation Proceedings,* 24(1): 27–8.

Sque, M. and Payne, S.A. (1996) 'Dissonant loss: The experiences of donor relatives', *Social Science and Medicine,* 43(9): 1359–70.

Strauss, A. and Corbin, J. (1990) *Basics of Qualitative Research: Techniques and Procedures for Developing Grounded Theory.* Newbury Park, CA; SAGE.

Whittaker, M. (1990) 'Bequeath, bury or burn?', *Nursing Times,* 86(40): 34–7.

REPORT 4

Arguing about Racism in Discussion Forums about Gypsies: A Reflective Account of a Discourse Analysis Study

Simon Goodman and Lottie Rowe

This reflective report provides an example of a discourse analytic study. The study addresses the ways in which opposition towards Gypsies is debated, with particular regard to whether or not this opposition constitutes racism or prejudice. Data from internet discussion forums about Gypsies were subjected to critical discursive psychological analysis. The analysis demonstrated that opposition towards Gypsies can be presented as racist. However when such accusations were made, contributors to the forums responded with criticism and dissociated themselves from being presented as racist. Nevertheless there was an acceptance that opposition to Gypsies may constitute prejudice. This prejudice was presented as an inevitable result of Gypsies' behaviour and appeared to be deemed acceptable. Across the report, reflections are offered on discourse analysis (what it offers that other approaches do not), aspects of discourse analytic research relevant to the study (the use of internet data and associated ethical issues) and on writing up discourse analytic research (what to include in a literature review and how much data to cite when presenting analyses).

Introduction

This report addresses the ways in which opposition towards Gypsies is debated, with a focus on whether or not this opposition constitutes racism or prejudice. First we show that Gypsies are a vulnerable group who are subject to prejudice and discrimination. Next we introduce the discursive literature on prejudice, with particular attention given to developments that have shown that making accusations of racism may be as problematic as racist comments themselves. As a result of this, we make the case for addressing the ways in which talk about racism and prejudice is managed in an online discussion forum about Gypsies.

The term 'Gypsy' (which will be used throughout this report) refers to Travellers and Romany people, who are recognized as an ethnic group in the United Kingdom under the Race Relations Act 1976 (amended in 2000). There is a wealth of literature that shows that Gypsies are a vulnerable group who suffer discrimination throughout Europe (for example, Marcu and Chryssochoou, 2005) and in the UK (Ellis and McWhirter, 2008). Gypsies are nevertheless presented negatively in media and political spheres (Schneeweis, 2010).

Throughout its history, discursive approaches within psychology have focused on the ways in which prejudice and racism are managed in talk. Billig (1988: 95) described the 'norm against prejudice' in which it was demonstrated that speakers will avoid being labelled as prejudiced because this can make them appear irrational (Edwards, 2003). In their review of (critical) discursive literature on talk about prejudice, Augoustinos and Every (2007: 125–34) identify five major strategies that are used by speakers to avoid being seen to violate these norms. They described these strategies as the 'denial of prejudice', 'grounding one's views as reflecting the external world', 'positive self and negative other presentation', 'discursive deracialization' and 'liberal arguments for "illiberal" ends'.

There is, however, a problem with the way in which the terms and concepts of 'prejudice' and 'racism' are used within social psychology, including discursive psychology. The two terms are often used interchangeably with few attempts at differentiating them. Augoustinos and Every (2007), for example, offer one of the most detailed reviews of the discursive literature in this field and refer to 'the language of "race" and prejudice', using the two interchangeably. The seminal study in this area, entitled 'mapping the language of racism', refers to talk designed to 'dodge the identity of prejudice' (Wetherell and Potter, 1992: 211). Figgou and Condor (2006) point out that there is no commonly agreed definition of prejudice and instead they focus on how members of the public make sense of this and racism.

Discursive psychology has been used to address talk about Gypsies directly. Tileagă (2006) showed how such talk can be extremely prejudiced, with Gypsies (the victims) being blamed for prejudice towards them on the grounds that they are (viewed as) not just different from 'us' but also a morally inferior group that does not belong in the host nation (in this case, Romania). Leudar and Nekvapil (2000) addressed the representation of Gypsies in televised debates held in the Czech Republic. Like Tileagă, they found Gypsies to be presented as different from the majority group on the grounds that they were considered not to be normal. More recently Rowe and Goodman (2014) addressed discussion forum posts in the UK and found that Gypsies were presented as different, immoral and likely to be criminal and were described in dehumanizing ways that legitimized their harsh treatment and further exclusion from society.

However, in addition to these features of race and prejudice talk, it has also been demonstrated that there is increasingly a norm against making accusations of prejudice and racism (Goodman, 2010; van Dijk, 1992). The norm against prejudice is presented as victimizing majority groups because it is seen as preventing their freedom of speech and shutting down debate (Goodman and Burke, 2010). Those who make accusations of racism are open to criticism for what Lewis (2004) describes as 'playing the race card' and for being unfair. Burke and Goodman (2012) showed that public online discussions (in this case, on Facebook) can contain examples of talk that displays no regard or orientation to the norm against prejudice and instead can be seen as examples of 'old', unguarded prejudice where few of the strategies outlined by Augoustinos and Every (2007) are used. What this means is that discursive literature has demonstrated that (a) Gypsies can be presented in a particularly negative and prejudicial light and (b) online forums can be arenas for discussions that contain a reduced or absent norm against prejudice. Therefore an analysis of discussion forums about Gypsies promises to be a fertile source of unguarded race talk. The purpose of the present research is to build upon the discursive literature on the social construction of Gypsies while also focusing on the ways in which talk about prejudice and race are managed in this setting.

> **BOX R4.1** **What to include in a discourse analysis literature review?**
>
> It can be tricky deciding what to include in a literature review when writing up a discourse analysis study. What we chose to do here was to start by 'locating' the issue, which for us is prejudice and racism towards Gypsies. That meant providing evidence for Gypsies' harsh treatment. This section was kept very concise for this report but unfortunately there is plenty of evidence for this type of treatment. To make your argument in the literature review, you can use literature from a range of sources, including discourse analytic research but equally from quantitative studies. Next we turned to our theoretical and methodological approach which is discursive psychology. It is always good to argue what your chosen approach offers that other approaches do not and you may want to use this to critique existing literature about your topic. Make sure you finish the introduction with a statement of your research aims.

Method

The data in this report come from a larger project, which is the first discursive research that addresses the ways in which Gypsies are represented in the United Kingdom (see Rowe and Goodman, 2014). The data set consisted of three internet discussion forums. The first of these followed an article on *The Independent* newspaper's website, entitled 'No Blacks, no dogs, no Gypsies', which highlights the prejudicial treatment of Gypsies in the UK. [1] The second forum followed an article on *The Sun* newspaper's website entitled 'Paradise lost to

---

[1] http://www.independent.co.uk/news/uk/home-news/no-blacks-no-dogsno-gypsies-860873.html [at the time of writing, the comments accompanying the article are no longer accessible].

> ## BOX R4.2 — Collection and selection of internet data
>
> The data selection process was led by the research topic. We conducted a search for internet discussion forums related to newspaper articles and television programmes that focused on Gypsies and Travellers. We adopted this approach because the media has been a dominant component of previous research regarding the presentation of Gypsies and discussion forums provide opportunities for people to respond to relevant articles or programmes. These forums can give access to a diverse collection of views. Usually we know little for certain about individual contributors' backgrounds because contributions are usually made anonymously, with contributors using pseudonyms. This need not be a major problem because we are trying to get a sense of the common and diverse ways in which Gypsies are discussed rather than trying to get a representative sample of participants. Another advantage of discussion forums is that they allow for the collection of interactional discourse (that is, discussion between people) without any intervention from the researcher shaping the discussion. They can therefore be regarded as 'naturally occurring' data (see Chapter 10 in this volume for more on the debate about the use of 'naturally occurring' and researcher-generated data in discourse analytic research). Overall, as sources of data, discussion forums (especially newspaper discussion forums) are non-restrictive, free, readily available and easy to access.

JCB gypsies', which described the local response to Gypsies laying the foundations for a permanent caravan site.[2] The third forum followed an article on the website 'Foreigners in the UK', entitled 'Gypsy child thieves: controversy over BBC documentary'[3] which responded to a television documentary called 'Gypsy child thieves'[4] and argued that the documentary represented Gypsies in unfair and prejudicial ways. Data were collected in the summer of 2010 and the comments were left between May 2009 and June 2010. The posts are presented here as they appeared in the discussion forums so any spelling or grammatical errors remain. The only alteration is that line numbers have been added to help keep track of data during the analysis (and to make it easier for us to show readers what our interpretations relate to). Links to the original forum sites can be found in the footnotes in this report, although, at the time of writing, *The Independent*'s forum is no longer available to view.

---

[2]http://www.thesun.co.uk/sol/homepage/news/article2446669.ece.

[3]http://www.foreignersinuk.co.uk/blog-videoblog-gypsy_child_thieves_controversy_over_bbc_documentary_1383.html.

[4]http://www.bbc.co.uk/programmes/b00mkjyd.

Initial analysis of the data identified interesting talk about what is meant by prejudice and racism, which is analysed in detail here. The approach to analysis that we adopted here is critical discursive psychology (Wetherell, 1998) (for more on this, see Chapter 10 in this volume). Attention is paid to what is accomplished by the comments in the discussion forums, that is, their 'action orientation' and function, rather than using them as ways of trying to assess what the contributors may or may not think. As this analysis gives specific attention to the ways in which 'racism' and 'prejudice' are made topics of discussion and are then managed in discussion, extracts were chosen based on explicit arguments about the use of these concepts. Therefore the extracts featured in this analysis are all of those that contain explicit references to and include arguments about, 'race', 'racism' or 'prejudice'.

BOX R4.3

Ethical considerations: should you gain permission and consent before using data from online sources?

A key ethical question to think about when using discussion forums as a data source is whether there is a need to gain permission and consent from those who own or manage the forums. As we saw in Chapter 3 in this volume, obtaining consent from research participants is normally a core consideration for ethical research. However, the data collected for this project were available online within the public domain and membership of the discussion forum was not required in order to view the comments. Therefore we did not seek explicit permission and consent from owners or managers of the forums. Furthermore, the contributors' user names were not altered in our report because it was assumed that these were pseudonyms rather than contributors' real names. These decisions reflect standard practice with this type of publicly available data. Different considerations arise when the data are in some sense 'semi-public'. For example, Burke and Goodman's (2012) discourse analytic research used data from Facebook but permission was obtained from the administrators of relevant Facebook groups before using data from those groups.

Findings

Three distinct ways of talking about racism and prejudice were identified. These are (1) making direct accusations of racism; (2) responding to accusations of racism; and (3) attempts to reposition racism. Each of these will be addressed briefly in turn. Readers who wish to see a more extensive analysis are directed to the article in which we originally presented this research (Goodman and Rowe, 2014).

Direct accusation of racism

This first section of the analysis addresses the ways in which direct accusations of racism were made in the discussion forums. The extract below, which contains a direct accusation of racism, is taken from the forum on *The Sun*'s website.

Extract 1: *The Sun* – bessie83

1	What a racist bunch of idiots. Gypsies are recognised as a distinct ethinic minority!
2	GOD FORBID they build on land they own! Is this not what people do with land
3	they own. God forbid they would want basic sanitation for their children and
4	washing facilties. Of course they pay road tax and insurance on cars, im sure
5	gypsies have to abide by laws like anyone else. The ignorant attitudes on this
6	forum are appalling and enrage me!!

This post begins with an explicit and insulting accusation directed towards all those who have posted previously on this discussion forum. Here the racism is presented as self-evident and as unacceptable to the extent that it merits insulting people who have made such comments because it so strongly violates the norm against prejudice (Billig, 1988). After the initial comment, the writer goes on to account for why these comments are deemed to be so offensive by presenting Gypsies as an ethnic minority. It therefore follows that members of ethnic minorities are constructed as people who should be protected from racism, a point that is emphasized through the use of the exclamation mark (line 1). The contributor then goes on to suggest that Gypsies should be free to build on their own land, a point that is made with the sarcastic use of the phrase 'GOD FORBID' which is emphasized through the use of the capitalized form (which tends to denote shouting in online communications). A rhetorical question is used to suggest that Gypsies building on their own land is reasonable. The appeal to the interests of Gypsy children presents a moral argument for right of Gypsies, similar to that identified in the support of asylum seekers though the use of appeals to supporting families (Goodman, 2007). As in other examples, Gypsies are presented as being law-abiding citizens (lines 4–5) who make a positive contribution to their country through the paying of taxes. The post ends by accusing those who are deemed to be making the 'racist' comments of ignorance, which is a common feature of more direct accusations of racism in online settings (Burke and Goodman, 2012). Those comments are presented in a very negative light ('appalling' – line 6) and are deemed worthy of a negative emotional response.

This analysis has shown that in these forums there are examples of direct accusations of racism directed towards those who oppose Gypsies. The next section, however, demonstrates the ways in which other participants in the forums respond to such accusations.

Responding to accusations of racism

This next section begins with a direct response to the previous extract, in which making accusations of racism is strongly criticized.

Extract 2: *The Sun* – Thicko

1   Bessie83 – You are clearly the ignorant one here. Branding people racist is so
2   pathetic and old.

This extract begins by directly addressing 'bessie83', the poster responsible for the previous extract. The contributor here takes issue with the reference to ignorance (extract 1, line 5) and turns it around so that 'bessie83' is presented as ignorant instead. The reason for this counter-claim comes next, in the charge that making accusations of racism is problematic (here 'pathetic' and 'old'). This post therefore demonstrates an example of the orientation to accusations of racism as problematic (for example, Goodman, 2010). It is noteworthy that the contributor here does not engage with any of bessie83's other arguments that are based around a more positive and sympathetic portrayal of Gypsies; it is only the explicit accusation that is singled out for criticism. This adds further weight to the existence of a taboo about making accusations of racism. Indeed, in this post, the lack of awareness of this taboo displayed in the previous post is used as the grounds to challenge and insult the author of the accusation. This analysis provides an example of a contributor going to rhetorical lengths to deny racism and to suggest that making accusations of racism is problematic and unacceptable.

BOX R4.4	How much data to present in discourse analysis reports?

It can be difficult to decide how much data to include in a report on research which used discourse analysis. You need to provide data extracts to illustrate and ground your analyses and interpretations. When you have analysed data from people engaged in conversation or discussion, you will be focusing on how they negotiate whatever it is that you are interested in (such as constructions of Gypsies, racism and prejudice) through their talk. This means that you will usually need to provide data extracts in which two or more speakers negotiate together. These extracts may be quite lengthy.

Regardless of whether you are writing a dissertation, a journal article or a book chapter, you will always have to conform to a word limit. This can mean that you have to compromise about how many data extracts to include, which can leave you dissatisfied about how thoroughly you have grounded your analyses in data for the reader. This applies in this present short report where we have only been able to present a few brief data extracts. More broadly, you will need to make a subjective decision about what needs to be included in your report. It is often impossible to include all your interesting findings in one report, so it can make more sense to focus on one or two elements that most powerfully address your research question and do these really well. In the analysis that we have presented in this report, it was necessary to include three sections as they develop to tell the 'story' that we considered to be interesting. In the original article (Goodman and Rowe, 2014), we have at least two extracts in each section to show that there are common (arguably generalizable) features of each of the strategies that we identified.

This dilemma about how to fit the presentation of your analyses within what always feels like a restrictive word limit is not specific to the reporting of discourse analytic research. Whether you have done IPA, thematic analysis, grounded theory, narrative analysis or discourse analysis, you will need to make strategic decisions about what to focus on when presenting your work (and what to report only in outline or omit altogether) and how much data to cite.

Repositioning racism as prejudice

In this final extract, racism is once again denied but this time prejudice towards Gypsies is not denied; instead it is accepted.

Extract 3: *The Independent* – kuma2000

```
1    Maybe it is prejudice. But its prejudice derived from experience not hearsay. But it
2    is NOT racism. That is throwing in a buzzword that is designed to provoke a
3    reaction of denial, you could do the same thing by saying "all people who hate
4    Travellers are paedophiles" and get a similar immediate reaction. My multiple
5    experiences of different Traveller groups found them to be people who have a
6    complete disregard for the people around them. They expect us to provide free
7    campsites for them and to pay to clean up the filth and mess they leave around our
8    houses and workplaces when they decide to leave and to turn a blind eye to the
9    things that go coincidentally go missing when they are around
```

This extract begins with a partial acceptance of the suggestion that opposition to Gypsies is prejudiced. This is signalled through the term 'maybe' which is a 'hedging' term that neither fully denies nor confirms that this is the case. However, the next sentence does concede that this opposition is caused by prejudice (signalled through the 'but') which changes the meaning of the previous 'maybe' to an acceptance. This prejudice is accounted for in a way that is designed to present the speaker as rational rather than bigoted on the grounds of 'experience' (line 1). Claims which invoke experience to support them are difficult for others to argue against, especially if they cannot make similar claims to relevant experience to support their position. What this means here is that prejudice based on 'hearsay' (line 1) is deemed irrational and wrong whereas prejudice based on experience is understandable and acceptable. Interestingly, this statement is followed with an explicit denial that this opposition is racist (line 2) which is emphasized through the capitalization of 'NOT' (line 2).

As in the previous extract, accusations of racism are presented as unreasonable (Goodman, 2010; van der Valk, 2003) – indeed, more so than experience-informed prejudice. Accusations of racism are presented as a simplistic way of making a point and gaining a 'reaction' (line 3) that requires a denial (line 3). As is demonstrated in this extract and throughout the analysis, it is the case that accusations of racism require a denial (Augoustinos and Every, 2007; Billig, 1988). The reference to 'buzzword' (line 2) suggests that these accusations are simplistic and easy to make but that they are also unwarranted. After this criticism, the writer goes on to liken accusations of racism to accusations of being a sex offender (line 4), something that is claimed would also require a denial. While it is the case that there is a norm against paedophilia as there is against racism, by drawing a comparison between the two it is suggested that racism is a baseless and unfair accusation to make that will be damaging to those at whom it is directed. The implication here is that accusations of racism are made in situations (such as those where groups like Gypsies are criticized) where there are no grounds for making such claims. Here the 'racism' is removed from opposition to minority groups.

A number of reasons for taking issue with Gypsies are given, based in personal experience. Gypsies (here 'Travellers') are presented as the unreasonable group because they have no regard for others. They are presented as freeloading (lines 6–7) and dirty (line 7) and as thieves (line 9). Throughout this post, an 'us and them' distinction is used to position Gypsies as very different to and worse than settled communities. Although racism is denied, it is conceded that opposition is due to prejudice (albeit prejudice grounded in personal experience) and Gypsies are nevertheless presented in a particularly negative way.

Discussion

In the first extract, it was shown that what has been described as the norm against prejudice (Billig, 1988) was operating so that the harsh treatment and criticism of Gypsies can be labelled as problematic and, in particular, racist. This norm was invoked by contributors to the forum who were arguing for a more positive stance towards Gypsies. Here racism is presented as extremely negative and as the grounds on which to justify anger, shock and resistance. The norm against prejudice towards other groups is invoked to bolster the strength of a norm against prejudice towards Gypsies.

In the second extract, it was shown how contributors to the forums deal directly with accusations of racism in a way that presents the accusations as unwarranted and unfair. In this case accusations are presented as problematic because they are baseless insults that prevent proper engagement with an issue. This post contains a counter-insult (including ignorance and being pathetic) but contains no rhetorical effort to suggest that there is no prejudice or hatred directed towards Gypsies. This means that it is only 'racism' that is rejected, not hatred or prejudice. So while the label 'racism' is strongly rejected, there is a lack of orientation to the norm against prejudice, as prejudice towards Gypsies remains unchallenged.

BOX R4.5	**Embracing the messiness of talk – what discourse analysis offers that other methods cannot**

One of the great things about discourse analysis is the way in which issues that can be methodological problems for other methods and approaches (both qualitative and quantitative) become the main focus of interest. Where varying attitudes might cause a problem for a questionnaire study and IPA alike, discourse analysis expects and embraces variation because it is where this variation occurs that controversies and debates can be really understood (Potter and Wetherell, 1987). In our research, having people simultaneously claim that something is prejudiced and not racist provided the opportunity to look at how contributors to discussion forums (and therefore members of the public with an interest in these issues) understand and construct these topics. This was seen to be done in ways that appear to justify the harsh treatment of a minority group in a previously unidentified way. No other research approach would have allowed us to gain this understanding.

It is the final extract that contains the most striking finding which is that there is an acceptance that opposition to Gypsies may indeed be due to prejudice but explicitly not racism. This suggests a hierarchy of opposition to out-groups whereby racism is the most extreme form. This is signalled by the post orienting to racism as problematic. No posts contained an acceptance that the writer is racist or any suggestion that racism is acceptable. There is therefore evidence in this data of a norm against *racism*. However, next in this hierarchy comes prejudice, something oriented to as less severe than racism and something that is not denied. Within the final extract in this analysis, there is a distinction (see Billig, 1985) made between prejudice based on 'hearsay' and prejudice based on experience, so in this data set the hierarchy seems to be racism, prejudice based on hearsay and experience-informed prejudice. It is this experience-informed prejudice that is presented as acceptable and something that does not require a denial. The lack of rhetorical work to deny prejudice towards Gypsies could demonstrate that prejudice against Gypsies is socially acceptable. Acknowledging prejudice in the service of denying racism is a novel finding. This has implications for (social) psychologists in general: it has been shown that it is important to make a proper distinction between prejudice and racism.

These findings have major implications for the discursive literature on prejudice and racism. While the taboo against prejudice (Billig, 1988) has remained a consistent and robust finding throughout discursive psychology, this research has shown that in the specific context of discussion forums about Gypsies in the UK, the taboo against prejudice does not seem to operate. Instead there is a hierarchy of prejudices where only racism is deemed too extreme to acknowledge (van Dijk, 1993), whereas prejudice towards Gypsies is not denied but rather is presented as an inevitable outcome that is blamed on the actions of the Gypsies themselves. This has worrying implications for the treatment of Gypsies, who have been shown to be a particularly vulnerable group of people. It appears that when it comes to Gypsies, the norm against prejudice is suspended so that this talk is an example of 'discourse that denies, rationalizes and excuses the dehumanization and marginalization of, and discrimination against' Gypsies (Every and Augoustinos, 2007: 412), much to the detriment of this group and those who campaign for their rights.

SUMMARY

This report has provided an illustration of how a discourse analysis study might be conducted and presented, with reflections on discourse analysis, aspects of the research process and writing up discourse analytic research. Although we used a particular form of discourse analysis (critical discursive psychology), research which has used other forms could be presented in much the same way. We hope that this report, alongside Chapters 10 and 11, helps to demystify discourse analysis for readers, shows how discourse analysis can produce important, new insights on contemporary issues and encourages readers to undertake their own discourse analytic research.

References

Augoustinos, M. and Every, D. (2007) 'The language of "race" and prejudice: A discourse of denial, reason, and liberal-practical politics', *Journal of Language and Social Psychology*, 26(2): 123–41.
Billig, M. (1985) 'Prejudice, categorization and particularization: From a perceptual to a rhetorical approach', *European Journal of Social Psychology*, 15(1): 79–103.

Billig, M. (1988) 'The notion of "prejudice": Some rhetorical and ideological aspects', *Text: Interdisciplinary Journal for the Study of Discourse*, 8(1–2): 91–110.

Burke, S. and Goodman, S. (2012) '"Bring back Hitler's gas chambers": Asylum seeking, Nazis and Facebook – a discursive analysis', *Discourse & Society*, 23(1): 19–33.

Edwards, D. (2003) 'Analyzing racial discourse: The discursive psychology of mind–world relationships', in H. van den Berg, M. Wetherell and H. Houtkoop-Steenstra (eds), *Analyzing Race Talk: Multidisciplinary Approaches to the Interview*. Cambridge: Cambridge University Press. pp. 31–48.

Ellis, G. and McWhirter, C. (2008) 'Land-use planning and Traveller-Gypsies: Towards non-prejudicial practice', *Planning and Practice Research*, 23(1): 77–99.

Every, D. and Augoustinos, M. (2007) 'Constructions of racism in the Australian parliamentary debates on asylum seekers', *Discourse & Society*, 18(4): 411–36.

Figgou, L. and Condor, S. (2006) 'Irrational categorization, natural intolerance and reasonable discrimination: Lay representations of prejudice and racism', *British Journal of Social Psychology*, 45(2): 219–43.

Goodman, S. (2007) 'Constructing asylum seeking families', *Critical Approaches to Discourse Analysis across Disciplines*, 1(1): 35–49.

Goodman, S. (2008) 'The generalizability of discursive research', *Qualitative Research in Psychology*, 5(4): 265–75.

Goodman, S. (2010) '"It's not racist to impose limits on immigration": Constructing the boundaries of racism in the asylum and immigration debate', *Critical Approaches to Discourse Analysis across Disciplines*, 4(1): 1–17.

Goodman, S. and Burke, S. (2010) '"Oh you don't want asylum seekers, oh you're just racist": A discursive analysis of discussions about whether it's racist to oppose asylum seeking', *Discourse & Society*, 21(3): 325–40.

Goodman, S. and Rowe, L. (2014) '"Maybe it is prejudice ... but it is NOT racism": Negotiating racism in discussion forums about Gypsies', *Discourse & Society*, 25(1): 32–46.

Leudar, I. and Nekvapil, J. (2000) 'Presentations of Romanies in the Czech media: On category work in television debates', *Discourse & Society*, 11(4): 487–513.

Lewis, A. (2004) '"What group?" Studying whiteness in the era of "colour blindness"', *Sociological Theory*, 22(4): 623–46.

Marcu, A. and Chryssochoou, X. (2005) 'Exclusion of ethnic groups from the realm of humanity: Prejudice against the Gypsies in Britain and in Romania', *Psicología Política*, 30: 41–56.

Potter, J. and Wetherell, M. (1987) *Discourse and Social Psychology: Beyond Attitudes and Behaviour*. London: SAGE.

Rowe, L. and Goodman, S. (2014) '"A stinking filthy race of people inbred with criminality": A discourse analysis of prejudicial talk about Gypsies in discussion forums', *Romani Studies*, 24(1): 25–42.

Schneeweis, A. (2010) 'Talking differences: Discourse about the Gypsy/Roma in Europe since 1989', *Humanities and Social Sciences*, 70(9): 32–52.

Tileagă, C. (2006) 'Representing the "other": A discursive analysis of prejudice and moral exclusion in talk about Romanies', *Journal of Community & Applied Social Psychology*, 16(1): 19–41.

van der Valk, I. (2003) 'Political discourse on ethnic minority issues: A comparison of the right and the extreme right in the Netherlands and France (1990–97)', *Ethnicities*, 3(2): 183–213.

van Dijk, T.A. (1992) 'Discourse and the denial of racism', *Discourse & Society*, 3(1): 87–118.

van Dijk, T.A. (1993) 'Denying racism: Elite discourse and racism', in J. Solomos and J. Wrench (eds), *Racism and Migration in Western Europe*. Oxford: Berg. pp. 179–93.

Wetherell, M. (1998) 'Positioning and interpretative repertoires: Conversation analysis and post-structuralism in dialogue', *Discourse & Society*, 9(3): 387–412.

Wetherell, M. and Potter, J. (1992) *Mapping the Language of Racism: Discourse and the Legitimation of Exploitation*. Hemel Hempstead: Harvester Wheatsheaf.

REPORT 5

The Effects of Surfing and the Natural Environment on the Well-Being of Combat Veterans: A Reflective Account of a Narrative Analysis Study

Nick Caddick, Brett Smith and Cassandra Phoenix

The aim of this report is to provide the reader with an insight into how one form of narrative analysis – dialogical narrative analysis (Frank, 2010, 2012) – might be conducted and written up as a journal article or dissertation. The report summarizes research conducted by Caddick, Smith and Phoenix (2015) on the effects of surfing and the natural environment on combat veterans experiencing post-traumatic stress disorder. The original project used narrative to explore the veterans' life stories and the role of surfing in their post-trauma lives. The project also integrated insights from phenomenology to explore in greater depth the physical and sensory details of the veterans' surfing experiences and how these were storied by the participants. This report provides a truncated version of the original paper, interspersed with reflections on the process of doing a dialogical narrative analysis.

Introduction

The concept of 'Blue Gym' (Depledge and Bird, 2009) captures the notion of being active in natural-water environments and encapsulates various forms of activity such as swimming or surfing in the sea, kayaking and fishing in lakes and rivers, or simply walking along the coast. As Smith and Sparkes (2012: 343) suggested, 'this moves traditional notions of the gym as an indoor, machine-filled contained physical place and space to conceptualising it as part of our multi-sensory natural environment, city surroundings or maritime culture'. The Blue Gym thus conveys an environment and set of activities through which people might become active and connect with nature in ways that could positively influence their health. However, because there is currently very little research in this area, the capacity of the Blue Gym to influence *psychological* health and well-being is empirically unknown.

Our purpose in this research was to explore how surfing – as one application of the Blue Gym concept – could influence well-being among a group of combat veterans experiencing post-traumatic stress disorder (PTSD). PTSD is the term used to describe the psychological and emotional distress that some combat veterans experience following traumatic events in war. Research conducted with combat veterans has revealed that PTSD is associated with diminished well-being, poorer mental and physical health functioning and increased risk of suicide (for example, Jakupcak et al., 2009). Such findings powerfully illustrate the negative personal consequences of war for some veterans and underscore the need to provide support for those experiencing PTSD.

Moreover, the need for support is reinforced by suggestions that the prevalence of PTSD among US troops returning from Iraq and Afghanistan could be as high as 31 per cent (Tanielian and Jaycox, 2008). In the UK, research has indicated that the rate of PTSD among combat-deployed troops is around 6.9 per cent (Fear et al., 2010). However, given the widely reported influence of stigma in restricting service members – both active and retired – from seeking treatment for PTSD (for example, Green et al., 2010), this figure is likely to underestimate the scale of mental health need among UK combat veterans.

The central research question we explored was: 'What effect did surfing and the natural environment have on veterans' well-being?' Furthermore, we considered how and why these effects occurred. We aimed to answer these questions by engaging with veterans' personal stories and by seeking detailed descriptions of their lived experiences of surfing. Accordingly, we chose a narrative approach.

BOX R5.1 Reflecting on the introduction

As with many qualitative studies published as a realist tale (Sparkes and Smith, 2014), we have begun by introducing the reader to the background of the study and the context of the research. As part of this, we defined key terms like 'PTSD' that will recur throughout the report. However, we decided that it was important to introduce the particular version of narrative analysis we were working with. Given that the field of narrative inquiry is methodologically diverse with many different varieties of analysis (see Holstein and Gubrium, 2012), we felt it was incumbent on us as researchers to describe the assumptions underpinning our approach to narrative as part of our introduction. This was particularly so given that our approach included a relatively novel strategy of combining narrative with phenomenology in what we characterized as a 'phenomenologically inspired narrative analysis' (for more on phenomenology, see Chapters 2 and 4 in this volume). Narrative researchers can avoid confusion about what is meant by 'narrative' by introducing their approach early in their write-up.

A narrative approach involves studying the stories people tell of their lives and experiences (Smith and Sparkes, 2009) (see Chapters 12 and 13 in this volume). Narrative is an important topic for qualitative health researchers because, as Frank (2010) suggested, stories are more than simply passive representations of people's lives; they *do* things. Narratives have the capacity to act on, in and for people in ways that can have both positive and dangerous implications for their psychological health. Narratives act on people in the sense that they constitute certain emotions, beliefs and practices as appropriate in the context of a particular story while others are necessarily rejected or set aside. They act by shaping our awareness of what good psychological health is and can be and also what behaviours are seen as important for promoting psychological health.

Like Frank (2010: 21), we reject an understanding of narrative whereby 'stories imitate life that has already happened and now is being represented in the story'. Rather, we see stories as shaping what becomes experience. This said, we readily acknowledge that people's everyday experience is of a physical world in which their embodied actions – their fleshy, physical and sentient capabilities – have the power to influence their lives. People's experiences, therefore, also influence the stories they tell to represent those experiences. As Frank (2010: 21) put it, 'mimesis [imitation] happens, but as a reciprocal process. Life and story imitate each other, ceaselessly and seamlessly, but neither enjoys temporal or causal precedence.' Thus, narrative shapes experience and experience also shapes narrative, continuously and recursively.

Focusing purely on narrative, however, can sometimes obscure the fleshy physicality of people's lived experience, subsuming it as the product of a story. Our desire was to understand not only how stories shaped the veterans' surfing experiences and influenced well-being but also the visceral and embodied qualities of veterans' active engagement with surfing and the Blue Gym. Accordingly, we attempted to draw out veterans' embodied and sensory experiences of surfing using phenomenological theory and principles, primarily the work of Merleau-Ponty (1962). We thus describe our approach as a phenomenologically inspired narrative analysis.

Method

Sampling and participants

We used purposive sampling to recruit participants for this study from a UK-based veterans' surfing charity. Fifteen male combat veterans (aged between 27 and 60 years) gave informed consent to participate in the study. Ten out of the 15 had been diagnosed with PTSD. Being officially diagnosed with PTSD was not a requirement for inclusion in our study given that PTSD is a contested category of disorder and could arguably be viewed as the medicalization of veterans' suffering (Summerfield, 2004). Regardless of diagnosis, however, all the participants referred to themselves as living with PTSD. One additional participant was a former member of the civilian emergency services who was diagnosed with PTSD and was a member of the charity. Ethical approval for the research was granted by a university ethics committee.

Data collection

Our research design was an iterative process of data collection and analysis, which included the write-up of our findings (Frank, 2012; Sparkes and Smith, 2014). To begin, we used two forms of data collection concurrently to generate rich, storied data. The first was interviews. All participants were involved in semi-structured life history interviews, conducted face-to-face between Nick Caddick and the participants, either in a participant's home or in the charity's headquarters. In each of these encounters, Nick encouraged participants to tell stories about how they had lived their lives over time, providing us with detailed insights into their personal and social lives (Sparkes and Smith, 2014). He used a semi-structured interview guide in a flexible manner to help stimulate reflection on important topics.

The second method was participant observation (Sparkes and Smith, 2014). This entailed the researcher (Nick) observing and participating in the daily activities of the veterans during 18 of the charity's twice weekly surf camps and during three residential weeks in which Nick actively immersed himself in the group environment and joined in their activities which included surfing each day, coastal walks and yoga/meditation sessions. Following a period of observation, Nick documented the findings in field notes, resulting in approximately 90 hours of observational data. We used the method of participant observation because it enabled us to gain insight into the mundane, typical and occasionally extraordinary features of everyday life in the context of the group (Sparkes and Smith, 2014). Furthermore, combining interviews with participant observation was useful for us to build a more complex account of participants' lives and the socio-cultural worlds they inhabited.

BOX R5.2	Collecting data and inviting stories

Interviewing for narrative research projects generally works best when the researcher remains open to the participant and invites her or him to tell stories about their life. This often begins with what is called a 'grand tour' question or invitation such as 'Tell me about your life'. While it is often useful to draw from a list of questions as prompts for topical discussion, too much structure in an interview guide can easily disrupt the flow of participants' storytelling. The researcher needs to be willing to follow the participants' lead rather than rigorously pursuing answers to particular questions in the way that a political interviewer might do. If interviewing on sensitive topics, it is also good ethical practice to allow the participant her or himself to define the boundaries of what she or he wishes to talk about and what stories to tell (for more on ethics in qualitative research, see Chapter 3 in this volume).

It is equally worth pointing out that stories are not simply told in interview settings: they are lived and enacted in everyday life. In this study, combining interviews with participant observation enabled us to remain alert to the ways in which the stories participants told in the interviews guided their actions in and beyond the social environment of the charity. For example, observing how the veterans responded to the activity of surfing and how they interacted with each other afterwards can be conceptualized as stories being lived and embodied in practice within the social milieu. Considering how veterans' actions formed part of their unfolding stories was a key component of this study's methodology.

Data analysis

We analysed our data through the lens of dialogical narrative analysis (DNA) (see Chapters 12 and 13 in this volume). In a DNA, as described by Frank (2010, 2012), the analyst examines stories not as mere products of telling but as 'actors' that do things for and to people. The analyst first considers what type of story is being told and how that story is structured. He/she then seeks to understand 'the mirroring between what is told in the story – the story's content – and what happens as a result of telling that story – its effects' (Frank, 2010: 71–2). Furthermore, in DNA stories are understood as artful representations of people's lives (Frank, 2012). Recognising this, the dialogical narrative analyst attempts to understand the reasons why a person chooses to represent their life using a particular story and what the storyteller does by telling that story.

The iterative process of doing the DNA (see Frank, 2012) began with Nick immersing himself in the data by reading and closely re-reading the interview transcripts and field notes to gain familiarity with the data. He then marked up the transcripts and field notes with conceptual comments which included, for example, notes on the type of stories being told by the veterans and how and why the stories were told in this way. Next the researchers collectively considered the data in relation to various dialogical questions (Frank, 2012), which we asked to illuminate the effects that stories were having on the veterans' lives. Such questions included 'What resources does the storyteller draw upon to shape their subjectivity?' and 'What is at stake for the teller in a particular story?' (Frank, 2012). In addition to these dialogical questions, we asked how the veterans' stories were grounded in their embodied and sensory experiences of surfing and the natural environment (Hockey and Allen-Collinson, 2007). We thus sought to incorporate within our analysis a phenomenology of the body and the senses, revealing through their stories how the veterans experienced their being-in-the-world in relation to surfing and the elements (Hockey and Allen-Collinson, 2007; Merleau-Ponty, 1962). Throughout the analysis, Nick used theoretical and procedural memos to record emerging analytical ideas and interpretations of the data. One role of the other researchers (Brett and Cassandra) in this process was to act as 'critical friends' who each provided a different theoretical sounding board and encouraged reflection on interpretations as they emerged in relation to the data.

BOX R5.3	A method of questioning

Frank (2010: 72) suggested that 'some methods are more useful for the questions they offer than for any procedures they prescribe'. Dialogical narrative analysis is best conceptualized as a method of questioning rather than a set of procedures to follow. Asking questions about the stories that participants tell and enact helps us to consider how these stories might be acting in their lives. As shown in Chapter 13 in this volume, such questions can include 'What sense of identity is being shaped by the participant's story?', 'What resources does the participant draw on to construct their story?' and 'Who does the participants' story connect them to or disconnect them from?' Answering such questions can feel daunting given the lack of procedural guidance in DNA as a method. Perhaps the best way of seeking answers is simply to write. Unlike methods where writing occurs at the end of the project as a way of reporting findings, DNA prioritises writing itself as a form of analysis. The researcher should write continuously throughout the analytic process, musing on possible answers to the questions they pose about participants' stories. Then, as their analytical thoughts begin to emerge through drafting and re-drafting, these will feed into the writing of the final report.

Findings

Experiencing respite from PTSD

All the participants spoke at length of the suffering they encountered associated with PTSD. Consistent with symptoms of PTSD (American Psychiatric Association, 2000), this suffering typically involved the traumatic reliving of combat events through nightmares and flashbacks, a sense of being constantly anxious or on alert, problems with anger and/or alcohol and a profound sense of morbid sadness. The veterans experienced these symptoms as an exhausting cycle of suffering that dominated their everyday lives and kept PTSD at the forefront of their thoughts and awareness. There was, however, one activity – surfing – that enabled the veterans to push PTSD into the background and experience a sense of respite from suffering, as exemplified in the following veteran's comments:

It frees you up. It's freedom for those two or three hours, kind of like a bit of respite. It takes your mind off it. Just leave all that away somewhere on the beach and then, we'll deal with that later. But for now, when we're surfing, we're going to have a laugh. And there's not a lot you can do to not have a laugh – it's kind of the antidote to PTSD in a way. You know, get your wetsuit on, go for a paddle, ride a wave and it's like PTSD doesn't exist for that short time, which is all good in my book.

BOX R5.4 — Selecting stories for analysis

For Frank (2012), selecting the stories on which to focus your analysis is a crucial issue in DNA. If you have a relatively homogeneous group of participants (as we did because all participants were members of the same charity), you may hear the same story or stories repeated time and time again by the participants. In this case, selecting the story on which to focus your analysis mainly involves identifying that story (see Chapter 13 for guidance) and considering what the story is about. If you have multiple participants belonging to different groups or subcultures, you may hear different stories being told. The choice of which stories to focus on can be made through the practical wisdom derived through analytic experience – what Flyvbjerg (2001) refers to as 'phronesis'. This involves hearing how stories you have collected speak to the original research interest, representing those stories in writing and then revising which stories are chosen for analysis as the writing and the arguments develop.

Respite, as articulated by the participants, can be described as a positive feeling of release from everyday struggles associated with PTSD. The notion of respite conveys the temporary absence of trauma-related thoughts and feelings, bringing about a much-needed relief from suffering. Respite allowed the veterans to forget about PTSD or to place it on hold while they focused on enjoying the surfing experience. The story they told can thus be summarized as follows: 'I suffer from PTSD but, when surfing, for these few hours, PTSD is placed in the background and laughter/enjoyment is possible. Surfing provides a break from suffering.' Accordingly, experiencing respite did not mean that veterans expected their problems to disappear forever by going surfing. Rather, surfing provided the veterans with a welcome release or escape from the distressing PTSD symptoms that encompassed their experience of everyday life.

As part of their stories of cultivating respite through surfing, the veterans emphasized the need to go surfing regularly. Regular surfing was regarded throughout the charity's subculture as necessary for disrupting the cycle of PTSD symptoms that would otherwise remain a continuous or uninterrupted source of suffering. This notion of regularity that characterized the veterans' stories seemed to lend itself to the telling of what Riessman (1993) termed a 'habitual narrative'. This is a type of narrative in which events occur over and over and consequently there is no peak in the action. For these veterans, surfing was the repetitive event at the centre of a habitual narrative that organized their experiences temporally around regular periods of respite from PTSD. That said, the veterans also recognized that respite only 'worked' while surfing and did not extend beyond the time spent in the water.

BOX R5.5 — What to include in the findings section

What you include in the findings section will depend on what features of participants' stories appear most relevant to the effects that these stories are having in the participants' lives. You may wish to begin (as we did in this report) simply by providing a description of the dominant story or stories told by the participants. Illustrative quotations can be used to highlight the main content of the story. From there, you may continue to focus on the content of the story (*what* participants said) and how this shapes participants' everyday actions and the meanings they give to these actions. Alternatively, the structure of participants' stories (*how* they are told) may also be relevant to the work these stories do in participants' lives, thus warranting analytical attention. For example, the temporal structure of veterans' respite stories (that is, a repetitive or habitual narrative with surfing as the recurring focus of action) had the important effect of focusing participants' lives firmly in the present.

Researchers might also utilize a useful tactic called 'analytical bracketing' (Gubrium and Holstein, 2009) to alternately focus on the content and structure of stories as part of a DNA. As Sparkes and Smith (2014: 136) described, 'this is the process of moving back and forth between the *whats* and *hows* of narrativity' (emphasis in original). This gives the researcher the space needed to focus in depth on one aspect of stories while holding the other temporarily in abeyance. The researcher then 'brings the results together to produce a complex picture of narrative life'.

Furthermore, the veterans' stories gave a sense of the embodied sensations that helped to constitute the experience of respite. Consider, for example, the following exchange between the interviewer and one of the participants:

Interviewer: Can you describe what sort of effect surfing has on you psychologically?

Participant: It's just a fantastic feeling of forgetting about all my problems, worries, just forget about it and just do it. And it's just great. I always tell that to others, you know, just get down there and get in there and you'll know what I'm talking about. Because it's great.

Interviewer: And what do you think it is about surfing that's so good and makes you feel that way?

Participant: Well, it's the atmosphere, the surroundings, and also the sound I suppose as well – of the waves – because that can be used for relaxation. It calms you, helps calm you down. And the smell – there's no smell, you know, it's clean, fresh air. And then you're just focused on your waves and your board.

As Merleau-Ponty (1962) made clear, we live the world through our bodies. For the veterans, respite from PTSD was grounded in their physical bodies and channelled through the various senses, notably the aural, visual, haptic (touch) and olfactory (smell) senses. Also evident, though mentioned less frequently, was gustatory perception in the salty taste of the sea water that the veterans occasionally swallowed. The role of the senses in cultivating respite through surfing is illuminated by Merleau-Ponty's notion of 'bodily intentionality', that is, the directedness or intentional object of consciousness (what we are conscious of at any particular moment). For Merleau-Ponty, sensory perception is tied to bodily movement 'and all bodily movement is accompanied by intentionality which lies at the core of perception' (Hockey and Allen-Collinson, 2007: 117). As the veterans' stories suggest, when they moved throughout the seascape with its constantly fluid and shifting modality, the intentionality of their consciousness was no longer dominated by PTSD. Rather, it was directed outwards towards the sensory stimulations of the ocean.

Effects of surfing on well-being

Going surfing and experiencing respite influenced the veterans' sense of well-being in two key ways. First, by pushing PTSD into the background of their lives, the experience of respite through surfing protected the veterans' well-being against some of the more serious problems (such as suicide) that can be associated with PTSD. For example, another veteran commented:

It's just that escape, isn't it? Get out of that cycle of all the symptoms for a few hours. And it shows that if you don't do it, if you don't go, you end up going back downhill again, everything starts getting worse again. That's it, if you stop, you don't know where you're going to end up. A few guys who haven't been for a long time have had serious problems. You know, they come back in and they're alright. They've not cured anything but you can see the difference.

Veterans' stories of surfing as respite worked to keep the chaos of suffering far enough at bay. As Frank (2013) explained, 'chaos' is an anti-narrative whereby the teller of the story imagines life never getting better and life is swallowed up by the hopelessness of chronic suffering. As the comments above suggest, regular surfing prevented the veterans from entering a downward spiral in which they felt overwhelmed by their suffering, thus avoiding chaos. Indeed, the habitual narrative of surfing as respite from PTSD provided the veterans with an important alternative to the chaos narrative. Moreover, for some veterans, the importance of forestalling chaos was nothing less than life-saving given their reported previous contemplation of suicide as a way of ending their suffering.

In addition to holding off chaos, a second effect of surfing on well-being centred on the positive emotions it generated for the veterans. Consider, for example, the following field note recorded by Nick Caddick in August 2012 after one of the charity's weekly surf camps:

Great surf session today with the guys. As we left the water and threw our boards down on the beach, I observed two veterans high-five each other while enthusiastically discussing the best waves they caught that day. It was clear from this brief exchange that these veterans had a good time in the water, the broad grins across their faces revealing much about their enjoyment of the experience.

The veterans themselves also testified how the activity of surfing evoked in them feelings of pleasure and joy. In the words of another veteran:

The feel good effect it has is fantastic really for me. I mean, I just come out of there [sea] – one, I'm pretty knackered, and two, you got that feeling of just like 'Ahhhh, God', you know, 'That was so good'. But that feeling of – it's not just being in the water, it's like a washing away [of PTSD], you know, with the water. And especially when it gets a bit rough and you get turned over by the waves a few times, it feels like it's just pummelling it out of you or just washing it out of your system a little bit.

Addressing our central research question, these comments reveal that going surfing and experiencing respite provided the veterans with a positive boost to their well-being. Also evident was the way in which being physically immersed in the ocean environment was an intrinsic feature of the emotional benefits derived from surfing. Indeed, the body's haptic ('touch') connection with the ocean was strongly emphasized and was portrayed by the veterans as charged with emotion, for example in feeling one's troubles being 'pummelled out' by the force of the waves. Moreover, the positive emotions generated through surfing were not only experienced at the bodily level; they were also framed by the veterans' stories of surfing as respite from PTSD. This is evident in the above comment whereby the bodily feelings evoked in this veteran by his surfing experiences are couched in respite terms (for example, in feeling PTSD being washed out of his system).

How did surfing influence well-being?

The veterans' stories also revealed how surfing influenced well-being and facilitated respite from PTSD. One way in which surfing worked to facilitate respite for the participants was by keeping them focused on the present:

> For me, it's not just the couple of hours in the water. It kind of starts Monday/Tuesday and sort of doesn't really finish till I get home Wednesday. And then Thursday/Friday – fucking hell – I'm still thinking about what I did Wednesday. And then Saturday/Sunday, it's like. 'Aaaaahhhhh, fucking hell.' Yeah, so Saturday I get fucking suicidal. But do you know what I mean, you get to the point where you think, 'Aaaaahhhhh, fucking hell, Wednesday's miles away.' And then Monday, you're thinking 'Yay, only two more sleeps and it's surfing day.' So yeah, it's really good. In all, I think I've probably got more out of this in three months than I've had out the NHS [UK's National Health Service] in fucking eighteen months.

Regular surfing facilitated respite by helping the participants stay focused on experiences in the present and avoid dwelling on the traumatic memories hidden in their past. A useful way of conceptualizing this finding is through the notion of shifting time tenses (Phoenix et al., 2007) that framed the telling of participants' respite stories. For example, the problems associated with PTSD can be understood in part as a reliving of the past in the present. Regularly experiencing respite through surfing worked for the veterans by keeping the past in the past and the present in the present. That is, going surfing enabled the participants to experience time in the present and keep the traumatic memories of the past from entering their thoughts and narrative consciousness.

Discussion

Our purpose in this report was to examine the effects of surfing and the natural environment on the well-being of combat veterans. The evidence we have presented is the first to indicate that surfing and the Blue Gym could have a role to play in promoting veterans' well-being. We have also extended previous knowledge in the area of physical activity, combat veterans and PTSD (see Caddick and Smith, 2014) by highlighting how nature-based physical activity can influence the well-being of combat veterans. Specifically, we showed that experiencing regular respite and embodying this narrative through surfing can elevate well-being in combat veterans in two key ways. The first was by preventing decline into a state of embodied chaos (Frank, 2013) whereby the hopelessness of chronic suffering becomes unbearable. The second was through the positive emotions evoked by going surfing and connecting with the ocean environment.

Our research adds to the emerging literature on nature-based physical activity (for example, Mitchell, 2013) by showing how benefits to well-being are grounded in the

> ### BOX R5.6 — Concluding the analysis
>
> Concluding a DNA may well include making evaluative comments on what the stories you have analysed are doing both on and for the participants. It is likely that this will also include some reference to the conclusions drawn from previous studies in the topic area. It is worth remembering though that any ending to a DNA, whilst not necessarily tentative, must always be provisional. As indicated in Chapter 13, this is because DNA holds to a commitment of people and their stories as *unfinalized* (Frank, 2012). This means that analysis is never viewed as the 'last word' on participants' stories. The ending to a DNA should thus always remain open not only to alternative interpretations of participants' stories but also to other possibilities of how these stories might evolve and change in the future. As Frank (2012: 50) put it, 'the dialogue always continues'.

participants' embodied lived experiences of movement in and through nature. Drawing on phenomenological perspectives (for example, Merleau-Ponty, 1962), we showed that benefits to well-being are not primarily cognitive, as researchers sometimes suggest (for example, Berman et al., 2008) but are derived from fully embodied contact with and active participation in nature. In surfing, there is an intertwining of the body with the natural world that results in embodied and sensory pleasures through the multi-sensorial stimulation of being active in nature.

Furthermore, our findings highlight the usefulness of veterans' stories of respite as an alternative to the dominant medical model approach to PTSD treatment. A medical model treats PTSD as an illness to be cured or as some damaged portion of the mind or brain that requires fixing through therapy and/or psychopharmacology. It makes the problematic assumption that distress can be cured through such means – which might not be the case (Cromby et al., 2013). Accompanying the medical model is a powerful narrative that acts to shape and constrain people's stories about (and experiences of) mental health problems. This has been termed the 'restitution narrative' (Frank, 2012) and follows the basic storyline of 'Yesterday I was healthy, today I'm sick, but tomorrow I'll be healthy again'. Like the medical model that spawned it, the restitution narrative becomes problematic when a cure is not forthcoming.

The veterans in this study rejected the medical model and the notion of medical cure and instead chose to tell respite stories. They believed that their memories could not be wiped and therefore the shadow of combat trauma was always likely to remain with them in one form or another. Instead, they saw their task as one of trying to live with or adapt to PTSD as best they could. Bury's (1991) notion of adaptation to chronic illness might usefully be applied here. Following Bury, respite stories constituted a form of positive action that veterans undertook to adapt to and counter the effects of their suffering. Moreover, in pushing PTSD into the background, respite stories helped to normalize PTSD so that it was partially or temporarily bracketed off and its impact on the veterans' health and identities could be limited. Respite stories might, therefore, increase the narrative options available to veterans who are locked into a medical restitution narrative that no longer works for them. That is, should medical treatments fail make a difference to their suffering, there is another type of story to fall back on.

SUMMARY

This report has provided an illustration of how one form of narrative analysis (a dialogical narrative analysis) might be performed. It is important to note that there are many other versions of narrative analysis available in the diverse methodological field of narrative. Readers interested in this particular version are encouraged to use Chapter 13 of this book as well as the references provided in this report as key introductory readings for DNA. It is hoped that this report may serve as a useful example of how DNA could be conducted and how a DNA report could be written up – but not as a rigid guide.

References

American Psychiatric Association (2000) *Diagnostic and Statistical Manual of Mental Disorders*. Revised 4th edn. Washington, DC: American Psychiatric Association.

Berman, M.G., Jonides, J. and Kaplan, S. (2008) 'The cognitive benefits of interacting with nature', *Psychological Science*, 19(2): 1207–12.

Bury, M. (1991) 'The sociology of chronic illness: A review of research and prospects', *Sociology of Health and Illness*, 13(4): 451–68.

Caddick, N. and Smith, B. (2014) 'The impact of sport and physical activity on the well-being of combat veterans: A systematic review', *Psychology of Sport and Exercise*, 15(1): 9–18.

Caddick, N., Smith, B. and Phoenix, C. (2015) 'The effects of surfing and the natural environment on the well-being of combat veterans', *Qualitative Health Research*, 25(1): 76–86.

Cromby, J., Harper, D. and Reavey, P. (2013) *Psychology, Mental Health and Distress*. Basingstoke: Palgrave Macmillan.

Depledge, M.H. and Bird, W.J. (2009) 'The Blue Gym: Health and wellbeing from our coasts', *Marine Pollution Bulletin*, 58(7): 947–8.

Fear, N.T., Jones, M., Murphy, D., Hull, L., Iversen, A.C., Coker, B., Machell, L., Sundin, J., Woodhead, C., Jones, N., Greenberg, N., Landau, S., Dandeker, C., Rona, R.J., Hotopf, M. and Wesseley, S. (2010) 'What are the consequences of deployment to Iraq and Afghanistan on the mental health of the UK armed forces? A cohort study', *The Lancet*, 375(9728): 1783–97.

Flyvbjerg, B. (2001) *Making Social Science Matter: Why Social Inquiry Fails and How It Can Succeed Again*. Cambridge: Cambridge University Press.

Frank, A.W. (2010) *Letting Stories Breathe: A Socio-Narratology*. Chicago: University of Chicago Press.

Frank, A.W. (2012) 'Practicing dialogical narrative analysis', in J.A. Holstein and J.F. Gubrium (eds), *Varieties of Narrative Analysis*. Thousand Oaks, CA: SAGE. pp. 33–52.

Frank, A.W. (2013) *The Wounded Storyteller: Body, Illness and Ethics*. 2nd edn. Chicago: University of Chicago Press.

Green, G., Emslie, C., O'Neill, D., Hunt, K. and Walker, S. (2010) 'Exploring the ambiguities of masculinity in accounts of emotional distress in the military among young ex-servicemen', *Social Science and Medicine*, 71(8): 1480–8.

Gubrium, J.F. and Holstein, J.A. (2009). *Analyzing Narrative Reality*. Thousand Oaks, CA: SAGE.

Hockey, J. and Allen-Collinson, J. (2007) 'Grasping the phenomenology of sporting bodies', *International Review for the Sociology of Sport*, 42(2): 115–31.

Holstein, J.A. and Gubrium, J.F. (eds) (2012) *Varieties of Narrative Analysis*. Thousand Oaks, CA: SAGE.

Jakupcak, M., Cook, J., Imel, Z., Fontana, A., Rosenheck, R. and McFall, M. (2009) 'Posttraumatic stress disorder as a risk factor for suicidal ideation in Iraq and Afghanistan war veterans', *Journal of Traumatic Stress*, 22(4): 303–6.

Merleau-Ponty, M. (1962) *Phenomenology of Perception*. Trans. C. Smith. London: Routledge & Kegan Paul.

Mitchell, R. (2013) 'Is physical activity in natural environments better for mental health than physical activity in other environments?' *Social Science & Medicine*, 91(R1–R2): 130–4.

Phoenix, C., Smith, B. and Sparkes, A.C. (2007) 'Experiences and expectations of biographical time among young athletes: A life course perspective', *Time & Society*, 16(2–3): 231–52.

Riessman, C.K. (1993) *Narrative Analysis*. Newbury Park, CA: SAGE.

Smith, B. and Sparkes, A.C. (2009) 'Narrative inquiry in sport and exercise psychology: What can it mean, and why might we do it?' *Psychology of Sport and Exercise*, 10(1): 1–11.

Smith, B. and Sparkes, A.C. (2012) 'Disability, sport and physical activity: A critical review', in N. Watson, A. Roulstone and C. Thomas (eds), *Routledge Handbook of Disability Studies*. London: Routledge. pp. 336–47.

Sparkes, A.C. and Smith, B. (2014) *Qualitative Research Methods in Sport, Exercise and Health: From Process to Product*. London: Routledge.

Summerfield, D. (2004) 'Cross-cultural perspectives on the medicalization of human suffering' in G.M. Rosen (ed.), *Posttraumatic Stress Disorder: Issues and Controversies*. Chichester: John Wiley. pp. 233–45.

Tanielian, T. and Jaycox, L.H. (2008) *Invisible Wounds of War: Psychological and Cognitive Injuries, their Consequences, and Services to Assist Recovery*. Santa Monica, CA: RAND Corporation.

GLOSSARY

action orientation   a core feature of how discourse analysts view language – as performing particular social actions or functions in talk or writing, such as justifying, questioning or accusing.

anecdotalism   a non-systematic analytic practice involving reading through the data and immediately identifying some patterns, labelling these as 'themes' and selecting data extracts to support these. Anecdotalism produces a poor-quality thematic analysis.

anonymization   removing or disguising information that could identify research participants.

axial coding   an aspect of grounded theory analysis that involves hypothesizing possible relationships between categories and testing these against data.

beneficence   achieving the greatest good through research.

'Big Q' qualitative research   refers to the use of qualitative techniques, the quality of the research narrative, the 'fit' between the research question and the philosophical perspective adopted, and the method of investigation and analysis undertaken, within a qualitative paradigm that emphasizes contextualized understandings and rejects notions of objective reality or universal truth.

categories   labels given to meaningful units (words, phases, sentences or larger segments of text) that have been identified in a data set during the coding process in grounded theory analysis. 'In vivo' categories have labels that use participants' actual words.

central organizing concept   refers to a core idea or concept that underpins a theme.

code   a label given to a unit of meaning in the data (a word, phrase, sentence or larger segment of text) that captures a feature of that unit that has been noted by the researcher as being relevant to a guiding research question.

code book   the complete list of code words/labels for a research study and the meanings assigned to them.

coding drift   a risk associated with the coding stage of analysis when the researcher starts to code data in light of new analytic insights but overlooks data relevant to these new codes that were considered earlier.

coherence   an indicator of high-quality qualitative research. Coherence refers to the quality of the research narrative, the 'fit' between the research question and the philosophical perspective adopted, and the method of investigation and analysis undertaken.

commitment   an indicator of high-quality qualitative research. Commitment involves demonstrating prolonged engagement with the research topic.

confidentiality   refers to steps that the researcher takes to protect the privacy of research participants and ensure that any information they provide during research cannot be used by others to identify them in research outputs.

consequentialism   ethics concerned with the outcome of a course of action.

constant comparison   a basic process in grounded theory analysis that involves examining segments of data against existing categories to discern similarities and differences and to determine whether some existing categories need to be amended in light of the data or whether new categories need to be created.

context   the social systems and feedback loops within which an individual is embedded and through which they make sense of, construct and are constructed by their worlds.

contextual constructionism   the assumption that all knowledge is context specific and influenced by the perspective of the perceiver.

core category   in the latter stages of grounded theory analysis, a core category (or core categories) is identified which potentially explains all or most subsidiary categories.

critical discourse analysis   a version of discourse analysis that is concerned with how the abuse of social power, dominance and inequality are enacted, reproduced and resisted in text and talk in social and political settings.

critical discursive psychology   a version of discourse analysis that attends to the detail of linguistic interaction in a particular context and to broader patterns in collective linguistic sense-making.

critical realism   the assumption that a reality exists independent of the observer but we cannot know that reality with certainty.

data familiarization   a vital initial stage of thematic analysis that involves reading and re-reading the data to develop a deep and familiar sense of the semantic, obvious meanings of the data.

debriefing   providing participants with additional information about the research after they have taken part in it and asking for their feedback.

deductive   a term that describes an approach to research that begins at the level of theory and the creation of hypotheses and proceeds to test these hypotheses against data to generate logical conclusions. This is sometimes called a 'top-down' approach because it involves moving from a level of generality to increasing levels of specificity.

description/descriptive account   an account of the data which answers the question of what are the reported experiences of the participants.

dialogical narrative analysis   a form of narrative analysis that examines how a story is put together from narrative resources and the effects that the story has in people's lives.

dialogical questions   types of questions that the researcher asks of the data in narrative analysis to open up the social, cultural and relational dynamics of stories.

discourses   sets of written or spoken linguistic material that have a degree of coherence in their content and organization and that perform constructive functions in broadly defined social contexts.

discursive objects   the phenomena of interest to a discourse analytic research project, which seeks to explore how these phenomena are constructed in talk, writing and other forms of text.

discursive psychology   a version of discourse analysis that views language as a form of social action, addresses the social functions of talk and considers how these functions are achieved.

discursive resources   the array of categories, rights, obligations and activities that people draw upon when talking about or constructing a particular discursive object.

double hermeneutic   a term that describes when the researcher is attempting to make sense of the participant attempting to make sense of the topic under investigation.

empiricism   a theory of knowledge that claims that our knowledge of the world must arise from the collection and categorization of our sense perceptions/observations of the world.

epistemological constructionism   the assumption that knowledge is constructed and fallible.

epistemology   a branch of philosophy that is concerned with questions about what constitutes valid knowledge and how we can obtain it – in other words, questions about *how* we can know and *what* we can know.

explanation/explanatory account an account of the data that addresses the question of why or how the reported participant experiences came about.

Foucauldian discourse analysis a version of discourse analysis that is concerned with the availability of discursive resources within a specified cultural context and the implications for people within that context. These implications tend to be examined in terms of identity and selfhood, ideology, power relations and social change.

gem a small extract of data that powerfully and succinctly illuminates the phenomenon being examined in interpretative phenomenological analysis.

goodness of fit a criterion by which the outcome of grounded theory research is evaluated. It refers to the extent to which the categories generated through analysis are applicable to the data.

hermeneutics a philosophical and practical concern with the process of interpretation.

homogeneous sample a purposively selected sample where participants share significant characteristics.

hot cognition the process involved when an individual is engaged with trying to make sense of something that is important, current and affectively laden.

hypothetico-deductivism a theory of knowledge that focuses on identifying theoretical claims (hypotheses) that are false and thereby developing a clearer sense of the truth.

idiographic research research that seeks to examine individual cases in detail to understand an outcome.

idiography an approach committed to understanding each case on its own terms.

impact and importance an indicator of high-quality qualitative research that refers to the theoretical, practical and socio-cultural impact of the study.

inductive a term that describes an approach to research that begins at the level of data and proceeds from there to discern patterns in the data and link these patterns to existing theory or use them to create new theory. This is sometimes called a 'bottom-up' approach because it involves starting with the specific (that is, the data) and moving up from this level towards conceptual and theoretical levels.

informed consent the (ongoing) process by which people who have been invited to take part in research decide whether to accept that invitation and agree to the research procedures after the nature of the research and its requirements have been clearly explained to them.

interpretative framework a researcher's theoretical commitments, understandings, experiences and emotional investments (both personal and professional) that they bring to bear on their research and which can shape their research in fruitful ways.

latent codes these capture the implicit (covert) meanings in data, the assumptions or logic frameworks that underpin the overt content.

macro ethics ethical considerations that focus on the wider societal implications of research.

meaning-making the process of making sense of (understanding and explaining) our world.

memos records of the thought processes of the researcher on specific aspects of a grounded theory analysis and accounts of how analytic decisions were made. These play a vital role in the development of a grounded theory.

meso ethics ethical considerations that focus on relationships with knowledge communities.

micro ethics ethical considerations that focus on fieldwork details.

mixed methods research research that uses qualitative and quantitative methods in combination to address a research question.

naïve realism in its simplest form, the assumption that reality can be discovered by the use of appropriate methods of inquiry.

narrative a resource that culture and social relations make available to us and that we use to help construct our stories and understand the stories that we encounter.

narrative constructionism an approach that conceptualizes human beings as meaning-makers who use narratives that their social and cultural world has passed down to interpret, direct and communicate life and to configure and constitute their experience and sense of who they are.

narrative constructivism an approach that conceptualizes narrative as a cognitive structure or process that is to be found inside the mind.

narrative foreclosure a situation in which the story one tells about one's life is seen as the only possible story that could be told.

narrative habitus dispositions or habitual ways of acting that have developed and been sustained by the stories we have taken on board over the years.

narrative identity a fluid and continual process of constructing and performing a social identity through the stories we tell about our lives.

narrative resources the plots or storylines that society and culture make available to us and from which we selectively draw to construct the stories we tell.

narrative theme a pattern that runs through a story or set of stories.

nomothetic research research that seeks generalizable findings that uncover laws to explain objective phenomena.

non-maleficence causing the least possible harm in research.

ontological relativism the assumption that psychological and social phenomena are multiple, created and dependent on us rather than existing independently of human conceptions and interpretations.

ontology a branch of philosophy that is concerned with questions about what constitutes 'reality' and how we can understand existence.

open coding identifying and labelling meaningful units of text, which might be a word, phrase, sentence or larger section of text.

'Other' (a member of) a group that is constructed in opposition to the norms in a particular culture.

over-coding this refers to a practice in qualitative analysis where stories in data are broken down into much smaller, more 'manageable' chunks and many different codes are assigned to these. Narrative analysts try to avoid doing this and aim instead to preserve the integrity of stories.

phenomenology a philosophical approach concerned with attempting to capture subjective experience, as far as possible, in its own terms. 'Phenomenology' also refers to the application of this approach in human science research.

pluralistic analysis the application of different qualitative methods to a single data set with the aim of producing rich, multi-layered, multi-perspective analyses.

positioning a discourse analytic interpretation of the concept of identity (see 'subject positions').

positivism a theory of knowledge which claims there is a direct correspondence between things in the world and our perception of them, provided that our perception is not skewed.

radical constructionism   the assumption that data do not reflect reality but that reality is constructed through language (see also 'social constructionism').

realism   the assumption that a reality exists independent of the observer which can be accessed through research.

reflexivity   the acknowledgement by the researcher of the role played by their interpretative framework (including theoretical commitments, personal understandings and personal experiences) in creating their analytic account.

relational ethics   an approach to ethics that locates ethical action in the context of relationships between people (also termed 'ethics of care').

relativism   the assumption that 'reality' is dependent on the ways we come to know it.

reviewing themes   an important stage of thematic analysis that involves checking that themes 'work' in relation to the coded data and the entire data set.

rigour   an indicator of high-quality qualitative research. Rigour refers to the completeness of the data collection and analysis.

saturation   an aspect of grounded theory analysis that refers to gathering examples of meaningful units of text from interview transcripts until no new examples emerge of the categories that have been identified through the analysis. Saturation is reached when the theory that has been developed through analysis can fully explain all variations in the data.

scientific method   an approach to knowledge that assumes that a researcher can obtain accurate information about the psychological and social worlds by striving for objectivity, neutrality and precise measurement in hypothesis-testing.

semantic codes   these capture the surface meanings in data, the overt meanings articulated by a participant.

semi-structured interview   an interview that starts from an interview schedule but that moves flexibly to follow up the concerns and interests of the participant.

sensitivity to context   an indicator of high-quality qualitative research. The researchers should make clear the context of theory and the understandings created by previous researchers using similar methods and/or analysing similar topics; the socio-cultural setting of the study; and the social context of the relationship between the researchers and the participants.

situationism   ethics concerned with the particular case.

'small q' qualitative research   refers to the use of qualitative techniques within a broadly quantitative framework or paradigm.

social constructionism   a critical stance towards the ways in which we understand the world and ourselves, which are seen as having been built up through social processes, particularly through linguistic interactions.

social critique   a contribution that discourse analysis and other critical analytic approaches can make to social and political practice by questioning the status quo and thus empowering oppressed groups and guiding reform.

speaking position   this term can be understood broadly or specifically or both. It can refer to the ways in which the social position of 'researcher' or 'writer' shapes what a researcher or writer can say and do. More specifically the term can refer to the researcher's interpretative framework and the ways in which this is believed to have shaped their research questions and data generation and informed their analysis.

story analyst standpoint   a standpoint within narrative analysis where the researcher places narratives under analysis and communicates results in the form of a realist tale to produce an analytical account of narratives.

story   a specific tale that a person tells and that they create from the narratives available to them.

storyteller standpoint   a standpoint within narrative analysis where the analysis is the story and the story is communicated in the form of a creative analytical practice.

subject positions   positions provided within a discourse for users of that discourse. By adopting, rejecting or negotiating these positions, the user of the discourse is constructed as a subject.

subtheme   a subtheme shares a central organizing concept with a theme but highlights one particular aspect of it.

superordinate theme   a high-level theme in IPA research that incorporates existing themes and organizes them to provide a representation of the data. A study's superordinate themes collectively provide an answer to its research question.

symbolic interactionism   a perspective within sociology that holds that people act towards things based on the meanings those things have for them, that these meanings are derived from social interaction and that these shared meanings are influential in society.

thematic map   a diagrammatic representation of themes and the relationships between them.

theme   a pattern of meaning in a data set that is typically made up of a number of codes that cohere around a central organizing concept.

theme definition   a theme definition describes the key concept encapsulated in a theme and also highlights the analytic interpretation of data relevant to the theme.

theme-ing   the identification of patterns and structural elements in stories found in data.

theoretical coding   an aspect of grounded theory analysis that involves shifting from a descriptive level of coding and reformulating some categories in a conceptual way in light of the relationships that are discerned between categories. This is also known as selective coding.

theoretical integration   an aspect of grounded theory analysis that refers to identifying one core category (or sometimes more than one) and relating it to all the other subsidiary categories to determine its explanatory power. Links with existing theory are also established and developed.

theoretical sampling   a process of ongoing data collection for the purpose of generating theory, where previous analysis influences decisions about subsequent data to be collected. This approach to sampling is characteristic of grounded theory research.

theoretical sensitivity   in grounded theory research, this refers to making links between the emergent grounded theory and existing theories or theoretical concepts, which may further develop the emergent theory.

transparency   making the various decisions and steps in qualitative research visible to readers. This allows other researchers to follow and understand the processes which shaped the research, particularly the analysis. Transparency can be thought of as a marker of good qualitative research.

typology   a collection of stories that provide an overview/summary of the findings of a narrative analysis.

virtue ethics   ethics concerned with the character of the person acting/behaving.

REFERENCES

Abell, J. and Walton, C. (2010) 'Imagine: Towards an integrated and applied social psychology', *British Journal of Social Psychology*, 49(4): 685–90.

Alcoff, L. (1994) 'The problem of speaking others', in S. Orstrov Weisser and J. Fleischner (eds), *Feminist Nightmares – Women at Odds: Feminism and the Problem of Sisterhood*. New York: New York University Press. pp. 285–309.

Alcoff, L.M. (2006) *Visible Identities: Race, Gender and the Self*. New York: Oxford University Press.

Allport, G.W. (1962) 'The general and the unique in psychological science', *Journal of Personality*, 30(3): 405–22.

Anderson, E. and McCormack, M. (2015) 'Cuddling and spooning: Heteromasculinity and homo-social tactility among student-athletes', *Men and Masculinities*, 18(2): 214–30.

Ansara, Y. G. and Hegarty, P. (2012) 'Cisgenderism in psychology: Pathologizing and misgendering children from 1999 to 2008', *Psychology & Sexuality,* 3(2): 137–60.

Antaki, C., Billig, M., Edwards, D. and Potter, J. (2003) 'Discourse analysis means doing analysis: A critique of six analytic shortcomings', *Discourse Analysis Online*, 1(1). Retrieved 5 September 2015 from http://www.shu.ac.uk/daol/articles/v1/n1/a1/antaki2002002-t.html.

Aronson, J. (1994) 'A pragmatic view of thematic analysis', *The Qualitative Report*, 2(1) (http://www.nova.edu/ssss/QR/BackIssues/QR2-1/aronson.html).

Atkinson, J.M. and Heritage, J. (eds) (1984) *Structures of Social Action: Studies in Conversation Analysis*. Cambridge: Cambridge University Press.

Atkinson, P. (2010) 'Negotiating the contested terrain of illness narratives – an appreciative response', *Sociology of Health and Illness*, 32(4): 661–2.

Bakhtin, M. (1984) *Problems of Dostoevsky's Poetics*. Translated and edited by C. Emerson. Minneapolis, MN: University of Minnesota Press.

Bamberg, M. (2011) 'Who am I? Big or small— shallow or deep?', *Theory & Psychology*, 21(1): 122–9.

Bamberg, M. and Georgakopoulou, A. (2008) 'Small stories as a new perspective in narrative and identity analysis', *Text & Talk*, 28(3): 377–96.

Bartlett, D. and Payne, S. (1997) 'Grounded theory – its basis, rationale and procedures', in G. McKenzie, J. Powell and R. Usher (eds), *Understanding Social Research: Perspectives on Methodology and Practice*. London: Falmer Press. pp. 173–95.

Basinger, E.D., Wehrman, E.C., Delaney, A.L. and McAninch, K.G. (2015) 'A grounded theory of students' long-distance coping with a family member's cancer', *Qualitative Health Research*, 25(8): 1085–98.

Baxter, L.A. (1991) 'Content analysis', in B.M. Montgomery and S. Duck (eds), *Studying Interpersonal Interaction*. New York: The Guilford Press. pp. 239–54.

Benner, P. (1985) 'Quality of life: A phenomenological perspective on explanation, prediction, and understanding in nursing science', *Advances in Nursing Science,* 8(1): 1–14.

Benton, T. and Craib, I. (2001) *Philosophy of Social Science*. New York: Palgrave.

REFERENCES

Billig, M. (1988) 'Methodology and scholarship in understanding ideological explanation', in C. Antaki (ed.), *Analysing Everyday Explanation: A Casebook of Methods*. London: SAGE. pp. 199–215.

Bochner, A.P. and Riggs, N.A. (2014) 'Practicing narrative inquiry', in P. Leavy (ed.), *The Oxford Handbook of Qualitative Research*. Oxford: Oxford University Press. pp. 195–222.

Boyatzis, R.E. (1998) *Transforming Qualitative Information: Thematic Analysis and Code Development*. Thousand Oaks, CA: SAGE.

Bramley, N. and Eatough, V. (2005) 'An idiographic case study of the experience of living with Parkinson's disease using interpretative phenomenological analysis', *Psychology & Health*, 20(2): 223–35.

Braun, V. and Clarke, V. (2006) 'Using thematic analysis in psychology', *Qualitative Research in Psychology*, 3(2): 77–101.

Braun, V. and Clarke, V. (2012) 'Thematic analysis', in H. Cooper (ed.), *APA Handbook of Research Methods in Psychology. Vol. 2, Research Designs*. Washington, DC: APA Books. pp. 57–71.

Braun, V. and Clarke, V. (2013) *Successful Qualitative Research: A Practical Guide for Beginners*. London: SAGE.

Braun, V., Clarke, V. and Rance, N. (2014) 'How to use thematic analysis with interview data', in A. Vossler and N. Moller, N. (eds), *The Counselling and Psychotherapy Research Handbook*. London: SAGE. pp. 183–97.

Breakwell, G.M. (1986) *Coping with Threatened Identities*. London: Methuen.

Breakwell, G.M. (1996) 'Identity processes and social changes', in G.M. Breakwell and E. Lyons (eds), *Changing European Identities: Social Psychological Analyses of Social Change*. Oxford: Butterworth Heinemann. pp. 13–27.

Brinkmann, S. and Kvale, S. (2008) 'Ethics in qualitative psychological research', in C. Willig and W. Stainton-Rogers (eds), *The SAGE Handbook of Qualitative Research in Psychology*. London: SAGE. pp. 263–79.

British Psychological Society (2009) *Code of Ethics and Conduct*. Leicester: British Psychological Society.

British Psychological Society (2010) *Code of Human Research Ethics*. Leicester: British Psychological Society.

British Psychological Society (2013) *Ethics Guidelines for Internet-mediated Research*. Leicester: British Psychological Society.

Brockmeier, J. (2012) 'Narrative scenarios: Toward a culturally thick notion of narrative', in J. Valsiner (ed.), *The Oxford Handbook of Culture and Psychology*. Oxford: Oxford University Press. pp. 439–67.

Bruner, J. (1990) *Acts of Meaning*. Cambridge, MA: Harvard University Press.

Bryant, A. and Charmaz, K. (2007) 'Grounded theory in historical perspective: An epistemological account', in A. Bryant and K. Charmaz (eds), *The SAGE Handbook of Grounded Theory*. Thousand Oaks, CA: SAGE. pp. 31–57.

Buetow, S. (2010) 'Thematic analysis and its reconceptualization as "saliency analysis"', *Journal of Health Service Research & Policy*, 15(2): 123–5.

Bundon, A. 'Authors, audiences, and advocates … But athletes first: Blogging and the Paralympic movement'. http://elk.library.ubc.ca/bitstream/handle/2429/45647/ubc_2014_spring_bundon_andrea.pdf?sequence=1 (accessed 3 March 2014).

Burkitt, I. (2014) *Emotions and Social Relations*. London: SAGE.

Burman, E. and Parker, I. (eds) (1993a) *Discourse Analytic Research: Repertoires and Readings of Texts in Action*. London: Routledge.

Burman, E. and Parker, I. (1993b) 'Introduction – discourse analysis: The turn to the text', in E. Burman and I. Parker (eds), *Discourse Analytic Research: Repertoires and Readings of Texts in Action*. London: Routledge. pp. 1–13.

Burr, V. (2015) *Social Constructionism*. 3rd edn. Hove: Routledge.

Caddick, N., Phoenix, C. and Smith, B. (2015) 'Collective stories and well-being: Using a dialogical narrative approach to understand peer relationships among combat veterans experiencing post-traumatic stress disorder', *Journal of Health Psychology*, 20(3): 286–99.

Caddick, N., Smith, B. and Phoenix, C. (2015a) 'The effects of surfing and the natural environment on the well-being of combat veterans', *Qualitative Health Research*, 25(1): 76–86.

Caddick, N., Smith, B. and Phoenix, C. (2015b) 'Male combat veterans' narratives of PTSD, masculinity, and health', *Sociology of Health & Illness*, 37(1): 97–111.

Camp, D.L., Finlay, W.M.L. and Lyons, E. (2002) 'Is low self-esteem inevitable in stigma? An example from women with chronic mental health problems', *Social Science and Medicine*, 55(5): 823–34.

Carey, R.N., Donaghue, N. and Broderick, P. (2010) '"What you look like is such a big factor": Girls' own reflections about the appearance culture in an all-girls' school', *Feminism & Psychology*, 21(3): 299–316.

Chamberlain, K. (2000) 'Methodolatry and qualitative health research', *Journal of Health Psychology*, 5(3): 285–96.

Chamberlain, K. (2011) 'Commentary: Troubling methodology', *Health Psychology Review*, 5(1): 48–54.

Charmaz, K.C. (1990) '"Discovering" chronic illness: Using grounded theory', *Social Science & Medicine*, 30(11): 1161–72.

Charmaz, K. (2014) *Constructing Grounded Theory*. 2nd edn. London: SAGE.

Christ, T. (1970) 'A thematic analysis of the American business creed', *Social Forces*, 49(2): 239–45.

Clarke, A.E. (2003) 'Situational analyses: Grounded theory mapping after the postmodern turn', *Symbolic Interaction*, 26(4): 553–76.

Clarke, N.J., Willis, M.E. Barnes, J.S., Caddick, N., Cromby, J., McDermott, H. and Wiltshire, G. (2015) 'Analytical pluralism in qualitative research: A meta-study', *Qualitative Research in Psychology*, 12(2): 182–201.

Clarke, V. and Braun, V. (2013) 'Teaching thematic analysis: Overcoming challenges and developing strategies for effective learning', *The Psychologist*, 26(2): 120–3.

Clarke, V. and Kitzinger, C. (2004) 'Lesbian and gay parents on talk shows: Resistance or collusion in heterosexism?' *Qualitative Research in Psychology*, 1(3): 195–217.

Clarke, V. and Smith, M. (2015) '"Not hiding, not shouting, just me": Gay men negotiate their visual identities', *Journal of Homosexuality*, 62(1): 4–32.

Clarke, V. and Spence, K. (2013) '"I am who I am": Navigating norms and the importance of authenticity in lesbian and bisexual women's accounts of their appearance practices', *Psychology & Sexuality*, 4(1): 25–33.

Coffey, A. and Atkinson, P. (1996) *Making Sense of Qualitative Data*. Thousand Oaks, CA: SAGE.

Corbin, J. and Strauss, A. (2015). *Basics of Qualitative Research: Techniques and Procedures for Developing Grounded Theory*. 4th edn. Thousand Oaks, CA: SAGE.

Coyle, A. (1996) 'Representing gay men with HIV/AIDS', in S. Wilkinson and C. Kitzinger (eds), *Representing the Other*. London: SAGE. pp. 72–7.

Coyle, A. and Wright, C. (1996) 'Using the counselling interview to collect research data on sensitive topics', *Journal of Health Psychology*, 1(4): 431–40.

Cromby, J. and Standen, P. (1996) 'Psychology in the service of the state', *Psychology, Politics, Resistance*, 3(Spring/Summer): 6–7.

Cronin, A. (2008) 'Focus groups', in N. Gilbert (ed.), *Researching Social Life*. 3rd edn. London: SAGE. pp. 226–44.

Crossley, M. (2000) *Introducing Narrative Psychology*. Buckingham: Open University Press.

Dallos, R. and Draper, R. (2010) *An Introduction to Family Therapy: Systemic Theory and Practice*. 3rd edn. Buckingham: Open University Press.

Dapkus, M.A. (1985) 'A thematic analysis of the experience of time', *Personality Processes and Individual Differences*, 49(2): 408–19.

Davies, B. and Harré, R. (1990) 'Positioning: The discursive production of selves', *Journal for the Theory of Social Behaviour*, 20(1): 43–63.

Davies, B. and Harré, R. (1999) 'Positioning and personhood', in R. Harré and L. van Langenhove (eds), *Positioning Theory*. Oxford: Blackwell. pp. 32–52.

Denison, D. (2008) 'Clues to language change from non-standard English', *German Life and Letters*, 61(4): 533–45.

Denzin, N.K. and Lincoln, Y.S. (2011a) 'Introduction: The discipline and practice of qualitative research', in N.K. Denzin and Y.S. Lincoln (eds), *The SAGE Handbook of Qualitative Research*. 4th edn. Thousand Oaks, CA: SAGE. pp. 1–20.

Denzin, N.K. and Lincoln, Y.S. (eds) (2011b) *The SAGE Handbook of Qualitative Research*. 4th edn. Thousand Oaks, CA: SAGE.

de Visser, R. and Smith, J.A. (2006) 'Mister in-between: A case study of masculine identity and health-related behaviour', *Journal of Health Psychology*, 11(5): 685–95.

Dewe, M. and Coyle, A. (2014) 'Reflections on a study of responses to research on smoking: A pragmatic, pluralist variation on a qualitative psychological theme', *Review of Social Studies*, 1(1): 21–36.

Doucet, A. and Mauthner, N.S. (2012) 'Knowing responsibly: Ethics, feminist epistemologies and methodologies', in T. Miller, M. Birch, M. Mauthner and J. Jessop (eds), *Ethics in Qualitative Research*. 2nd edn. London: SAGE. pp. 122–39.

Douglas, K. and Carless, D. (2015) 'Finding a counter story at an inclusive, adapted, sport and adventurous training course for injured, sick, and wounded soldiers: Drawn in–drawn out', *Qualitative Inquiry*, 21(5): 454–66.

Duncombe, J. and Jessop, J. (2002) '"Doing rapport" and the ethics of "faking friendship"', in M. Mauthner, M. Birch, J. Jessop and T. Miller (eds), *Ethics in Qualitative Research*. London: SAGE. pp. 108-23.

Dwyer, S.C. and Buckle, J.L. (2009) 'The space between: On being an insider–outsider in qualitative research', *International Journal of Qualitative Methods*, 8(1): 54–63.

Eatough, V. and Smith, J.A. (2008) 'Interpretative phenomenological analysis', in C. Willig and W. Stainton Rogers (eds), *The SAGE Handbook of Qualitative Research in Psychology*. London: SAGE. pp. 179–94.

Eatough, V., Smith J.A. and Shaw, R. (2008) 'Women, anger, and aggression: An interpretative phenomenological analysis', *Journal of Interpersonal Violence*, 23(12): 1767–99.

Economic and Social Research Council (2015) *Framework for Research Ethics* (http://www.esrc.ac.uk/_ images/framework-for-research-ethics_tcm8-33470.pdf).

Edley, N. and Wetherell, M. (1999) 'Imagined futures: Young men's talk about fatherhood and domestic life', *British Journal of Social Psychology*, 38(2): 181–94.

Edwards, D. and Potter, J. (1992) *Discursive Psychology*. London: SAGE.

Elliott, R., Fischer, C.T. and Rennie, D.L. (1999) 'Evolving guidelines for publication of qualitative research studies in psychology and related fields', *British Journal of Clinical Psychology*, 38(3): 215–29.

Ellis, C. (2004) *The Ethnographic I*. Walnut Creek, CA: Altamira Press.

Esin, C., Fathi, M. and Squire, C. (2014) 'Narrative analysis: The constructionist approach', in U. Flick (ed.), *The SAGE Handbook of Qualitative Data Analysis*. London: SAGE. pp. 203–16.

Fallowfield, L. (2001) 'Participation of patients in decisions about treatment for cancer (editorial)', *British Medical Journal*, 323(7322): 1144.

Farvid, P. and Braun, V. (2006) '"Most of us guys are raring to go anytime, anyplace, anywhere": Male and female sexuality in *Cleo* and *Cosmo*', *Sex Roles*, 55(5–6): 295–310.

Feldman, M., Skoldberg, K., Brown, R. and Horner, D. (2004) 'Making sense of stories: A rhetorical approach to narrative analysis', *Journal of Public Administration Research and Theory*, 14(2): 147–70.

Fine, M. (1994) 'Working the hyphens: Reinventing the Self and Other in qualitative research', in N.K. Denzin and Y.S. Lincoln (eds), *Handbook of Qualitative Research*. Newbury Park, CA: SAGE. pp. 70–82.

Finlay, L. and Gough, B. (eds) (2003) *Reflexivity: A Practical Guide for Researchers in Health and Social Sciences*. Oxford: Blackwell.

Finlay, W.M.L. and Lyons, E. (2000) 'Social categorizations, social comparisons and stigma: Presentations of self in people with learning difficulties', *British Journal of Social Psychology*, 39(1): 129–46.

Finlay, W.M.L. and Lyons, E. (2001) 'Interviewing people with intellectual disabilities: A review of question phrasing, content and the use of self-report scales', *Psychological Assessment*, 13(3): 319–55.

Finlay, W.M.L. and Lyons, E. (2002) 'Acquiescence in people with mental retardation', *Mental Retardation*, 40(1): 14–29.

Fiske, S. and Taylor, S. (1991) *Social Cognition*. 2nd edn. New York: McGraw Hill.

Flowers, P., Smith, J.A., Sheeran, P. and Beail, N. (1997) 'Health and romance: Understanding unprotected sex in relationships between gay men', *British Journal of Health Psychology*, 2(1): 73–86.

Foss, C, and Ellefsen, B. (2002) 'The value of combining qualitative and quantitative approaches in nursing research by means of method triangulation', *Journal of Advanced Nursing*, 40(2): 242–8.

Foster, C., Eeles, R., Ardern-Jones, A., Moynihan, C. and Watson, M. (2004) 'Juggling roles and expectations: Dilemmas faced by women talking to relatives about cancer and genetic testing', *Psychology and Health*, 19(4): 439–55.

Fowler, D.D. and Hardesty, D.L. (eds) (1994) *Others Knowing Others: Perspectives on Ethnographic Careers*. Washington, DC: Smithsonian Institution Press.

Fox, A.P., Larkin, M. and Leung, N. (2011) 'The personal meaning of eating disorder symptoms: An interpretative phenomenological analysis', *Journal of Health Psychology*, 16(1): 116–25.

Frank, A.W. (2006) 'Health stories as connectors and subjectifiers', *Health*, 10(4): 421–40.

Frank, A.W. (2010a) *Letting Stories Breathe*. Chicago: University of Chicago Press.

Frank, A.W. (2010b) 'In defence of narrative exceptionalism', *Sociology of Health and Illness*, 32(4): 665–7.

Frank, A.W. (2012) 'Practicing dialogical narrative analysis', in J. Holstein and J. Gubrium (eds), *Varieties of Narrative Analysis*. London: SAGE. pp. 33–52.

Frank, A.W. (2013) *The Wounded Storyteller: Body, Illness and Ethics*. 2nd edn. Chicago: University of Chicago Press.

Freeman, M. (2010) *Hindsight: The Promise and Peril of Looking Backward*. Oxford: Oxford University Press.

Freeman, M. (2011) 'Stories, big and small: Toward a synthesis', *Theory and Psychology*, 21(1): 114–21.

Freeman, M. (2014) 'Qualitative inquiry and the self-realization of psychological science', *Qualitative Inquiry*, 20(2): 119–26.

French, D.P., Maissi, E. and Marteau, T.M. (2005) 'The purpose of attributing cause: Beliefs about the causes of myocardial infarction', *Social Science & Medicine*, 60(7): 1411–21.

Freud, S. (1909/1955) 'Notes upon a case of obsessional neurosis', in J. Strachey (ed. and trans.), *The Standard Edition of the Complete Psychological Works of Sigmund Freud* (Vol. 10). London: Hogarth Press. pp. 151–318.

Frost, N. (ed.) (2011) *Qualitative Research Methods in Psychology: Combining Core Approaches*. Maidenhead: Open University Press.

Frost, N.A. and Nolas, S.M. (2011) 'Exploring and expanding on pluralism in qualitative research in psychology', *Qualitative Research in Psychology*, 8(2): 115–19.

Frost, N., Nolas, S.M., Brooks-Gordon, B., Esin, C., Holt, A., Mehdizadeh, L. and Shinebourne, P. (2010) 'Pluralism in qualitative research: The impact of different researchers and qualitative approaches on the analysis of qualitative data', *Qualitative Research*, 10(4): 441–60.

Frost, N. and Shaw, R. (eds) (2014) 'The place of qualitative methods in mixed methods research [Special issue]', *Qualitative Methods in Psychology Bulletin*, 17: 1–69.

Gergen, K.J. and Gergen, M.M. (1983) 'Narratives of the self', in T.R. Sarbin and K.E. Scheibe (eds), *Studies in Social Identity*. New York: Praeger. pp. 254–73.

Gibbs, G. (2008) *Analysing Qualitative Data*. London: SAGE.

Gilhooly, K. and Green, C. (1996) 'Protocol analysis: Theoretical background', in J.T.E. Richardson (ed.), *Handbook of Qualitative Research Methods for Psychology and the Social Sciences*. Leicester: BPS Books. pp. 43–54.

Giorgi, A. and Giorgi, B. (2008) 'Phenomenology', in J.A. Smith (ed.), *Qualitative Psychology: A Practical Guide to Research Methods*. 2nd edn. London: SAGE. pp. 26–52.

Glaser, B.G. (1978) *Theoretical Sensitivity*. Mill Valley, CA: Sociology Press.

Glaser, B.G. (1992) *Emergence vs Forcing: Basics of Grounded Theory Analysis*. Mill Valley, CA: Sociology Press.

Glaser, B.G. and Strauss, A.L. (1965) *Awareness of Dying*. New York: Aldine.

Glaser, B. and Strauss, A. (1967) *The Discovery of Grounded Theory: Strategies for Qualitative Research*. New York: Aldine.

Goodman, S. and Burke, S. (2010) '"Oh you don't want asylum seekers, oh you're just racist": A discursive analysis of discussions about whether it's racist to oppose asylum seeking', *Discourse & Society*, 21(3): 325–40.

Goodman, S. and Rowe, L. (2014) '"Maybe it is prejudice … but it is NOT racism": Negotiating racism in discussion forums about Gypsies', *Discourse & Society*, 25(1): 32–46.

Graham, H. (1986) *The Human Face of Psychology*. Milton Keynes: Open University Press.

Green, C. and Gilhooly, K. (1996) 'Protocol analysis: Practical implementation', in J.T.E. Richardson (ed.), *Handbook of Qualitative Research Methods for Psychology and the Social Sciences*. Leicester: BPS Books. pp. 55–74.

Griffin, C. (2007) 'Being dead and being there: Research interviews, sharing hand cream and the preference for analysing "naturally occurring data"', *Discourse Studies*, 9(2): 246–69.

Griffin, M. (2010) 'Setting the scene: Hailing women into a running identity', *Qualitative Research in Sport & Exercise*, 2(2): 153–74.

Gubrium, J. and Holstein, J. (2009) *Analysing Narrative Reality*. London: SAGE.

Gubrium, J. and Holstein, J. (2014) 'Analytic inspiration in ethnographic fieldwork', in U. Flick (ed.), *The SAGE Handbook of Qualitative Data Analysis*. London: SAGE. pp. 35–48.

Guest, G., MacQueen, K.M. and Namey, E.E. (2012) *Applied Thematic Analysis*. Thousand Oaks, CA: SAGE.

Hadfield, J., Brown, D., Pembroke, L. and Hayward, M. (2009) 'Analysis of accident and emergency doctors' responses to treating people who self-harm', *Qualitative Health Research*, 19(6): 755–65.

Hagerty, R.G., Butow, P.N., Ellis, P.M., Dimitry, S. and Tattersall, M.H N. (2005) 'Communicating prognosis in cancer care: A systematic review of the literature', *Annals of Oncology*, 16(7): 1005–53.

Hallam, R., Ashton, P., Sherbourne, K. and Gailey, L. (2008) 'Persons with acquired profound hearing loss (APHL): How do they and their families adapt to the challenge? *Health: An Interdisciplinary Journal for the Social Study of Health, Illness and Medicine*, 12(3): 369–88.

Hammersley, M. (1999) 'Some reflections on the current state of qualitative research', *Research Intelligence*, 70: 16–18.

Hammersley, M. (2014) 'On the ethics of interviewing for discourse analysis', *Qualitative Research*, 14(5): 529–41.

Hammersley, M. and Traianou, A. (2012) *Ethics in Qualitative Research: Controversies and Contexts*. London: SAGE.

Harcourt, D. and Frith, H. (2008) 'Indication of cancer status: Women's experiences of an altered appearance during chemotherapy', *Journal of Health Psychology*, 13(5): 597–606.

Harper, D.J., O'Connor, J., Self, P. and Stevens, P. (2008) 'Learning to do discourse analysis: Accounts of supervisees and a supervisor', *Qualitative Research in Psychology*, 5(3): 192–213.

Harré, R. and Secord P. (1972) *The Explanation of Social Behaviour*. Oxford: Blackwell.

Heath, H. and Cowley, S. (2004) 'Developing a grounded theory approach: A comparison of Glaser and Strauss', *International Journal of Nursing Studies*, 41(2): 141–50.

Henwood, K.L. (1996) 'Qualitative inquiry: Perspectives, methods and psychology', in J.T.E. Richardson (ed.), *Handbook of Qualitative Research Methods for Psychology and the Social Sciences*. Leicester: BPS Books. pp. 25–40.

Henwood, K. and Pidgeon, N. (1994) 'Beyond the qualitative paradigm: A framework for introducing diversity within qualitative psychology', *Journal of Community & Applied Social Psychology*, 4(4): 225–38.

Hepburn, A. (2006) 'Getting closer at a distance: Theory and the contingencies of practice', *Theory & Psychology*, 16(3): 327–42.

Hepburn, A. and Potter, J. (2011) 'Threats: Power, family mealtimes, and social influence', *British Journal of Social Psychology*, 50(1): 99–120.

Hepburn, A. and Wiggins, S. (2005) 'Size matters: Constructing accountable bodies in NSPCC helpline interaction', *Discourse & Society*, 16(5): 625–45.

Hepburn, A. and Wiggins, S. (eds) (2007) *Discursive Research in Practice: New Approaches to Psychology and Interaction*. Cambridge: Cambridge University Press.

Holland, S., Williams, A. and Forrester, D. (2014) 'Navigating ethical moments when researching substance misuse with parents and their children', *Qualitative Research*, 14(4): 411–27.

Holliday, A. (2007) *Doing and Writing Qualitative Research*. 2nd edn. London: SAGE.

Hollway, W. (1989) *Subjectivity and Method in Psychology: Gender, Meaning and Science*. London: SAGE.

Holstein, J. and Gubrium, J. (2012a) *Varieties of Narrative Analysis*. London: SAGE.

Holstein, J. and Gubrium, J. (2012b) 'Introduction', in J. Holstein and J. Gubrium (eds), *Varieties of Narrative Analysis* London: SAGE. pp. 1–11.

Holton, G.J. (1973) *Thematic Origins of Scientific Thought: Kepler to Einstein*. Cambridge, MA: Harvard University Press.

Hopkins, P.E. (2009) 'Women, men, positionalities and emotion: Doing feminist geographies of religion', *ACME: An International Journal for Critical Geographers*, 8(1): 1–17.

Horne, G., Seymour, J. and Payne, S. (2012) 'Maintaining integrity in the face of death: A grounded theory to explain the perspectives of people affected by lung cancer about the expression of wishes for end of life care', *Social Science & Medicine*, 49(6): 718–26.

Horton-Salway, M. (2007) 'The "ME Bandwagon" and other labels: Constructing the genuine case in talk about a controversial illness', *British Journal of Social Psychology*, 46(4): 895–914.

Howitt, D. (2013) *Introduction to Qualitative Methods in Psychology*. 2nd edn. Harlow: Pearson.

Hussain, Z. and Griffiths, M.D. (2009) 'The attitudes, feelings, and experiences of online gamers: A qualitative analysis', *CyberPsychology & Behavior*, 12(6): 747–53.

Hutchby, I. and Woofitt, R. (2008) *Conversation Analysis*. 2nd edn. Cambridge: Polity Press.

Huxley, C.J., Clarke, V. and Halliwell, E. (2014) 'A qualitative exploration of whether lesbian and bisexual women are "protected" from sociocultural pressure to be thin', *Journal of Health Psychology*, 19(2): 273–84.

Hydén, L.-C. (2014) 'Bodies, embodiment and stories', in M. Andrews, C. Squire and M. Tamboukou (eds), *Doing Narrative Research*. 2nd edn. London: SAGE.

Jaspal, R. and Breakwell, G.M. (eds) (2014) *Identity Process Theory: Identity, Social Action and Social Change*. Cambridge: Cambridge University Press.

Jaspal, R. and Nerlich, B. (2014) 'When climate science became climate politics: British media representations of climate change in 1988', *Public Understanding of Science*, 23(2): 122–41.

Jefferson, G. (1990) 'List construction as a task and resource', in G. Psathas (ed.), *Interaction Competence*. Lanham, MD: University Press of America. pp. 63–92.

Jingree T. and Finlay W.M.L. (2008) '"You can't do it ... it's theory rather than practice": Staff use of the practice/principal rhetorical device in talk on empowering people with learning disabilities', *Discourse & Society*, 19(6): 705–26.

Jingree, T. and Finlay, W.M.L. (2013) 'Expressions of dissatisfaction and complaint by people with learning disabilities: A discourse analytic study', *British Journal of Social Psychology*, 52(2): 255–72.

Joffé, H. (2011) 'Thematic analysis', in D. Harper and A.R. Thompson (eds), *Qualitative Methods in Mental Health and Psychotherapy: A Guide for Students and Practitioners*. Chichester: Wiley. pp. 209–23.

Josselson, R. and Lieblich, A. (eds) (1993) *The Narrative Study of Lives (Vol. 1)*. London: SAGE.

Karlsen, M.L., Coyle, A. and Williams, E. (2014) '"They never listen": Towards a grounded theory of the role played by trusted adults in the spiritual lives of children', *Mental Health, Religion & Culture*, 17(3): 297–312.

Kidder, L.H. and Fine, M. (1987) 'Qualitative and quantitative methods: When stories converge', in M.M. Mark and L. Shotland (eds), *New Directions in Program Evaluation*. San Francisco, CA: Jossey-Bass. pp. 57–75.

King, N. (2010) 'Research ethics in qualitative research', in M.A. Forrester (ed.), *Doing Qualitative Research in Psychology: A Practical Guide*. London: SAGE. pp. 98–118.

Kitzinger, C. and Wilkinson, S. (1996) 'Theorizing representing the Other', in S. Wilkinson and C. Kitzinger (eds), *Representing the Other*. London: SAGE. pp. 1–32.

Krippendorf, K. (2013) *Content Analysis: An Introduction to its Methodology*. 3rd edn. Thousand Oaks, CA: SAGE.

Kurz, T., Augoustinos, M. and Crabb, S. (2010) 'Contesting the "national interest" and maintaining "our lifestyle": A discursive analysis of political rhetoric around climate change', *British Journal of Social Psychology*, 49(3): 601–25.

Liebert, R. and Gavey, N. (2009) '"There are always two sides to these things": Managing the dilemma of serious adverse effects from SSRIs', *Social Science & Medicine*, 68(10): 1882–91.

Lieblich, A., Tuval-Mashiach, R. and Zilber, T. (1998) *Narrative Research: Reading, Analysis and Interpretation*. London: SAGE.

Lincoln, Y.S. and Guba, E.G. (1985) *Naturalistic Inquiry*. Newbury Park, CA: SAGE.

Livia, A. (1996) 'Daring to presume', in S. Wilkinson and C. Kitzinger (eds), *Representing the Other*. London: SAGE. pp. 33–42.

Loopstra, C., Strodl, E. and Herd, D. (2015) 'A qualitative analysis of how parents assess acute pain in young children', *Health Psychology Open*, 2(1): 1–12.

Lopes, P.N., Coyle, A. and Gallie, J. (2014) 'Emotion and self-regulation in deliberate personal change: A case study analysis', *Psicologia: Revista Associação Portuguesa de Psicologia (Journal of the Portuguese Psychological Association)*, 28(1): 19–31.

Lyons, A.C., Madden, H., Chamberlain, K. and Carr, S. (2011) '"It's not really us discriminating against immigrants, it's more telling people how to fit in": Constructing the nation in immigration talk in New Zealand', *Journal of Community & Applied Social Psychology*, 21(1): 14–27.

Lyons, E., Chrysanthaki, T. and Barrett, M. (2006) 'The role of perceived discrimination and political trust in fostering social cohesion: The minority perspective', paper presented at the International Society of Political Psychology 29th Annual Scientific Meeting, Barcelona, 12–15 July.

Madill, A. and Gough, B. (2008) 'Qualitative research and its place in psychological science', *Psychological Methods*, 13(3): 254–71.

Madill, A., Jordan, A. and Shirley, C. (2000) 'Objectivity and reliability in qualitative analysis: Realist, contextualist and radical constructionist epistemologies', *British Journal of Psychology*, 91(1): 1–20.

Mankayi, N. (2008) 'Morality and sexual rights: Constructions of masculinity, femininity and sexuality among a group of South African soldiers', *Culture, Health & Sexuality*, 10(6): 625–34.

Marks, D. (1996) 'Able-bodied dilemmas in teaching disability studies', in S. Wilkinson and C. Kitzinger (eds), *Representing the Other*. London: SAGE. pp. 64–7.

Marks, M.R., Huws, J.C. and Whitehead, L. (2015) 'Working with uncertainty: A grounded theory study of health-care professionals' experiences of working with children and adolescents with chronic fatigue syndrome', *Journal of Health Psychology*, 'online first' version. doi: 10.1177/1359105315583367.

Marquand, D. (1991) 'Civic republicans and liberal individualists: The case of Britain', *European Journal of Sociology*, 32(2): 329–44.

Mason, J. (2006) 'Mixing methods in a qualitatively driven way', *Qualitative Research*, 6(1): 9–25.

Mauthner, N.S. (2012) '"Accounting for our part of the entangled webs we weave": Ethical and moral issues in digital data sharing', in T. Miller, M. Birch, M. Mauthner and J. Jessop (eds), *Ethics in Qualitative Research*. 2nd edn. London: SAGE. pp. 157–75.

Mayer, F.W. (2014) *Narrative Politics: Stories and Collective Action*. Oxford: Oxford University Press.

Maykut, P. and Morehouse, R. (1994) *Beginning Qualitative Research: A Philosophic and Practical Guide*. London: The Falmer Press.

McAdams, D. (2013) *The Redemptive Self*. 2nd edn. Oxford: Oxford University Press.

McLean Taylor, J., Gilligan, C. and Sullivan, A.M. (1996) 'Missing voices, changing meanings: Developing a voice-centred, relational method and creating an interpretive community', in S. Wilkinson (ed.), *Feminist Social Psychologies: International Perspectives*. Buckingham: Open University Press. pp. 233–57.

Mead, G.H. (1934) *Mind, Self and Society*. Chicago: Chicago University Press.

Medved, M.I., Brockmeier, J., Morach, J. and Chartier, L. (2013) 'Broken heart stories: Understanding Aboriginal women's heart problems', *Qualitative Health Research*, 23(12): 1613–25.

Merino, M.-E. and Tileagă, C. (2011) 'The construction of ethnic minority identity: A discursive psychological approach to ethnic self-definition in action', *Discourse & Society*, 22(1): 86–101.

Meyrick, J. (2006) 'What is good qualitative research? A first step towards a comprehensive approach to judging rigour/quality', *Journal of Health Psychology*, 11(5): 799–808.

Miles, M.B. and Huberman, A.M. (1994) *Qualitative Data Analysis: An Expanded Sourcebook*. 2nd edn. Thousand Oaks, CA: SAGE.

Miles, M.B., Huberman, M. and Saldaña, J. (2014) *Qualitative Data Analysis: A Methods Sourcebook*. 3rd edn. Thousand Oaks, CA: SAGE.

Milgram, S. (1963) 'Behavioral study of obedience', *Journal of Abnormal and Social Psychology*, 67(4): 371–8.

Miller, T. and Bell, L. (2012) 'Consenting to what? Issues of access, gate-keeping and "informed" consent', in T. Miller, M. Birch, M. Mauthner and J. Jessop (eds), *Ethics in Qualitative Research*. 2nd edn. London: SAGE. pp. 61–75.

Miller, T., Birch, M., Mauthner, M. and Jessop, J. (eds) (2012) *Ethics in Qualitative Research*. 2nd edn. London: SAGE.

Millward, L. (2012) 'Focus groups', in G.M. Breakwell, J.A. Smith and D.B. Wright (eds), *Research Methods in Psychology*. 4th edn. London: SAGE. pp. 411–37.

Moran, D. (2000) *Introduction to Phenomenology*. London: Routledge.

Moran-Ellis, J., Alexander, V.D., Cronin, A., Dickinson, M., Fielding, J., Sleney, J. and Thomas, H. (2006) 'Triangulation and integration: Processes, claims and implications', *Qualitative Research*, 6(1): 45–59.

Mullings, B. (1999) 'Insider or outsider, both or neither: Some dilemmas of interviewing in a cross-cultural setting', *Geoforum*, 30(4): 337–50.

National Institute for Clinical Excellence (2004) *Guidance Manual: Improving Supportive and Palliative Care for Adults with Cancer*. London: National Institute for Clinical Excellence.

Nind, M., Wiles, R., Bengry-Howell, A. and Crow, G. (2013) 'Methodological innovation and research ethics: Forces in tension or forces in harmony?' *Qualitative Research*, 13(6): 650–67.

Nolas, S.-M. (2011) 'Pragmatics of pluralistic qualitative research', in N. Frost (ed.), *Qualitative Research in Psychology: Combining Core Approaches*. Maidenhead: McGraw Hill/Open University Press. pp. 121–44.

Oguntokun, R. (1998) 'A lesson in the seductive power of sameness: Representing Black African refugee women', *Feminism and Psychology*, 8(4): 525–9.

Oliver, P. (2010) *The Student's Guide to Research Ethics*. Maidenhead: Open University Press.

Page, R. and Thomas, B. (eds) (2011) *New Narratives: Stories and Storytelling in the Digital Age*. Lincoln, NE: University of Nebraska Press.

Palmer, R. (1969) *Hermeneutics*. Evanston, IL: Northwestern University Press.

Parker, I. (1992) *Discourse Dynamics: Critical Analysis for Social and Individual Psychology*. London: Routledge.

Parker, I. (2002) *Critical Discursive Psychology*. Basingstoke: Palgrave.

Parker, I. (2005) *Qualitative Psychology: Introducing Radical Research*. Maidenhead: Open University Press

Parker, I. and Burman, E. (1993) 'Against discursive imperialism, empiricism and constructionism: Thirty-two problems with discourse analysis', in E. Burman and I. Parker (eds), *Discourse Analytic Research: Repertoires and Readings of Texts in Action*. London: Routledge. pp. 155–72.

Parsons, J. and Lavery. J. (2012) 'Brokered dialogue: A new research method for controversial health and social issues', *BMC Medical Research Methodology*, 12: 92.

Payne, S. (1992) 'A study of quality of life in cancer patients receiving palliative chemotherapy', *Social Science & Medicine*, 35(12): 1505–9.

Payne, S., Seymour, J.E., Chapman, A., Chau, R. and Lloyd, M. (2004) 'Attitudes and beliefs about end-of-life care in the Chinese community: Challenging stereotypes', *Palliative Medicine*, 18(2): 153.

Peel, E., Parry, O., Douglas, M. and Lawton, J. (2006) '"It's no skin off my nose": Why people take part in qualitative research', *Qualitative Health Research*, 16(10): 1335–49.

Phoenix, C. and Orr, N. (2014) 'Pleasure: A forgotten dimension of physical activity in older age', *Social Science and Medicine*, 115(Aug): 94–102.

Phoenix, C. and Smith, B. (2011) 'Telling a (good?) counterstory of aging: Natural bodybuilding meets the narrative of decline', *The Journals of Gerontology Series B: Psychological Sciences and Social Sciences*, 66(5): 628–39.

Phoenix, C., Smith, B. and Sparkes, A.C. (2007) 'Experiences and expectations of biographical time among young athletes: A life course perspective', *Time and Society*, 16(2–3): 231–52.

Phoenix, C. and Sparkes, A. (2009) 'Being Fred: Big stories, small stories and the accomplishment of a positive aging identity', *Qualitative Research*, 9(2): 219–36.

Pidgeon, N. (1996) 'Grounded theory: Theoretical background', in J.T.E. Richardson (ed.), *Handbook of Qualitative Research Methods for Psychology and the Social Sciences*. Leicester: BPS Books. pp. 75–85.

Plummer, K. (ed.) (1981) *The Making of the Modern Homosexual*. London: Hutchinson.

Pomerantz, A.M. (1986) 'Extreme case formulations: A new way of legitimating claims', *Human Studies*, 9(2–3): 219–29.

Popper, K.R. (1969) *Conjectures and Refutations*. London: Routledge & Kegan Paul.

Potter, J. (1996) *Representing Reality: Discourse, Rhetoric and Social Construction*. London: SAGE.

Potter, J. (1997) 'Discourse analysis as a way of analysing naturally occurring talk', in D. Silverman (ed.), *Qualitative Research: Theory, Method and Practice*. London: SAGE. pp. 144–60.

Potter, J. (2003) 'Discourse analysis', in M. Hardy and A. Bryman (eds), *Handbook of Data Analysis*. London: SAGE. pp. 607–24.

Potter, J. (ed.) (2007a) *Discourse and Psychology: Volume I Theory and Method*. London: SAGE.

Potter, J. (ed.) (2007b) *Discourse and Psychology: Volume II Discourse and Social Psychology*. London: SAGE.

Potter, J. (ed.) (2007c) *Discourse and Psychology: Volume III Discursive Psychology*. London: SAGE.

Potter, J. and Hepburn, A. (2005) 'Qualitative interviews in psychology: Problems and possibilities', *Qualitative Research in Psychology*, 2(4): 281–307.

Potter, J. and Wetherell, M. (1987) *Discourse and Social Psychology: Beyond Attitudes and Behaviour*. London: SAGE.

Price, J. (1996) 'Snakes in the swamp: Ethical issues in qualitative research', in R. Josselson (ed.), *Ethics and Process in the Narrative Study of Lives*. Thousand Oaks, CA: SAGE. pp. 207–15.

Radley, A. and Chamberlain, K. (2001) 'Health psychology and the study of the case: From method to analytic concern', *Social Science & Medicine*, 53(3): 321–32.

Rasmussen, M.L. (2004) 'The problem of coming out', *Theory into Practice*, 43(2): 144–50.

Reason, P. and Rowan, J. (eds) (1981) *Human Inquiry: A Sourcebook of New Paradigm Research*. Chichester: Wiley.

Redmond, C., Larkin, M. and Harrop, C. (2010) 'The personal meaning of romantic relationships for young people with psychosis', *Clinical Child Psychology and Psychiatry*, 15(2): 151–70.

Reicher, S. (2000) 'Against methodolatry: Some comments on Elliott, Fischer, and Rennie', *British Journal of Clinical Psychology*, 39(1): 1–6.

Reis, E. (2009) *Bodies in Doubt: An American History of Intersex*. Baltimore, MD: Johns Hopkins University Press.

Rennie, D.L. (2000) 'Grounded theory methodology as methodical hermeneutics: Reconciling realism and relativism', *Theory and Psychology*, 10(4): 481–502.

Rhodes, J. and Smith, J.A. (2010) '"The top of my head came off": An interpretative phenomenological analysis of the experience of depression', *Counselling Psychology Quarterly*, 23(4): 399–409.

Rich, A. (1980) 'Compulsory heterosexuality and lesbian existence', *Signs: Journal of Women in Culture and Society*, 5(4): 631–60.

Richardson, L. (2000) 'Writing: A method of inquiry' in N.K. Denzin and Y.S. Lincoln (eds), *Handbook of Qualitative Research*. 2nd edn. London: SAGE. pp. 923–48.

Ricoeur, P. (1970) *Freud and Philosophy*. New Haven, CT: Yale University Press.

Riessman, K. (2008) *Narrative Methods for the Human Sciences*. London: SAGE.

Rowlands, J. (2005) 'To tell the truth', *Cancer Nursing Practice*, 4(5): 16–21.

Sam, D.L. and Berry, J.W. (2010) 'Acculturation: When individuals and groups of different cultural backgrounds meet', *Perspectives on Psychological Science*, 5(4): 472–81.

Saldaña, J. (2011) *Ethnotheatre: Research from Page to Stage*. Walnut Creek, CA: Left Coast Press.

Sarbin, T.R. (1986) (ed.) *Narrative Psychology: The Storied Nature of Human Conduct*. New York: Praeger.

Saunders, B., Kitzinger, J. and Kitzinger, C. (2015) 'Participant anonymity in the internet age: From theory to practice', *Qualitative Research in Psychology*, 12(2): 125–37.

Schegloff, E.A. (1997) 'Whose text? Whose context?' *Discourse & Society*, 8(2): 165–87.

Schiff, B. (2013) 'Fractured narratives: Psychology's fragmented narrative psychology', in M. Hyvärinen, M., Hatavara and L. C. Hydén, L.C. (eds), *The Travelling Concept of Narrative*. Amsterdam: John Benjamins. pp. 245–64.

Sedgwick, E. (1990) *The Epistemology of the Closet*. London: Penguin.

Senior, V., Smith, J.A., Michie, S. and Marteau, T.M. (2002) 'Making sense of risk: An interpretative phenomenological analysis of vulnerability to heart disease', *Journal of Health Psychology*, 7(2): 157–68.

Shaw, R. and Frost, N. (2015) 'Breaking out of the silo mentality', *The Psychologist*, 28(2): 638–41.

Shepherd, R., Barnett, J., Cooper, H., Coyle, A., Moran-Ellis, J., Senior, V. and Walton, C. (2007) 'Towards an understanding of British public attitudes concerning human cloning', *Social Science & Medicine*, 65(2): 377–92.

Shinebourne, P. and Smith, J.A. (2009) 'Alcohol and the self: An interpretative phenomenological analysis of the experience of addiction and its impact on the sense of self and identity', *Addiction Research & Theory*, 17(2): 152–67.

Short, N., Turner, L. and Grant, A. (eds) (2013) *Contemporary British Autoethnography*. Rotterdam: Sense Publishers.

Sidnell, J. and Stivers, T. (eds) (2013) *The Handbook of Conversation Analysis*. Malden, MA: Wiley-Blackwell.

Silver, C. and Fielding, N. (2008) 'Using computer packages in qualitative research', in C. Willig and W. Stainton-Rogers (eds), *The SAGE Handbook of Qualitative Research in Psychology*. London: SAGE. pp. 334–51.

Silver, C. and Lewins, A. (2014) *Using Software in Qualitative Research: A Step-by-Step Guide*. 2nd edn. London: SAGE.

Sinister Wisdom Collective (1990) 'Editorial', *Sinister Wisdom*, 42(4): 1–6.

Skloot, R. (2010) *The Immortal Life of Henrietta Lacks*. London: Macmillan.

Smith, B. (2013a) 'Disability, sport, and men's narratives of health: A qualitative study', *Health Psychology*, 32(1): 110–19.

Smith, B. (2013b) 'Sporting spinal cord injuries, social relations, and rehabilitation narratives: An ethnographic creative non-fiction of becoming disabled through sport', *Sociology of Sport Journal*, 30: 132–52.

Smith, B., Allen Collinson, J., Phoenix, C., Brown, D. and Sparkes, A. C. (2009) 'Dialogue, monologue, and boundary crossing within research encounters: A performative narrative analysis', *International Journal of Sport and Exercise Psychology*, 7(3): 342–58.

Smith, B., Papathomas, A., Martin Ginis, K.A. and Latimer-Cheung, A.E. (2013) 'Understanding physical activity in spinal cord injury rehabilitation: Translating and communicating research through stories', *Disability & Rehabilitation*, 35(24): 2046–55.

Smith, B., and Sparkes, A. C. (2006) 'Narrative inquiry in psychology: Exploring the tensions within', *Qualitative Research in Psychology*, 3(3): 169–92.

Smith, B. and Sparkes, A. (2008) 'Contrasting perspectives on narrating selves and identities: An invitation to dialogue', *Qualitative Research*, 8(1): 5–35.

Smith, B. and Sparkes, A.C. (2011) 'Multiple responses to a chaos narrative', *Health: An Interdisciplinary Journal for the Social Study of Health, Illness & Medicine*, 15(1): 38–53.

Smith, B., Tomasone, J. R., Latimer-Cheung, A. E. and Martin Ginis, K. A. (2015) 'Narrative as a knowledge translation tool for facilitating impact: Translating physical activity knowledge to disabled people and health professionals', *Health Psychology*, 34(4): 303–13.

Smith, J.A. (1993) 'The case study', in R. Bayne and P. Nicolson (eds), *Counselling and Psychology for the Health Professionals*. London: Chapman Hall. pp. 249–65.

Smith, J.A. (1996) 'Beyond the divide between cognition and discourse: Using interpretative phenomenological analysis in health psychology', *Psychology & Health*, 11(2): 261–71.

Smith, J.A. (1999) 'Towards a relational self: Social engagement during pregnancy and psychological preparation for motherhood', *British Journal of Social Psychology*, 38(4): 409–26.

Smith, J.A. (2003) 'Validity and qualitative psychology', in J.A. Smith (ed.), *Qualitative Psychology: A Practical Guide to Research Methods*. London: SAGE. pp. 232–5.

Smith, J.A. (2004) 'Reflecting on the development of interpretative phenomenological analysis and its contribution to qualitative psychology', *Qualitative Research in Psychology*, 1(1): 39–54.

Smith, J.A. (2011a) 'Evaluating the contribution of interpretative phenomenological analysis', *Health Psychology Review*, 5(1): 9–27.

Smith, J.A. (2011b) 'Evaluating the contribution of interpretative phenomenological analysis: A reply to the commentaries and further development of criteria', *Health Psychology Review*, 5(1): 55–61.

Smith, J.A. (2011c) '"We could be diving for pearls": The value of the gem in experiential qualitative psychology', *Qualitative Methods in Psychology Bulletin*, 12: 6–15.

Smith, J.A. (ed.) (2015) *Qualitative Psychology: A Practical Guide to Research Methods*. 3rd edn. London: SAGE.

Smith, J.A., Flowers, P. and Larkin, M. (2009) *Interpretative Phenomenological Analysis: Theory, Method and Research*. London: SAGE.

Smith, J.A., Harré, R. and van Langenhove, L. (1995) 'Idiography and the case study', in J.A. Smith, R. Harré and L. van Langenhove (eds), *Rethinking Psychology*. London: SAGE. pp. 59–69.

Smith, J.A. and Osborn, M. (2015) 'Interpretative phenomenological analysis', in J.A. Smith (ed.), *Qualitative Psychology: A Practical Guide to Research Methods*. 3rd edn. London: SAGE. pp. 25–52.

Smith, J.A., Stephenson, M., Jacobs, C. and Quarrell, O. (2013) 'Doing the right thing for one's children: Deciding whether to take the genetic test for Huntington's disease as a moral dilemma', *Clinical Genetics*, 83(5): 417–21.

Smith, M. (2005) *Philosophy and Methodology in the Social Sciences*. London: SAGE.

Sools, A. (2013) 'Narrative health research: Exploring big and small stories as analytical tools', *Health: An Interdisciplinary Journal for the Social Study of Health, Illness & Medicine*, 17(1): 93–110.

Sparkes, A.C., Perez-Samaniego, V. and Smith, B. (2012) 'Social comparison processes, narrative mapping, and their shaping of the cancer experience: A case study of an elite athlete', *Health: An Interdisciplinary Journal for the Social Study of Health, Illness & Medicine*, 16(5): 467–88.

Sparkes, A.C. and Smith, B. (2008) 'Narrative constructionist inquiry' in J. Holstein and J. Gubrium (eds), *Handbook of Constructionist Research*. London: Guilford Publications. pp. 295–314.

Sparkes, A.C. and Smith, B. (2012) 'Narrative analysis as an embodied engagement with the lives of others', in J. Holstein and J. Gubrium (eds), *Varieties of Narrative Analysis*. London: SAGE. pp. 53–73.

Sparkes, A.C. and Smith, B. (2014) *Qualitative Research Methods in Sport, Exercise and Health: From Process to Product*. London: Routledge.

Spector-Mersel, G. (2011) 'Mechanisms of selection in claiming narrative identities: A model for interpreting narratives', *Qualitative Inquiry*, 17(2): 172–85.

Spector-Mersel, G. (2014) '"I was … Until … Since then …": Exploring the mechanisms of selection in a tragic narrative', *Narrative Works*, 4(1): 19–30.

Speer, S.A. (2002) '"Natural" and "contrived" data: A sustainable distinction?' *Discourse Studies*, 4(4): 511–25.

Spohrer, K. (2011) 'Deconstructing "aspiration": UK policy debates and European policy trends', *European Educational Research Journal*, 10(1): 53–63.

Sque, M. and Payne, S.A. (1996) 'Dissonant loss: The experience of donor relatives', *Social Science & Medicine*, 43(9): 1359–70.

Steffen, E. and Coyle, A. (2011) 'Sense of presence experiences and meaning-making in bereavement: A qualitative analysis', *Death Studies*, 35(7): 579–609.

Steffen, E. and Coyle, A. (in press) '"I thought they should know...that daddy is not completely gone": A case study of sense-of-presence experiences in bereavement and family meaning-making', *Omega: Journal of Death and Dying*.

Stephens, C. and Breheny, M. (2013) 'Narrative analysis in psychological research: An integrated approach to interpreting stories', *Qualitative Research in Psychology*, 10(1): 14–17.

Stewart, D.W. and Shamdasani, P.N. (2014) *Focus Groups: Theory and Practice*. 3rd edn. Thousand Oaks, CA: SAGE.

Strauss, A. and Corbin, J. (1990) *Basics of Qualitative Research: Techniques and Procedures for Developing Grounded Theory*. Newbury Park, CA: SAGE.

Suffla, S., Seedar, M. and Bawa, U. (2015) 'Reflexivity as enactment of critical community psychologies: Dilemmas of voice and positionality in a multi-country photovoice study', *Journal of Community Psychology*, 43(1): 9–21.

Tajfel, H. and Turner, J.C. (1986) 'The social identity theory of intergroup behavior', in S. Worchel and W.G. Austin (eds), *The Psychology of Intergroup Relations*. Chicago: Nelson-Hall. pp. 7–24.

Tamboukou, M., Andrews, M. and Squire, C. (2014) 'Introduction: What is narrative research?', in M. Andrews, C. Squire and M. Tamboukou (eds), *Doing Narrative Research*. 2nd edn. London: SAGE. pp. 1–26.

Terry, G. and Braun, V. (2009) '"When I was a bastard": Constructions of maturity in men's accounts of masculinity', *The Journal of Gender Studies*, 18(2): 165–78.

Terry, G. and Braun, V. (2011) '"It's kind of me taking responsibility for these things": Men, vasectomy and "contraceptive economies"', *Feminism & Psychology*, 21(4): 477–95.

Terry, G. and Braun, V. (2012a) 'Structural impediments to sexual health in New Zealand: Key informant perspectives', *Sexuality Research and Social Policy*, 9(4): 317–26.

Terry, G. and Braun, V. (2012b) '"Sticking my finger up at evolution": Unconventionality, selfishness, resistance and choice in the talk of men who have had "pre-emptive" vasectomies', *Men and Masculinities*, 15(3): 207–29.

Terry, G. and Braun, V. (2013) '"We have friends, for example, and he will not get a vasectomy": Imagining the self in relation to others when talking about sterilization', *Health Psychology*, 32(1): 100–9.

Thompson, A., Larkin, M. and Smith, J.A. (2011) 'Interpretative phenomenological analysis and clinical psychology training: Results from a survey of the group of trainers in clinical psychology', *Clinical Psychology Forum*, 222: 15–19.

Toerien, M. and Wilkinson, S. (2004) 'Exploring the depilation norm: A qualitative questionnaire study of women's body hair removal', *Qualitative Research in Psychology*, 1(1): 69–92.

Triandis, H.C. (1996) 'The psychological measurement of cultural syndromes', *American Psychologist*, 51(4): 407–15.

Triandis, H.C., Leung, K., Villareal, M.J. and Clack, F.I. (1985) 'Allocentric vs. idiocentric tendencies: Convergent and discriminant validation', *Journal of Research in Personality*, 19(4): 395–415.

Turner, A., Barlow, J. and Ilbery, B. (2002) 'Play hurt, live hurt: Living with and managing osteoarthritis from the perspective of ex-professional footballers', *Journal of Health Psychology*, 7(3): 285–301.

Turner, A.J. and Coyle, A. (2000) 'What does it mean to be a donor offspring? The identity experiences of adults conceived by donor insemination and the implications for counseling and therapy', *Human Reproduction*, 15(9): 2041–51.

Turpin, G., Barley, V., Beail, N., Scaife, J., Slade, P., Smith, J.A. and Walsh, S. (1997) 'Standards for research projects and theses involving qualitative methods: Suggested guidelines for trainees and courses', *Clinical Psychology Forum*, 108: 3–7.

Urquhart, C. (2013) *Grounded Theory for Qualitative Research: A Practical Guide*. London: SAGE.

Ussher, J. (1991) *Women's Madness: Misogyny or Mental Illness?* London: Harvester Wheatsheaf.

Uwannah, V. (2015) 'A portfolio of academic, therapeutic practice and research work including an investigation of the experiences of Pentecostal Christians with mental health conditions within a congregational setting'. Unpublished PsychD portfolio (Practitioner Doctorate in Psychotherapeutic and Counselling Psychology), University of Surrey.

Verey, A. and Smith, P. (2012) 'Post-combat adjustment: Understanding transition', *Journal of Aggression, Conflict and Peace Research*, 4(4): 226–36.

Vignoles, V.L., Chryssochoou, X. and Breakwell, G.M. (2004) 'Combining individuality and relatedness: Representations of the person among the Anglican clergy', *British Journal of Social Psychology*, 43(1): 113–32.

Wetherell, M. (1998) 'Positioning and interpretative repertoires: Conversation analysis and post-structuralism in dialogue', *Discourse & Society*, 9(3): 387–412.

Wetherell, M. and Edley, N. (2009) 'Masculinity manoeuvres: Critical discursive psychology and the analysis of identity strategies', in N. Coupland and A. Jaworski (eds), *The New Sociolinguistics Reader*. Basingstoke: Palgrave Macmillan. pp. 201–14.

Wetherell, M. and Potter, J. (1992) *Mapping the Language of Racism: Discourse and the Legitimation of Exploitation*. Hemel Hempstead: Harvester Wheatsheaf.

Wetherell, M., Taylor, S. and Yates, S.J. (eds) (2001a) *Discourse Theory and Practice: A Reader*. London: SAGE/Open University Press.

Wetherell, M., Taylor, S. and Yates, S.J. (eds) (2001b) *Discourse as Data: A Guide for Analysis*. London: SAGE/Open University Press.

Whiffin, C., Bailey, C., Ellis-Hill, C. and Jarrett, N. (2014) 'Challenges and solutions during analysis in a longitudinal narrative case study', *Nurse Researcher*, 21(4): 20–26.

Widdicombe, S. (1993) 'Autobiography and change: Rhetoric and authenticity of "Gothic" style', in E. Burman and I. Parker (eds), *Discourse Analytic Research: Repertoires and Readings of Texts in Action*. London: Routledge. pp. 94–113.

Widdicombe, S. (1995) 'Identity, politics and talk: A case for the mundane and the everyday', in S. Wilkinson and C. Kitzinger (eds), *Feminism and Discourse: Psychological Perspectives*. London: SAGE. pp. 106–27.

Wiggins, S. (2009) 'Managing blame in NHS weight management treatment: Psychologizing weight and "obesity"', *Journal of Community & Applied Social Psychology*, 19(5): 374–87.

Wiggins, S. and Potter, J. (2008) 'Discursive psychology', in C. Willig and W. Stainton Rogers (eds), *The SAGE Handbook of Qualitative Research in Psychology*. London: SAGE. pp. 73–90.

Wiles, R. (2013) *What Are Qualitative Research Ethics?* London: Bloomsbury.

Wilkinson, S. (1996) 'Feminist social psychologies: A decade of development', in S. Wilkinson (ed.), *Feminist Social Psychologies: International Perspectives*. Buckingham: Open University Press. pp. 1–18.

Willig, C. (ed.) (1999) *Applied Discourse Analysis: Social and Psychological Interventions*. Buckingham: Open University Press.

Willig, C. (2011) 'Cancer diagnosis as discursive capture: Phenomenological repercussions of being positioned within dominant constructions of cancer', *Social Science & Medicine*, 73(6): 897–903.

Willig, C. (2012) *Qualitative Interpretation and Analysis in Psychology*. Maidenhead: Open University Press.

Willig, C. (2013) *Introducing Qualitative Research in Psychology*. 3rd edn. Maidenhead: McGraw Hill/Open University Press.

Willig, C. and Stainton-Rogers, W. (eds) (2008) *The SAGE Handbook of Qualitative Research in Psychology*. London: SAGE.

Winter, D.G. and McClelland, D.C. (1978) 'Thematic analysis: An empirically derived measure of the effects of liberal arts education', *Journal of Educational Psychology*, 70(1): 8–16.

Wodak, R. and Meyer, M. (2009) 'Critical discourse analysis: History, agenda, theory and methodology', in R. Wodak and M. Meyer (eds), *Methods of Critical Discourse Analysis*. London: SAGE. pp. 1–33.

Woodrum, E. (1984) '"Mainstreaming" content analysis in social science: Methodological advantages, obstacles, and solutions', *Social Science Research*, 13(1): 1–19.

Woodward, R. and Jenkings, K.N. (2011) 'Military identities in the situated accounts of British military personnel', *Sociology*, 45(2): 252–68.

Yardley, L. (2000) 'Dilemmas in qualitative health research', *Psychology and Health*, 15(2): 215–28.

Yardley, L. (2008) 'Demonstrating validity in qualitative psychology', in J.A. Smith (ed.), *Qualitative Psychology: A Practical Guide to Research Methods*. London: SAGE. pp. 235–51.

Yin, R. (1989) *Case Study Research*. Rev. edn. Newbury Park, CA: SAGE.

Yuval-Davis, N. (2013) 'A situated intersectional everyday approach to the study of bordering', EUBorderScapes Working Paper 2. Retrieved 5 September 2015 from http://www.euborderscapes. eu/fileadmin/user_upload/Working_Papers/EUBORDERSCAPES_Working_Paper_2_Yuval-Davis.pdf.

Zimbardo, P.G. (1973) 'On the ethics of intervention in human psychological research: With special reference to the Stanford prison experiment', *Cognition*, 2(2): 243–56.

NAME INDEX

SUBJECT INDEX

identity *cont.*
  as social performance, 230–2
  and storytelling, 230–1
idiocentrism, 192–3
idiographic research, 14–15, 52, 54, 199, 370
'immersion' in a data set, 106, 158
impact of research, 23, 26, 370
in vivo categories and codes, 136, 151
independent audit, 62
individualism, 191–3, 196, 198–9
inductive analysis, 15, 89, 105, 127, 242, 370
'indwelling', 216
inferring of meaning, 131
informed consent, 37–8, 40–1, 370
'insider' perspective, 248–9, 310
interpretative frameworks, 16, 20, 71, 371; *see also*
    reflexivity in research; 'speaking positions'
interpretative phenomenological analysis (IPA), 6, 15,
    47, 50–83, 87–8, 241, 243, 246–50, 254, 293–4, 303
  aims, 50
  analysis stage, 59–64, 69-76
  commitment to the person, 51
  data collection, 55–6
  desirable qualities in, 64–5
    'interpretative' coding, 91
  research questions for, 53
  sampling for, 54–5, 59
'interpretative repertoires', 165–6, 191
'interpretative violence', 40, 42
'interpretive omnipotence', 209
inter-rater reliability, 86–7
intersubjectivity, 120, 242
interviews, 48
  semi-structured, 48, 55–9, 128, 148, 373
  structured, 56

journals, academic, 292, 297

language
  action orientation of, 166–7
  and construction of reality, 163, 165, 167, 173
  different views of, 160–1
  in an everyday setting and in an institutional
      context, 167
  functions of, 175–8, 242
  power of, 179
  used in social situations, 131–2
latent codes, 89, 91, 101, 105, 108, 110, 371
liberal individualism, 166
literature reviews, 99, 126–7, 148, 294, 308, 313, 323, 342

macro ethics, 34, 371
marginalized groups, 38, 309–10

masculine identity, 107
meaning-making, 5, 204, 371; *see also* sense-making
measurement in psychology, 13
memos made by researchers, 90, 138, 142, 153–4, 215, 371
meso ethics, 34–5, 371
method
  as distinct from methodology, 87
  taken as a heuristic guide, 213–14
'methodolatry', 27–30
micro ethics, 34, 371
mixed-methods research, 4, 28–9, 241, 244–5, 318, 371

naïve realism, 242, 371
narrative
  definition of, 371
  as distinct from stories, 204–5, 207, 214, 223
  ideal types of, 220
  typology of, 219
narrative analysis, 6, 47–8, 87, 202–39, 241, 243, 246–7,
    250, 255, 354, 356, 365
  definition of, 207
  differences from other forms of qualitative
      analysis, 210
  different standpoints in relation to, 207–9
  different types of, 213
  difficulties with and weaknesses of, 203, 211–12
  guide to application of, 213–21
  reasons for choice of, 209–12, 221
  strengths of, 210–11
  theoretical approaches to, 204
  underpinning philosophical assumptions of, 203, 207
narrative constructionism, 202, 204, 206–7, 243, 371
narrative constructivism, 204, 243, 371
narrative exceptionalism, 212
narrative foreclosure, 236, 371
narrative identity, 231–2, 239, 372
narrative resources, 205, 218, 231–3, 239, 372
narrative structure, 228
narrative themes, 216–17, 372
'narrative under-analysis', 209
'naturalistic' research, 14
'naturally occurring' data, 127–8, 132, 172, 343
nomothetic research, 14, 52, 372
'noticing' process, 107, 151, 245
NVivo, 135, 148, 175; *see also* software for qualitative
    analysis

objective reality, 4, 13, 15, 86
objectivity, 12, 23, 142, 167
  scientific, 179
online research, 39–40, 344
ontological relativism, 204, 372
ontology, 11–12, 15–18, 164, 372